A MAN MADE TO MEASURE

Elaine Crowley was born in Dublin. She left school at fourteen and became an apprentice tailor. At eighteen she went to England and joined the A.T.S. She married a regular soldier in 1949 and spent part of her married life in Egypt and Germany. Since 1963 she has been living in Port Talbot.

Elaine Crowley has six children, three girls and three boys, and numerous grandchildren. Once her children were at school she did a variety of jobs – Avon lady, dinner lady and part-time sewing machinist making sleeping bags. In 1969 she went to work in the personnel department of the British Steel Corporation in Port Talbot. After nine years there she took voluntary redundancy and began writing. At first she wrote articles and had several accepted. But this form of writing was not satisfying enough and she began work on a novel, *Dreams of Other Days*, which achieved a best-selling success on its publication in 1984. *A Man Made to Measure* is her second novel.

A Man Made to Measure

Elaine Crowley

PENGUIN BOOKS

Penguin Books Ltd, 27 Wrights Lane, London W8 5TZ (Publishing and Editorial)
and Harmondsworth, Middlesex, England (Distribution and Warehouse)
Viking Penguin Inc., 40 West 23rd Street, New York, New York 10010, USA
Penguin Books Australia Ltd, Ringwood, Victoria, Australia
Penguin Books Canada Ltd, 2801 John Street, Markham, Ontario, Canada L3R 1B4
Penguin Books (NZ) Ltd, 182–190 Wairau Road, Auckland 10, New Zealand

First published in Great Britain by Century Hutchinson Ltd 1986
Published in Penguin Books 1987 (twice)

Printed and bound in Great Britain by
Cox & Wyman Ltd, Reading
Filmset in Linotron Times by
Rowland Phototypesetting Ltd,
Bury St Edmunds, Suffolk

For my mother
who told me stories

Chapter One

'High-class dressmaker, late of Pim's, Georges Street, Dublin. Modish costumes and dresses made to measure. Satisfaction assured,' Dolly Devoy read aloud from the printed card hanging in the window of the tenement house.

'What's modish?' Bid Dunne asked.

'God, you're awful ignorant. Everyone knows what that means – the latest from London and Paris!'

'Isn't it grand to have brains,' Bid said, not offended by Dolly's sharp answer: she was used to her friend's sarcastic remarks. 'Anyway, we'd better go in. She can see us through the lace hangings and will wonder what we're gawping at.'

'I hope I'm doing the right thing,' Dolly said, looking down at the brown paper parcel she held. 'I paid five and eleven a yard for this and I don't want it ruined.'

'Well, you haven't much option. You've worn out every other dressmaker in the city with your fussiness. It's Miss Murtagh or no one.'

'You've a terrible cheek. I know what I want, that's all. Not like some people whose taste is all in their mouth.'

'Don't I know it, you're always telling me. Shut up now and come in if you're coming.'

They stepped into the narrow hall, keeping their distance from the red raddled walls and knocked on the first door in the passage. After a second knock the door opened narrowly and part of a face was seen that asked, 'Yes, what is it?'

'A girl in work recommended you and I was wondering if

7

you'd make me a frock,' Dolly said in the pleasing voice she used to strangers.

The door opened wider; now the elderly woman was in full view. She smiled with relief. 'Oh, is that what it is? I do have to be careful. You never know who knocks on your door. Young fellas sometimes trying to frighten the life out of me, or women from up in the house wanting a lend. And I like to keep myself to myself. But come in, do.'

Dolly and Bid followed her into the room, Dolly's eyes taking everything in. The table with a length of stuff laid out, brown paper pattern pieces pinned to it. A tailor's dummy with metal handles at bust and waist for altering its size, small boxes full of buttons, spools of thread and pieces of tailor's chalk.

There was a sewing machine under the window and next to it, on a table, a tall paraffin lamp. The glass globe of the lamp was decorated with a garland of roses similar to the brilliantly coloured flowers which wreathed the word 'Singer' on the machine. The room smelled of new material, paraffin, machine oil and the stew simmering in an iron pot on the hob.

'You must be jaded with the heat,' the dressmaker said and invited them to sit down. Dolly and Bid sat on a small hard sofa covered in black leatherette, out of which the horse hair stuffing poked bristles.

'And you said it was a girl from work recommended me?' Miss Murtagh asked.

'It was, Mamie McCarthy,' Bid said.

'Then you work in Jacobs?'

'That's right. Bid's on the mixing loft and I'm in the office,' Dolly replied before Bid could answer.

'They make lovely biscuits. But I'm sure the work must be killing in this weather.'

'It's very hot in the bakehouse, isn't it, Dolly? Dolly worked there until last week, didn't you?' Bid looked innocently at

8

her friend and thought – put that in your pipe and smoke it, letting on you've always been an office girl.

Dolly looked daggers at her, then turned away and spoke to the dressmaker. 'I'd want the frock in an awful hurry. I'd have to have it by next week. I'm singing in a concert in Jacobs' Hall.'

'You're a singer! Imagine that! A good voice is a gift from God.'

Dolly undid the parcel, exposing the material. "Panne velvet!' Miss Murtagh exclaimed. 'It's beautiful. I love velvet, though it's hard to work on. Isn't it a gorgeous shade – apple green, it'll go well with your dark colouring. What way were you thinking of having it made?'

'The skirt to the floor, there's oceans of stuff. And falling from under the bust. And the neck to about here.' Dolly used her hands as well as her voice to describe how she wanted the dress. 'And the sleeves . . .'

'Wait now for a minute,' the dressmaker interrupted. 'I've a pattern book, I'll show you.'

Dolly leafed through the book, chose a style, changed her mind and picked another, eventually settling for a mixture of two designs, the low neck of one and the flowing skirt of a different dress. Miss Murtagh marked both pages with pieces of paper, then began to measure Dolly. She talked while she slipped the tape round Dolly's bust, waist and hips and measured her length. 'You won't be hard to fit, anyway. You're a fine girl, built to proportion. Some people have terrible queer shapes. Hold still now while I get the length of your arm.'

She talked as she wrote the measurements in a red shiny covered notebook along with Dolly's name and address and, when she had finished, added, 'Isn't the world in a terrible state all the same. What do you think of the animosity in the North over the Home Rule Bill?'

Dolly and Bid regarded her blankly. Then Bid agreed that it was terrible right enough.

9

'Terrible isn't the word!' Miss Murtagh replied. 'Do you know the Protestants up there will fight if the Bill comes off. And Carson's at the head of it. They've thousands of Ulster Volunteers armed to the hilt. Bought from the Germans so I've heard tell. That money came out of no ordinary pocket. All the big bugs are behind it. Look at what it could lead to – Irishmen fighting Irishmen. Sure if them in the North hadn't started their Volunteers our own lads wouldn't have bothered. Now there's hundreds of them, too. Though God help them they're at a disadvantage, nothing but wooden rifles and letting on things.'

'Is that so?' Dolly said, not having heard half of what the woman was saying, not interested, her mind on what the apple green velvet would look like finished, and if it would be ready in time.

'Oh, that's a fact. And a woman I know, a great reader, was telling me that on top of everything else there could be a war over the other side.'

'Listen, we're in an awful hurry, we'll have to go. You won't let me down, sure you won't?'

'I won't. Come in on Tuesday for a try on, and it'll be ready on Thursday. But like I said – velvet's hard to work on, then there's thread and buttons and a band of canvas to make the hem stand straight! I'd have to ask seven and sixpence. Will that be all right?'

'That'll be grand,' Dolly said.

'Would you have time for a cup of tea, it'd be no trouble?'

'Thanks all the same, we have to go.' Behind Miss Murtagh's back Dolly made a face at Bid, warning her not to say yes to the tea.

'Oul wans are all the same. She'd have kept us for hours blathering about the war and the Volunteers,' Dolly said when they had left the dressmaker's. Bid agreed, then suggested they walk home by way of Westland Row railway station and see the people going off to England. Along the way, a man

10

riding a bicycle and carrying a ladder on his shoulder looked back as he passed them.

'You've clicked. It must be your hobble skirt,' Bid said. The man on the bike wobbled and nearly fell off.

'The price of him if he landed in the middle of the road with his baldy head stuck in the rungs – giving me the eye! He's old enough to be my father.'

The man righted himself and rode faster; soon he was out of sight. Bid laughed and said, 'You wouldn't be saying that if it was Jem O'Brien giving you the eye.'

'That's different, he's only eighteen the same as myself. Though he's taking that long about throwing his eye my way I'll be ninety before he does.'

Bid linked her arm through Dolly's and adjusted her steps to Dolly's mincing ones. 'It's a wonder the circulation to your feet isn't strangled in that skirt. But you're right about Jem, he's very slow. Still I bet he'll make a move the night of the concert – between your singing and the apple green matching your eyes he won't know what hit him. Will you go out with him if he asks you?'

'I might.'

'What do you mean – you might? He's gorgeous. That's your trouble, you never know what you want.'

'Oh, but I do,' Dolly said complacently. 'And in any case he can't dance.'

'I hate you when you look like that, like a bloody cat,' Bid said staring at Dolly. 'What is it you do want, anyway?'

'That's for me to know and you to find out.'

'Keep your secrets – I don't care. But listen – if you do start a line with Jem, put in a word for me. With him and Kevin being pals we could make up a foursome.'

A long line of hansom cabs passed them heading for the station. 'Wouldn't it be marvellous to be going away. Riding in a cab all dressed up with the trunks and bags full of new clothes. Going off to England,' Dolly said.

11

'Did you hear what I said about me and Kevin?'

'Of course I did, and I will if I go out with Jem. Oh Bid, look at that!' Dolly squeezed Bid's arm. 'There! Look!'

From a turning in front of them, an open-topped, silver-grey Rolls Royce emerged and stopped at the junction as the cabs streamed by.

'Let's have a closer look,' Dolly urged, and, despite her hobble skirt, moved quickly dragging Bid with her. They stopped at the kerb and looked into the car. Two men were in the front, one stout and elderly at the wheel, the other young and dressed in a grey uniform. Both men were wearing motoring goggles. In the back sat two women, their faces and hats shrouded by motoring veils reaching to their shoulders.

'You know who that is, Delahunt the MP,' Bid said.

'Did you ever see anything like it?' Dolly stood entranced, looking after the car pulling into the road. 'Imagine owning that, and did you see the gear of the wans? They must be off to England.'

'They live out in Foxrock, so what would they be doing going this way?'

'Sure they could have been in town or something before they went. A lot of the gentry go to England in May and June, I bet you that's where they are going.'

'That was his wife and daughter. And the fella in the cap the driver, only that's not what you call him.'

'The chauffeur, you mean.'

'I knew it was something like that. He's a bloody oul bags, that Delahunt. Remember he was in all the papers last year during the lock-out. He's an MP, one of them Protestant ones on the side of the landlords and employers. My father said if the likes of Delahunt had his way, Connolly, Larkin and everyone on strike would have been hanged.'

'You're as bad as Miss Murtagh with all your information – wars and strikes. I never knew you were that interested.'

12

'No more than yourself I'm not, but I couldn't forget the strike. Neither should you, for weren't we locked out of Jacobs? You'd better cross or we'll be here all night. Eight months my father was locked out and not a penny coming in.'

They darted in between a couple of cabs and crossed the road. On the other side Dolly admitted, 'The strike was terrible all right. What did you think of Delahunt's daughter – wasn't she gorgeous?'

'All I saw was the veil.'

'But you could make out her features and her hat. That was a beauty, real ostrich feathers and a lovely pink. And talking about hats, mine is a show,' Dolly said as she caught sight of herself in a shop window they were passing. She pulled Bid up to it, let go her arm and began rearranging her hat.

The shop front was painted black, its windows filled with funerary urns, white waxy lilies, mourning cards deckle-edged in black and masses of green foliage. Bid glanced in, then away. Next door was a monumental mason's; tombstones met her gaze. 'Jasus, what a fecking place to stop! That's all I need, tombstones and wreaths looking up in my face. It's bad enough funerals passing you every five minutes of the day without stopping to admire the trimmings. Do you know, I think more people die in Ireland than anywhere else.' She tugged at Dolly's arm, forcing her away from the window.

Outside the railway station, barefooted boys competed with porters to carry luggage in and out of the building. Other equally poor boys called in raucous voices the latest editions of the evening papers. Dolly and Bid watched the comings and goings, commenting on the women and their clothes, admiring some, making a laugh of others.

'That'll be you and Jem in a few years' time – love's young dream!' Bid said, nudging Dolly and pointing to a couple leaving the station.

'Up from the country,' Dolly said, looking at the red-haired

13

woman and the tall, pale-faced young man. 'A pair of bog trotters.'

The couple were arm-in-arm and deep in conversation. The young man carried an old valise bound with a strap, and the woman had a basket on her arm and was holding a brown paper parcel tied with twine, hanging by loops from her fingers.

'She looks years older than him,' Bid said.

'Maybe she's his mother!' Dolly laughed, though not loudly. The couple passed by, hesitated for a moment looking up and down the street. Then they turned right and walked on.

'So this is Dublin,' Bessie Maguire said. 'The buildings are very tall.'

'This is nothing, wait'll you see the rest of it,' Liam replied. 'There's taller ones still, statues lining the streets and bridges, half a dozen or more over the Liffey, all with fancy work and lamps on them. And Sackville Street is wider than a four acre field. Do you know it's a fact you could pass someone on the other side that you knew well and not recognize him?'

Imagine that! Bessie was very impressed. They walked for a while longer along the street, which stretched way ahead of them. Bessie stopped. 'The string is cutting into my fingers, I'll have to change hands.' When she changed over the basket and the parcel, she said, 'Mightn't it be as well to check we're on the right road?'

'We will in a minute. I'm enjoying the stroll. It's grand to have you beside me in Dublin. I'm that proud of you. And I never saw you in anything as nice as the navy blue costume. You look lovely.'

'Sure I wore this the day we were married.'

'Did you now? And I never noticed. But that day I was so overcome with joy I saw nothing but your face.'

'Men all over – and me spending a fortune on the costume!'

'Small fortunes we had then, but wait till tomorrow. Wait

14

till I get my hands on a real one. I'll take you to one of the grand shops in Grafton Street and deck you in diamonds.'

Bessie smiled indulgently at her husband, her soft face and blue eyes full of love. But when she spoke her voice had a cautious note. 'Liam, love, maybe we'd better not build our hopes too high till after we've seen the solicitor.'

'The divil a fear of disappointment. Amn't I,' he paused to recall the unfamiliar wording of the solicitor's letter, 'amn't I the sole beneficiary of the aunt's estate? An estate! Sure that could be as big as the one your master had at home, with acres and acres of land, hundreds of cows, horses and everything, to say nothing of the mansion itself.'

'All the same, if your aunt had a place like that isn't it queer no one ever heard tell of it?'

'And sure how would they? The week I was born she left and that's twenty-five years ago. And never a word from her until the solicitor's letter saying she was dead, Lord have mercy on her.'

'Maybe you're right, but an estate in a place that's full of buildings and that, where would be the room?'

'Ah for God's sake, Bessie, don't be cross hackling every word out of my mouth!'

Liam's face flushed with annoyance. He was very excitable lately. She wouldn't disagree with him any more, for in a minute he could forget they were in a street surrounded by strangers and raise his voice to convince her he was right. That was youth for you. No doubts about anything. Ready to believe anything. Throw caution to the wind. That was the difference ten years between them made. She was full of doubts and fears. Only in bed, in the dark, lying in Liam's arms, listening to the words he whispered had she respite from them, forgot that she had seen Liam an infant in his mother's arms. Had answered the door to him when he came as a child to play with her brothers. Had never given him a thought as she went about her work in the Big House, happy in her own

15

way, grateful for her position as assistant cook. And as the years passed, putting aside her longing for a husband, knowing that husbands for girls without dowries were hard to come by.

She hadn't noticed Liam growing, changing from boy to man until the Sunday of the hurling match. She was home that day. Her mother had gone to gossip with a neighbour, her father was asleep by the fire. There wasn't a sound, only the ticking of the clock. Then she heard someone whistling. A tune she didn't know, but a lovely, happy sound. A shadow fell across the threshold and a voice asked, 'Is Mikey 'ithin?'

'He's not. He's gone down to the match,' she replied, going to the door, screwing her eyes against the glare when she stepped into the sunshine. She looked up at him, surprised that she had to. Only yesterday he wasn't up to her shoulder, now he towered above her. And why, when she had seen him a thousand times before, was his smile now different? And the voice she had heard whimpering with the pain of a cut knee, raised in childish argument with her brothers, why was that now low with a caress in it so that when he asked, ''Tis your day off?' she felt as if something warm had touched her.

'It is,' she replied.

'Will you be watching the match, so?'

She shook her head and laughed. 'My mother would think I'd gone mad, and the boys be put out – not many girls watch the match.'

'No,' he agreed. 'Well, I'd better be going.'

'Goodbye then.' She watched him go up the boreen.

'Who was that?' her father asked when she came in.

'Liam Maguire, calling for Mikey.'

'A queer thing at this hour of the day. Sure wouldn't he know well Mikey's gone this hour or more? I wonder what brought him here?'

Bessie didn't know and it never entered her head that it was to see her. Not until her next day off when Liam found another excuse to call. There was no one except herself in the

16

house when he came. She asked him in and gave him a glass of buttermilk. He talked about his father's farm and how he wished he had a place of his own.

'You will one day, sure you're only young.'

'It's when you're young you want it. From morning till night I'm out in the fields and all I get is pocket money.'

'Isn't that how it is? Isn't it the same for all farmer's sons? But it'll be yours when the time comes. You're lucky, it's a fine farm. At least you won't have to take the boat like my brothers. My father has worked hard all his life and never managed to increase our bit of land by an inch.'

While she talked she was watching his face and wishing she was a young girl with a comfortable farmer for a father and a matchmaker arranging a wedding between her and Liam.

'Would you come for a walk with me, Bessie?'

She was astounded by the request. 'How could I do such a thing like that?'

'On your two feet. It's easy, I'll show you.' He stood up and demonstrated, putting one foot before the other. 'That's how.'

She laughed out loud, and he continued walking slowly towards her, stopping in front of her, putting out his hands, resting them on her shoulders. 'Like that, it's easy. God, Bessie, don't be letting on you don't know why I've been calling. Do you know I saw you a while back, one day before the first Sunday I called. Honest to God, I didn't know you. Well – like – I knew you all right. But still it was as if I was seeing you for the first time. Do you know what I mean?'

She meant to say, 'Stop your fooling and go along now.' But she didn't. Instead she said, 'I do. For the same thing happened to me. Oh, but it's foolishness, so say no more about it.' She made an attempt to move from him, but his hands tightened on her shoulders and he bent his head towards her. 'No, Liam! Now stop that!' She turned her face away though she longed to kiss him. But it was madness and she

17

would have no part of it. 'Let go of me this minute and take yourself home.'

He let her go but wouldn't budge from the kitchen until she agreed to meet him that evening. Casting aside all her arguments – 'Sure it'll be easy. You don't have to be back at the House till morning. Slip out when everyone's asleep. I'll be in the ten acre field, by the trees. Not a soul will see us and you'll be back and not one the wiser.'

In the bed which she shared with her young sister she lay and listened for everyone to fall asleep. From behind the curtain which divided the girls from the boys, she heard her brothers talking. It seemed as if they would never stop, but gradually all became silent. She slipped from the bed, groping on the chair for her clothes.

'What's up, Bessie?' the sleepy voice of her sister asked.

'Nothing, love. I'm going to the meeting of the waters. Go back to sleep.'

She tiptoed to where the bucket stood just clear of the hanging, able to be reached by boys and girls and drawn to their side of the loft. She drew it out in case the child was still awake, and waited. When she was sure that the little girl slept she replaced the pail, climbed down the ladder, crept past the room where her parents lay and went out. In the yard she put on her blouse and skirt, then ran all the way to the ten acre field.

He enfolded her. 'You came. I was afraid you wouldn't. I've been here this long time. Oh you came!' He covered her face with kisses. Her heart that had raced with her to the field continued to race. He kissed her mouth for a long time.

'No one has ever done that before,' she said when he took away his lips. 'No one has ever kissed me.'

'Not in your whole life?'

'Not in my whole life.'

'Then you'll never go short again,' Liam said.

In the summer night with the moon shining, the smell of

18

honeysuckle on the air, a sky full of stars and Liam kissing her, Bessie forgot their age difference, his father's farm and the murder there would be if it was discovered she was out in the middle of the night. She surrendered herself to pleasure she had never known existed until Liam's passionate caresses moved from her lips and neck, and his fingers began with urgency to undo her blouse. Then, as fast as a falling star, she fell to earth. 'Don't do that. No! Stop! You can't do things like that.'

'Sure I won't hurt you. I only want to touch you. Let me, love.'

'You can't. Things like that are a sin. And I'm a sinner putting temptation in your way.' She buttoned her blouse with shaking fingers. 'I shouldn't have come. I must have been mad.'

'You're sorry you came.' Liam's voice had a pleading note in it. 'Don't tell me that. Don't tell me you regret it.'

'Regret it, ah no. Not if I live to be a hundred could I regret or forget tonight.'

'Will you come again, so?'

'Walk a bit of the way with me and I'll tell you.'

'Don't go yet.'

'I have to. My sister could wake and disturb the house. I have to.'

They began to walk home. 'Well,' Liam said, 'you were going to tell me.'

'It was a madness that made me say yes and come here tonight. I'm years older than you, and haven't a dowry to bring a husband. Being older than you is bad enough, but being penniless as well, your parents would never agree to that. But, do you see, I had to. I wanted to walk in a summer's night holding a man's hand. To have his arm around me, to have him kiss me. I have my feelings and when you asked me to meet you I gave into them.'

'Was that all it was then – you wanting to be held and kissed

19

by a man? And I suppose what you're telling me is that any man would have done?'

'I wish that was the truth. Wouldn't that be easy. But, God forgive me, I've never stopped thinking about you since the first day you came. Like someone who's lost their mind I've been. Seeing your face before me every waking minute. Not able to close my eyes in case the memory went and didn't come back in my dreams. Ah no, Liam, another man wouldn't have done at all.'

'Then, for the Lord's sake, what are you on about? I love you. We'll get married and to Hell with them all. And say no more about your age, sure what has that to do with anything?'

After that, Bessie didn't need much persuasion. When she was with him she forgot all the obstacles in their way. Meeting in the dead of night, slipping out of her home, or on other occasions from the Big House, running through the silent fields, all heightened the excitement of their being together.

Now she let Liam fondle her breasts, kiss and see them as well as he could by whatever light was in the sky. But that was as far as she would allow him to go despite his protestations that it wasn't natural for a man to be halted so. When she was alone she suffered agonies of conscience for her sin of impurity, and those of Liam's for which she was the cause. Each time she resolved that soon she would go to confession, but always postponed the going, knowing that she could not truly promise to cease allowing Liam the liberties she joyously granted him.

She never knew how someone found out that she and Liam were meeting. Unaware that the secret was out, one morning while passing the Maguires' farm she saw Liam's mother by the gate. She had a small churn of milk in her hands. 'It's a grand day Mrs Maguire, thank God,' Bessie said, thinking as she saluted the woman how like Liam she was and experiencing a feeling of affection towards the older woman as she saw the likeness.

'Grand day is it? Well – it won't be when I've finished with you. You whipster! How dare you open your mouth to me. A sack you should have over your head. Carrying on with my son. I know all about your goings-on in the ten acre field. You – an oul wan leading an innocent child astray. Ah, well may you look taken aback and the colour drain from your cheeks.'

'Mrs Maguire – me and Liam, we were going to tell . . .'

'Don't you Mrs Maguire me – you're not fit to recognize a respectable woman. Or were you hoping to trap my son and have the same title yourself? That before long you'd warm your arse on my hearth, was that it?'

Bessie wanted to run away, but her legs wouldn't obey the signals her brain sent to them, and so she stood rooted while Mrs Maguire spat forth a stream of venom.

'An O'Halloran. The daughter of a labouring man that him, nor his seed, breed nor generation ever owned an inch of land, and it's a farmer's son you're looking for.'

Though her legs might not have the power to move, Bessie thought, I haven't lost the use of my tongue and I'll not stand silent while she makes mock of my people. 'I never gave your land a thought. You and your likes might find that hard to believe for I've heard tell you'd kill for it. And maybe the O'Hallorans don't own an inch of land. And maybe it's a fault and then again maybe it's not. They're decent respectable people. I'm proud to belong to them.'

'Fine words and speeches from the labourer's daughter. Learned from listening to them above in the House. But I'll fine speech you.' Mrs Maguire advanced towards Bessie. She was close now. Bessie could see the rough skin of her face, the veins mottling her cheeks, the eyes she thought like Liam's, narrowed, glinting with hatred. Fear released the limbs which surprise had paralysed and she stepped back. Mrs Maguire came on, lowering the churn she carried, one hand on its neck, the other grasping the bottom, aiming it at Bessie.

'Don't! For God's sake have a bit of sense,' Bessie cried as the woman swung back the churn, then heaved it forward, sending the foaming milk cascading over Bessie.

''Tis a pity to waste it on you,' Liam's mother screamed. 'Manure it should have been. Go now from here before I leave the churn's imprint on your skull.'

She would, too, Bessie thought, blinking her eyes free of the cloying milk, she's like someone demented. She turned and began to walk as quickly as her shaking legs would allow.

Mrs Maguire followed her along the road screaming after her. 'You're an oul wan! When I was your age I'd been married for years with children running round me. Look at you – an oul wan! Look at the breasts of you all bolstered up letting on you're a girl. But you'll never have him. Never! I'll see to that. I'll have you run out of the Parish.'

'You've gone very quiet,' Liam said. 'Are you all right, the basket isn't too heavy?'

'No, the basket's grand. I was just thinking how lucky I am to have you for a husband,' Bessie replied.

'If them at home had had their way you wouldn't. By now you'd have been in America. But I'd have followed you and found you wherever you were.'

'Would you have done that, Liam? Would you have followed me across the sea?'

'To the ends of the earth, astoir.'

'I thought I'd lost you once your mother found out. I could have stood my ground if it was only lack of a dowry stood between us. But it was the age. Telling me I was an oul wan. I got it into my head it was the truth. I was too old for you. Even my own mother said the same thing. After your mother threw the milk over me I ran all the way home. It was a warm day and the milk dried tight on my face, but was clammy under my clothes. I was crying with shame and anger. I wanted comfort. Someone to take my side. And do you know what

22

she said when I told her about you and me and the scene with your mother? She said what more could I expect. Ten years on the side of a woman was too much, especially when the woman was a poor one. And that when I'd be full of aches and pains and the gaminess gone out of me, you'd still be a strip of a lad. "And what about children, there's that to consider. You'll soon be past having them, and 'tis well known that the old cow doesn't fall as easy as the young one." My own mother said that to me! And I believed her. She was saying what everyone would say. And if she wasn't with me – who could I count on?'

'Me, didn't you think of that?'

'I did, but I thought they'd get at you, your parents and the priest. That's why I decided to go to America, for I couldn't have stayed in the Parish with us separated.'

'Well, thank God you didn't. And thank God for the inheritance. We bested them all. And never let me hear you mention your age again for I never give it a thought.'

That it may always be so, Bessie said to herself – and the Light of Heaven to your Aunt Hetty for remembering you in her will.

Liam slowed his pace, put down the valise and wiped a hand across his sweating face. 'Maybe we should ask this man coming where Denzille Street is,' he said.

'I think we should,' Bessie agreed, hiding her concern, for Liam's face had gone the colour of chalk. The man said they were going in the wrong direction and pointed them back the way they had come.

They found the lodging house, a narrow, three-storeyed building with yellowed lace curtains covering the downstairs window. Two little girls sat on the kerb making piles of the summer dust and further along the gutter Bessie saw what appeared to be the mangled remains of a black cat. The smell was awful and she covered her nose with a handkerchief as they went up the shallow steps and Liam knocked on the door.

'Excuse me ma'am,' he said to the woman who answered. 'We were looking for a room for me and the wife.'

The woman scanned them before answering: 'Five shillings a night in advance. The breakfast's at eight in the morning and no going upstairs after.'

'Right, we'll take it.'

'Come in.'

Liam and Bessie followed her into the hall and along a drugget-covered passage, moving out of the way of a large castor oil plant that reached its shiny green leaves into the narrow hall, and beyond to where the passage widened and the stairs began. Pointing up them the landlady said, 'It's the right-hand door on the first landing. The key's in the lock,' and held out her hand for the money.

The room faced the street. Bessie went to the window and looked out. 'There's an undertaker's across the road and a hearse going out,' she said. 'I hope that's not bad luck.'

'What gave you that idea? It's never unlucky to see a funeral,' Liam said, coming to stand beside her, putting an arm round her waist. He kissed the side of her face and his hand moved to fondle her breast.

'All the same I don't like it, nor the black cat either. They can be good or bad luck.'

'You're not still doubting my fortune are you, thinking the black cat and the hearse will alter it?'

'No,' Bessie said, moving out of his embrace, 'don't be paying any attention to me and my notions.' She went to the iron bedstead where they had put their luggage. 'Mind you, at the same time I'm not setting my hopes too high.' She took off her hat. The dusty sunbeams made a halo round her head.

'Your hair is beautiful, like a flame,' Liam said, coming towards her, his hands outstretched. 'Let me touch it, warm my poor cold hands on it.'

'I hate it. It's red rusty like a shovel left out in the rain, and

24

keep your hands to yourself, they've a way of straying from the hair of my head. Put away the bags instead.'

Liam sulkily did her bidding. But his bad humour didn't last longer than the time it took to stow the baggage in the cupboard, and he was smiling when he suggested that they should ask the landlady for a cup of tea, then ramble into town and find the lie of the land for tomorrow.

'Are you sure you're not too tired?' Bessie inquired, remembering how he had looked earlier on in their walk.

'Not a bother on me. Come on down, I've a terrible thirst.'

The landlady refused them tea. Bed and breakfast she reminded them was her business, not light refreshments.

'But ma'am, we've not had a cup since leaving home this morning,' Liam pleaded.

'There's an eating house down the way. Not a stone's throw from here – you'll get all your orders there.'

'That's Dublin people for you,' Bessie said when they were in the street. In the eating house they had soda bread, brown and white and two cups of strong tea.

'One and six,' said the girl who served them. When she had left the table Bessie and Liam said together, 'And that's Dublin prices.' They laughed and said they were entitled to make a wish for saying the same thing at the same time. 'I hope your Aunt Hetty's estate is a big one,' Bessie wished aloud. 'We'd need a fortune to live in Dublin.'

'You shouldn't have let me know your wish, now it won't work. But it will, of course. I don't believe in all them superstitions.'Twill be a fortune.' He caught hold of and squeezed Bessie's hand. 'Listen, will I ask the girl where Molesworth Street is?'

'Do,' Bessie replied, smiling at him fondly.

The girl's directions were long and imprecise, so that soon they were lost and had to ask the way again.

'Aren't they gorgeous houses!' Bessie exclaimed when at last they turned into the street where the solicitor had his office. They walked slowly along the terrace of mellow red-bricked houses admiring the uniformity of the sash windows, the arched fanlights, the wrought iron balconies round some of the upstairs windows, stopping now and then to read brass nameplates fastened to ornate railings or mounted on walls. Eventually they found what they were looking for. 'T. R. Geoghan,' Bessie read out. 'That's him, but to be sure take a look at the letter.' From his pocket Liam took the letter and together they read it and were satisfied they had come to the right place.

'Wouldn't it be grand if he was open,' Liam said.

'Wishing won't make it so. But at least tomorrow we'll have no trouble finding him. Put the letter safe and we'll go back for I'm tired now.'

Before getting into bed Bessie pulled back a corner of the mattress and examined the wooden corner where the spring was fastened. 'What's that you're doing?' Liam asked.

'What I should have done before we took the room. Looking for bugs.'

'Much good it would do to find them now, unless you fancied a night in the undertaker's yard.'

Bessie ignored his comment, bent closer and sniffed audibly. 'It smells of paraffin. If there were any, they'd be dead, it kills them.'

'God bless your nose,' Liam said, coming to stand by her. 'I can smell nothing but the lovely sweet smell of yourself.'

They undressed, then knelt and said their prayers. In bed Bessie lay with her head on Liam's chest and heard his thundering heart. His hands caressed her. Their touch became more urgent. All the while she talked, asking questions. Questions to which she always wanted the same answer. Did he love her? Did he regret leaving the farm, marrying her?

'Haven't I told you a thousand times and more. I'd be happy anywhere with you. And if you'd refused me I'd have gone a

26

bachelor to my grave. God, you're a terrible woman talking at a time like this!' He shifted so that Bessie's head lay back on the pillow. 'Is it only tormenting me you are with the questions or don't you like what I'm doing to you?'

'Tormenting you was all it was for I like it well enough.'

'So then stop talking.'

Dolly said 'good night' to Bid and walked up the street towards her home. It was beginning to get dark and she thought how the houses didn't look so bad in the falling dusk. The dirt wasn't so noticeable either, nor the shabbiness of the women standing round the open hall doors. But the smells were the same: onions frying in stale fat, gusts of porter rushing into the warm evening every time a public house door swung open, and the stink of unwashed bodies sweating in the summer heat. As she neared her own house the street widened, there were fewer pubs and the smells were overlaid with more pleasant and unusual ones. For further up the street lived the Jews. She could smell burnt feathers from the chicken butchers' – a clean, acrid smell, and frying oil, and a faint whiff remained from the barrels of pickled cucumbers that had stood outside Ordman's all day. They were nice smells – she liked them, as she liked the duck loaves and bagels, the sour sweet cucumbers and the fish her mother fried in pennyworths of the cooking oil.

But the lift her spirit received was soon lowered when she reached her own home, two rooms in a three-storeyed tenement. Fifty other people shared the house with Dolly and her family. The house had been built early in the previous century, when the street was still part of the outlying town. Dolly often wondered whom it had belonged to then, tried to envisage how different life would have been when only one family owned so many rooms . . . when there were fields all round and when everything was green and clean. For now, though a house on the opposite side of the street had enough

27

land to graze a couple of cows whose milk they sold from a front room converted to a dairy, all else was houses.

A long dark passage led from the front door to the backyard where a cold water tap dripped incessantly, sliming the stones round the shore green and making hazardous the filling of kettles and buckets. Close to the tap in a wooden shack was the lavatory, its deep conical pan set into a wooden seat that ran from wall to wall. The women of the house took turns to drench it with dirty suds on washday.

Beyond the pipe and wooden shack lay the remains of the original owner's garden. Long gone to wrack and ruin, only the roses remained, returned now to the briar, but sweet smelling and in their season growing in profusion along the crumbling wall. New babies in battered bassinets were put into the garden for air and if they survived convulsions and fevers, learnt to crawl and took their first steps through the stinging nettles and long coarse grass. Sometimes a tenant kept a pig in the garden until the smell of pig-swill became too much for the other occupants. Then, after angry words and nearly coming to blows, the pig would vanish – until the next time.

As she entered the passage, Dolly was overcome with a feeling of loathing for the house which even the smell of wild roses could not dispel. She hated everything about the place – the ever-open hall door with gossiping women congregated round it, the garden draped with rope lines festooned with babies' dingy arse-rags. She hated the night noises: coughing, hawking men, crying infants, quarrelling voices, creaking bed springs, the shrieks of women giving birth, or men and women in their death agony. And she hated the courting couples in the hall leaning against the walls saying their good nights. But most of all she felt hate and shame for the times when she watched furtively for the passage to be empty, then the frantic rush with the bucket, newspaper-capped for decency's sake, out to the lavatory to empty its contents. She pushed open the door of the room used as kitchen, living room and where her father and brother slept on chair beds since she had grown too big to share the room with Richard. The room was clean, bright and cheerful. A good fire burned in the blackleaded grate, the steel hobs were burnished and above the fireplace a tassel-fringed chenille mantelcloth decorated the shelf. Seated round the table covered with a matching chenille cloth over which a smaller white one was laid, Dolly's parents and brother were seated drinking tea and eating bread and butter.

'You're awful late,' Dolly's mother said, getting up and going to the hob where on top of a pot, two plates, one upended over the other were keeping her dinner warm.

'The bit of food will be destroyed. What kept you, and we dying to tell you the news?'

'What news?'

'About Richard, child, don't tell me you forgot,' her father said.

'Oh God!' Dolly put her hands up to her face. 'I did. I forgot all about it. Dick, I'm sorry. But you passed. Didn't you pass? I know you did. I can tell. Didn't I do the Nine Fridays for you. Oh Dick, I'm delighted.' She went to her brother and hugged him.

'Well now,' said her father, his thin face flushed with pleasure, 'what do you think of that? Isn't that one in the eye for them that thought I had notions of grandeur keeping my son at school? But wasn't I right? I knew he had it in him and that the Brothers would bring it out. He passed with flying colours and has a place in the Civil Service.'

Richard winked at Dolly, and they both smiled at their father's boasting. She sat down and began her dinner of stuffed lamb's heart, cauliflower and potatoes. Her mother made fresh tea and Dolly noticed that she was unusually quiet. Her father continued to extol the virtues of education and the teaching abilities of the Irish Christian Brothers. When he

29

paused for a minute Dolly took advantage of it and asked Richard to tell her more about the results and where he would be working.

'London. The War Office.'

'London! England, you'll be going to England! That's marvellous. When?'

'Next month if all goes well with the medical, please God.'

Dolly ate a bit of her dinner, then asked, 'Ma – when Dick goes can I have the chair bed back?'

Bridget, about to pour out the tea, stopped, the spout of the pot wavering, tea spilling, staining the cloth. 'Now look what you were the cause of. You think of no one but yourself. A bed of your own – the first thought in your head.'

'And what's wrong with wanting a bed of my own? In any case, then you and Father could have the double one back. I hate sleeping with you. I can't turn over but you're telling me to lie still.'

'That's because you're like a bloody eel. Don't think I wouldn't be just as pleased to get rid of you, but it's the bringing of it up now. Bringing it up weeks before Richard goes. Not a word about him going away from home. Oh no. Nothing but looking to your comfort. A selfish, spoiled little girl, that's what I reared.'

Dolly's face became sulky, but she didn't answer her mother. Instead she concentrated on dissecting the sheep's heart. Cutting away the opening into the valves which after stuffing her mother had sewn up with white cotton. Spearing a piece of the fatty substance, holding it aloft on her fork, her expression changing from sulkiness to one of disgust. 'I hate that. Look at the threads hanging from it. It makes me feel sick.'

Pity about you. If I'd known your stomach was that delicate it's smoked salmon and bagels I'd have got for you.'

'Richard tried to coax Dolly into better humour, promising to write to her when he went away. Even take her over for

30

a holiday when he had saved up. But she wouldn't be humoured, got up from the table and said she was going to lie down.

'Well, I tried anyway,' Richard said. 'Listen, I promised Maggie and Tom I'd drop down for half an hour. Will I see you later on in Fitz's, Da?'

'You will. Go on now, the fresh air will do you good.'

After Richard had left for his sister Maggie's house, Johnny said to his wife, 'Passing the examination was the best thing for him. Getting away from here will be the makings of him.'

Bridget said nothing. She was thinking. Her husband continued talking. 'He was beginning to get ideas. I could see the way his mind was working. There last year when Carson's Ulster Volunteers was set up to prevent Home Rule I could tell the way he was thinking. Though I suppose it was the lock-out that had the greatest influence on him. He had great admiration for Connolly. When the strikers were injured by the police and Connolly formed the Irish Citizen's Army, I was afraid of my life he'd join. That would have put paid to his education.'

'That's right,' Bridget said, knowing he was content so long as now and then she said something, anything, and went back to her thoughts. God knows she didn't begrudge Richard his chance, nor the sacrifice keeping him at school had meant. But she wasn't convinced that staying in school and becoming a clerk was what he wanted. But his father was. Morning, noon and night, on at him to better himself, pay attention to his copy books, listen to the Brothers. They knew what was what.

He was talking again. 'Nothing surer than he'd have got mixed up in something. Didn't I find the leaflets amongst his exercise books. Them of Connolly's – *Reasons Why You Should Join The Citizen's Army*. And then MacNeil's *Enrol Under The Green Flag*.'

'You did, aye.'

31

'I did, and all the information about the fellow Pearse, the schoolteacher. I'm telling you if I hadn't had the strong hand on him in one of the organizations he'd have been. And God only knows what them fellas will get up to if the Home Rule Bill isn't passed. But he's going to the right place now.'

Poor Richard, robbed of his childhood. Night after night bent over the fecking oul exercise books. And where would it get him in the end? 'I was wondering if you had a shilling to spare, Bridget?' Johnny's question broke in on her wonderings.

'For what?' she asked. She knew well for what, but it satisfied her to make him explain.

'The least I can do on a night like this is buy my son a drink. And there'll be them in Fitz's watching points. Ready to say, "Look at that now, educating his son and not able to stand his round." Could you make it two shillings?'

Bridget rooted in her purse, counted out the money and said, 'Between you and her 'ithin on the bed you have me fleeced.'

'You'll have it back a-Saturday. The weather's holding, no fear of me being knocked off. Grand weather this for the building,' Johnny said, taking the money and going.

Lying on the big bed in the parlour Dolly thought about Richard leaving home. She was sorry he was going. She would miss him. But he was lucky going to live in England. Everyone in England was rich. They'd have no tenement houses there. Maybe one day she would be a famous singer and go to London. The choirmaster in Jacobs said her voice was good enough to be trained. Gradually her bad humour evaporated. She thought of the coming concert and what she would sing, and hoped the apple green dress turned out all right. Maybe Jem O'Brien would pluck up the courage to ask her out. And if he did she would go. He wasn't bad. Better than any of the others in the crowd. Though his mother was a dealer in the big market and sold fish. But he was nice. And you had to have a fella. Jem would do for the time being. One day she was bound to meet someone marvellous and get her voice trained. She lay imagining what it would be like to sing on a proper stage. Not Jacobs' Hall, but a real one with gorgeous curtains and people in the gilt boxes, like the Gaiety, maybe. With everyone throwing flowers and calling 'Encore, Encore'. She fell asleep and dreamed she was an opera singer.

Chapter Two

The Delahunts, as Bid had supposed, were heading for Kingstown and the mail boat which would take them on the first stage of their journey to Sussex. There they would be guests of Lord and Lady Whitehead to whose son, Stephen, Alice was soon to become engaged.

Staying in the English countryside during June when the London Season was at its height was unusual and most unfortunate, Lady Delahunt thought as the Rolls drove to the harbour. But unavoidable; Lady Whitehead's frail health kept her in the country and the dear children had to get to know each other before the engagement was announced. So Horsham it had to be. But there would be plenty of other Seasons after Alice was married. In a few years, for Lord Whitehead must be close to seventy and not robust, Stephen would inherit the title and Alice become one of London's leading hostesses. The best in the land would flock to her drawing room. Her entertaining would be the talk of the town. Happily Lady Delahunt dreamed of the glittering prize Alice had won.

'Look! There goes the train. Aren't the servants lucky old things. I wish I could have travelled out on it,' Alice said as the mail train passed them near Blackrock.

'I rather like trains. But for such a short trip the car is more comfortable. Anyway, you'll have plenty of train rides when we get to the other side,' Lady Delahunt replied.

At Kingstown, while Sir Arthur stopped to talk with some-

34

one on the quayside, Alice and her mother boarded, were greeted by the steward and shown to adjoining cabins where the servants had unpacked for the crossing. Coming into Alice's cabin her mother suggested they should go up on deck until the boat sailed.

Little yachts with brightly coloured sails bobbed gently on the water, seagulls wheeled in the sky. 'It's a lovely evening, so we'll have a good crossing, thank heavens. Your father is still gossiping, I see.'

'I wish we weren't going,' Alice said.

'Oh good, he's taken his leave. He's coming aboard. What on earth do you mean you wish you weren't going?'

Alice didn't answer her mother immediately but looked up at the sky and the wheeling seagulls, then down to where the gangplank was being drawn up.

'Well! And why do you wish you weren't going to Horsham may I ask?'

'Nella's coming home from Paris tomorrow. I haven't seen her for almost a year. There'd have been so much to talk about.'

'Nonsense. You'll be far too busy enjoying yourself to give Nella a thought.' And a good thing too, Lady Delahunt said to herself. Nella Sugden was an unsettling influence. One of those frightful modern young women like Constance Gore Booth who had married that Polish Count Marievicz. Really frightful women who meddled in things that didn't concern them. Constance getting mixed up in the politics, founding the Fianna Boy Scouts and helping that fellow Connolly during the strike. And Nella preaching socialism to Alice, women's suffrage, insisting that parents had no right to choose a girl's husband! Her father had done the right thing packing her off to Paris. The pity was she hadn't stayed there.

The boat was moving out of the harbour, the gulls following it. Lady Delahunt stopped thinking about Nella and, taking hold of Alice's arm, said it was getting chilly. They should go

35

inside, she didn't want Alice catching a chill. Obediently, Alice allowed herself to be led away, although she would have preferred to stay on deck and watch the Dublin hills fade into the distance. Her thoughts were still on Nella's arrival the next day. She hated missing it. Nella was wonderful company.

'I'll sit with you for a while. We can chat until Papa comes. He must have found someone else to detain him.' Lady Delahunt took off her hat, patted her hair and sat beside Alice. 'Aren't you terribly excited about seeing Stephen, darling?' Her small face smiled at her daughter.

'I suppose so.'

'Really, there're times I could shake you. Can't you show a bit more enthusiasm? Here you are young and beautiful, with trunks of the most divine clothes on board and tomorrow you're seeing your future husband. What more could any girl want?'

'I don't know him.'

'Of course you do. You've known him all your life.'

'I've known the gardener all my life, but that doesn't mean I'd want to marry him. Anyway I haven't seen him for years.'

'Well, really! I've never heard you talk like this before. Never known you to question me. What can you be thinking of?'

'Actually I was thinking about Nella. How chic she will be after her stay in Paris. I suppose being so beautiful helps.'

'Alice, don't try my patience. And Nella is neither chic nor beautiful. She's too flamboyant and has dreadful hair.'

'But Mama, you said Nella's hair was magnificent. You described it as Titian.'

'You imagined that.' Lady Delahunt's mouth was tight-lipped. 'Her hair is red. Ginger. Foxy. Beside you, she looks common. Your face, like mine, is delicately featured. If Nella had our features and colouring, for not many women have truly black hair, especially with blue eyes, you might describe her as a beauty.'

'Well, I think she's beautiful. And I'm not madly excited about seeing Stephen. Even when I was younger I didn't like him. I see no reason why it should be different now.'

Lady Delahunt took a deep breath, counted to ten and said, 'Let's not discuss it any more. It's time to get ready for dinner. See you presently.'

Left alone, Alice admitted to herself that she had lied to her mother. She was looking forward to seeing Stephen again. Nella, who had been in love dozens of times, said it was the most indescribable feeling. Making you want to dance and sing. Tell the whole world about it. Your heart hammering at the sight of the one you were in love with. Sheer ecstasy. Alice had never felt like that in anyone's presence. Still, she told herself, maybe that was because she was younger than Nella. And maybe tomorrow when she saw Stephen the magic would happen.

'Do you want the fry or the plain breakfast?' the landlady asked the next morning.

'The fry please,' Liam replied.

'It costs extra.'

'How much?' Bessie asked.

'A shilling each.'

'We'll have the plain breakfast.'

'But I'm starving,' Liam protested when the woman left the room.

'It won't do you a bit of harm, and after we've been to the solicitor we'll have a grand feed.'

The woman brought tea and bread with butter scraped thinly on it. While Liam and Bessie ate she stayed in the dining room moving the chairs in and out around the tables, flicking at real or imaginary crumbs with a not very clean tea towel.

'She's doing that to discourage us from lingering,' Bessie said in a low voice, 'so hurry up and finish.'

37

'There's ages to kill before the appointment. How'll we put it in?'

'I noticed a chapel near the railway station. We could get an hour's Mass, then saunter slowly to the office.'

During Mass, Bessie prayed that all would go well at the solicitor's, that Liam wouldn't be too disappointed if it wasn't all he expected and that God would grant them health and happiness.

At the solicitor's a young woman asked if they had an appointment, and then invited them in. In the hall Bessie noticed the brown linoleum so highly polished you could, she was sure, see your face in it, and the shining brass rail along the wall to prevent people rubbing against the flocked wallpaper.

'In here,' said the woman, and they followed her into a downstairs room. 'Sit down and I'll tell Mr Geoghan you're here.'

'That's one of them typewriting machines and a telephone, too,' Liam whispered, pointing to the secretary's desk.

'I've seen the likes before,' Bessie whispered back.

'You would of course, at the Big House. They had all the newfangled things.' He smiled at Bessie and she knew he was nervous. She was, too. She caught hold of his hand and squeezed it.

The girl returned and said Mr Geoghan would see them now. She held open the door for them.

'Ah, Mr Maguire.' The solicitor, a thin man wearing rimless spectacles, stood up and held out his hand. 'I'm delighted to meet you. How are you?'

Thank God he talks the same as us anyway, Bessie thought. Liam won't be as nervous as he would if the voice of the man was English. People couldn't help the way they spoke but an English accent had a queer effect all the same.

'And this is?' Mr Geoghan asked.

'The wife. This is Bessie,' Liam replied.

'Well now, is that so? I didn't know you were married.

38

Didn't know that at all. Your aunt, Lord have mercy on her, never mentioned that fact at all, though many's the chat we had about you.'

'We only married a while back, since the aunt died, God be good to her.'

'So that's it. Well, I'm delighted to meet you, Mrs Maguire.' He shook hands with Bessie, then invited them both to sit down.

'Now then, let me see,' Mr Geoghan said and began studying the file he had open on the desk. 'As well as being your aunt's solicitor I'm also the executor of her will.' When he looked up from the papers he was smiling and Bessie saw that he had gold in one of his teeth. She had seen the like before in the mouths of the gentry and wondered as she had then what happened to the gold in people's teeth when they died.

'Your aunt left you everything she had except for a sum to the Redemptorist Fathers for masses for her soul. There's a house and the sum of forty pounds. You'll have these papers to sign, then it's all yours. The house is vacant. A grand little place, furnished and in a good location near the river.' Mr Geoghan began detaching forms from the file, filled his fountain pen and was about to push the papers across the desk when Liam spoke.

'There'll be the estate as well, sir, you didn't mention that.'

'That *is* the estate, the house and the money.'

'But sir!' Liam was searching his pocket, taking out the letter, handing it over. 'Do you see, sir, you've said it there about the aunt's estate.'

Mr Geoghan's tooth flashed. 'Ah, Mr Maguire, estate is a word with more than one meaning. In legal terms it means the belongings, money, property of someone deceased. What was it you thought your aunt had left you?'

'An estate! 'Twas what you said, there in black and white.' He waved the letter in front of him, his voice rising. 'There it is, look, there, do you see?'

Bessie caught hold of his waving arm. Her heart bled for

39

his disappointment. For the shame she knew he was feeling at showing his ignorance. For the first time since entering the room she spoke. 'Sure it was only a misunderstanding, love. And isn't a house and forty pounds a grand thing to have? And wasn't the mistake an easy one to make. Didn't I think the very same as yourself?'

'Oh, yes, indeed, it happens every day in the week,' Mr Geoghan said. 'People are always misunderstanding solicitors' letters. People from all walks of life. You'd be surprised at the number it happens to.'

'Did you hear that Liam, it's always happening. And, just think, we own a house in Dublin. Sure that's grand. We can do anything with a house of our own and forty pounds,' Bessie said.

'You could indeed. Your aunt at one time considered opening a shop. She went as far as having the parlour window knocked out and a big one put in though the venture never came off. Still, as your wife says there's great possibilities in owning property.' The solicitor looked at the watch hanging from a thin gold chain across his breast. Bessie realized they were overstaying their appointment and squeezed Liam's arm, hoping to convey this to him.

'I'll want your signature here, and here,' Mr Geoghan said, coming around the desk. Liam wrote his name on the lines indicated. 'Now, that's that. You'll want the keys and the cheque, of course. Or maybe cash would be better? Have you a bank account?' Liam who hadn't spoken since making his protest shook his head.

'Cash then's the thing. Let's see what I've got in hand.' He took out his wallet and went through it. 'Twelve pounds. I don't carry much on me, but there might be the difference in here.' He opened a black and red metal box. 'If you don't mind silver I think I can make it. That's another five pounds in notes.' He counted out the rest in crowns and florins. It made a heavy pile of silver.

'If you could oblige us with an envelope, sir?' Bessie asked.

'Certainly. No trouble at all.' The solicitor made the coins into a parcel, which Bessie put well down in her basket.

'You take the notes Liam,' she said, 'and then we'd better go and not keep the man all day.'

'No hurry,' the solicitor lied and smiled, displaying his gold. 'But don't go without the keys and I'll give you directions how to get there. Do you know Dublin?'

'I was here before, many times,' said Liam.

Once only for a few hours, Bessie thought, but didn't contradict him.

'You'll have no bother finding it, so. Turn right from here and head for the Liffey. You'll get a tram there that will take you up the quays.' He shook hands with them. 'It was a pleasure to meet you. I hope you'll be very happy in Dublin.'

Outside, Liam leant against the railings looking dejected. 'Well, didn't I make a right eejit of myself. An estate! I thought I had an estate. Honest to God I did.' He looked like a small boy feeling sorry for himself and like a small sulking child Bessie decided to treat him.

'Come on now, Liam Maguire, we'll have none of this. If there's any eejits going it's the likes of solicitors who can't write plain English. All he had to do was write what you were actually going to get. But there's no harm done. And no one thinks any the worse of you. What in God's name would we have done with an estate? You the Master and me the Mistress! Can't you just see us, done up to the nines and never a minute's peace between one thing and another. A fine pair we'd have made.' She saw the beginnings of a smile. In a minute she knew he'd be over his disappointment.

'It was only that I wanted to give you everything,' he said, straightening up. 'It's not many diamonds forty pounds will buy.'

'Diamonds my eye! What would I do with diamonds? And haven't I got the best jewel of all in you. Come on now, let's

41

move. And there is one thing we can afford with the money.'

'What's that?'

'The grand feed.'

'We can too, and I'm starving.' The smile was all over his face. She took his arm. 'Do you know what,' she said, 'you're the loveliest man in the world and I love you.'

'If the street hadn't all the people passing I'd kiss you this minute. Let's go for the food, then we'll find the house and hansel it.'

'You think of nothing but that and food. I don't know what sort of man I married.'

The Delahunts travelled through the night on the boat train from Holyhead, crossed London by hansom cab to Victoria and set off again by train for Sussex.

'Why, I do believe that's Stephen come to meet us!' Lady Delahunt exclaimed as the train arrived at Whitehead's Halt. 'Doesn't he look lovely, Alice? Wake up, Arthur!' She shook her husband who came to with a start.

Alice looked out of the window and saw Stephen. It must be him for there was no one else on the platform except a railway man. And she thought how she would never have recognized this tall fair man as the boy she remembered who had come to Ireland when she was a child. He was older than herself and Nella and hadn't paid much attention to either of them when they met at children's parties to which they were all invited.

She remembered too that when she was fourteen her parents had been invited to Rudgewick Park, how excited her mother had been, the preparations for the visit – then at the last minute Lady Whitehead had been taken ill and the visit cancelled. Her mother had been inconsolable for days and Alice had thought what a fuss she was making about nothing. And couldn't understand her mother's chagrin the following year when Nella and her family went to Sussex and they

42

weren't invited. Once she had overheard a conversation between her mother and father: 'The Whiteheads are looking her over. I'll die if they choose that awful Nella,' her mother had said. And her father had replied, 'It's nothing of the kind. Sugden's interested in land the Whiteheads have for sale. It's business, that's all.'

'Then why has that wretched girl gone with them?'

'Keep her out of trouble.'

At the time Alice hadn't understood what the conversation was about, but when last year they went to the Whiteheads' London home she knew it was her turn to be looked over. Stephen was still in Europe and his name was only mentioned in passing by his mother, but Lady Delahunt made it quite clear to Alice why she was there. And now she was in Horsham and Stephen was a young man, smiling and waving as the train halted.

Lady Delahunt had kept the window closed because of smuts, now Sir Arthur wide awake struggled with the leather strap fastening. Succeeding, he opened the window, leant out and waved to Stephen who was hurrying to their carriage.

'Lady Delahunt, Sir Arthur, Alice, how splendid to see you,' Stephen said after opening the door. He helped the women to alight and asked if they had had a good journey and if the crossing was smooth.

'Like the proverbial mill pond,' Sir Arthur replied.

'My dear, dear boy.' Lady Delahunt kissed Stephen on both cheeks. 'It's been such a long time. Let me look at you.' She held him at arms' length. A thought went through her mind. Unlike most young men in their twenties he hadn't filled out. He was quite boyish-looking. It disconcerted her vaguely, but only for a moment. 'How good of you to meet us, we weren't expecting it.' He was very handsome and elegant.

'No, well the carriage was to have been sent, but knowing your interest in cars, Sir Arthur, I thought it might be rather fun to meet you in the Packard. Papa tells me you have a Rolls.'

'I have. She's a beauty. Wouldn't consider any other machine.'

'Every man to his taste,' Lady Delahunt said and beckoned Alice who was hovering in the background. 'Come along, darling. You go ahead with Stephen, I must see the servants leave nothing behind.'

'Is this your first time in Sussex?' Stephen asked as he and Alice emerged from the Halt.

'Yes,' Alice said shyly.

'You'll like it. There's plenty to do. Marvellous riding. And Papa will let me have the car. I'll take you for drives – we'll go to Brighton. Of course there's no one else staying, everyone's in London.'

'Mama explained that your mother's health confines her to the country. Actually, I'm glad. Oh, not about your mother's health, I didn't mean that. I mean I love the country. Is she ill now?'

'She doesn't complain. Something beastly wrong with her back.' Stephen opened the car door. 'I'd ask you to ride in front with me, but I expect your father will want a front seat.'

'I'm sure he will,' Alice agreed.

Sir Arthur and Lady Delahunt came out of the station followed by their servants and a porter pushing a trolley laden with trunks, hat boxes, bags and shooting sticks.

'The trap will be here presently,' Stephen said, showing Lady Delahunt into the car. They were about to drive off when she remembered their motoring veils; a servant had to be called and told to bring them. Only when the ladies' faces were protected did the car drive away from the station.

Sir Arthur monopolized the conversation, talking to Stephen about his stay in Europe, telling him how wise he was to have got out before it was too late. Once or twice Lady Delahunt attempted to get a word in edgeways but didn't succeed until they had turned through the gates of Rudgewick Park and were driving along the avenue of magnificent lime

44

trees. 'How beautiful they are! My favourite trees.' On and on she went about the trees and Alice wished she would shut up. Stephen would think her an awful bore.

No sooner had Lady Delahunt paused for breath when the house came into view and she was off again. 'What a magnificent house! Such brickwork! Simply breathtaking! I adore sandstone corners, their way of highlighting the doors and windows, so delightful against the red brick. Tudor, isn't it, Stephen?'

'Actually I'm a bit of a duffer about that sort of thing. It was built in 1577, that's over the door, but I'm not sure who was on the throne then.'

'Elizabeth,' Alice said.

'Of course,' her mother agreed, 'but I'd still class it as Tudor.' No one contradicted her and she became silent and gazed through the window rapturously taking in every detail of the house's façade and imagining the time when Alice would be its mistress.

Chapter Three

Jacobs' Hall was thronged. Jem O'Brien sat in the audience never once taking his eyes from the stage. In a minute Dolly would appear. As she sang he could feast his eyes on her. He loved her. He had from the moment four years ago when they had both started at Jacobs. He thought about her all day, and dreamt up schemes as to how he could approach her, ask her to go out with him. But in his heart he knew it was useless – Dolly would never give him a rec. Not someone like her – the most gorgeous girl in the world. Dolly could have anyone she fancied. And of one thing he was certain – she didn't fancy him.

Kevin McEvoy, a mate of Jem's to whom in a rash moment he had confided his secret adoration of Dolly now nudged him with his elbow. 'I bet you're getting all excited O'Brien, eh?'

'Shut up! It's going to start. There's the MC,' Jem said in a low voice.

Up the side steps leading to the stage climbed Mr McGurk, a mixer of cakes, more familiar to the audience in flour-dusted overalls. Now he wore his best navy blue serge suit, and his hair was flat with hair oil. A round of applause greeted his ascent. He let it die then stepped forward. 'Ladies and gentlemen, it gives me great pleasure to welcome you here tonight for our annual concert. Many of the singers and musicians you already know – old favourites who have delighted you through the years. But tonight we have as well a few newcomers, and it's one of these, a young girl and a grand singer who'll open the concert. Ladies and gentlemen – give a big hand for Dolly Devoy!' Almost before Mr McGurk finished his speech Jem began to clap, followed by everyone else and from the audience rose cries of 'Come on Dolly'.

Mr McGurk stepped behind the curtains as they began to part, revealing Dolly in her apple green velvet. Jem swallowed the lump in his throat. Beside him Kevin whispered, 'Jasus, she's gorgeous right enough!' Someone behind him hissed 'Shhh!' Jem thought Dolly was lovelier than ever. It was the first time he had seen her hair loose. She's beautiful, like one of them singers on the Gaiety, he thought.

Mr McGurk led her forward, she bowed and smiled. 'Dolly is going to give us that old favourite by Balfe, *There Is A Flower That Bloometh*.' The audience applauded, the MC left the stage and Dolly moved back to stand by the piano. The accompanist began to play and Dolly to sing.

Jem clasped his hands together. She could sing as well as everything else! He had heard tell she had a voice. But he'd never dreamt it was such a voice. It was sweet and clear and strong, could go high and low, every note was true, and the feeling she put into it! He was sweating with emotion. He was sure she was looking at him, singing just for him.

The song finished, the audience clapped, stamped their feet and called for an encore. Mr McGurk appeared again and held up a hand. 'Now then, let's be fair,' he cajoled. 'There's others waiting their turn. But I promise you won't be disappointed, Dolly will oblige again later on.' Dolly left the stage and the concert proceeded.

During the interval Kevin told Jem he was mad if he didn't chance his arm and send round a note to Dolly. 'Sure what have you got to lose, and if she refuses it won't be to your face. Go on, here's a pencil, and that young fella'll run round with it.'

'Ah God, I don't know.'

'Go on. Write, "Dear Dolly," then something about the

47

song, and the frock, mots like that. And ask her if she'll meet you after. And ask her if she'll bring Bid. And that we'll take them for ice cream wafers. Go on. Here.'

'Well, all right then, but she'll never come,' Jem said and took the pencil. Kevin found a bit of paper and gave it to him.

'Wet it, it's copying ink, lick the shaggin' pencil. Hurry up, the interval's nearly over.'

Resting the paper against the wall Jem moistened the pencil leaving a purple stain on his lips and wrote:

'Dear Dolly, I was wondering if you'd care for a wafer after. You sang lovely. And if you come would you ever bring Bid. Kevin has a smack for Bid. Don't refuse, please, if you can, come. Jem.'

'Eh, commere you. Take this round the back to the stage and knock on the door. Say it's for Dolly Devoy and you want an answer. There's a penny for yourself and if you don't come back I'll lambaste you in the morning,' Kevin said, handing the coin and note to a young boy.

The order of artistes was altered during the second half of the concert.

'That's because Dolly is going to do the last number,' Kevin whispered, 'and if that young fella's run off with the penny I'll break his bloody neck.'

Dolly sang *Danny Boy*, and this time did an encore, singing *A Nation Once Again*. The audience joined in, got to its feet singing with her, 'And Ireland long a province be a nation once again,' their voices full of fervour. Jem was outside of himself, lost in the spectacle of Dolly, her arms outstretched, imagining they beckoned him, the smile was for him alone. She was telling him, yes, she would come, she would be his sweetheart.

A tug at his sleeve brought him down to earth, and Kevin's voice was saying, 'I've just seen that little fecker, he's at the back of the hall. I'm going before he makes off.'

The curtain came down. Dazedly Jem left his seat and followed the crowd out.

'You did it. Be Jasus you must have the four-leaved clover. Look at this, she wrote back. She's going to meet you.'

Kevin was waving a sheet of paper. Jem grabbed it and read:

'Dear Jem, Thanks very much for the note. Me and Bid will come for an ice wafer. Wait outside the Peter Street entrance. Dolly.'

He couldn't believe it. Dolly Devoy was going to meet him. He felt ten feet tall. Then he felt nervous. And then nearly died when he put his hands in his pockets and discovered he only had two threepenny bits. 'I never changed the money out of my working clothes. That's all I have,' he said, holding out the little silver coins.

'I've half a crown, we'll be all right, that'll buy three wafers apiece,' Kevin said. 'Come on, let's be at the door before they come out. You'd never know with mots, they might have only done it for a laugh. But if we're there we'll collar them. I fancy a court with Bid Dunne, they say she's a grand court.'

Jem went with him, hoping against hope that the note wasn't a cod; telling himself that Dolly wouldn't go that far for a laugh. They seemed to wait for ages before the girls came out. He had expected to see Dolly in green velvet with her hair flowing free and was disappointed that she wore a coat and dress and her hair was coiled.

'You sang grand,' Kevin said.

'Thanks very much,' Dolly replied. 'I don't know what I'd have done without Bid giving me encouragement in between. I had a sore throat. I don't think I did justice to the songs.'

'Oh, but you did. You were marvellous. You should have heard what everyone was saying.' Jem forgot his nervousness. 'Honest to God I've never heard singing like it.'

'Do you think so, really?'

49

'Honest to God – you were terrific.'

'Well, are we ready then?' Kevin asked. The girls looked at each other, giggled, then said they were.

The four of them started off together, but after a while Kevin and Bid walked in front. Alone with Dolly, Jem became tongue-tied again. And Dolly gave him no help. He was glad the ice cream shop was close. There Kevin would get the talk going again.

Sitting on the wooden benches round the splintery table stained from raspberry juice, Dolly smiled and said it was nice of Jem to have asked her out. His tongue unlocked before her green-eyed smile and he asked what she would have, and Bid, too.

'You're very good-natured with my money, O'Brien. A great one inviting people out for wafers and only a tanner on him.'

Jem's face went the colour of the raspberry sauce. That was the night out finished. Dolly definitely wouldn't bother her head about a fella who asked her out and didn't have the price of an ice cream on him. But to his surprise Dolly turned on Kevin. 'There's no call for that. I didn't come for the sake of a wafer, and I don't think much of you trying to show him up.'

'For God's sake I was only joking.'

'Joking or not I don't like it, and not if I was dropping would I eat your wafers. If you want to take me home Jem, you can.' He was up off the chair like a shot.

'I'll see you tomorrow Bid, good-night,' Dolly said and ignored Kevin.

One good thing anyway, Dolly thought as they walked away, I don't have to let on I live in Rathmines or Rathgar with Jem O'Brien.

'I was thinking when you were singing that you were as good as anyone on the Gaiety, better even.'

'Mr Hicks, the man in charge of Jacobs' choir, says I should have my voice trained.'

'Would you not?'

'I might.'

He searched his mind for something else to say. 'I thought your frock was lovely. I was a bit disappointed when you came out in your ordinary things.'

'Thanks very much! There's nothing ordinary about anything I wear.'

'I didn't mean it like that.' Now he had offended her. It wasn't safe to open his mouth. He was an awful gaum. He walked on with her in silence.

After a while she said, 'You're very quiet.'

'I was thinking.'

'And what were you thinking about?'

'If I'd have the nerve to ask you out again.'

'I wouldn't eat you. And if you are you'd better hurry up, I'm nearly home.'

'Will you then, come out on Friday, and I'll make sure to bring the money.'

Dolly laughed. 'All right then. Where will I see you?'

'Wherever you like.'

'At the Pillar, at half-seven, and thanks for walking me home.'

He waited until she went into the hall, then walked away as though stepping on air. He had walked Dolly Devoy home. He had an AP with her. She was going to be his sweetheart.

Bessie and Liam's house was on the quays, halfway between the Four Courts and the Phoenix Park. Further up the river, barges were laden with barrels of Guinness' porter and sailed down to the docks. Bessie saw them when she stopped whatever she was doing and went to the window for a breath of air. She saw the swans, sailing up and down, and they reminded her of the river at home, the quietness of the place, the smell of it in the summertime. And she wondered if she would ever get used to living on the quays in Dublin, become

51

used to the smell of the brewery always on the air, the noise and the bustle. And she wondered too if she would ever get the house in order. Every room had an accumulation of rubbish, newspapers that went back years, empty cardboard boxes, lengths of string looped and tied, drawers crammed with letters, picture postcards, broken Rosary beads and cotton reels with only a few strands of thread. There were mountains of old-fashioned clothes, lace-up boots and shoes and dozens and dozens of empty glass jars and bottles. Liam's Aunt Hetty could never have thrown out anything in her life.

But for all her irritation at the clutter and nostalgia for the country, Bessie wouldn't have swapped one minute of her new life with Liam. After his initial disappointment that a house and forty pounds was all he'd inherited, he couldn't get over his luck. With his easy good-humoured manner he made her days happy, and in bed convinced her she was the most beautiful woman God ever created. She loved him passionately and had no cause for complaint until the day he brought her home the ring.

It was in a little box lined with white satin. The ring had a wide frontpiece on which in a thin spidery script the letters *Mizpah* were carved. 'How much did you give for that?' Bessie asked, unable to contain her annoyance. Though she regretted it as soon as she spoke, for Liam looked as if she had struck him.

'Thirty-five shillings – why, don't you like it? It's nine carat gold. Look,' he said, taking the box from her and plucking the ring from its nest of satin. 'Do you see the writing on it? The man in the shop told me what it means. It's from the Bible. About people being separated. And one of them says, "May the Lord watch between me and thee when we are separated one from the other." I thought you'd love it.'

'Oh darling, I do. It's lovely. Only forty pounds won't last kissing time if you buy me presents like that.'

'Ah for God's sake there's still plenty left.'

'It's all we have to live on. The ring is gorgeous but we can't afford presents. We should be thinking of ways to stretch what's left. Or how we'll manage once it's gone. It's something we weren't used to. You were kept on the farm and me above in the House. Now we've rates and firing, not to mention food. And it's you that has the fine appetite!' Here she paused and laughed, hoping to take the sting out of her lecture.

Liam thought for a minute, then said, 'I suppose you're right enough. I'll go out first thing in the morning and look for a start.'

'That might be easier said than done. I don't suppose there's much work in Dublin no more than anywhere else. And there'll be few positions, not decent ones, anyway, for me now that I'm a married woman. In the best houses you have to live in.'

'Then that's out,' Liam said definitely. 'I didn't get married to sleep on my own. I'll provide for you.'

'Sure I know you would. But I was thinking maybe we could start a business.'

'Like what?'

'An eating house. Serving decent food and not fleecing the customers. We're in the right locality with all the people passing up to the Park and Zoological Gardens, and then there'd be the soldiers going back to barracks of a night.'

'It sounds grand. Do you think we could succeed?'

'I think we could. Sit down here and we'll go through it.' Bessie moved aside a bundle of newspapers and made room for the two of them on the sofa. 'Do you see this room? It's big enough to turn a coach and four and there's the shop window your aunt had put in. It could be the dining room. We'd want a counter and tables and chairs. Then we'd have to have things for the kitchen, bigger pots and the like, and more delft. But supposing you got a bit of work, even casual, we could live off that and with what's left of the inheritance

53

get what we'd need for the business. There's no scarcity of secondhand things in Dublin.'

Suddenly the roles were reversed – it was Liam's voice that had the cautious note as he pointed out to Bessie the pitfalls of the venture she planned. 'We mightn't do any trade at all. Soldiers with a drink taken can be very contrary. And how could you manage to cook all them meals, supposing that people *did* come in?'

'People have to eat. There's nothing like a day in the Park for giving them an appetite – and you're the fine big man, wouldn't you be able to handle any soldier the worse for drink. And as for the cooking, haven't I helped cook for sixty before now in the House. Elaborate dishes at that, so a mutton stew, bacon and cabbage and apple cakes after that would be child's play. Besides, later on we could get a girl in to help. It'll be a success, I know it.' She talked persuasively, dismissing one by one any other objections Liam raised, and when she had finally convinced him leant over and kissed him. 'I'm sorry about the ring. It's gorgeous and I'll treasure it always. Now then, come on, and we'll shift out the rubbish,' she said standing up, 'and if you hear the rag man, tell me.'

Later in the day she helped Liam carry out the bottles, jam jars and clothes belonging to his aunt for which she could find no use. The rag man gave coloured balloons, celluloid windmills and coppers in exchange for rags and bottles. The sticks of the windmills were wedged between a board and the back of the cart. Their red and blue and white sails whirled round and round as a breeze blew off the Liffey. Bessie wished she had children, their eyes would dance with joy at the sight.

'What'll you have?' Jack the Rag asked.

'The money.'

'Fourpence,' the rag man said and handed Bessie the coppers.

*

As her mother had foretold, Alice was having such a good time she hardly ever thought of Nella. Stephen was marvellous company and the days flew by, each one filled with pleasant activities. They rode and swam, went for drives in the Packard and boating on the river. Stephen told her of the places he had visited in Europe, describing the sights and cities in such a way that while he talked she could see them.

One day he suggested they should take bicycles and go for a ride. Alice confessed that she didn't know how and besides, she hadn't anything suitable to wear. Stephen brushed aside all her excuses. 'It's easy, I'll teach you and I'm sure Mama's maid will be able to find something for you to wear.'

The maid brought a voluminous pair of bloomers to Alice's room. 'I wouldn't be seen dead in them,' Alice laughed, holding the garment in front of her.

'You'd be surprised, Miss – when they're on they don't look too bad. Some ladies can look very elegant in them.'

'Well, I suppose it would be a lark. All right then, I'll try them.' When Stephen saw her in the bloomers he burst out laughing and Alice didn't mind a bit and took that as another sign of how much she liked him. If anyone else had done so, she would have been mortified. Stephen helped her to mount, held onto the saddle and told her what to do with her feet. Up and down the path they went until she discovered he had let go of the saddle and she wobbled and fell off. He helped her up. Watching him bending and stretching she thought again, as she had when she watched him punting, how graceful and beautiful he was; and that she was falling in love with him. And when he smiled at her she was convinced that he, too, was in love with her.

But in the evenings she doubted that he felt anything for her. After dinner on the day they arrived his mother had said, as the women were about to leave the table, 'Dear Alice, I'm sure you would like some air. Listening to your Mama and me gossiping while we embroider is tedious for a young girl.

55

Why not take a stroll in the garden? Be a dear boy, Stephen, and go with her.'

It became a joke between Alice and Stephen, so that each evening as Lady Whitehead rose and repeated almost word for word her little speech, they dared not look at each other.

The gardens were beautiful. The air heavy with the smell of roses, the murmuring of a stream that divided the formal gardens from the park. Sometimes a bird flew from out of the trees which in the dusk looked mysterious, so that Alice imagined them waiting for darkness when their spirits would emerge to walk as she and Stephen were. And she mused how lovely it would be to tell Stephen her thoughts while she strolled with his arm round her. But in fact they kept a distance from each other and talked only of the day's happenings.

Each evening she felt sure that this time Stephen would say something about their life together, let her know that he was at least aware of the plans for their marriage. That it had gone beyond the stage of tentative arrangements between their parents.

By the end of the first week when he had said not a word that could be interpreted as more than the courtesy of a host towards his guest, she complained to her mother.

'I've got to know him now and I've accepted the fact that I'm to marry him. And I thought he had done the same. Now I'm beginning to wonder if he has been let in on the secret. I might just as well walk in the garden with another girl – a friend – or you.'

'Don't be so impatient, darling. Of course Stephen knows he is to marry you. He may be a little shy, that's all. He will propose when the time is right.'

'He will, I suppose – when you and his Mama tell him the time is right,' Alice retorted.

Pleased that Alice was eager for the proposal, Lady Delahunt allowed her rudeness to go unchecked, though the thought crossed her mind that Stephen was taking his time.

56

But to Alice she said, 'We'll be here for ages yet, and before we leave you and Stephen will be unofficially engaged. Then later we'll invite him over to Dublin and announce it. Don't you worry about a thing, it will all be taken care of . . .'

So Alice made the most of the days and waited for an evening when by the rose arbour Stephen would kiss her, hold her and ask her to marry him. One day while driving to Brighton Alice said, 'It's awfully generous of your father to let you have the car.'

'It's the Prodigal Son thing, I expect. He sent me off to Europe for a year and I stayed for three.'

'Yes, I know. Why? I mean – what made you stay so long?'

'I fell in love with Paris. Have you been?'

'No, but I'd like to,' Alice replied, not adding that it was Paris her mother suggested for their honeymoon.

'Paris is glorious, you must go. I've seen a lot of other capital cities, but Paris is different. There's an air about it, a magic. It's impossible to describe. You feel free, as if anything was possible there,' Stephen said and then became silent. Alice studied his profile. He really was terribly goodlooking. Such beautiful features, his skin smooth like a girl's, his hair adorable. She wondered what he would do if she reached out and touched it? Probably crash the car. I'd better not. But I do like him. Love him perhaps. Being married to him would be rather nice.

When they were married they would have a car. She imagined days of sunshine, driving with him, listening to his voice. Riding bicycles together, laughing at each other. Going to Paris with him. Being happy with each other. Of course there would be other things too, and babies. Suddenly she felt warm all over and strangely excited. She would sleep with Stephen and they would do all the things she vaguely knew about. Her heart was beating quickly, she was aware of it. This was how Nella had described being in love. Forgetting her earlier fear, she stretched out a hand and placed it on his

57

gauntleted one. Briefly he took his eyes from the road and smiled at her. And she told herself, that yes, she was in love, and that sleeping with Stephen would be nice.

They were in Brighton driving along the Front towards the Pavilion when Stephen said, 'I met your friend Nella in Paris.'

'Nella! What a funny thing – I was just thinking about her. When? You know she's back in Dublin now.'

'Let me see, when was it? Six months ago. In a restaurant. She recognized me – it was such a surprise.'

'I expect you talked and talked – it must have been exciting. I wonder why she never mentioned it in her letters.'

'Forgot probably. It was such a brief encounter, we were both with friends. She did invite me to visit her, but unfortunately something came up and I couldn't.'

'A pity. I'm sure you'd have enjoyed it,' Alice said, and wondered who the friend had been. And felt a stirring of what she supposed must be jealousy. He was probably in love with someone else. Someone he wanted to marry. An exquisite Parisienne. Someone exotic, as different from herself as one could imagine. She would ask Nella as soon as she got to Dublin. Then she reminded herself that by then she would be engaged to Stephen. She wouldn't ask Nella. Once Nella described the girl, she would come alive. It was better to forget her, pretend she didn't exist. Once they were married she would devote herself to making Stephen forget she had ever existed.

On the last Sunday in June Alice accompanied her family and Stephen's to church. She was enchanted by the approach along the Causeway lined on either side by charming houses. How lovely, she thought, to be married here instead of in St Patrick's in Dublin. Patrick's was such a cold gloomy place and the surroundings appalling. Those dreadful houses facing it, so many dirty ragged children and poor women. They always gathered near the cathedral door when there was a wedding. It was so depressing. But of course for her to be married anywhere except in Dublin and Patrick's was out of the question. That is, she reminded herself, if she were to be married at all. Another week had gone by and Stephen still had not proposed, nor once attempted to hold her hand, much less kiss her. She hoped her mother knew what she was doing, otherwise she would be returning to Dublin as unattached as when she had left it.

Some young people had been invited to luncheon. Afterwards, everyone went into the garden where beneath the giant Cedar of Lebanon, servants had arranged wicker chairs, small tables, a chaise longue for Lady Whitehead and numerous cushions and rugs. Everyone agreed it was too hot to do anything but laze. The women and girls wore exquisite day dresses of voile, gauzy and light in pastel colours, and their hats were large and lavishly decorated with flowers.

'What a glorious day,' Lady Delahunt remarked, her expression radiant. Everything was going according to plan. Alice was obviously smitten with Stephen. Though, she thought to herself, she must mention to Lady Whitehead that Stephen needed jogging slightly – he must propose soon. She sighed contentedly. Everything was wonderful, the company delightful, the world absolutely marvellous.

After a while the young people became restless, and when Stephen suggested a game of tennis they went indoors to change. The women talked about fashion and repeated the latest gossip. Lord Whitehead settled his silver head more comfortably against the chair and stretched his long elegant legs which disturbed the black labrador whose muzzle was resting on his lap. The dog shifted, laid his muzzle across his master's ankles and slept. From the tennis courts came the twang of rackets against balls and the voice of someone calling the score.

Sir Arthur continued talking. 'Sometimes when I stand to address the House about Ireland and the situation in Europe I get the feeling I'm talking to myself.'

'Europe seems less likely to erupt than it did a year ago,' Lord Whitehead said and was immediately sorry he had done so. For Arthur, once started on politics, was inclined to go on.

'I fear Europe less than the situation here and in Ireland. Our navy will take care of foreigners.' Lord Whitehead made what he considered were appropriate noises. 'Damned trade unionists – nothing but a vehicle for the Bolsheviks. Dreadful state of affairs – shop stewards trying to run the country.'

Lord Whitehead closed his eyes. *Politics!* So soon after luncheon! 'I mean to say, it's not good enough! Miners, railwaymen and transport workers forming a tripartite alliance. Don't you agree?'

'Of course, dear chap.' Lord Whitehead opened his eyes and began fondling the head of the labrador. 'His sight's failing – happens to the breed – go blind early, don't you know.'

'A pity.' Sir Arthur glanced quickly at the dog and away. He wasn't to be side-tracked by canine defects. 'What is the world coming to when people like shop stewards are attempting to wrest power from our hands. The Transport Union, that's Connolly's lot. He's a dangerous man. You know he's formed a movement – the Irish Citizen's Army.'

'Aimed at the working classes. I read about it somewhere.'

'Dissatisfied fellows have flocked to it – malcontents.'

'There are so many movements in Ireland – the Irish Republican Brotherhood, the Connolly thing, Gaelic Leagues and Associations, one can hardly keep up. But Redmond seems a sensible chap. He's conceded at least four of the Ulster counties be excluded from Home Rule.'

'Redmond's all right, pity the rest aren't like him. Have you considered what will happen if the Bill doesn't get through the Lords?'

'It won't,' Lord Whitehead said, wearily.

'Of course it won't – and quite right too! Only this time there'll be trouble in Ireland. There are many opposed to

60

Redmond – a hard core that nothing but an independent Ireland will satisfy. They are just waiting for the right moment.'

'Wouldn't doubt it,' Lord Whitehead agreed. Good manners forbade him telling Arthur to give the subject a rest. But really he did work himself into a lather. Quite puce in the face, and on such a lovely afternoon, too. He must steer him onto a safer subject. 'I shouldn't worry too much, old chap – we'll survive – the old order will prevail. Always has. Always will. As that fellow Darwin says, "the survival of the fittest". Think on the bright side. We are forming our own alliance – young Stephen and Alice – ensuring that the stock is maintained, what.'

Lady Delahunt's eyes shone with pleasure at the mention of her daughter's name. Stephen and Alice! In her mind she began arranging the invitation list, drafting the announcement for *The Times*. Saw before her Alice and Stephen in Patrick's Cathedral pledging themselves to one another. She was suffused with joy, breathless, flushed.

'Are you too warm, dear?' Stephen's mother inquired.

'No, I'm quite well, thank you,' Lady Delahunt assured her hostess.

'Do you know I think we'll have tea a little early.' Lady Whitehead raised an arm and waved. In a very short time three maids came bearing trays with the silver tea service, plates of cucumber sandwiches, pale golden scones, pots of honey, butter, cream and jam.

That evening during dinner Lord Whitehead was called to the telephone. Returning to the dining room he announced to the company that his brother, who was holidaying in Germany, had just rung with the news that Archduke Francis Ferdinand and his Duchess had been assassinated earlier in the day. And that rumour was rife that the assassination would lead to a European war.

'How ghastly,' Lady Whitehead said. 'Such a pretty woman.

I saw her last year in Vienna. Such a devoted couple. Where did it happen?'

'Sarajevo.'

The meal continued with Lady Whitehead telling Alice and her mother what she knew about the assassinated Duchess, and the men discussing whether or not the incident would spark off a war in which England would be involved.

'Whether or not, I'll take no chances. I'm afraid this visit must be cut short.'

Lady Delahunt gasped. 'But Arthur you can't – you mustn't.'

'A bit hasty don't you think,' Lord Whitehead commented. 'If there is a war, which I'm not convinced there will be, it's hardly likely to happen overnight.'

'Nevertheless we'll go home. I have business interests and I know Ireland. England's difficulty is Ireland's opportunity – they'll seize the moment. You'll forgive us, Margaret, and you too, Herbert.'

Lady Delahunt fumed inwardly. Perhaps there was a war coming, and perhaps the Irish would rebel, but surely to God not before the end of the week! Not before Stephen actually proposed to Alice. Then she suddenly realized the implications of war. Stephen would join the army. That could delay the wedding. Oh, it wasn't fair! Only a moment ago everything had been so *certain*, so *safe*.

Alice woke early on the day they were to leave Horsham and lay contemplating the previous evening. She and Stephen had walked as usual in the garden. How she had hoped that this being their last evening together he would be bound to mention their engagement. And all he talked about was the threat of war. Explaining the political situation in Europe. Telling her that Europeans were more politically aware than the English. In every café on every boulevard in Paris people would be discussing the situation. It was one of the things he had loved about Paris.

Just before they said good night, Stephen had suggested that in the morning early they should go for a last ride and eagerly she had agreed. Though after leaving him her spirits sank and she became convinced that the morning would bring no miracle. There would be a gallop on the Downs, no more than that.

She had gone to her mother's room and cried. Telling her in between sobbing that she was sure Stephen didn't love her. That she knew he didn't find her attractive. That he didn't even like her. 'I wish I'd never come. I'm ugly. I hate myself. I'm glad we're going home tomorrow.'

'You silly girl. Of course he loves you and will marry you. It's just an unfortunate time, that's all. His mind is full of war and heroic deeds. Men are like that. And your father hasn't helped matters by rushing us home. You be patient and it will all come right, you'll see. Go to bed and who knows what will happen in the morning.'

Now it was morning and Alice felt as disconsolate as the night before. She longed to go back to sleep and waken up at home. For it to be a time before Stephen was ever mentioned as her future husband. Not to have her mind swinging all the time between whether he loved her or didn't.

But it was no use daydreaming. That wouldn't help anything. She got up and went to the window. It was a glorious morning full of sunlight and the singing of birds. Despite herself she began to feel happy and hope rose again in her.

Stephen was at the stables, the horses were saddled. 'It's a pity you're going today,' he said as they rode out. 'There was so much I had planned for us.' *What?* she wanted to ask him, wording her question lightheartedly, yet in such a way that he would understand she wanted a comment about his intentions. But how to do it? While she searched for the right words Stephen said 'I'll tell you what – let's have a race, shall we?'

The moment was gone, Alice knew. She agreed to the race.

'From here to those trees. I'll count to three, ready?'

Alice said she was. Then they were off galloping, Stephen in front, then she passing him.

'Well done,' Stephen said, coming to where she waited. 'You won.'

'You let me.'

'I didn't, honestly.' He smiled and she thought how handsome he was and how much she loved him.

'You're a fraud, you held back.'

'Well, maybe just a little bit,' he admitted. 'Look – if we ride along here there's a gap in the trees and there's the most marvellous view.' They stopped at the gap and admired the view. 'There's something else I want to show you.' They moved on to another gap and the beginning of a slight incline. 'Follow me down. In the spring it's very marshy around here but after all the fine weather it's all right now,' Stephen called back.

Spread at the bottom of the incline was a field of buttercups glistening in the sunlight. Alice gasped. 'It's beautiful. I've never seen so many growing together. It's like a golden cloth thrown over the field.'

'I thought you'd like it.' Stephen dismounted and helped Alice down. They stood close. Maybe now he'll put his arms around me, kiss me and tell me he loves me. She waited expectantly. Stephen stepped back. 'I'll tell you what, I'll pick you an enormous bunch.' She wanted to say 'Don't, they'll die. I'm going home in a few hours, what'll I do with them? Leave them alone!'

He went into the field and she watched him, wishing he had gathered the flowers from the edge, and not crushed so many beneath his feet. She wished he had stayed and kissed her.

Her mare rubbed its head against her. She stroked it and talked to it. 'He doesn't like being alone with me for long. That's why he's picking flowers. I don't want them. They're nicer in the field. It was an excuse to get away from me.' The mare's ears pricked up, hearing the sound of an approaching horse before Alice did. Then she caught the sound too but could see nothing because of the trees. She looked towards the field. Stephen had stopped picking and was walking back, his feet flattening more blossoms. He arrived at the field's edge as the horse and rider came down the incline.

'Robbie! Hello.'

'Hello, Stephen. I didn't know you were back.'

'Yes, I've been home for a few weeks,' Stephen said, raising his hand that held the flowers as if he meant to wipe his forehead. 'I'm so hot; here, Alice.' He gave her the bunch of buttercups. 'Oh, this is Alice, a friend from Dublin.' Robbie smiled at her. A dazzling smile. She wondered who he was. Was he foreign, Italian perhaps? He was so dark, such eyes and the white, white teeth. The smile lit his face and seemed to radiate from it, reaching into her, warming her.

Robbie dismounted and came towards her, his hand outstretched. She felt excited and flustered and knew she was blushing. His touch was pleasant and afterwards she thought he had squeezed her hand but wasn't sure.

'I hope you're enjoying yourself.'

'Oh, yes, I am.'

'Alice is going home today,' Stephen said.

'What a pity when we've just met. I see you've had him picking flowers. I've never known him do that before.' Alice thought they must be friends, he was so friendly, so familiar with Stephen. Picking a flower from her hands he asked if she liked butter, while all the time his eyes were regarding her face. She giggled when he tilted her chin and held the flower beneath it and laughed delightedly when he said, 'Yes, you do like butter,' even though she sensed that Stephen wasn't joining in the fun.

When he spoke his voice had an edge to it. 'It was good to see you Robbie, but we must go now.'

'Yes, of course,' Robbie said and presented Alice with the flower. 'Sorry it's not a forget-me-not. Goodbye, Stephen.'

65

'Who is he?' Alice asked, watching him ride up the slope.

'A fellow from Southwater.'

'Is he a friend?'

'He was when we were children, before I went away to school. I've seen him about from time to time. His father has a lumber business, they sometimes buy wood from the estate, that sort of thing.'

'He's rather unusual,' Alice said.

'Very. What my mother would call a man who doesn't know his place.'

'His place?'

'Over-familiar, doesn't touch the forelock, you know like that thing with the flowers.'

'Yes, I suppose you're right,' Alice said, not meaning it, thinking about Robbie's smile and the effect it had had on her. And how the place seemed dim since he went as if the sun had gone behind a cloud. As though from a distance she heard Stephen say, 'Not that he'd care what my mother thinks of him or what anyone thinks of him. It's all part of his charm, I suppose. They say he has a way with women.' Alice said nothing but wished that Stephen had a way with women.

'Well, we'd better set off, I suppose,' Stephen said. After they had been riding for a while he noticed that she didn't have the buttercups. 'You forgot the flowers.'

'So I did. I must have dropped them when your friend was playing that silly game,' she said but didn't add that she had kept the one Robbie had held under her chin.

Robbie rode home, knowing that when he arrived his father would be waiting. There would be a row, all the usual accusations hurled at him. At the first opportunity he was clearing out. He had only stayed this long for his mother's sake. Let Jack and Herbert work the business, let them inherit it. They danced to his father's tune. No one would ever call the tune for him.

'Where the bloody hell have you been? You knew I wanted help with this load,' his father roared as Robbie came into the yard. 'You're good for nothing. You won't work here, you don't work in school, most of the time you're not there. But it's finished. I'm not throwing my money away – you're not going back. And another thing, if you ride out once more when I need you here I'll shoot that bloody horse.'

Robbie looked at his fuming father, a vein throbbing at the base of his neck, red-faced, the colour raised by his temper reaching his bald head tinging it pink. Robbie wondered as he often had what his mother had seen in this man to make her leave her home and family in Dublin and bury herself in a place like Southwater.

'You're an idle, vain, good-for-nothing. And don't think I haven't heard about your goings-on. One of these days you'll be looking down the barrel of a shotgun and I hope the girl's father has the guts to pull the trigger.'

Her husband's furiously raised voice brought Robbie's mother into the yard. 'What's the matter now? Why are you always on at him?'

'It's a pity you didn't go on at him a bit more in his rearing. You ruined him. From the minute he was born you made more fuss of him than his brothers, gave him more attention than anyone. Turned his head with all the praise. Interfered when I tried to make something of him. Well, I hope you're satisfied. Look at him – an arrogant, insolent pup!'

Robbie's mother looked at him and they smiled at each other. Her eyes that were so like his flashed their message: Don't heed him. He's jealous of you. Now that you're grown up more than ever. But he always was. Maybe it's because you look like me and my family. I love you. More than him, she says. It wasn't always so. Let him say what he likes. Don't answer him back. I'll get round him about your schooling. I want you to be educated. I don't want you to spend your life

67

chopping and pollarding trees. I don't want you finishing up here.

'Listen, Father, I'm sorry, I forgot you wanted the timber loaded. In any case I thought Jack and Herbert were about.'

'Jack and Herbert, they're no great shakes, but I'll say this for them, they're workers. Jack and Herbert were off to Chichester with a load while you were out gallivanting.'

'I didn't know that. Look – I said I'm sorry. Give me five minutes to unsaddle the horse and I'll be with you.'

'A lot of good that'll be with the day half-gone.' His father's voice was becoming quieter. He'd leave him now to his mother who would calm him completely. Now turning the horse towards the stables he said, 'I won't let you down again.'

'Don't make me promises. Don't gabble about not letting me down. I know you. You're not capable of keeping your word to anyone.'

'Ah now, that's not fair,' his mother was saying, moving close to her husband, taking his arm, at the same time signalling to Robbie to go. He went, patting the horse's neck, telling it with luck it might survive – for he wouldn't be around much longer to endanger its life.

Chapter Four

Alice thought how small their William and Mary house looked after the vastness of Rudgewick Park. But the unfavourable comparison only lasted a moment. She was home and delighted. The journey from Horsham had been wretched – Mama in low spirits at the hastiness of their departure, Papa taciturn and the sea rough. And her own humour hadn't been of the best, brooding all the time over Stephen's behaviour, and, as one weary hour followed another, more convinced that he was in love with someone else. The only bright memory was of Robbie. Now, however, she had something pleasant to contemplate. Nella had sent a message – she was calling tomorrow.

Her maid found the buttercup amongst Alice's things. 'What shall I do with this, Miss?' she asked. 'It's an old flower. Will I throw it out?'

'Yes,' Alice said, then changed her mind. 'No, don't. I'll press it. Fetch me some tissue paper and I'll want a heavy book – let me see now, which one?' She found a suitable one, smoothed out the crumpled petals into a semblance of their former self. It would be a keep-sake. Sometimes when she was down-hearted she would look at it and remember that field of gold and Robbie coming down the incline and feel the warmth of that smile again.

Nella arrived after lunch. 'Oh Nella, I'm so delighted to see you. You were gone so long.'

'You're a fine one!' Nella pretended to be annoyed. 'Away on holidays and not even a picture postcard! And fancy going off the night before I arrived! Deserting me! Spoiling my homecoming!'

'I know and I'm sorry.' She hugged Nella. 'It couldn't be helped – I had to go. I'll tell you all about it.' She took her arms from round Nella and stood a little way back gazing admiringly at her. 'You look divine! Your dress is marvellous! And your hair really *is* Titian.'

'Why, of course it is,' Nella said, touching her hair. 'What made you think it might be otherwise?'

'Oh nothing, I'd just forgotten how glorious it is. But your dress! I'm green with envy. Turn round, let me see it.'

Nella obligingly pirouetted. 'It's unbelievably beautiful. I've never seen anything like it. The tunic's shaped like a bell! Fancy one shoulder being black and the other white! And the colours of the embroidery, all those shades, delicious looking pinks and greens and lemons. They remind me of sherbet. It's really superb. I love the bell-shaped line over the long black satin skirt. From Paris of course.'

'Of course. A Poiret, influence of the Ballet Russe.' Nella sat and Alice did, too. 'You've simply got to see the Ballet – such dancing, such shapes, such fabulous colours. You haven't lived until you've seen it.'

Alice held up her hands. 'Don't. Don't tell me any more, you make me so envious. But do tell me, what brought you home?'

Nella shrugged. 'I thought I could paint – it turned out otherwise, and I missed Dublin.'

'Gosh, you're the last person I would have imagined being homesick. You never said so in your letters.' Alice remembered something else which Nella hadn't mentioned in her letters and was just about to ask for details of her meeting with Stephen and what his friend was like when Nella took from her bag an elaborately enamelled cigarette holder. Drawing out a cigarette from a matching case, she lit it and blew a perfect smoke ring.

'You smoke! How *avant garde*! You'll scandalize Dublin society.'

'That's not all I do,' Nella said and blew another ring. 'But enough about me. What about this holiday with the Whiteheads, I'm dying of curiosity.'

So she told Nella about Stephen and their engagement.

'Stephen! Not Stephen Whitehead – you're not engaged to him!'

'I would have been, unofficially anyway, only Papa got the wind up about a war in Europe and the Irish starting trouble, so he rushed us home. But why are you looking so shocked?'

'Shocked, I'm not shocked,' Nella lied. 'Surprised, disappointed. I thought I'd talked sense into you. My God, I spent hours trying to make you realize you're a person in your own right, not a chattel in the marriage market. Didn't you listen to one word?'

'You know very well I did. It sounded great stuff. But in the long run I'm not like you. I haven't got your courage. And besides, I don't really mind marrying someone my parents choose. They love me, they would only choose someone who would make me happy. You don't believe me, I can see by your face. You look worried. Don't be, Nella. And anyway, it may all come to nothing. Stephen showed not the slightest interest in me. Perhaps Paris liberated him. Perhaps like you he won't consider his parents' wishes.'

If you only knew just how liberated Stephen is, Nella thought and felt pity for Alice. She was such an innocent. Surely her parents must have an inkling of the kind of man they had chosen for a son-in-law. Of course the Whitehead title would be very alluring. One that went back, unlike Sir Arthur's which was a Union one. What was she to do about it? Blurt out the truth to Alice – spell out the sordid business? Thank God there was nothing official yet. Maybe there would

71

be a war and maybe . . . No, she didn't wish that. Stephen was a kind, gentle person, she didn't wish him dead. The thing was to work on Alice. Make her see she could do anything she chose with her life.

'Do you think it might have?'

'Might have what?'

'Oh Nella, you haven't been listening! Do you think Paris liberated Stephen?'

'Probably, but it doesn't matter since you're not engaged, nor madly in love.'

Again Alice was tempted to ask for details of the exotic Parisienne, but decided that the less she knew about her the better. So instead she suggested that she and Nella go to her room and talk there. 'There's so much still to talk about. And Mama will be back shortly, she comes straight in here to recover from her calls. She loves the view.' The two girls looked out at the rose garden, then Nella lit a new cigarette and Alice said, 'That's another reason for going to my room. Mama would have a fit if she found you smoking.'

'Liam, Liam, come out and give the boy a hand with the things,' Bessie said, going into the kitchen where Liam was whitewashing the ceiling.

'What have you bought this time?' he said, coming down the ladder, going to kiss her.

'Don't, this is my best coat,' Bessie backed away. 'You're a terrible man, there's more whitewash on you than the ceiling.'

'I never let on to be a painter,' Liam said, grabbing hold of her and kissing her. 'God, you were gone for hours,' he said, letting her go. 'My belly thinks my throat is cut.'

She pretended indignation. 'Useless, that's what you are, not able for a bit of brush work, nor to cook a bit of something. Now give over and help the boy in with the stuff.'

The chairs and tables were brought in and the boy went back and returned with a large wicker basket filled with cooking utensils. Bessie gave him a shilling and thanked him.

'Well, what do you think?' she asked.

Liam appeared to study the furniture critically, trying out a chair, rocking a table. Bessie looked on, knowing if he did find any faults she'd have to stand over him while he made repairs. For big and strong as he was, with nails, hammers or paint brushes he might as well have been a two year old.

'They were a great bargain. I got them at an auction down on the quays, and the man threw in the basket for nothing. Five pound for the lot.'

'Five pound!' He pretended to be aghast.

'I got them for a song,' Bessie said. 'They're all sound. No worm in them and with a bit of varnish they'll be like new.'

'What about my dinner?'

'Don't always be thinking about your stomach. Listen till I tell you the rest. I saw the paper for the room and I found a shop that'll sell me peas and custard powder and dry goods at cost. And the man there was telling which is the best place to buy meat. And to go early in the morning to the big market for vegetables. They're fresh up from the country and cheap. Aren't you excited, Liam?'

'I'm hungry.'

'May the divil fire you. Come into the kitchen with me and while I cook you something I'll tell you the rest of my plans. It's going to work out. I'm positive. We'll have an eating house that'll be the best in Dublin. Wait'll you see.' She took off her coat and hat and put on an apron. 'Word of it will get around. That's the best recommendation. I'm telling you we'll make a fortune. Here, before I peel the potatoes wash that whitening off yourself.'

While he was drying his hands on the roller towel she put her arms around him. 'If you only knew how happy I was going around everywhere today. Knowing that it was all to give us a good life together. I kept thinking how lucky I was. How good God was to send you to me. I love you. And pay

73

not a bit of attention to me giving out about the painting and that, it's only my way.'

He turned to her. 'I know it well. Do you think I'd put up with it otherwise? But there's one thing I can't and won't stand for.' His tone was serious.

Had she done something unknowingly that had upset him? 'What is it?' she asked and her voice was as serious as his.

'I won't put up with being starved. Make me my dinner immediately or I'm off.' He was laughing.

'Oh God, for a minute you gave me a fright,' she laughed with him, then reached up and kissed him. 'Go in and sit down and before you know it I'll make you a feed fit for a king.'

'Your future is secure now,' Richard's father said when his son passed his medical. He pushed to the back of his mind the fear that a war might be declared between England and Germany. Bridget, like the majority of people in Ireland and England was unaware of the situation in Europe. Her fears for her son were that he might lose his faith, sleep in damp beds and get into bad company.

'A life of prosperity, that's what's in front of you and a pension at the end. Not like me and your mother relying on the few shillings Lloyd George has granted. Though thank God for it and spare us to see seventy and receive it. You'll end your days beholding to no one.'

'Will you shut up and let the child enjoy today instead of looking to the pension,' Bridget said exasperatedly.

'I'm only speaking the truth. A man has to look to the future.'

'Then it's a bloody pity you don't look to ours instead of spending every penny in Fitz's.'

Word came that Richard would start work on the fifth of August 1914. He would travel to London on Saturday the first. Lodgings had been found for him in Westminster.

74

Maggie bought him a raincoat which cost fifteen and eleven, and two sticks of shaving soap which she said were from his nephew. Everyone said the coat was a grand fit. Maggie told him to smell the soap, it was gorgeous, the girls would be mad about it. Richard said thanks and kissed her and was surprised to see her eyes, in which he had only seen laughter, filled with tears.

Dolly, who had been saving for a new skirt which Miss Murtagh was to make, spent the money on a cardigan in a marline mixture of blue and grey. Richard's eyes were grey-blue and the colour would suit him.

His mother got his clothes ready, washing and pressing and mending and constantly reminding him not to travel in his best suit, and the minute he got to his lodgings to give it a good shake before hanging it up so the creases would fall out. Then he'd be as smart as a new pin on his first day in the office.

In the pocket of his suit she put two pound notes and a pair of Third Order Scapulars hanging on brown tape. The brown squares of woollen cloth were meant to be worn one next to his chest and one on his back. She knew he would laugh if she gave them to him now and asked him to wear them and pray to St Francis. But she hoped that finding them when he was in a strange room, maybe a bit lost and lonely, they would remind him of his faith and that Someone was always watching over him.

On the day Richard was leaving, his father went up to the Hazard and ordered a cab. 'You won't let me down: 97, Clanbrassil Street, for the North Wall. The son is going over. Into the Civil Service – the War Office.' The jarvey said he wouldn't let him down.

Maggie, Tom and Christie came long before Richard was to leave. Bridget was very agitated, checking and rechecking that Richard had everything, telling him not to forget his Rosary beads, the new shirt, the bottle of Holy Water and his bacon sandwiches. She was glad of the child getting under her feet, giving her an excuse to scold him for it distracted her mind from its grief. Johnny kept going in and out to the door watching for the cab. It came at last and the family piled in. The men squeezed along one seat and the women on the other. The neighbours gathered round the door and called good wishes: the children scutted on the cab for a little way down the street.

Along New Street, across the Poddle, past St Patrick's Cathedral and on to Christ Church went the cab. Then down Wine Tavern Street and along the Liffey. Dolly kept looking through the window, watching the sky, hoping the clouds would blow away, that it wouldn't rain. Jem was taking her to the Fair. He had suggested the Zoological Gardens, but she had told him that by the time the boat sailed it would be too late for that. 'Let's go to the Fair instead. I love the swinging boats and the hobby horses.'

The cab slowed down on the side of the Liffey opposite Bachelor's Walk. Looking towards it Bridget blessed herself and said, 'Lord have mercy on the poor unfortunates who lost their life there last week.'

'Lord have mercy on them,' the other passengers said and crossed themselves.

'Mown down,' Tom said. 'Murdered for making a jeer of the soldiers who'd been out in Howth trying to stop the arms coming in. And they turned and opened fire on the crowd. I'm telling you it's a terrible thing when you can't shout and mock without being murdered. Bring out the army when our lads tried getting in a few rifles. But that wasn't the case in the North. No one lifted a hand to stop the guns coming into Larne for Carson's Volunteers.'

'The curse of God on the same guns in whose ever hands they are! They'll be the cause of death and destruction for some poor mother's son. And I believe the Germans have been selling to the two sides,' Bridget said.

76

'It's right enough,' Tom said. 'In the long run it's money makes the world go round.'

'You're well out of it all, Richard,' Johnny said as the cab turned down Eden Quay and felt a great sense of relief that Richard, please God, would be out of harm's way in England. All the rumours of war might come to nothing. He wouldn't think about it.

The clouds blew away, the sun came out and Dolly was impatient to set off for her appointment with Jem. Maggie held Christie in her arms, showing him the boat and the seagulls and telling him to wave 'Day, Day,' to Richard.

'God Bless you and keep you,' Bridget said and kissed her son.

'Look after yourself and don't forget to write.' His father shook Richard's hand. 'You'll do well for yourself over there.'

Dolly hugged her brother. 'I'll miss you.'

'You will in your eye. You'll be that delighted having a bed to yourself you'll never give me a thought. Go on now, let me board the boat before they haul up the gangway.'

The fairground was beyond the Croppy's cemetery. Passing it, Jem asked if she'd learnt that poem about *The Croppy Boy*. Dolly hadn't.

'God, it used to give me the shivers thinking about the boy going to confession and all the time the priest was a soldier dressed up. And him telling him everything about the rising.' He began to recite. '"*Good men and true in this house who dwell, To a stranger bouchal I pray you tell, Is the priest at home? or where may he be seen? I would speak a word with father Green.*" The last line – that was the one that really frightened me. "*The robes were off and in scarlet there Stood a yeoman captain with fiery glare.*" Wasn't that a terrible thing all the same?'

'It's only a poem,' Dolly said dismissively.

'I know, but it happened really. In Wexford in ninety-eight.

77

The poor croppys – they're buried in there. They used to have their hair cut short, you know to show they had sympathy with fellas in France that started the revolution, that's why they have the name.' He began to recite again. '"*With fiery glare and with fury hoarse. Instead of a blessing he breathed a curse.'Twas a good thought boy, to come here and shrive, For one short hour is your time to live.*"'

Dolly thought – he's a fecking eejit, not a bit romantic. What do I care about Croppy boys? Then she heard the fairground music, the organ on the Hobby Horse playing the *Gold and Silver Waltz*. She began to lilt it. She could see the naphtha flares around the stalls and the boats swinging to and fro, and see the people going in and out of tents and hear the girls squealing when the boats went high, and smell the lovely scent of crushed grass. She caught hold of Jem's hand, 'Oh, come on,' she urged. 'Oh come on, let's hurry, let's run.'

She felt very tender towards him on the way home. Now and then as they walked towards the city she glanced at him and thought what a nice face he had and how, though he wasn't tall, he had a good carriage. She liked a man to hold himself well. And he was very good-natured, not minding how many rides she had had on the boats and horses. Maybe tonight she would let him come into the hall, but not for long.

'Are you hungry?' he asked at the very moment she was deciding how many times he should kiss her.

'No,' she replied. 'Are you?' And she thought that no matter how nice he was, there wasn't a bit of romance in him. There was she thinking about kissing and all he had on his mind was food.

'I am. There's a new place – an eating house, it's supposed to be good.'

'An eating house! What do you take me for! You could be poisoned in one of them places.'

'This one's not like that, by all accounts. Someone was

telling me you could eat off of the floor, it's that clean and the food's as good as you'd get at home.'

They stopped outside the eating house. The large window had a crisp white lace hanging. Dolly peered through. 'It doesn't look too bad, at least they've chairs and tables, not oul benches.'

'Do you want to risk it?'

'All right, but I'll only have a cup of tea or a glass of mineral.'

'Good evening.' Bessie behind the counter smiled at them. 'Did you want something to eat or only tea?' she inquired.

'Only tea for me. What about you, Jem?'

'The smell is making me wallfalling with the hunger,' Jem said, sniffing appreciatively.

'That's what we've got.' Bessie pointed to a small blackboard on a shelf behind the counter. The dishes and prices were itemized in chalk. 'Mutton stew. Meat Pie. Rashers and Eggs. Apple cake. Bread pudding. Tea. Milk. Minerals,' Jem read aloud.

'The stew is lovely. I do bacon and cabbage and sometimes ribs, but that's only in the daytime,' Bessie told them.

Dolly's eyes roamed over everything looking for faults. She saw that the apple cake was beneath a gauze, metal-ribbed cover and the cups and saucers stacked on the counter were spotless. She *is* clean, she thought, though how would you know what the kitchen is like? Or where she buys her meat? Carrion maybe, sheep and cows that fell out of their standing from disease.

'I'll have the stew, apple cake and two cups of tea, please,' Jem said.

Dólly decided to risk the cake. Telling herself that the flour might be adulterated with chalk but that wouldn't kill you and there wasn't much tampering anyone could do with the fruit.

'If you sit down I'll bring the food in a minute,' Bessie said.

They sat and Dolly continued her scrutiny. The red linoleum

79

with a Turkish pattern was clean and polished; the green and white American cloth on the tables like new. The wallpaper looked new, too. It was cream-coloured with a trelliswork design up which pink and white roses climbed. She couldn't find a fault.

Bessie served them. 'That'll be one and a penny,' she said. Jem paid her and Dolly asked if they had been open long.

'Nearly a month. The first week custom was slack, but it's picking up, thanks be to God.'

'You're not from round here?' Dolly said.

'No, from down the country. We're not long up.'

'Do you like the city?'

'I do, what little I know of it. Sure I don't get much further than the market. Liam, that's my husband, he loves Dublin. And is getting to know it inside out. It's no wonder, he's worked all over the place, driving cattle, carrying coal, labouring, everything. This week he's doing night porter in a hotel.'

'Is that so?' Dolly said.

'He doesn't pause for breath,' Bessie sighed. 'Still they say hard work never killed anyone. I'll leave you now to your food and I hope you enjoy it.'

'Country people – they'd teach you how to live. Grabbers. Not here five minutes and set up in business,' Dolly said when Bessie was out of earshot.

On the fourth of August, war was declared between England and Germany. It was Tuesday and a Bank Holiday. Crowds had gone to the seaside and into the country. Robbie Brightwell was at a fair on the Downs, Richard was settling into his lodging-house and preparing for work the following day. At the fair *Alexander's Ragtime Band* was playing. It suddenly stopped as a man with a megaphone mounted the steps to the hobby horses. He waited for the horses to come to a standstill before making the announcement that England and Germany were at war. There was a stunned silence then a wild cheer went up. Strangers spoke to each other. Crowds descended on the beer tent. A few older people looked anxiously around as if waiting for directions. But the general atmosphere was one of rejoicing.

Richard's landlady came up to tell him. 'Didn't you hear the stop press? We've gone to war. Everyone's making for the Houses of Parliament. Put your coat on – you wouldn't want to miss this!' Richard followed her downstairs where the other lodgers were gathered in the hall and together they set out for the Houses of Parliament. There was a big crowd cheering and singing. Richard thought he was having a nightmare. Only a little while ago his father was congratulating him on going to England where he would be safe. What lay in store for him now, he wondered. Men in the crowd were talking about finding a recruiting office, joining up, doing their duty. He wondered what his mother and father would make of the news.

When Bridget heard she rounded on Johnny. 'You were afraid of him getting mixed up in anything here. Well, now I hope you're satisfied! You couldn't wait to get him to England. Oh no. "You'll be safe in England," you told him. You didn't want him joining any of the organizations. What'll he have to join over there, answer me that if you can!'

Johnny, who was as shocked and worried as his wife, put on a brave face. 'You're working yourself up for nothing. Stop crying and listen to me. Richard's a Civil Servant. He's at the War Office. He'll have to join nothing. Them fellas won't have to go in the army. Who do you think would do all the clerical work if they did? I'm telling you, he'll never have to join up.'

Sir Arthur Delahunt spoke from recruiting platforms lending weight to the opinion of John Redmond, leader of the Irish Nationalist Party, that self-respecting Irishmen must support England's championing of small nations. Explaining that

Home Rule had to be shelved until the following year or however long the war lasted. Assuring the assembled crowd that with the might of the British Navy and the heroic stance of the fighting men of Great Britain the war would soon be over. And afterwards, Ireland's loyalty would not be forgotten: Home Rule would be assured. The response was tremendous. Irish Volunteers who had flocked to defend their part of Ireland against the threat of Carson's men from the North now flocked to fight for England.

Liam attended one of the recruiting drives. 'In Belgium, German soldiers are raping women. Infants are being impaled on soldiers' bayonets and waved about like flags. What decent man can stand by, knowing such atrocities are being committed? What Irishman who prizes the freedom of small nations, who honours women and loves children can sleep in peace, knowing that such abominations take place?' Sir Arthur Delahunt thundered. Liam was deeply moved. 'I say to you – *enlist today*! Let your heart dictate. Think of your own women and children. Enlist today and by Christmas we'll have defeated the Hun . . .'

Liam joined in the clapping at the end of Sir Arthur's speech. The band struck up a military march. Men stood taller, began to move, some away, some in time to the drumbeat towards the recruiting tent. Liam was filled with a desire to right the wrongs done to Belgian women and children. Like someone drugged, he began walking in the direction of the tent. He was startled suddenly by someone hitting him on the back. Looking round he recognized a man he had worked with recently. 'I thought it was you,' the man said. 'Which way are you going? For a minute I thought you were heading for the recruiting sergeant!' The man laughed.

'No,' Liam said, 'I was only walking this way. All the same that's a terrible thing happening in Belgium.'

''Tis if it's the truth. How are we to know? Haven't the

82

English always been the great liars. Small nations how are you? Aren't *we* a small nation? Haven't *we* been pillaged down the centuries? What about *our* freedom? Any Irishman who joins up is mad. Here is where they should be. Redmond will take some of the Irish Volunteers into the British Army, but thank God he won't get them all. Enough will remain to fight for our own cause.'

Away from the feverish excitement of the crowd and the enticement of the drum Liam considered what he had nearly done. In a moment's madness he could have deserted Bessie, left her alone, struggling to make a go of the eating house. He was grateful to his friend for the timely slap on the back. 'Let's have a jar, it's great meeting you again,' he said. 'There's a pub round the corner.'

One morning, not long after war had been declared Robbie returned from riding to find his father pacing the kitchen and his mother crying.

'Out gallivanting,' his father shouted. 'I've said it before – I'll shoot that bloody horse. I suppose you knew all about it.'

'About what?'

'Jack and Herbert are gone. I went up to call them and they weren't there.'

'Did you know about it, Robbie?' his mother asked, trying to control her tears.

'You don't think he'd tell you! Sit down,' he ordered Robbie. 'They couldn't wait – two weeks into war and they've run off to join up.'

'Join the army? Jack and Herbert?' Robbie was genuinely surprised.

'Don't act the innocent with me, and don't say another thing until I've finished. I've spent my whole life building up this business. Who do you think it was for? Myself? Well, it wasn't! Like a fool I was doing it for my sons. And what happens now? I'll have to take men on. I'm not made of money. So if you think I'm wasting any more of it on school fees you're mistaken. One more report that you're not attending and out you come. *Do you hear me?*'

'Promise your father,' his mother pleaded. 'It's for your own sake.'

What had she ever seen in him? Robbie wondered. What made her run away with him? Leave Dublin which she told him was a beautiful city? With so many things to do. Theatres and concerts, bands in the park, the streets full of fashionable people and beautiful buildings. To leave all that for a village in Sussex! He hated him. If it wasn't for his mother he would tell him what he could do with the school fees and the business.

'Do you hear me Robbie, promise your father.'

'All right,' Robbie said. And for the first week of the new term he kept his promise. On the following Monday he went to Chichester. 'How old, son?' the recruiting sergeant asked. 'Eighteen,' Robbie replied, his eyes not wavering.

'Right. Sign here for the King's shilling.'

'I wasn't going to tell you, I was going to do a bunk like Jack and Herbert, but I couldn't. I couldn't bear the thought of leaving without saying goodbye. I'm sorry, Mother, but I had to join up. You know I've always had this thing about the army – about wanting to see the world. And now everyone's going. You want to, you want to go out there and bash the Hun. I hate school, Mother, and working in the business would be worse.'

'But Robbie, you're only sixteen – you can't be a soldier.' His mother's face was pale but she didn't cry. She wanted to plead: Don't leave me, Robbie. I love you too much. You're my life. If you go away I'll die. Instead she said, 'You're too young. They'll find out, they won't keep you.'

'No they won't, not unless you or Dad tell them. Nobody bothers if you're big enough and look older. You wouldn't tell them, you wouldn't do that, Mum.'

Her instinct told her, Yes, do tell. Stop him going. You

84

didn't bear him and love him to let him go, a child still, to be a soldier. But for how long could she keep him against his will, seeing the resentment in his eyes, knowing that at the first opportunity he'd be gone?

'You wouldn't, Mum?' Robbie asked again.

'No,' she said. 'I wouldn't do that. Though I wish you'd waited. I'm glad you told me. I'd have found it hard to forgive if you had just gone.' He smiled at her and she knew that she could forgive him anything.

'What about Dad – will he do anything?'

'No,' she replied without hesitation, 'he won't get in touch with the army, but you've made your bed now and you can lie on it – that'll be his attitude. Don't be surprised if when you write he doesn't reply and don't expect to be welcomed back with open arms when you get leave.'

The dining room smelled of delicious food and freshly made coffee – the Delahunts were having breakfast. Sir Arthur was reading the *Irish Times*, following the progress of the British Expeditionary Forces. Lady Delahunt was sorting the morning mail. Alice gazing through the window appeared to be fascinated by the pony, ropes trailing from its neck fastened to the fringes of the drawing room carpet which it pulled face down through the dewy grass of the paddock so that the exquisite Persian rug might be refreshed. In reality, Alice was oblivious of the scene outside. Her mind was occupied with the post her mother was sorting into little piles. Amongst them she hoped would be a letter from Stephen.

It was weeks since she had heard from him and then only the briefest note. Such a note she had told herself required no reply. After receiving it she had gone to her room where she tore the letter into shreds, vowing that never again would she write to him. Later her mother came to talk to her, to persuade her to be patient, to make allowances for Stephen whose mind was preoccupied with thoughts of war. She must write a nice cheerful letter, take the poor boy out of himself. Men looked to women for that sort of thing. And Alice allowed herself to be persuaded and wrote a light-hearted letter, in which she described Nella's Parisian clothes, how she caused many a raised eyebrow in Dublin drawing rooms and that she was now considering going to London to nurse wounded soldiers.

She also wrote about her visits to Horsham, repeating things she had said in an earlier letter. Telling him how she often thought about the marvellous times they had shared. She hoped he would soon come to Dublin so that she could return some of the hospitality he had shown her. Dublin, she wrote, was all agog with the war. Everyone giving lavish parties and dances to send off the young men going to fight.

Redmond the Irish Nationalist politician had presented colours to the Irish Regiments leaving for France. They marched away singing '*It's a long way to Tipperary*'. Everyone was singing the song, at all the parties, even the messenger boys whistled it as they rode their bicycles. He really must come over soon. She signed the letter '*Much love*' and sent it off.

For weeks she waited in vain for a reply. 'Men are like that,' her mother consoled, 'dreadful letter writers. Look at Papa – he leaves all the personal correspondence to me,' on the few occasions Alice complained. Nella hid her relief that the romance was foundering behind a barrage of flippant remarks. 'Men are idiots when it comes to writing letters. Give them a sword or a gun and they're away but the sight of pen and ink causes paralysis.'

'For you, dear.' Alice looked away from the window. Her mother was holding out a letter. From the delighted expression on her face Alice knew it must be from Stephen. 'It's not from Horsham, the postmark's rather blurred, but definitely not Horsham,' Lady Delahunt said, handing over the envelope.

Alice opened it, quickly scanned the one page and exclaimed: 'He's joined the army!' She read the single sheet, folded it and put it back in the envelope.

'Come on, darling, don't keep me in suspense. What does he say?'

'Nothing much, really. Only that he'll come here for Christmas and then he thinks the war will be over. He never mentioned our engagement.'

'Well, he wouldn't. You don't write and ask someone to become engaged. I mean to say if that had been the case there would have been no need for the visit to Horsham. He has to ask you in person. It will all come about quite properly at Christmas. Don't you agree Arthur?'

Lady Delahunt had to repeat her question before Sir Arthur looked up from the paper and said, 'What's that?'

'Stephen says the war will be finished by Christmas. He's coming to Dublin then, and they'll become engaged.'

'A capital idea. By then we'll have the Hun running back to Berlin,' Sir Arthur said and returned to his paper.

Alice consoled herself that Christmas was no time away. She and Stephen would become engaged then and be married the following summer. And in the meantime there was lots to do. Her mother organized a 'sewing circle'. The nursery was cleared, tables and chairs brought in from attics and garden sheds and on Tuesday afternoons between two and four o'clock, friends, acquaintances, the wives of local businessmen and Alice knitted comforts for the troops or stitched yards of gauze into suitable shapes for surgical dressings. The ladies wore white overalls and covered their hair with nurses' veils. Nella, when invited to join the 'circle', refused.

'Actually,' she said when Alice asked her, 'I've decided to do the real thing. I'm off to Guy's next week. Dublin is driving me crazy. One feels so useless here. I mean to say – your Mama and all those women play acting.'

'I wish I could come with you,' Alice said.

'Why don't you? We'd have a super time. And think of the

87

comfort we'll be able to give. Real nurses are all very well, but let's face it, our young men won't want to be handled by just anybody. How would you like to waken up after a ghastly amputation and have some bucolic country girl hovering over you?'

'If I were that ill I wouldn't care.'

'Oh Alice, don't be obtuse, you know perfectly well what I mean.' Then Nella's tone altered, became coaxing. 'Seriously, you should come. Say that you will.' And she thought while she waited for Alice's reply, you might fall in love with a nice, normal man and not throw yourself away on Stephen.

'Mama would never let me. Anyway I'm not sure I could nurse. I feel faint at the sight of blood.'

'You'd get used to it. Think about it. Ask your Mama. The world is changing. Nursing's quite respectable now.'

'I'll ask, but it's a waste of time. The world may be changing but Mama hasn't caught up with it yet.'

Dolly was worn out and at her wit's end trying to ring the changes in her wardrobe. 'I've never known a young girl get so many dresses and blouses made,' Miss Murtagh said when once again Dolly arrived with a parcel of stuff. 'And you're not getting enough sleep, either.'

'It's all the hooleys. Between fellas going off to the war, and others getting married and having parties before they go, I'm worn out.'

'I suppose you're always called on to sing.'

'Well, of course I am!' Dolly looked amazed that Miss Murtagh should ask such a question.

'You'd want to mind your voice, not overstrain it.'

'I do swally two raw eggs before I go out.'

'The best thing for it, and never be without a piece of St Blaize's flannel, it's miraculous for the throat.' Miss Murtagh undid the parcel, smoothed the paper and folded the string.

'They'll come in handy,' she said, putting them in a drawer. 'And tell me, who is the hooley for this time?'

'Jackie Dempsey, a friend of Jem's. He's a nice fella. His poor mother's a widow and he's her only son. Do you think the heliotrope will suit me?'

'It'll be gorgeous. Sit down and I'll make you a cup of tea.'

Nowadays when Dolly came without Bid she never refused the tea. Bid was an awful jeer and laughed behind Miss Murtagh's back. Said she was stuck up. Bid couldn't tell the difference between being stuck up and respectable. Bid was very common. Dolly enjoyed the time spent with Miss Murtagh. It was very peaceful, especially when she talked about her childhood. Though sometimes she went on about the war and the nerve of England letting Irishmen do the dirty work for them. Last time she had moidered her brain going on about how, thank God, not everyone was as easily taken in as Redmond's Volunteers. There were men like James Connolly and Patrick Pearse. Men who knew a Rising was necessary. They were working for it, ready to lay down their lives for it. To spill their blood to revive poor Ireland sucked dry by the English vampire.

Dolly hoped that this evening she'd give all that a rest, and was delighted when, after Miss Murtagh had made tea and they were sitting before the fire, she talked about when she was young. Telling Dolly of the lovely house they had lived in in Ranelagh. Describing the flight of steps up to the hall door and how every morning the maid scrubbed them and polished the brass knocker shaped like a lion's head. There were red plush hangings and brass fenders you could see your face in. And every bedroom had matching jugs and basins and even the soap dishes were the same. In the mornings the maid brought up hot water for washing, and at bedtime put hot jars for your feet.

The kitchen was always full of lovely smells. Ribs of beef and Limerick hams cooking, sometimes legs of mutton or silverside of corned beef. The stockpot simmering away and trays of bread and cakes coming out of the oven. There was a big settee that the dog and the babies lolled on. And the wall facing the range had meat covers hanging on it. Every one of them copper that had to be specially cleaned, for copper got verdigris and could poison you. You could see the flames of the fire dancing in them.

'It must have been lovely,' Dolly said.

'Oh, indeed it was,' Miss Murtagh said, getting up from the fire and moving around the cramped room, taking from a curtained recess that served as a cupboard a tin in which she kept biscuits. 'The loveliest home you ever knew. And we were as happy as the day was long. Sure we were only children. We knew nothing of the truth. Dada brought us bags of cachous every night. His breath smelled of them when he kissed us. How were we to know why he ate them. Some evenings if he wasn't too late home he'd gather us round the piano and sing for us. *Moore's Melodies* – he loved them, but the *Kashmiri Song* was his favourite.'

'I don't know that one,' Dolly said.

'You do. *Pale hands I loved beside the Shalimar*,' Miss Murtagh sang in a high sweet voice.

'Yes – you're right, I do. Only I didn't know the name. I love it, would you ever write out the words?' Miss Murtagh said she would and Dolly asked if her mother loved singing, and was it to her that her father sang the *Kashmiri Song*.

'It was, but she didn't like the singing. She'd never stand by the piano, and I used to think she was a spoilsport and how kind and good-humoured Dada was and hope that one day I'd have a husband as handsome and gay who sang to me. God help the sense of children! How were we to know he had her heart broken.'

'What was it again you said he worked at?'

'He was what you call an actuary. Something to do with insurance. A very important job that you had to be educated

90

for. And he earned a great salary. But it was all to no avail for the drink had hold of him, and in the end killed him.'

'Go way!' Dolly said. 'You never told me that before.'

'It's not something I talk about often, and there's very few I'd mention it to. It was a terrible disgrace. One night when he was drunk he fell in D'Olier Street and hit his head on the kerb. He was rushed to Jervis Street hospital and they opened his skull, but they couldn't save him. His poor head, they shaved off his lovely black curls and stitched where they cut with a thing like twine, great big stitches that puckered his skin.'

'The Lord have mercy on him, that must have been a terrible sight. Your poor mother – how did she take it?'

'She never overed it – the suddenness of his death, the shame of it, but there was worse to come. He didn't have a penny on himself, and him in insurance. There he was dead in the house and no money to pay the undertaker – not a brass farthing. And on top of having nothing for the funeral expenses he owed to everyone.'

'He wasn't buried a pauper? That didn't happen to him?' Dolly, brought up in a home where paying the society money was as important as paying the rent, asked.

'He was spared that, thank God, only because arrangements were made for everything to be sold. The house, furniture, everything had to go. We came down in the world with a bang. Out of Ranelagh, me out of the convent and out to work. Take my advice and never marry a man that drinks.'

'I mightn't marry anyone,' Dolly said.

'You could do worse. Except you've no trade at your hand. I could always earn my own living. Anyway be a sensible girl and don't rush into things.'

'I didn't realize I'd been here so long,' Dolly said, looking at the clock. 'I'd better make a move.'

Miss Murtagh went to the door with her. 'Do you know,' she said, catching hold of Dolly's arm. 'I made a mistake about you in the beginning – I thought you were an impertinent young one. And you're not at all. Underneath everything you have a kind heart. And listen, you're my best customer as well, so don't ever worry if you're short – the money will do anytime.'

'The money's no trouble,' Dolly lied, her pride offended. 'I'm never short,' not, she thought, while my mother has it, even if she gives out yards to me.

On the way home she went over in her mind all Miss Murtagh had told her. One time she would have been like me with everything before her. Thinking about fellas and parties. Hoping for a husband. Boasting about having a trade at her hand was only a consolation, looking back. She'd have given that up in exchange for a husband. Any woman would. It was terrible to be old and lonely. To have no one who cared whether you were alive or dead. She thought about her mother rich in so many things. Constantly needed by herself and Maggie. By her father, who even though she gave out to him, you could tell she wouldn't be without. Poor Miss Murtagh boasting about her independence. And what did she really have – nothing.

Dame Street when she came to it was crowded with people going to the theatre. The show in the Olympia was supposed to be good. Maybe she'd get Jem to take her next Saturday. Then she remembered they were going to a dance. Though why she'd agree she didn't know. That feckin eejit couldn't put a foot under him. Imagine not being able to dance! It was just as well he didn't mind other fellas taking her up.

Out of the corner of her eye she saw Kevin McEvoy linking a tall dark-haired girl. He was supposed to be seeing Bid tonight! The louser! He'd have left her standing like a fool and tomorrow tell her a mouthful of lies. She crossed the road to avoid him. Maybe Miss Murtagh was right after all. Between drunkards, liars and fellas not able to dance men weren't much to write home about.

Her cynicism stayed with her until she was almost at the house. First thing tomorrow she'd make inquiries about having her voice trained. One day she could be famous. Then she could snap her fingers at any man. She let her imagination roam until she considered the bit in between having her voice trained and appearing as a star – that mightn't be so nice. For a start she'd have to leave home – go God knows where. London would be all right. But supposing you had to begin in Cork or somewhere down the country. And live in lodgings! Anything could happen to a girl in lodgings. Maybe she shouldn't rush in things. Leave them as they were for the present. And she mustn't lump all men together – they weren't all tarred with the same brush. One day she would meet someone special. In her heart she knew it. He was there somewhere just waiting. For the rest of the walk home she conjured him up.

Chapter Five

Robbie did his basic training in Aldershot. The man in the next bed was a Londoner with a small wiry body who chain-smoked and guessed on the first evening that Robbie was under age.

'I am not,' Robbie said, sounding indignant when all he felt was frightened.

'Call me Arthur, Arthur Miller, though by the weekend I'll be nicknamed Dusty.' Arthur grinned. 'You can't kid me. What are you, sixteen?'

'How can you tell? The recruiting sergeant couldn't.'

Arthur's nicotine-stained fingers lit a cigarette from the butt of the previous one. 'They don't give a bugger. You were big enough, that's all they look for. Get paid on commission, see. Now me, I look at people's eyes. You can tell a lot from the eyes. Yours are like a child's, clear, bright and that. Sixteen, eh? I could just about be your Dad. Here, have a fag.'

Robbie smoked his first cigarette, fighting down the wave of nausea and dizziness. 'You wouldn't tell the Corporal or anyone?'

'Me? What would I do that for? Tell us about yourself. Where are you from? What did you do before?' Robbie told him.

'You'll be all right. Stick by me. I know my way around. Stands to reason, being from the city and working since I was twelve. You want to watch some of this lot. Some of them'll scrounge, fags and money. Take advantage of a kid. You and me'll be mates, right?'

'Right,' Robbie said and didn't feel resentful that Arthur assumed he needed looking after. There was something like-able about him. A feeling that increased as time passed and Robbie discovered that despite Arthur's warnings about scroungers he was a soft touch, so that it was to him they came for fags, a loan of boot polish and money.

On their first evening in the barrack room Arthur showed Robbie photographs of his wife. 'That's Lil, taken at South-end, and that's us in her Mum's garden. Good, aren't they? Taken with a five bob box camera.'

Robbie admired the pictures and asked how long Arthur had been married and if he had a family.

'Twelve years. No kids. That bothers Lil. Though maybe with the war it's as well,' he said, not very convincingly.

By the end of the week everyone else was calling Arthur, Dusty, so Robbie did, too. 'I suppose I ought to write to Lil,' Dusty said one evening as he and Robbie were making their beds, 'and don't forget to put your trousers under the blanket. No, not on the springs you daft sod! How many times do I have to tell you.'

Robbie folded the trousers into their crease and laid them on the three-sectioned mattress known as biscuits then put his blanket on top.

'Be like razors them creases tomorrow,' Dusty said. He was sitting on his bed, a cigarette in the corner of his mouth, his eyes screwed against the smoke, undoing a penny packet of notepaper and envelopes. 'Better get started, else she'll think I've done a bunk.'

Robbie went to the ablutions. When he came back Dusty was contemplating the notepad with a worried expression, a pencil instead of the usual cigarette sticking out of his mouth.

'Can't think what to say?' Robbie asked.

95

'Aye,' Dusty replied. Robbie lay on his bed reading. 'Oh sod it,' he heard Dusty swear.

'What's the matter?'

'I can't write a letter, can I? I've never written nothing since I left school.'

'You must have,' Robbie said in disbelief.

'Straight up I haven't. Only the forms when I joined up.'

'But you can write.'

'Of course I can and read.'

'Then it's easy. Just imagine you're talking to Lil and write down what you're saying.' Robbie went and sat beside him. 'Look, put the address there. Leave a few lines and start here. "*Dear Lil*" or whatever you want to call her.'

For nearly an hour Dusty huddled over his pad laboriously writing, stopping sometimes to light a cigarette or to ask Robbie to spell a word. A couple of sheets he tore up and started again. Then at last he said triumphantly: 'I did it. I finished it. It's not much good I suppose but I done it.'

'She'll love it and next time it'll be easier,' Robbie told him.

Robbie wrote to his parents. His mother replied by return post but nothing came from his father. Lil wrote regularly to Dusty who sometimes read out parts of her letters to Robbie. She had a job in munitions and was saving up for a house. It would be nice not living with her Mum.

The platoon was taking shape. Learning how to drill, how to march for long periods, how to handle arms and bayonet the enemy. In the evenings the soldiers speculated on when they'd go to France. Hoping the war would last long enough for them to have a go at the Hun.

Dusty said he wished he had joined the Artillery. 'I always wanted to be a gunner. You can't beat the Gunners.'

'A bloody sight safer too,' another soldier said. 'Not like us out there in front. It's no joke being in the Infantry.'

Robbie was making a good impression on his superiors. Being complimented on his turnout, his skill at handling weapons and his general demeanour. 'You should think about being a regular soldier,' he was advised. He thought a lot about it. The idea was very appealing. He would get promotion, travel. Yes, he liked the thought very much. India, Hong Kong, Singapore, Malaya. He might just become a regular soldier.

Towards the end of the training period he knew he had left Dusty far behind. But Dusty still believed he was showing him the ropes. And because Robbie liked and admired him so much, he kept up the pretence of deferring to the older man. Dusty had courage and determination. No matter how long it took or how difficult he found things, in the end he overcame them. He was a good mate.

Lady Delahunt let word leak out that Alice was to become engaged during the Christmas holidays. Then she heard that Stephen couldn't get leave. There was no reason for her to doubt this but all the same she decided to keep a closer eye on events between Alice and Stephen and took to reading the not very frequent letters he sent. Things were not as they should be, she concluded. His letters gave not the slightest hint that he considered Alice other than as a friend. However, she decided to wait a little longer before doing anything about it.

As the weeks passed Alice fumed inwardly as one after another her friends and acquaintances brought forward their wedding dates. It was horrid having to smile and lie when the brides and their mothers asked: 'And when are you taking the plunge? It's the least you could do for the poor brave boy.' She was sick of her mother's constant and unconvincing consolations that hasty marriages were often regretted. That Stephen couldn't bully the War Office into granting him leave. That it was all for the best. She wouldn't want to be married and then have him dashing off to France. She wouldn't want to be widowed when she was scarcely married.

Look at the casualty lists – every day the papers were full of them.

Lady Delahunt was equally sick of the hollow consolations, between one thing and another the proposed match between Alice and Stephen had brought less joy than she had anticipated. Alice was a beautiful young girl. Young men swarmed around her. Stephen, though a big fish, wasn't the only one in the sea. Ireland had plenty of eligible young men. Then she remembered Rudgewick Park and her vision of Alice as its mistress, Alice holding court in a London drawing room and dismissed the thought of another match. She had let too much time slip by. Two months into the New Year. She would write to Margaret: as Stephen's mother she would know how to bring him to heel.

Stephen received two letters – one from Horsham in his mother's spidery script, the other, forwarded from Horsham was postmarked Paris, the handwriting that of a child or near-illiterate. He didn't recognize it. Yet the sight of the French stamp and the cheap paper made his heart thump. Such a letter must concern Émile. It wasn't from Émile, it wasn't his writing and anyway Émile was at the Front, or had been when he last heard from him several weeks ago. He put aside his mother's letter and opened the other one.

'I write to tell you bad news of my brother. You were his friend. A long time ago I brought you news of him. Now I write to tell that Émile is dead since the fourteenth of January. He made me promise if he was killed to do this before he went to be a soldier.'

His beautiful Émile was dead! He said it aloud but it meant nothing. He repeated it again, trying to picture the laughing dark-haired boy he loved. The vitality of him stilled. The body he had worshipped devoid of life. Émile, whose hands and feet were small and slender, his bones fragile, the skin on his arms covered with silky dark hair that grew in whorls. Patterns he had loved to trace. Émile with whom for the first time in his life he did not feel a sense of shame and guilt. In the beginning he had believed this was because Émile did not belong to his class. Émile, he had reasoned, was a prostitute, it was a business transaction, no more. But even then, even the first time he knew that wasn't so. Émile not only gratified his body, Émile fulfilled a want that was in him. Émile was the other side of himself for which he had unknowingly been searching. For the first time in his life he felt whole. For the first time in his life he was happy. He should have settled for it. Not heeded his father's urging and his mother's pleading that he had stayed too long in Europe, that it was time he came home. Time he considered the future, marriage.

The letters from home became more urgent, more pleading. Making him unsettled, irritable, suspicious. For the first time since his relationship with Émile had begun, he started questioning it. Questioning his homosexuality. Was this what he wanted to be? Was this the way he wanted to lead the rest of his life? Wasn't it just a thing of the moment that the right girl could cure?

He found fault with Émile. Criticizing the things he had previously admired, his spontaneity, his gregariousness, his generosity, eventually accusing him of being unfaithful. In the aftermath of the quarrel he left for England. Once there, he regretted his decision and wrote imploring Émile's forgiveness and promising to return. And he would have. He knew that almost as soon as he arrived home and for certain when he couldn't respond to Alice.

Now it was too late. Émile was dead. He would never see him again. Émile was a Catholic. He hoped for his sake he had had time to confess. Not been blown to smithereens. Not gone to Hell, a fear Émile had often voiced as the punishment he would suffer if death claimed him before he could confess the sin of his love. Stephen cried thinking of him, imagining him bundled in a groundsheet for burial.

He put down the letter and lay on the bed, his mind so taken up with sadness he didn't hear the knock on the door. It opened and the face of Harrison peered round it. 'Good God, Whitehead! What's the matter? You look wretched. Are you ill?' Then the young subaltern realized Stephen was crying. 'I say, I'm sorry barging in like that.' His eyes looked away from Stephen's face and saw the open letter. 'Not bad news?'

'A friend killed in France, someone I was in school with,' Stephen lied.

'Rotten luck. An infantry chap?'

'No, a gunner.'

'Awful pity. I came to see if you were coming into the village, I don't suppose so now. Sorry again to have barged in and about your friend.' The young officer backed out of the room.

Stephen lay for a while longer thinking about Émile, indulging his sense of loss and grief then realized someone else might come to the room or he could be called and mustn't be seen in such a state. He got up and bathed his red puffy eyes and combed his tossed hair then returned the letter from Émile's brother to his locker and took out his mother's letter.

Appearing calm and presentable he sat and read the letter from Horsham.

'My Darling Boy,

It's so lonely here without you. No sooner were you back from France when this wretched war took you away again. Having someone young about the place was lovely. So many of the young men from the estate have gone to war. It's depressing to be surrounded by the old.

And having said all that I come to what might seem like

*interference and preaching. But please bear with me, dearest
Stephen. I must write so to you, much though I would like not
to. You have been casual to say the least in your attitude to
dear Alice. When you came home from France Papa and I
talked with you about a possible marriage between you and
Alice. You raised no objection, in fact you seemed rather keen
on the idea. Alice is a sweet, dear child who we would love to
have as a daughter-in-law. Her mother, when we first spoke
about the possibility of a marriage, told me how much Alice
had liked you years ago when you went to Ireland on holidays.
Of course I know she was only a child then, but still the
families have known each other for many years – that's a good
foundation for any marriage.*

*I'm sure there is no need to remind you that the Delahunts'
visit last summer was to be the forerunner of you and Alice
declaring your intentions publicly. However, you have rather
dragged your heels. This week I had a letter from Lady Delahunt who tells me that Alice is greatly distressed with what she
interprets as your change of heart. In fact the child is pining. I
know of course that you would never go back on your word.
But you must make this clear to the Delahunts and to Alice in
particular.*

*You are expected to marry her. Indeed, you are contracted
to do so. Not legally perhaps, but you are honour bound.
I'm sure there is a perfectly reasonable explanation for your
tarrying, and that your motives have been selfless. But be a
dear boy and right this matter as quickly as possible.*

*And now that I've done my duty hear my most true and
pressing reasons for wishing you to marry. You are our only
child, our most precious possession. I want a grandchild, a
child in whose face I may again see yours. A child for me to
hold and believe for a little while that I am young again. Foolish
women's reasons. For your papa a child means the Whitehead
name going on into the future. The line surviving, the feet of
your children treading the land we've held for generations. So*

101

be a darling, stop dragging your feet and make Alice and your devoted parents happy.'

A wife! A child! Oh God, what was he to do? Was this why Émile had to die – so that he was free to marry? That his parents could die happy, assured of their immortality. But what of Alice? Sweet gentle Alice, beautiful Alice who aroused nothing but his pity. Could he go through with it? Approach Alice on their wedding night as he had approached other girls to whom, before Émile, he had looked for proof that he was normal.

No, he couldn't. It was no use. He couldn't go through with it. It wouldn't be fair to Alice. He put away his mother's letter and lay down on the bed. His mind was a kaleidoscope of images – Émile's face the night they parted, the brother – a thin, undernourished boy delivering Émile's first letter, his eyes darting from his face to the plate of croissants on the table; a window with the sun shining through onto Nella Sugden's glorious hair the afternoon she had met him and Émile in the restaurant. Round and round in his head went the pictures, blurring, merging, becoming clear. Alice's face convulsed with laughter the day he taught her to ride the bike and she wore the bloomers, his mother at her desk writing to him, urging him to do the right thing by Alice.

– Ah, if only, he thought, there was someone I could ask for advice. But there was no one. No one he could confide in: no one to ask for help. Whatever decision he reached he must reach alone.

From London Nella wrote long letters, letters which at first were enthusiastic, full of praise for the nursing staff and admiration for the wounded. Then the tone of the letters changed and in graphic detail she described the dreadful wounds, the squalidness of the hospital wards, the surroundings in Southwark, and what dragons the sisters, matron and staff nurses were. How disapproving they were of girls like herself whom they saw as playing at nursing. And really they were most unfair and detailed the nursing aids the most degrading tasks. If it wasn't for the fact that she went to the theatre and out to dine occasionally she couldn't possibly stick it.

Poor Nella, Alice thought, how she must hate it all, she really was very brave. It made her feel quite useless when she assisted at her mother's sewing circle. Most of the women had sons or husbands serving at the Front. Alice listened to their conversations and marvelled at their courage and how proud they were of their men. She didn't know how they bore it. And felt that if she loved someone who was likely to be killed at any moment she wouldn't have the composure to sit and roll bandages or discuss the merits as to which parcel they were going to have sent out from the Army and Navy Stores. But as always she reminded herself that she was unlikely to be in that position. Stephen had not written now for several weeks. For all she knew, he could be at the Front. It must surely be time, he enlisted ages ago.

Then one morning a letter arrived. The post was late that day so her mother had already left the dining room. Alice opened the letter and read that Stephen was sorry for what must appear a dallying with her affections. That had never been his intentions. Times were not easy or normal. His intentions had always been what was best for her. She must believe that. He remembered with great pleasure their time together in Horsham. Lately it was often only the memory of her goodness and sweetness which had kept him sane. And if she thought that an extravagant statement it was only because she had no experience of how ghastly life in camp could be. But thank heavens it was almost over. In April or May he would probably go to France, but whenever it was he would have embarkation leave first. He could come to Dublin, maybe for a week.

They could get married. It seemed to be what everyone was doing. He was sorry he hadn't given her more notice. It wasn't that their marriage had been far from his mind. Hardly an hour passed that she and their future hadn't occupied his thoughts. Would she consider it? Would her mother approve of such a hasty marriage – it would of course cut down on all the ceremonies, etc.

Alice was overjoyed. He did love her. She was a fool to have ever doubted it. She reread the line about how their future had hardly ever been far from his mind, and she remembered the day in Brighton when she had reached out and touched him, the warmth that had spread through her as she imagined him her husband. Then she had longed for it to be so and did so now again. Of course it would be heartbreaking – just married and Stephen having to rush off to France. But so romantic, too. With her head full of the idea she went to find her mother.

Lady Delahunt was in the flower room surrounded by buckets of spring flowers – daffodils, bluebells, narcissi and grape hyacinths. 'Mama, I've had the most wonderful letter from Stephen. Oh Mama, he's asked me to marry him!'

'Why, darling, I'm so pleased for you. Not that I ever doubted the dear boy's intentions.' She must write to Margaret and tell her that Stephen had come up trumps, Lady Delahunt thought as she snipped a stem to the right length.

'He has leave soon, only a short one before he goes to the Front. He wants us to marry then.'

'Marry during his leave? Whatever can he be thinking of? Your wedding day is the most important one in your life, and war or no war it must be done properly. Why, you aren't even engaged yet! You must announce your engagement during this leave and then set a date for the wedding.'

'But Mama, you can't . . . that's not fair. It's almost a year since the marriage was first spoken of. Then the war came, everyone said it would be over soon. But it isn't, it could go on forever and anything could happen.'

'What nonsense you talk.' Lady Delahunt removed her gardening gloves and sat down in a cane chair motioning Alice to do likewise. But Alice said she preferred to stand. 'You and Papa and everyone said the war would be over by Christmas. Well, it isn't. Supposing it goes on and on, maybe Stephen will never get another leave. You can't stop me marrying him. It's not fair, it's not . . .'

'Stop that! You're becoming hysterical. Stop it at once and sit down. You're behaving like a scullery maid. And stop all this nonsense about the war lasting forever. We've suffered a temporary set-back, that's all. But we'll soon rout the Hun. Your father is convinced of it. So let's have no more talk of week-end marriages. I'd never forgive myself if I let you do such a thing. Everything shall be done properly. When Stephen comes over we'll discuss it all, set a date for your wedding, and by the time it arrives I can assure you all this dreadful war will be a thing of the past.'

'Stephen will be killed. I know it. He'll die without me ever being his wife.' Alice began to cry. 'He'll die and it will be all your fault. Nella is right. I am a fool. A fool, a pawn just being moved around to suit you and the Whiteheads.'

'How dare you! I have never heard such impertinence! I will not tolerate such behaviour. Go at once to your room, and when you've composed yourself write to Stephen telling him of my wishes, and then I shall expect an apology.'

If only, Alice thought, lowering her eyes before her mother's gaze, I had an atom of courage. If only I had the nerve to stare her out, then I might find the will to defy her, to write to Stephen, 'Yes, I'll marry you. I'll come to London and we'll marry there.'

'Do you hear me – go at once to your room.'

Thinking bitter thoughts, but not voicing them Alice went. Her mother put on her gloves and resumed her flower

arranging. Outwardly she appeared calm as she stripped sur-
plus leaves, filled vases and stood back to admire the effect, but
inwardly she was in turmoil. Alice, the daughter she thought
she knew, a sweet docile girl had almost rebelled. You could
see it in her eyes, in the set of her mouth. To question her
decision on when she should marry! To question her father's
opinion on how long the war would continue! Of course it was
all Nella's fault. Until she left to nurse they were inseparable.
Heaven only knew what other nonsense she had filled Alice's
head with. The sooner Alice was married the better. She
needed a husband to settle her, all young women did. But
that was no reason for rushing things. And of course Stephen
wouldn't be killed. That was unthinkable. One always had to
look on the bright side. Alice would have the most wonderful
wedding – it would be a day for Dublin to remember.

Usually, Richard's letters came in the afternoon post. Bridget
could curb her impatience from then until Dolly or Johnny
came home at tea-time to have them read. But this morning
a letter came just after they had left for work. She couldn't
wait for hours not knowing what it said, so putting on her hat
and coat she went down the street to Maggie's shop. It was
early so she knew they wouldn't be busy yet. Maggie was
weighing up butter into quarter pounds, beating and clapping
it into shape. Tom had just finished strewing the floor with
fresh sawdust which Christie was doing his best with the aid
of a hand brush to sweep away. 'You're a bold boy. Leave
that alone now or you'll have it flying over the butter and
bacon,' Bridget scolded.

'A demon,' Maggie said affectionately. 'What brings you in
so early, Ma?'

'This.' Bridget held up the letter. 'It'd go between me and
my rest waiting for this evening. I want you to read it.'

'Let me finish the butter and we'll go up and have a cup of
tea. While you're waiting you could put them cracked eggs

that's in the basin outside the door.' Bridget took out the cheap eggs and placed them amongst the heads of cabbage, baskets of potatoes, yellow turnips and the brine barrel with pigs' cheeks and ribs pickling.

'I'm ready now, come up Mother,' Maggie called and Bridget followed her up the stairs. 'I'll put on the kettle and then put you out of your agony. Hasn't he lovely writing,' Maggie said, looking at the envelope before opening it and beginning to read:

April 1915

'*Dear Ma, Da, and Dolly,*

How's everyone in Dublin? I think about you all at home and wish I was there. You'll have to excuse the writing, I'm balancing the pad on my knee and scribbling with a stylo.

Well, Da – it looks as if the Civil Service isn't as secure as you thought. I'll probably have to enlist. Have you read all the hu ha in the papers about women lately, well the Service is now employing them. No doubt the women think they've succeeded, that the publicity worked and they are about to get their rights. God help their senses. It suits the Government well enough to let them in – it's a ploy to release more men for the Forces.

We've had a circular round – "Your King and Country need you – we don't." Couldn't give a broader hint, could they? There's talk of conscription and the Service's line is, "Will you go or must you be fetched?" And promises that if you go the job will be kept, etc.

I can't help smiling at the irony of the situation, me likely to finish up as a British soldier! But all is not bad news and once you get used to the idea, it's nice having girls working here. There's more going on for a start. This week I was invited to a soirée (social evening) and danced for the first time in my life – the Sir Roger de Coverly, you should have seen me! Afterwards I walked this girl home. She's very nice. Her name is

107

*Emily. Now Ma, don't jump to conclusions. I'm not courting.
I must close now. Give my love to all and a kiss to Christie.*

*Your loving son
Richard.'*

'For God's sake, Mother, stop crying. The army thing might never come off,' Maggie said, handing back the letter.

'I knew it. I knew nothing good would come of him going to England. I knew something was in that letter.'

'You're meeting trouble halfway. He could feck the Civil Service up an apple tree and come home, so don't worry. I'll make another pot of tea.'

While Maggie filled the kettle she talked to her mother, wondering who Emily was. And if there was anything in it between her and Richard.

'I don't know,' Bridget replied. 'I only wish to God he'd met a girl here, then he might have thought twice about going away.'

'There wasn't much chance of that with Father's encouragement to go.'

'Bull driving's more like it. But when he comes in tonight I'll have something to say to him.' Bridget stood up. 'I won't delay you.'

'Sit down for a minute, Tom can manage all right. What's the latest with Dolly and Jem? Do you think anything will come of that?'

'I'd be surprised if it did. She treats him like dirt. How he puts up with her I don't know. She's a terrible young wan. Wanting her own way in everything. And she has me fleeced for money – her and her style. The few shillings she gives up she has back on the treblefold. I don't know what I'd do without the few shillings from Mrs Margolis. God bless her, five shillings into my hand for a bit of cleaning.'

'What Dolly needs is a kick in the shite and a houseful of children. That'd bring her to her senses. You ruined her, made a God of her.'

'Maggie you're like a tonic,' Bridget said and she was smiling.

'Listen, I'll stay for a bit longer, but you go down now and give Tom a hand. Send up Christie and I'll keep him from under your feet.'

Christie sat on his grandmother's lap and while she told him makey-up stories, she thought how it only seemed like yesterday when the child on her lap had been Richard. And now he was going to be a soldier. No matter what Maggie said about not meeting trouble halfway, she knew it as surely as if Richard stood in front of her wearing the King's uniform.

Members of the Boys' Brigade and Girl Guides had helped to collect the jumble, their mothers had baked cakes and scones and today the Sale was being held. The small stage in the church hall was festooned with red, white and blue bunting. A picture of King George V and Queen Mary looked down on the audience gathered to hear Sir Arthur, their local MP, address them and open the Jumble Sale.

'Ladies and gentlemen, we can arrange most things but not the weather. However, I'm sure it will take more than a bad day to deter our local residents from coming out to support you and your efforts to raise money for little luxuries that make our boys' stay in the trenches comfortable.' Sir Arthur paused and the audience clapped.

'As you know, it was my belief and the belief of those better informed than me that our boys would have been home by Christmas. Unfortunately, this was not so. But take heart, all along the Western Front they are fighting gallantly to bring this ghastly business to an end.'

Again the audience clapped. Sir Arthur took advantage of the pause to drink some water and his agent stepped forward holding up a hand for silence. 'Ladies and gentlemen,' he said. 'Sir Arthur has kindly agreed that before he declares the Jumble Sale open, if you have any questions he will answer them.'

A woman rose and asked: 'Sir Arthur, do you think some way might be found to curb the enthusiasm of the ladies distributing white feathers?' There was an angry buzz from the audience. The agent held up a hand until it subsided.

'I'm not sure I understand your question,' Sir Arthur replied. 'The white feather is the mark of the coward, of the shirker. These ladies are trying to prick the conscience of such men. Surely you can't object to that?'

'With the principle, no. But mightn't it be sensible for the ladies to ensure that the men to whom they gave the feathers were, in fact, able-bodied shirkers?'

'I believe they do.'

'That's not so. Last week my son who has a bad heart was harangued by a group of these women. I'm sure his is not the only case.'

The woman was taking up too much of the question time. The crowd showed their disapproval by shuffling their feet and half-heartedly stifling coughs. Sir Arthur said he was sorry that the woman's son had been harassed and promised to look into the incident. The agent looked at the clock and announced that there was time for only one more question.

'Sir Arthur, as you know the funeral took place recently of O'Donavan Rossa, a man notorious for his Fenian activities. A man considered so dangerous, such a threat to Ireland, that he was forbidden ever to live here again. His body was brought home from America.' While the man spoke, Sir Arthur's head was nodding in agreement. 'At his graveside Patrick Pearse made what I consider an inflammatory speech. A speech which in my opinion can have nothing but an unhealthy influence on certain citizens of Ireland.'

The man's lengthy statement was enthusiastically applauded. 'Well sir, what I would like to know is the government's attitude to such speeches, to Pearse, Connolly and their organizations.'

'One of constant vigilance, have no fear. We are not fooled by the various guises under which these organizations operate. We are not fooled by their claims to be cultural, Socialist or any of the other nonsense they spout. As long ago as nineteen-fourteen I drew attention to them in the House. Have no fear, these men and their organizations are constantly being observed. Thank you for your question and may I now declare this Jumble Sale open.'

By the time Sir Arthur left the hall the weather had improved. Coming out into the sunshine he said to his agent, 'The man back there said nothing about a part of Pearse's speech which made me go cold and then see red.'

'What did he say?' asked his agent.

'"The fools! The fools! The fools! They have left us our Fenian dead, and while Ireland holds these graves Ireland unfree shall never be at peace." I'm telling you, they are plotting something – I've felt that for a long time. Any doubts were dispelled on St Patrick's Day when they paraded through Sackville Street.'

'Oh come on, Sir Arthur – they've done that before. It was one of the things you mentioned in a speech in the House in nineteen-fourteen. No one takes them seriously. And anyway, the Volunteers are MacNeill's thing. MacNeill's a professor at the university, a peaceable chap. You're not suggesting he's about to lead a revolt!'

'That's the trouble, not many in authority do take them seriously. But I do and it's not MacNeill I'm concerned about. It's Connolly and Pearse. I'll tell you what I see happening – they'll join forces. MacNeill's Volunteers will welsh on him and go with them. Home Rule, if and when it's granted, isn't enough for them. They want what they describe as a Free Nation. You mark my words. No one is more aware of the saying "England's difficulty is Ireland's opportunity" than Pearse and his crew.'

*

111

From January 1915 every week Richard had sent his mother a money order for ten shillings. After cashing it she gave Johnny half a crown and saved the rest. When Richard got a holiday and came home he wouldn't go empty-handed. He came in May. She was overjoyed and wouldn't let herself acknowledge that his stay was only temporary.

Dolly complained about having to sleep again with her mother, but Bridget said nothing, knowing her bark was worse than her bite. Didn't it show in how she and Jem wanted to take Richard everywhere with them? Not that he went, preferring to spend his time seeing boys he had gone to school with. Boys more fortunate than him she thought, boys whose fathers had taken them away from school and put them to a trade. Living at home with no threat of the army hanging over them, nothing more serious than being accosted by the lunatics of women eager to see every young man in uniform. Women with more money and time than sense, mad about the King and England, a bloody pity they didn't take themselves over to live in England and not be going round giving out white feathers.

She cooked all Richard's favourite meals and made him lie on in the mornings, wakening him with thin bread and butter and his tea nice and strong. Several times she brought the talk round to the girl Emily. Asking what she was like, where she lived, how old she was, stopping short always of asking Richard if he was serious about her. One day she suggested to him that he should pack it in altogether. 'She's a nice girl, why would I do that.'

'You don't be follying what I'm saying at all. It was the job I was talking about, not the girl.'

Richard smiled at her. 'Mother,' he said, 'I'd forgotten your mind is like a grasshopper – jumping from one thing to the next. What would I do if I did?'

'There's plenty of work here since the war. You'd have no bother.'

'Oh I'm sure! Can you imagine me applying to Guinness' and they say, "What did you work at before?" "Well sir, I was in the Civil Service, only I was afraid of having to join the army, so I came home."'

'Guinness' isn't the only place.'

'All the firms' attitudes would be the same. They'd want references. Anyway, I like the Civil Service, I'm used to it.'

It's her, that one Emily. It's her keeping him over there, Bridget thought. 'Well, all I can say is you're a very foolish boy.'

'Ah, Mother, don't be worrying, the war'll be over before long.'

'I hope so for everyone's sake,' Bridget said.

'We've been going out for two years and I'm always in your place, why won't you come to mine?' Jem asked.

'I told you I don't like meeting strangers,' Dolly said.

They were in the park sitting on a bench, Dolly moving the fallen leaves round in a circle with the toe of her boot, wishing Jem would drop the subject of her going to his mother for tea.

'My mother's not really a stranger.'

'She is to me.'

'Yes, well all right, but she thinks it's very odd that I've never brought you home. You could come now, I said you might.'

How was she going to get out of this without saying out straight what was really keeping her from meeting his mother? That the minute she did he'd think it was the go-ahead. The next thing he'd be buying her a watch, then a ring and wanting to get married. That's the way it went. And she didn't want to get married but at the same time didn't want to lose him. The best thing was to pick a row with him – it would give her a breathing space. 'You've an awful cheek – there's nothing odd about me.'

113

'I didn't say there was. I was only saying what my mother must think.'

'And she's an awful cheek, too. I wouldn't care if you'd never come to the house, nor my mother either. We're not like that. And if you think I'm sitting here to be insulted you've another think coming.' She got up and began to walk towards the park gates.

Jem hurried after her. 'God, I never meant anything. Forget about coming over for your tea, it's all right.' Dolly allowed him to make it up to her and promised before she left him that evening that one day soon she would love to meet his mother.

When at Christmas she did visit his home, she expected to charm his mother immediately and was put out that Mrs O'Brien was unresponsive. She doesn't like me, Dolly thought. I can feel it. Well, I don't like her either. And she's making out to be more common than she is and giving me plenty of digs into the bargain, listen to her.

'I've no time for anyone who has ideas about themselves, or for some of the little girls that are in it nowadays. Little girls that marry and think that's that, I've a man – let him keep me. I've earned my living all my life and my mother before me. And thank God I can say the same thing about my daughters-in-law. Fine women, able to rear a family and sell in the market as well.'

'That's all very well if you're used to it,' Dolly said.

Jem's mother ignored her and continued, 'One of my neighbours' sons married a girl from the southside, a lazy young whipster. Had her first child and took to the bed. Lying on her arse a week after the child was born and her mother encouraging her. I'm telling you if she was belonging to me I'd have soon shifted her. Up and back in the market I was three days after my children were born.'

'Mother, will you for God's sake give over,' Jem said, wondering why his mother was behaving like this.

'I'm only saying what's in my mind,' Mrs O'Brien said.

Dolly thanked her for the tea and made an excuse about her mother not being well and she'd have to go.

Mrs O'Brien said to come again and Dolly said she would. Jem was full of apologies. 'I don't know what came over her, I'm terrible sorry.' Dolly said it was all right, maybe his mother was in bad humour. She wouldn't say a word against her. It suited her down to the ground the way Mrs O'Brien had received her, once she got over the blow to her vanity. Never again would she have to go there. For if and when Jem suggested it she would remind him of today.

'What did you do that for?' he demanded of his mother when he came back from seeing Dolly home.

'Because that wan's making a catspaw of you. A stuck up little nothing. Oh, give her her due she's smart and has a nice face and figure, but she's not for you. I'm telling you it'd be the poor lookout if you took her. She's full of herself. Get sense, son, and get that wan out of your mind. You want a girl of your own kind.'

Chapter Six

Robbie, now a corporal, Dusty and a young soldier sat against the sandbagged side of the trench, their feet on the duckboard. Mud oozed up through its slats. The soldier who had recently arrived as a replacement had red hair and was called Ginger. From further down the line came the sound of a mouth organ. Ginger whistled the tune and then began to sing softly in time to the music, '*There's a long long trail a winding*'. For a while there was no other sound except the mouth organ and the soldier's voice singing the plaintive, evocative air.

There were stars but no moon so that the barbed wire entanglements, the discarded bully-beef tins, the churned, scorched earth and the weary faces of the men weren't visible. And Robbie thought that at such times if it wasn't for the smells of your own body and those close to you, of the rats and the mud and the sweetish stench of bodies not yet buried, you could almost believe you were somewhere else. In the place of your dreams, where nightingales were singing and the world was sane.

Then a barrage of German artillery shattered the silence, the dreams and the soldier's singing stopped. 'Oh Jesus!' he said, crouching, his arms up over his head, 'Oh my God, that's the real thing.'

'It's OK. It's a long way off. You're all right,' Robbie assured him.

'Bloody replacements! You're all the same. Never been under fire, have you?'

The young man didn't reply and Dusty continued, 'Never had proper training, neither. Not like me and the Corporal. We was trained. None of your old men called off the Reserve to train us. No. We had the real McCay. Proper regular soldiers, pre-war blokes. That's what's wrong with you lot, eh.'

'I suppose so,' Ginger said. But Dusty wasn't listening. Dusty listened to no one any more.

'Real officers and NCOs we had. But Jerry made short work of us still. Thousands killed. Wiped out, thousands. All the best men, captains and corporals, the lot. They make anyone up now. Stay alive and you could be a corporal next week.'

'Here, have a fag,' Robbie said, offering his Woodbines, hoping to stop Dusty's bitter monologue. Dusty was bitter about everything. Dusty was going mad.

Ginger struck a match, lit his cigarette and Robbie's then offered it to Dusty who blew it out.

'Eh, what did you do that for? Lucifers don't grow on trees.'

'You don't give third lights.'

'It's unlucky,' Robbie explained.

The young man laughed. 'I don't believe in luck.'

'Wait'll Jerry's aiming at you, you'll believe in anything then. Anyway, don't burn a light that long, not in this trench, right?'

'It could point us out to a German sniper,' Robbie said.

'OK, sorry, I didn't know.'

A rat ran along the top of the trench, another followed it, then another, their feet skittering and making scratching sounds. 'What's that?' The cockiness in the soldier's voice was gone.

'Rats. They come in dozens, that's the advance party. Some of them are bigger than cats. All the good feeding! Stands to reason doesn't it, plenty of meat laying about.'

'Knock it off for Christ's sake, Dusty,' Robbie said.

For a few minutes Dusty kept quiet, then started again. 'Conscripted were you?'

117

'No, I wasn't. I volunteered.'

'They'll get all the buggers now they've got conscription. Come September they'll get the married ones as well.'

'Are you married?' Ginger asked Dusty.

'Not me mate.'

Dusty had been making that reply since he found out about Lil. Robbie remembered. Her letters stopped coming. Dusty was worried first that she was sick, then that she was dead, 'Killed in one of them Zeppelin raids they've had in London. That's what happened, I can feel it inside me.'

'The raids are miles from where Lil lives, besides someone would have sent word,' Robbie had told him.

'Who? My mum can't write, nor hers. No, something's happened to her. I've got to go home.'

'You'd have to have more proof than a feeling inside you to get compassionate leave.'

Dusty saw his Platoon Commander, explained his dilemma and was refused leave. Soon afterwards a letter did come, written by a neighbour of his mother's saying that the enclosed note was from Lil. Her Mum had passed it on to Dusty's mother.

It was a brief letter telling her mother she had gone to Newcastle and wouldn't be coming back. She loved Eric. He worked with her in the munitions factory, and had wanted her to go away with him for a long time. She was sorry for hurting Dusty but couldn't help it. Would her mother tell his mother.

'Don't take it too much to heart,' Robbie remembered having said as he gave the letter back to Dusty. 'It might all blow over.'

'Maybe,' Dusty replied with little conviction.

In the weeks that followed, Robbie was shocked by the transformation in Dusty. He became silent and morose, ate little of what food came up the line, chain-smoked, seeming to exist on tobacco and the rum ration. Where once he had been a wiry cheerful Cockney, now he was glum and

118

emaciated. Robbie wondered if the change in him was because of Lil, not able to comprehend that a woman could be responsible for such a breakdown. And when Dusty occasionally admitted to having blinding headaches Robbie ordered him to report sick.

'Well – how did you get on?' he asked when Dusty came back from the sick parade.

'Fuckin' Number Nines. Whatever I need it isn't purging. I threw them away.'

That was that. He'd sent him to the doctor, could do no more. Maybe it was Lil, maybe it was the trenches. He just didn't know. And you couldn't report him, silent and surly he might be, half-starved, but faultless when it came to his military duties, still a first-class soldier.

Ginger was rabbiting on, trying to engage Dusty in conversation. Robbie listened for a few minutes to Ginger talking about his Mum and Dad and heard Dusty's occasional grunted comments. Then they were both silent and Robbie let his mind return to Dusty and Lil, how after the arrival of the letter he had never mentioned her name again except on the night he had got drunk in the estaminet.

It was during a rest period when they had been withdrawn behind lines. On arrival they were bathed, deloused and issued with clean clothes and then had the evening free – to spend in the canteen or go to the estaminet. Dusty was for staying in the canteen but Robbie eventually succeeded in getting him to come to the makeshift French café which specialized in fried English food. 'Just think how a plate of egg and chips would go down, the best tonic in the world after all the tinned stew, hard tack and bully beef,' Robbie said.

'And sometimes there's a bit of spare,' another soldier, from the group gathered round Dusty, said.

The estaminet was a tin shack with smoke pouring from its chimney and the smell of frying fat everywhere. There was a stout woman cooking and a younger one serving. The egg and chips washed down with rough wine was the most delicious meal Robbie could remember eating since before the war. Even Dusty appeared to be eating with relish.

The girl on closer inspection was pretty and Robbie in a mixture of school French and broken English began flirting with her. After a few exchanges he suggested she should show him the countryside. She pretended indignance, tossing her head, looking away but remaining by the table. The soldiers sitting with him and Dusty egged him on, shouting encouragement. Their faces smiling, relaxed, like young men at home in a pub, the trenches put from their minds for a brief spell. Only Dusty called after Robbie and the girl a caution. 'Her old man could be waiting for you, a bloody frog ready to knife you. That or she'll give you a dose.'

Robbie ignored him and steered the girl into the night, towards a group of trees, stopping on the way to hold and kiss her, softening her up. She's a passionate little thing, a bit skinny. But all right unless she turns out to be a PT. Now the girl took his hand, leading him through the trees to a hollow lined with years of fallen leaves crumbled down into sweet-smelling softness.

She lay down and pulled him towards her, fingers searching for his buttons. He smiled into the darkness, no need for seduction here. He liked it better when they pretended reluctance. Still, you didn't look a gift horse in the mouth. Afterwards he lay back and reached to hold the girl, put her head on his shoulder, to lie for a while pretending they were lovers, to stroke and caress her and in a while repeat the performance at his own pace. But she was up from the ground adjusting her clothes, talking rapidly in French so that he could only understand a few words. She became impatient with his lack of understanding and insistently repeated, '*L'argent, l'argent.*'

'So it wasn't just my good looks, then?' Robbie said.

'Pardon, monsieur?'

'Forget it,' he said good-naturedly and gave her three francs.

The soldiers who had been sitting with Dusty were gone and he was very drunk. He must have really knocked it back, Robbie thought. I've been gone no time. He helped him back to billets, undressed him and put him to bed. Just before he fell asleep Dusty mumbled: 'It wasn't Lil's fault. He made her. That bloke made her do it. Lil wouldn't have run out on me. But I'll get him. I'll find him and kill the bastard.'

The next day Dusty was his gloomy self again. If he remembered having mentioned Lil's name he didn't let on.

Ginger's voice recalled Robbie to the present, 'When will I get leave, Corp?'

'You've only just come out!'

'Yeah, I know, but when will I get one?'

'There's a rota. You get it when your name comes up. It's supposed to be better organized now. Though I haven't had a turn yet. Still, you keep hoping, sometimes the hope of leave is the only thing that keeps you going. You'll have been added to the list, when you reach the top you're told. Word comes up with Daily Orders, then it's drop everything and away.'

'So if the war lasts it could be years before my turn.'

'Could be.'

'I never thought it would be like this. I knew there'd be fighting and that. It was why I joined up. But it's different to what I thought. Like coming up this morning I saw these soldiers. They were dead. Only I think they were drowned – in the mud – you know, not killed. Like I said, it's not what I expected. And all the trenches, miles of them zig-zagging all over the place as if a grave digger had gone mad. Then there's the rats. No one at home would believe it's like this.'

'You'll get used to it,' Robbie said. Poor sod, he'd get used to the rats and the lice, the rations that sometimes came on time and sometimes didn't and he'd learn to ignore Dusty's picking and the mud and constant weariness. But, Robbie wondered, how would he cope with fear? He'd never got used to that. Never got used to seeing the man beside him having his head blown off. Never got used to going over the top when the whistle blew. Waiting for it, his heart galloping and his legs weak, the helmet feeling too heavy and too tight. But you went, up and over, running, shooting, on and on, bullets flying, men falling, avoiding them, jumping over them, trampling on them. He had never got used to that.

'Don't think about things too much,' Robbie said, trying to reassure him, but the soldier said nothing and Robbie saw that, like Dusty, he was asleep. Well that was one good thing, being able to snatch sleep when you could. He settled himself and tried to do the same. But his mind raced. Thoughts of his mother and father, his brothers Jack and Herbert killed in a battle near Amiens, his chance of leave, chased each other round and round in his mind. Lately his mother hadn't written so often. His father never. Ah hell, it was no use trying to force sleep, the more you did the further away it fled. He opened his eyes and looked up at the stars. Millions and millions of them scattered as far as he could see. One fell, he watched its red streak until it vanished and he thought of his mother telling him that when a star fell it was a soul going to Heaven. How easy it was then to believe in souls and Heaven.

His mother looked up at the stars. She had written how sometimes she'd go out to look at them and pray that Jack and Herbert were up there, in Heaven and it consoled her. From far away he heard the whistle of a train. The sound of a train at night was such a sad lonely sound, like a cry. The cry of someone lost. He shivered. Jack and Herbert had loved trains. Once, long ago, they had all ridden on a train to Paris to visit his mother's sister. The train had stopped at Amiens. His mother told them there was a railway station in Dublin called Amiens. She wondered what this French town of the same name was like. Maybe on another trip to Paris they would stop off and see. And one day she would take them to

Dublin and show them the other Amiens that was a railway station.

Herbert and Jack were stopped at Amiens forever now. Where would he be stopped forever? Don't let me think about it, he prayed. Don't let me be a coward. Don't let me be killed. Let me sleep, please. He closed his eyes and the stars went away. Everything went away in the dark. When he was a child and the candle was blown out he cried because everything went away. He wanted to cry again.

'Easter's awful late this year and me dying for a day off,' Bid complained one day to Dolly at dinnertime.

'I know, not till April the twenty-third. My father says it's nearly the latest it can fall. Still, the weather might be nice. I hope so. Did I tell you about the new rigout I'm planning?'

'Twice already. What you didn't tell me is the latest about Richard.'

'He's definitely going into the army. My mother's demented. She wants him to come home.'

'Will he, do you think?'

'I'll read you his letter. I have it with me, I didn't get the chance to read it properly last night.'

'Go on then,' Bid said and Dolly read:

'I'm afraid my last letter was a little mixed-up so I'll try to make things more clear in this one. I think that sooner or later I'll be obliged to enlist. This morning the papers hinted at the possibility of conscription. And strange though it may seem to you knowing how I felt before coming to England, I think I'd prefer to be a volunteer. You'd have to be here to understand the feeling. Every time someone, a friend or acquaintance goes you feel as if by staying behind you are letting them down. It seems wrong that you should stay safe and sound while they go off to fight for you.

I could of course resign my position and come home. But

Ma, as I explained to you, what chance would I have of getting a job in Dublin once it was known that I'd thrown up a good job because I was afraid of being hurt. And in any case it is now impossible for anyone of military age to leave England without a passport signed by a magistrate. The passports won't be issued unless there is a valid reason for not joining the army. I'm not absolutely sure if these certificates are necessary in order to get into Ireland, but if not now they will be soon, of that I have no doubt.

So I have come to the conclusion that my best course is to volunteer. That way I will rid myself of feeling guilty, and an added bonus, as a volunteer I will draw my Civil Pay and have my place kept open for me after the war, please God. I know this will be a terrible blow to you both. But believe me I have no choice. Try to understand. There is also a further bonus to being attested sooner than later; I won't have to go until my class is called up or later if the Office wishes, so it could be ages yet.

Give my love to everyone at home and tell them to write to me.

Your loving son,
Richard.'

'He must have swallyed the dictionary – I never knew he could write like that. What did your mother say about the letter?'

'She was in a terrible state. First she blamed my father for ever encouraging him to go to England, then she changed her tune and blamed this girl Emily that Richard once mentioned in a letter. Me Ma says it's all her doing. That Richard's trying to impress her that's why he's talking about joining up. You know what me Ma's like – she had to find someone to blame. Like all mothers she thinks she knows the ins and outs of her children's minds. And to her way of thinking Richard would never do anything like joining the army without someone encouraging him. She threw the letter to one side. That's how

124

I was able to sneak it out, otherwise it would have been put away in my father's box. But by tomorrow she'll have got used to the idea and be making the best of it, praying all the harder for the war to be over before he has to go.'

'Your mother's right all the same – he's Irish, so why should he have to fight for England? Wouldn't it be terrible if they brought in conscription over here. Thank God I've no brothers and me father's too old.'

Dolly, fed up with talk of joining up changed the conversation, asking, 'What's the latest about you and Kevin? Has he said any more about getting married?'

Bid laughed. 'Only when he tries it on. And wouldn't I be a fool to believe him.'

'A three-quarter bred thick.'

'What about you and Jem?'

'Jem's not like that, but then I never lead him on.'

'They're all like that,' Bid said.

'Well, I think it's up to the girl. You have to make fellas respect you.'

'Listen to Saint Agnes! I hope you never forget yourself.'

'Don't worry, I won't.'

'You might if the fella was right.'

'The fella's got nothing to do with it,' Dolly said, getting up from the table. Bid was annoying her. She moved away.

'Where are you going? It's not time yet.'

'I've a lot to do. I'm going to be very busy after dinner.'

'Hmmm,' Bid scoffed. 'Writing on bits of paper! It's well for you. You want to be making oatcakes then you'd know what work is. Ah listen, I didn't mean to get your rag out. I'm sorry. Don't go yet. Tell us about your new rigout.'

'Oh, well, all right then.' Dolly sat down again and for the third time described what she was planning to wear for Easter.

He couldn't believe it – his turn for leave had come up – fourteen days. He was to set off immediately. Quickly, he got together his kit, rolling his groundsheet into the smallest possible roll, putting on his webbing, hanging his various pieces of equipment, not forgetting his gas mask, mess tin, tin hat, all the accoutrements of war. Laden he went to bid Dusty goodbye; Dusty, whose name had also come up on the roster, had refused his turn.

This time tomorrow I'll be home, Robbie kept thinking, in Blighty, in Southwater. The train to the port was packed with soldiers and officers singing, and quarrelling about seats and cushions, for the train was dilapidated. Seats were broken, windows smashed, and there were not enough places to sit and nothing to eat – except when they stopped at bigger stations and packs of sandwiches were pushed in at the windows by women who had set up canteens. But despite the discomforts the mood was one of jubilation. They were alive, they were on their way home.

At Folkestone and Victoria more voluntary canteen workers showered the returning soldiers with food, chocolate and cigarettes. On the way down to Sussex, Robbie thought of the surprise his mother would have. It would be dinnertime when he arrived. He would creep into the kitchen where she would be cooking. His father might be there, too. It would be nice to see him again, the old bugger.

The clean uniform he had been issued with at the point of disembarkation felt stiff and rough and irritated his skin. But still, that was better than the itching which plagued him at the front. He was vermin-free and his pocket had a certificate to prove it. He stretched comfortably and thought of how he would spend his leave.

The house looked smaller than he remembered it. Carefully, so as to make no noise, he opened the kitchen door. As he stepped over the threshold he knew that something wasn't right, something was missing. He went into the room, expecting to see his mother busy preparing food. There was no sign of her. Then he realized that there was no smell of food

126

cooking. The room itself was the same, though like the house it too seemed to have shrunk. 'Mother,' he called. There was no answer. A photograph on the mantelpiece caught his eye. It was of Jack and Herbert in uniform. He took it down and was staring at the faces smiling out of the sepia print when he heard the gasp of astonishment and turning saw his mother by the door, her face so changed but now filled with joy. 'Oh Robbie, Robbie!' Then she was in his arms and he was hugging her and kissing her hair, both of them crying and laughing. Then Robbie put his hands on her shoulders and held her away. She had become so old-looking and sick. He put down the picture and studied her again. She looked terrible. Her face thin and haggard, her eyes enormous.

'Well,' he said, making an effort to keep his tone teasing, 'I must say that was a great welcome home. There was I imagining half an ox at least roasting. I could smell it all the way down in the train and you weren't even here.'

'If only I'd known, but sure I didn't and was having a lie down.'

'Why, you never lie down!'

'Ah, I'm not as young as I was.'

'Are you not well?' Now his voice was anxious.

'Oh course I'm well. I get tired quicker, that's all. The doctor's given me a tonic.'

He held her close again. Tiredness, that's all ailed her and she was probably still grieving for Jack and Herbert, and maybe she wasn't eating properly.

She pulled away from him and told him to sit down. To let her cook for him. What would he like? Thank God they didn't have a shortage of food. There was that to be said for living in the country and his father related to all the butchers and shopkeepers. Would he like bacon, or chops, or would she make him a snack and put on a chicken, it wouldn't take her a minute to kill and pluck one.

He settled for bacon and eggs and a chicken for later. While

127

she cooked she bombarded him with questions, not waiting for answers. What was the journey like? What was France like? Was he tired? Why hadn't he told her he was coming?

'Oh Mother, you never change,' he said, delighted to see her bustling about, apparently not sick for all that she looked it. 'Tell me everything. All the news. What about Dad, you know he never writes. But how is he? Why isn't he here?'

'Him, don't mention him. I think he's gone mad. He spends more time in the woods than here.'

'He always did.'

'Not like this he didn't. Do you remember the little hut where he used to shelter if it came on to rain, well he's taken to sleeping there. Took out a paliasse and sometimes I don't see him from one end of the week to another.'

'What brought that about – was it, you know, Jack and Herbert?'

'I suppose so, though not in the way you'd expect. Not through grief. He never forgave any of you for joining up. I'm not saying I'd have wanted him going round with his chest stuck out boasting about his soldier sons. But when it was done it was done. God knows I broke my heart that any of you went. But it wasn't grief with him. It was anger. Rage that you'd done it without telling him. That you'd gone without a thought as to how he'd manage the business. That's all I'd hear, how all his life he'd worked to build up a business for you and it was thrown into his face. I'm telling you he's gone mad. He cares about nothing. Certainly not about me and as for the business it's gone to wrack and ruin when he could be making a fortune. There's a great call for timber because of the war. I think he's drinking out there. There's a mad streak in the Brightwell family. He had an old uncle, a cider-maker who fell down a well one night when he was stocious and drowned. Another oul lunatic like your father who took to living in the woods.'

Her spirited attack on his father exhausted her and Robbie

made her sit down while he finished the frying. 'Listen,' he said, 'I'll go out and surprise him, bring him back.'

'You'll do no such thing. I don't want him spoiling your first night at home and that's what he'd do.'

'Does he know you're not well?' he asked, still not believing her excuse of age and tiredness.

'I'd have to be stretched on the floor before he'd notice. Now stop worrying about me and him and my health and eat that food before it goes cold.'

Later he helped her catch a chicken and watched her wring its neck, pluck and clean it. And he reminded her of how often as a child he had seen her put baby chicks that weren't thriving inside her bodice to keep them warm.

'That was if they had a bad mother. You've a great memory all the same. You got that from me. Do you know, I can picture Dublin as if it was only yesterday I left it.' She laughed but not joyously. 'Looking back I do think I must have been mad eloping. Into army quarters in Aldershot. You've never seen anything like them in your life. No plaster on the walls, brick inside and out. No shops to buy your food from, everything supplied by the army. Rations they called them, like they did for the men. Lumps of beef that you wouldn't know which end of the cow it came from, your bread, everything and lumpy, weevily flour. And then when he finished we came here. Into the middle of nowhere. Me that was reared in the heart of Dublin able to walk into town in five minutes, in a lovely house with all my wants, me finishing up in Southwater.'

'Well, what made you do it?' Robbie asked. He was watching her as she poked the fire, pushing coals this way and that and he saw her face soften and heard when she spoke that the bitterness was gone from her face.

'Love,' she said. 'I fell in love with the handsomest man you ever saw. A fair, tall man on a big black horse. He had the bluest eyes I'd ever seen. They melted the heart in me. And the bricks and the lumpy beef and the lonely countryside didn't matter at all, for I had him.' She was crying quietly and Robbie let her.

'An old fool, that's what I was,' she said after a while and dried her eyes, 'an old fool.' Then she talked about ordinary things. And Robbie asked her about various people in the village and if she ever heard anything about the Whiteheads or Stephen.

She said no, that now his father didn't go to the estate any more she wouldn't hear. Robbie would have liked to go for a drink but felt guilty about leaving her alone. So he sat listening to her reminiscences of Dublin.

'I'd love to see it again. Would you take me? Robbie, you're not listening.' She asked him again.

'But why, Mother? There's no one belonging to you in Dublin.'

'I have relations, not that it matters. We could stay in a hotel.'

'It's out of the question. I don't want to spend my first leave on trains. You don't know what they're like nowadays. You'd never get a seat. Especially this weekend, it's Easter.'

'We could go in the morning before the holiday rush. Please, it's very important to me.'

'Why is it that important all of a sudden?'

'It just is.'

'Well, I'm sorry I can't do it.'

He felt awful for refusing her. She never asked for anything. But still he wasn't spoiling his leave for a silly whim. She made him feel so guilty just sitting there gazing into the fire, not saying anything. Why didn't she round on him, tell him he was selfish. That for once he could do something to please her. 'Look, you have to understand – I've been away for nearly two years. I just want to take things easy, enjoy myself. For God's sake why don't you say something.'

'It's all right. It doesn't matter. It was just a notion I had.'

'Oh Mother, don't cry. You never cry. Look I'll take you

130

to Brighton for the day, how's that, eh? Come on now, cheer up.' He went to her and put his hand on her shoulder. He felt her bones against his hand. She was so thin, he hadn't realized. So thin and so sick-looking and she was crying. There was something more wrong with her than tiredness. 'Listen, I'll go with you, but it'll have to be tomorrow otherwise we'll never get there.'

'God bless you, you don't know how happy you've made me. We'll go first thing in the morning. I'll write a note for your father.'

Had he guessed what ailed her, Robbie's mother wondered as the train made its way to Holyhead. Did she look so sick? Was that why the two soldiers gave up their seats? She wished he was settled down, married to a nice girl who would mind him. She'd die happy then. But Robbie wasn't the settling kind. And God help any little girl who thought he was.

'Try to sleep,' he said to her when the train left Euston. She didn't want to sleep, soon she'd be in her long sleep. She wanted to savour every minute of the journey. Look through the window, watch the countryside and towns rushing by, remark on them to Robbie, savour every single minute of the travelling and Robbie's company. That's what he didn't want, her talking all the time, demanding his attention. He wanted to be left alone to read or flirt as he was flirting with the girl sitting opposite. She knew every move of his. Through her half-closed lids she watched him working on the girl, flattering her, teasing her, making her blush and laugh. She was a pretty girl, a nice girl and like them all, falling for his charm.

What was it that he had? More than good looks. Lots of men had lovely eyes, smiles and handsome features. But he had something else. She supposed it was the ability to make a woman feel she was a woman. It was a gift she supposed, though who bestowed it she couldn't tell. The men who had it used it for their own ends. The way Robbie did. He collected women the way other people collected butterflies or stamps.

Only the people who collected stamps and butterflies looked after them, but Robbie, she knew, would never look after anyone but himself.

They stayed in a hotel the first night but after that his mother's cousins insisted on them coming to their place. Robbie was fussed over, plied with food, drink and showered with Holy medals and relics of saints to protect him. He fumed at the waste of his leave and thought of a city full of pretty girls which, if his relations and his mother had their way, he wouldn't even glimpse.

During Easter week Eoin MacNeill had found out that a Rising was planned. Confronting Patrick Pearse he asked if the evidence he had was true. Pearse admitted that it was. And MacNeill threatened that, short of informing Dublin Castle, he would do everything in his power to prevent it. However, later in the week he was told of the German arms deal and made to understand that with or without his blessing the Rising would go ahead. Reluctantly he went along with the plan.

Towards the Kerry coast steamed the *Aud*, a German vessel masquerading as a Norwegian ship. In her hold were the desperately-needed arms. Into Tralee Bay sailed the boat and steered course for a small uninhabited island, there to wait for nightfall when she would signal the watchers on the coast. The signals were sent but not acknowledged. For three days the *Aud* waited, signalling after dark, the green lights flashing to the shore. The coast remained in darkness.

Something was not right, the *Aud*'s captain decided and headed for open sea. There he was intercepted by a British Naval ship and ordered to set course for Queenstown Harbour. At its entrance the German scuttled the *Aud*. Down with her went the incriminating evidence, the thousands of rifles and rounds of ammunition on which a successful Rising depended.

Early the following morning a German submarine, bringing Sir Roger Casement back to Ireland to take part in the Rising, surfaced. An inflatable boat was lowered and Sir Roger and his companions made for Banna Strand where later in the day he was discovered in a ruined castle and arrested.

After breaking the German code, British Naval Intelligence alerted Dublin Castle that a Rising was to take place. Plans were made to arrest the leaders. But news of the *Aud*'s scuttling and Casement's arrest took the urgency out of the situation. Action could be postponed until after the Easter holiday.

James Connolly and Patrick Pearse were devastated by the news from Kerry. Nevertheless they decided to go ahead with the insurrection. MacNeill vehemently disagreed. He would not have anything to do with sending men out to be slaughtered. Connolly and Pearse changed the time of the Rising from Sunday to Monday: messages were sent down the country of the change of plan. The recipients were confused and doubly so when the *Sunday Independent* carried a notice signed by MacNeill that on no account was any action to be taken on Sunday, with no reference to manoeuvres being held on Monday. Those not seriously committed decided to forget about the business altogether.

Dolly flicked through the *Sunday Independent*. 'Don't disturb your father's paper, you know how he hates that,' Bridget said, turning from the fire where she was frying the breakfast.

'There's a play on in the Abbey by that fella Yeats, called *Cathleen Ni Houlihan*. Jem's always wanting to go to the Abbey, but I don't fancy it. I wouldn't mind seeing Gilbert and Sullivan in the Gaiety, or out to Fairyhouse. I'd love to see a horse racing.'

'You've got the inside falling out of the paper, tidy it before your father comes in from the yard or there'll be ructions.'

'All right, don't get your hair in a knot, I'm doing it.'

Johnny came in, picked up the paper and, not satisfied with its shape, smoothed and patted it to his satisfaction before beginning to read it. 'Well,' he said after a minute, 'amn't I the far-seeing man, listen to this. "*Owing to the very critical position, all orders given to Irish Volunteers for tomorrow, Easter Sunday, are hereby rescinded and no parades, marches or other movement of Irish Volunteers will take place.*" It's signed MacNeill himself. Now tell me what do you make of that? Well, I'll tell you. There was something planned for today. Something more than meets the eye. Them fellas have been cowhiffling behind MacNeill's back. Only he's got wind of it and put a stop to their gallop. I knew it all along. I'm a very far-seeing man.'

Bridget reminded herself that she had been to Mass and received the Blessed Sacrament. Her soul was in a state of Grace. She wouldn't lose her temper with Johnny. She wouldn't remind him, she wouldn't scream at him that it was a pity his far-seeing hadn't stopped Richard finishing up in France. No she wouldn't, though it was choking her not to. The oul booby. Instead she turned her attention to Dolly, warning her to watch the time for Mass and not to forget and break her fast or she couldn't receive.

'What do you think I am, mad or something? Why would I break my fast?'

'I was only reminding you. Hurry up now or you'll be going in late.'

Chapter Seven

From early morning the sun had spilled its radiance over the city, glinting sparks from granite buildings, reflecting itself in the broad river. It shone in through windows, waking people, enhancing their joy in being alive, giving credence to the miracle of Easter which they had celebrated the previous day.

In Liberty Hall James Connolly noticed that it was going to be a fine day, before addressing his men and confirming that at ten minutes to twelve they would leave Liberty Hall and begin their march to the General Post Office. And that as the Angelus proclaimed midday, throughout the city and in the country other groups would seize their objectives. Afterwards, looking through the window and seeing the river bathed in the life-giving sun, he shuddered at the prospect of what lay ahead. They were going out to be slaughtered, yet it had to be done.

Dolly saw the sunshine and thanked God for answering one of her prayers. Yesterday at Mass she had offered up her Holy Communion that today might be fine, then prayed for God to spare and bring Richard home safely from the Front, and lastly she prayed for the gift of purity in thought, word and deed.

She sang as she packed a brown velveteen bag with sandwiches and biscuits, and thought how lovely it was to be going on such a day to the Hill of Howth. Then she filled a basin with warm water and washed herself all over. She dressed, putting on her best underclothes, her pretty camisole with a deep lace edging, an apricot-coloured silk blouse with handkerchief cuffs, then stepped into the skirt of her brown tailor-made costume.

She took a long time doing her hair, brushing and combing, patting the glossy tresses into place. Then regarded with pleasure her long green eyes with tilting corners and her widely-spaced cheekbones. Her nose, she thought, was longer and flatter on the bridge than she would have liked, but overall she was satisfied with her reflection.

She put on a brown hat trimmed with apricot roses and cream ones the same colour as her skin, slipped on her jacket and lastly, so as not to soil them, her new soft kid, hand-stitched button boots. Boots for which she had paid three guineas, causing Maggie to exclaim when she heard the price, 'You're a feckin lunatic spending twice a man's wage on your feet!'

When she was fully dressed Dolly took down the looking glass, propped it against the leg of the table and began scrutinizing her feet, making heel and toe motions, first with one boot then the other, like someone dancing a gavotte, until her mother said if she didn't stop admiring herself she'd see oul Nick, and to put back the mirror and go out to meet Jem O'Brien if she was going.

Jem O'Brien noticed the sunshine as soon as he opened his eyes and was glad for the lovely day and that he was spending it with Dolly in Howth. Though it was still early he got up. He wanted to be in plenty of time to meet her; to arrive at the Pillar by quarter to twelve. It wouldn't do to be a minute late or Dolly would be in bad humour and the day ruined. And he mustn't forget to bring the old kettle.

While he dressed he thought about the day ahead. The ride out in the train from Amiens' Street. Him and Kevin sitting on one side, the girls done up to the nines facing them. Then

136

up the Hill of Howth in the open-topped tram. There was a grand view of the bay. Lovely flowers grew in Howth, yellow ones, gorse or broom, he could never remember which was which though Dolly often told him the difference. He'd have to ask her again.

They'd have great gas trying to get the fire going. Dolly getting her hair in a knot if the twigs weren't bone dry, and giving out yards if the nose of the kettle wasn't well-plugged with paper. She hated the tea to taste smoky. And after the picnic him and her going off on their own. He'd have to do plenty of coaxing before she'd agree to sit down, and then only after taking ages to arrange her skirt so it didn't crease, and him searching to make sure there were no Daddy Long-legs. And making the joke that it was as well for St Patrick, though she never laughed at it.

They'd lay staring up at the sky, breathing in the lovely air. Just the two of them as if they were the only ones in the world and the city was a million miles away. Him wishing they could stay there forever – him and Dolly, far away from Jacobs and the hooleys and dance halls that she loved and queened over: where he felt like someone with two left feet when he took her up to dance. And then she'd make excuses not to dance with him again, and he'd pretend not to mind. But he minded all right. He was mad jealous watching her in someone else's arms.

At home he practised the steps, la-la-ing the dance tunes, holding the sweeping brush, guiding it, leading it. It was easy and he'd be sure he had the hang of it and could surprise Dolly next time. But the next time he still made a bags of the real thing. If only she didn't love dancing so much, wasn't so good at it. Still, he was lucky she bothered with him, and no matter how many others she danced with, he took her home.

What she saw in him he'd never know, he thought, looking in the mirror at his pale face and grey eyes, combing back the fine dark hair that had a tendency to fall onto his forehead.

Saying to himself that he was very ordinary-looking. Not even a fine man, low-sized really. He straightened himself, stretching in an attempt to look taller. Right enough he was steeped to be Dolly's fella. She was any man's fancy. A lovely face and figure. Never a hair astray, neat and shining, her nails, her teeth, even her boots, always, even in work. Like a doll in a box. Perfect, so that often he was afraid to touch her, to disarrange her.

From downstairs his mother called. 'Are you coming down? Your breakfast's going cold.'

'I am, Ma. I'll be down in a minute.'

'Hurry up then,' his mother shouted, and he went down.

The sunlight streamed through the window of the room where Kevin McEvoy's brother Danny and his wife Josie lay sleeping. It fell warm and bright on the girl's face and woke her. Thinking it was a weekday and she should be out selling her fish, she sat up quickly before remembering thankfully that it was Easter Monday. Today she didn't have to go to the market nor push her cart through the street selling fresh herrings. She lay down again and moved as close as her pregnant belly allowed to her husband, slipping her hand beneath the arm that lay close to his side. In his sleep he caught her hand, enfolding it.

The sun also found its way into the room where Alice was being dressed for her wedding. Nella, who had long since abandoned nursing and was to be bridesmaid lounged on a chair, occasionally issuing orders to Alice's maid, and smoking one cigarette after another, elegantly handling her cigarette holder.

'Quick – put that out!' Alice said. 'Mama's coming, you know how she disapproves.'

Lady Delahunt came in and began to cough exaggeratedly and fan the air with her small, plump, bejewelled fingers.

'Really Nella, what can you be thinking of? Alice will arrive for her wedding reeking of tobacco.' She crossed the room to embrace her daughter. Alice turned from the mirror. Behind her mother's back Nella winked, made an apology and left the room.

'Wretched girl! I can never understand why you are friends.' Lady Delahunt sat down. 'She has a reputation for being fast, paints her face, smokes, bobs her hair and now this latest outrage – a flat of her own!'

Alice turned back to the cheval mirror, thinking how insipid she looked, compared to Nella. Her maid helped her into the fine cambric, hand-embroidered underwear worked by nuns who specialized in making expensive trousseaus. And she wondered at the strangeness of nuns working at creating such exquisite garments for occasions they could never experience. She raised her arms for the pin-tucked, beribboned camisole to be put on. Her mother's face seen through the mirror appeared old and worn, the corners of her mouth drooping, a preoccupied, worried expression on it. Today she shouldn't look like that. Her wish has been granted, soon she'll become the mother-in-law of an officer, gentleman and the son of a Lord. That's what she wanted. But perhaps it's sadness at losing me, Alice thought.

Lady Delahunt, unaware of Alice's scrutiny, pursued her bitter thoughts. Nella Sugden was an ill-mannered, badly brought-up baggage for all her parents' wealth and position. How dare she smoke in my presence. How dare she look at me with amused eyes! Or were they accusing? Accusing me as she had done when Stephen and Alice became engaged. What a time that was. Alice in a state because Stephen was going to Gallipoli instead of France. And then that dreadful business – the sinking of the *Lusitania*. It threw such a pall over things. Made one realize that civilians weren't safe from the abominable Hun. All those people drowned, over a thousand of the passengers, mostly American, women and children amongst them – a neutral ship torpedoed off the Irish coast! The guests hardly talked of anything else. All except Nella, of course. She had other things to say.

A fine sweat broke out on Lady Delahunt's forehead as she remembered some of the things Nella had to say. She dabbed at her face with a scrap of lace and cambric and tried to banish the memory, to concentrate on something pleasant. Her wedding outfit of pale lavender with ostrich trimming. But Nella's image, and the sound of her voice refused to be supplanted.

'How could you, how could you allow such a monstrous thing to take place? Alice getting engaged to Stephen Whitehead?'

'What are you talking about?' Lady Delahunt remembered how she had thought at first that perhaps Nella was drunk.

'You know perfectly well what I'm talking about. Stephen Whitehead is homosexual. It's written all over him.'

He wasn't, of course he wasn't. That was malicious nonsense. Although she had wondered; in Horsham when he met them at the station, and afterwards, when he didn't seem in a hurry to get engaged. But those fears were long laid to rest. Stephen was a gallant young man. A perfectly normal young man. And Nella Sugden was a disgraceful, dangerous girl to have as a guest in her house. She would ask her to leave at once. But no, that might not be the wisest course. Nella was quite capable of creating a scene; of involving Alice, perhaps, mouthing her unspeakable accusation. She would deal with it another way. Derision was always an effective weapon against the young.

'For a moment I thought you were drunk, but you're not dear, a little overwrought that's all.' Lady Delahunt smiled falsely at Nella.

'I'm not in the least overwrought. I'm concerned for Alice's happiness.'

'That's very sweet of you, but I can assure you Alice has never been happier.'

'Alice is a sweet naïve child who knows nothing of the world. You can't let this travesty of a marriage go ahead. You must call off the engagement!'

Lady Delahunt was pleased to see that Nella now *was* overwrought, almost hysterical. 'Do sit down, Nella. Let me get you some water.' Nella refused to sit or have a drink of water. 'I can't for the life of me think what possessed you to say such a wicked thing. Such a foul accusation!'

'Because Alice is my friend, because that gives me a right. Because you're her mother. You can't let her marry him! You mustn't! I should have spoken out ages ago. But I kept hoping something would happen to prevent a marriage. I care deeply for Alice, for her happiness.'

'You do have a penchant for caring, don't you Nella? You've been concerned for so many people, so many causes. Not so long ago it was the Suffragettes, then the Dublin strikers and when the war broke out you started nursing. Though I must say you tire rather quickly of your concern. It makes one suspect your motives and find it difficult to take you seriously. You need a husband, dear. Jealousy might just have something to do with your concern for Alice. Girls often feel like that if they are being passed over.'

'My God! You are incredible. I'm wasting my time. I'm going to speak to Alice, to her Papa.'

'You'll do no such thing. You haven't a shred of evidence for your vile accusation. Sir Arthur wouldn't listen to you, but Alice would and, false though your story is, can you imagine what an effect it would have on her? And now I think you had better go.'

Nella knew there was no point in arguing further. In a way she was as much to blame as Lady Delahunt. She should have spoken sooner. She turned to go.

'And one more thing,' Lady Delahunt said. 'If you breathe a word of this ludicrous accusation I'll see to it that the Whiteheads take you through the highest court in the land for defamation of character.' And of course she never did, Lady Delahunt thought. I put a stop to her lies. And today she's to be Alice's bridesmaid. What more proof is there that it was all a fabrication?

'Mama.' Alice's voice recalled Lady Delahunt from her tortured meanderings. 'Mama, you look so unhappy. I know the bride's mother is supposed to weep, but surely not until after the ceremony.' She smiled through the mirror at her mother.

'Do I, darling?' Lady Delahunt passed a hand across her face as if to erase its expression. 'I was thinking, that's all, and didn't realize my thoughts showed.'

While the maid laced up Alice's stays, she smiled again at her mother and said, 'They must have been unhappy ones, for you looked quite sad.'

'Oh, you know what Papa is like – always anticipating trouble. That strange notice in one of yesterday's papers – you know, the one he read aloud.'

'The one in the *Independent* signed by someone called MacNeill.'

'Yes, that's it. MacNeill is the man who started all this Irish Volunteer thing. The notice said something about all action being cancelled. So your father is convinced there's trouble brewing, an insurrection of some sort. It's all very tiresome really, and I don't understand any of it. But naturally it worried me in case something happened which would affect your wedding. That's all I was worrying about darling,' Lady Delahunt said and hoped the explanation would suffice.

The wedding dress was taken from its hanger. 'It's exquisite,' Alice's mother said. 'And it was a good idea of yours to have the bodice embroidered with seed pearls.' The dress was lowered over Alice's head. 'Yes, you are a clever girl, though not all your ideas are so good.' Lady Delahunt's laugh had an artificial ring to it. 'Remember how you suggested having buttercups in your wedding bouquet?'

'I remember,' Alice said as her head emerged from the white satin. 'You said it would be absurd.'

'Well, of course it would! Imagine at Dublin's most fashionable wedding – the bride carried buttercups! What would people think?'

Nella returning to the room paused by the partly-open door and overheard Lady Delahunt's remarks. 'Hypocrite – vile hypocrite.' She clenched her fists. 'Poor Alice – what will happen when she learns the truth?' she asked herself. 'And amn't I the biggest hypocrite letting this charade of a marriage go ahead. But how could I refuse her pleading for me to be bridesmaid? Hypocrites and cowards, the world is full of them. Please God, if You are up there, which I sometimes doubt, work one of Your miracles at this wedding feast and make Stephen into the man Alice is expecting.'

The maid smoothed the folds of Alice's gown into her waist and over her hips, then began to fasten the dozens of satin-covered buttons into their matching loops. 'Could you hold still a minute, please Miss Alice, I'm all fingers and thumbs and the satiny loops are that stiff.' Alice stood still, looking at, but not seeing her dazzling reflection. For before her eyes was another vision – a field of buttercups like gold in the morning sun and coming towards her a young man smiling an indolent smile, his brown eyes lazily regarding her.

Bessie's first thought when she opened her eyes and saw the sunshine was one of delight that the day was fine and sure to bring people flocking to the Park and Zoological Gardens Then, that she and Liam were blessed having their eating house on the quays: fresh air was a great appetizer. Today they would do a power of business.

'Holy Mother of God,' she said aloud, 'here am I thinking of nothing but the money and me married two years this very day. Liam,' she turned to him, reached a hand to touch him, then drew it back. 'I'll let him sleep awhile yet. That oul cough was at him all night, the rest will do him good.' She looked at his face propped on the pillows and thought how like a beautiful child he was when asleep, and she hoped that when God blessed her with a baby it would look like him. Have his pale clear skin and raven black hair.

She should get up, she told herself and get the range going under the cauldron of mutton stew. But the bed was comfortable and she liked lying next to Liam, studying his lovely face. If he hadn't had such a bad night she would reach and kiss him. Waken him with kisses. See his eyes open with delight in them and feel his arms go round her, and he roll her over and tell her he loved her, and that the morning was a grand time to make love, and return her kisses, and they all warm and easy, and his hands becoming urgent in their search for her. But this morning she would leave him lie.

She got up, being careful not to make a sound, easing her weight out of the bed so the springs didn't creak. By the side of the bed she knelt and said her morning prayers, thanking God for bringing her safely through the night, asking for His grace to guide her through the day, and her special prayer that when it was pleasing to His Will she should conceive a child.

When her praying was done she collected her clothes and tiptoed out of the room and went down to the kitchen. She lit the range and put on the kettle, dressed while she waited for it to boil, then, using some of the hot water, washed her face and hands in a tin basin. She wet the tea and sat to drink it, planning as she did the day ahead. There was the fat to lift from the mutton which she had cooked the previous night, potatoes to wash and peel, carrots and onions to chop. When Liam got up he could mix a dash of pipeclay and write up on the window what they had to eat. People liked to know what there was and how much it cost before coming in.

144

After drinking several cups of tea she began preparing food. The peas which had been soaking overnight she rinsed free of bread soda, covered them again in salted water and put them on to simmer. The stale bread had absorbed the water in which she had soaked it. She mashed down the crusts, put in sugar, two penny packets of spice, stirred in currants and sultanas, scooped the mixture into shallow greased tins and dotted the tops with margarine. She went briskly about her tasks, tidying after each one as she had been trained to do in the Big House, her thoughts flitting from one thing to another. How she must get a cough bottle from the chemist's and rub Liam's back and chest with warm camphorated oil. That the kitchen floor wanted scrubbing and the windows cleaning. And what good value she gave for money. She thought how happy she was and what a good husband Liam was. And that in a few years time they'd have enough money put by to start a small hotel. Plenty had done it before them. Plenty of country people, too. Near the railway station there was always call for clean, cheap lodgings. She put the kettle back on to make tea for Liam.

In Liberty Hall plans were being checked for the last time. Thomas MacDonagh and Michael O'Hanrahan were to take over Jacobs Biscuit Factory. Eamonn Ceannt would secure the South Dublin Union. Edward Daly capture the Four Courts and Eamon de Valera, Boland's Mill. Michael Mallin with Countess Markievicz as his second-in-command would set up their HQ in the College of Surgeons and seize St Stephen's Green.

These were the main objectives, if successfully taken approaches into Dublin were covered. If word had reached Volunteers in the country, and if the Germans sent aid, and if . . . ? Ah, what was the use of blinding himself with false hopes, James Connolly thought, the whole thing was doomed. Yet it had to go ahead. They had to Rise. All one could hope was that a spark of the fire that burned within these men waiting to go out would ignite, though at first it might only smoulder, the whole nation . . .

'Robbie, will you for heaven's sake stop pacing the room. Either sit down or go out for a walk, there's a park not far from here,' his mother said.

'Yes do,' one of the cousins echoed. 'It's a lovely morning, but take a raincoat, there might be a shower.'

Despite his bad humour at having been cooped up for days with his mother and her relations, Robbie smiled. They were such nice kind women, such an innocence about them. 'Soldiers don't have raincoats, only groundsheets, I don't think I'd better wear that.'

'Well, perhaps not.' The cousin giggled like a young girl.

'I thought I'd go into town. All my life I've heard about Dublin and here I am four days in it and haven't seen anything.'

'Oh indeed – there's plenty worth seeing, but with the holiday it'll be crowded. And we'd asked a friend, an old friend of your mother's, to tea; she's dying to see Fanny's son.'

He saw the disappointment on the cousin's face and on his mother's. He was sorry and all that, but he'd done his bit. He'd delivered his mother. He believed now she had blackmailed him into it, for since her arrival she didn't look at all sick. Talking nonstop with her relations, laughing and joking, recalling all they had done as girls. While he sat around stuffed with food and bored to death. Whether they liked it or not he was going into town.

His mother, recognizing the set expression on his face, knew it was useless to try and dissuade him. 'I suppose you're right. It might be a long time before you get the chance again,' she said and the cousins took their cue from her. They told him where and what tram to get, what to look out for on the way into the city, what to see when he arrived and how to get back.

He rode on the tram until he saw a canal bridge and ahead a busy street and guessed he was on the outskirts of the city.

'Where are we?' he asked the conductor.

'Coming up to Portobello Bridge, the barracks is round the corner. Are you getting off?'

'Yes,' Robbie said, 'but it's town I'm heading for, not the barracks.'

'You'd be better going on to the Pillar.'

'I fancy the walk.'

'It's a grand day for it,' the conductor said as he rang the bell.

Richmond Street and Camden Street were full of pretty girls all dressed up. Robbie walked along, aware of their glances, basking in their admiration, listening to their laughter, looking into shop windows at his reflection, admiring himself.

The Bleeding Horse, he stopped to look up at the graphic pub sign. He'd never seen one like that before. He sauntered on, a bleeding horse, blood pouring from its neck, pictures and statues in shop windows, blood pumping from Sacred Hearts. So many shops – bookshops, cake shops, pork shops, secondhand clothes shops. Wax pigs on their hind legs holding trays of sawdust pies, plates of cakes and the bread pudding his mother made and told him in Ireland it was called gur cake. Boots and shoes and silk and satin frocks, moulting fur coats and glassy-eyed stone marten neckties. And by most of the shop windows, beautiful girls pretending great interest in the wares, though from the corners of their eyes they watched the men passing. He wished he had more time. He knew he would like Dublin.

On the way he sampled a couple of public houses, enjoyed the porter and the friendly atmosphere. The men spoke to

147

him and discovering he wasn't stationed in Dublin gave him advice as to what he should see. 'If you go outta here and turn right you'll be in Dame Street. You could go left and see the Castle or right and Trinity'll be facing you. From there it's not a stone's throw to the Liffey and Sackville Street's the widest in Europe, did you know that?' Robbie said he didn't, bought a pint for the man who gave him the information and went.

The Castle, he decided could wait and turned right. Everywhere he looked there were beautiful women, women alone, in twos and threes, on the arms of men, riding past in cabs and on hackney cars, standing in groups talking and laughing, blocking the pavements so that often he had to walk around them or step off the path. There was all the buzz and colour and gaiety of London but something else besides. People here, he thought, smile more, are more relaxed. There's an ease about them – you could feel it lapping around you. You didn't feel a stranger.

On top of a tram that swayed towards the city Dolly and Bid paid their fares to the Pillar, admired each other's new clothes, looked out through the window, remarked on the glorious weather and speculated as to what sort of a day they would have in Howth with Jem and Kevin. They were in deep conversation when the tram stopped outside the Balast Office. Suddenly, without finishing what she was saying, Dolly jumped up and, pulling Bid with her, ran down the stairs and jumped off the tram just as the conductor rang the bell and the tram began to move.

'What did you do that for? You could have got us both killed,' Bid protested, breathless from her hurried descent. 'We should've gone on to the Pillar. Now we'll be late,' she said, looking up at the Balast Office clock, 'and all because you wanted your own way as usual.'

'They'll wait,' Dolly said dismissively. 'And anyway I felt

148

like a walk over the Bridge.' She smiled and linked her arm in Bid's.

'Jem'll wait. I'm not so sure about Kevin,' Bid replied as they crossed onto the Bridge.

The Bridge was crowded with passing people, with groups gathered talking, laughing, enjoying the sunshine. By the kerb a man played '*Oh, Oh, Antonio*' on a barrel organ. Two little girls with hands joined swayed in time to the music. Against the Bridge's parapets British soldiers leant, their caps pushed back at rakish angles, top tunic buttons undone, eyeing the passing women, making flirtatious remarks to those unaccompanied by men. Bid in her virgin blue costume, frilly blouse, beads, bangles and brooches galore, large breasts pushed provocatively forward returned their glances and giggled encouragingly. Dolly nudged her sharply with an elbow. 'Will you stop it. You're making a show of us. Do you want to get your name up – laughing and tricking with soldiers?'

'Shut up you, you're a bloody oul killjoy,' Bid said good-naturedly. 'And anyway, I don't know why you're giving out the pay about soldiers – isn't your own brother one?'

'That's a different thing altogether,' Dolly replied as they crossed into Sackville Street, and thought – honest to God, that wan's awful common.

'Well what d'ye think of that? Not a sign of them and us rushing like a pair of eejits,' Bid said as they neared Noblett's, a sweetshop opposite the Pillar where Jem and Kevin should have been waiting to take them to Howth.

Dolly was raging. 'They'd better hurry up. I'm not hanging around for any fella.'

'All the same, wouldn't it be terrible if they let us down,' Bid said. 'I was really looking forward to it, the sea air and that, and the appetite it gives you, you know.'

'I only know that I'm fit to be tied. I'll die if anyone sees us and guesses we've been left standing.'

149

'Ah, for God's sake don't meet trouble halfway. They're only a few minutes late.'

'I don't care. Listen, commere.' Dolly took hold of Bid's arm. 'Let on we're looking at the Easter eggs.' She moved with Bid up to the window and pretended to be admiring the sugar eggs garlanded with flowers and greetings piped in pink and blue. Using the window for a mirror Dolly adjusted her hat.

Around the foot of the Pillar people waited for trams to take them out of town. British officers hailed side cars and helped flashily-dressed women to mount. Spring flowers spilled over the dealers' baskets and men bought bunches of violets for their girls. Through the shop window Dolly could see all the activity and envied the girls whose day out was assured.

It was almost noon when Robbie reached the Pillar and noticed two unusually attractive girls who seemed to be quarrelling. The dark one was certainly annoyed. What a gorgeous figure she had! He'd take a bet she was a tartar. He came nearer. The fair one was prettier, but it was the other one he fancied. They appeared to have settled their difference and were now turning to look into the shop window. Great! He'd do the same.

'It's lovely weather,' he said, standing behind Dolly. Out of the corner of her eye she had seen him approach. Quickly she turned to look at him, noticing how handsome he was and that he was in uniform.

'I said it's a lovely day.'

'Do you mind! I'm not in the habit of talking to strangers,' she said in a cutting voice. Glancing quickly round and back again. Thinking, my God he's gorgeous. What a face! The two eyes dancing out of his head. But for all that she was having none of his freemaking. Wait'll she saw Jem O'Brien, she'd kill him for putting her in such a predicament. Never in her life had she seen anyone like this fella. He was a picture.

What a pity he wasn't a civvy, someone she met at a dance and would have an excuse to get to know.

'I only said it was a nice day. I thought the Irish were friendly.'

Dolly couldn't think of a smart answer though she was dying to. Bid, who had taken everything in, nudged her and whispered, 'You've got off your mark.'

'Shut up,' Dolly hissed and hoped the soldier didn't hear her. If only, she thought, I could get into talk with him, without seeming forward. She longed for a good look at his face again and to hear him speak. His accent was lovely. Englified. Her mind was frantically searching for an excuse to speak to him when an elderly, low-sized man wearing a flat cap and a muffler pushed past Robbie and stood beside Dolly at the window.

'It's a grand day thank God, a grand day. I wouldn't mind being up the Park, there's a horse running I'd put a bob on if I had it.' He clapped his hands and thanked God again for the weather.

Through the window Dolly saw Robbie shrug, smile and walk away. She could have cried. She could have throttled the old man who was talking across her to Bid, saying that when he was a chiseller he never had no sugar eggs, no indeed he didn't.

A bloody oul toucher that's what he was and not if he was wallfalling would she give him a farthing. And that eejit Bid talking to him, asking him if he had seen two fellas earlier on.

'No, I didn't. But sure how could I? Amn't I only after coming myself this minute. Why, were you meeting them?'

'No,' Dolly said, 'we always stand outside Noblett's on Easter Monday.'

'Don't mind her, mister, we were supposed to be meeting them.'

'Maybe they went for a ramble,' the man suggested, 'the day is early yet.'

'It's twelve by Cleary's clock. I'm not waiting another minute,' Dolly announced.

'Bedad you're right, and there's the Angelus to prove it.' Dolly, Bid and the man hurriedly made the sign of the Cross, then the man still looking towards the clock said, 'Eh, but commere, look at that.' He caught hold of Dolly's arm, his voice full of excitement.

'Look at what?' Dolly asked impatiently.

'That! There! Coming out of Abbey Street. There!' Dolly's eyes followed the direction of his pointing finger and saw the traffic stop and a column of men march across the wide street.

'The Volunteers, so what, aren't they always marching?' Dolly pulled her arm away from the man's grip.

'Ah, but this looks different. I'd say there's going to be trouble. Someone was telling me there was supposed to be trouble yesterday, but MacNeill cancelled it. Did you know that?'

'I didn't and what's more I'm not interested.'

The old man ignored Dolly's remarks, caught hold of her arm and Bid's. 'Come on,' he urged. 'You don't want to miss this, let's have a dekko.'

'We might as well,' said Bid and reluctantly Dolly allowed herself to be led across Henry Street to where they could get a better view of what was happening.

The marching men headed towards the General Post Office. Some passersby stopped to watch, others, assuming that it was just another of the Volunteers' marches, walked on about their business.

'That's James Connolly,' the little man said, pointing to a stocky figure wearing a bush-hat at the head of the procession. 'God bless him, the only man who gives a damn for the working man of Ireland. And that's Pearse, the pale fella. He's all for the Irish, has a school where they only speak it, but he's not a patch on Connolly.'

'Will you look at the get-up of them,' Dolly said gazing at

152

the contingent in their ill-matched uniforms and weapons. 'You'd think grown men would have more sense.' The column halted outside the Post Office. More people were stopping to watch. A command rang out, the column broke ranks and charged into the building. Now crowds came from everywhere. Soon Dolly and Bid were surrounded by people.

'I wonder what they've gone in there for?' a woman in the crowd asked. And a man replied quickly, 'For their allowance, ma'am. What did you think they wanted – stamps?'

'I was just wondering, that's all,' the woman said. 'There was no call for a snotty answer.'

Another man said contemptuously, 'What allowance? Who'd give them an allowance?'

'For all their marching and drilling. You didn't think they were doing it for nothing and half of them up from the country,' the first man said.

'Bedad you're right there. Live in your ear, country fellas would,' a different voice said, then asked earnestly, 'But commere, tell me something, out of whose pocket is this allowance coming? That's what I'd like to know.'

'Eff off, you gobshite,' the first man said good-humouredly.

The crowd was increasing. Dolly was being pushed and jostled and offended by the language. 'I'm not staying here. There'll be millia murder in a minute. Did you hear what that bowsie's after saying?' she asked Bid.

'Ah, you me arse Dolly Devoy. He's only cursing, it won't kill you. I think it's great gas, I'm enjoying myself. Go on home if you want to, but I'm staying,' Bid said.

The crowd was beginning to enjoy itself, too. Comments about the Volunteers, most of them derisory sallied back and forth. Occasionally, someone tried to say something in their defence, but their voices were quickly drowned beneath a storm of ribald abuse. The police stood about making no attempt to interfere and the little old man who had spoken earlier to Dolly and Bid was separated from them.

153

Then suddenly, the doors of the Post Office were flung open and the staff, dishevelled and astonished-looking came running out, calling as they came: 'They've taken over! They're smashing everything! They're taking over the country!' And almost at the same time a shower of glass fell from the upstairs windows. The crowd drew back until the glass had stopped falling then took up their positions again.

'Ye dirty crowd of corner boys! Lettin' on to be soldiers. May God blast the lotta you. It's out in France you should be like my lovely son and his father,' a woman in a black shawl screamed. And a man shouted defiantly: 'Take over the country how are ye? I'd like to see ye try it.'

'For Jasus' sake will you look at that, up there, on the roof!' another voice shouted. Heads tilted back, looked up and saw a pole on which a flag slowly ascended. For a moment it hung listlessly until a gust of wind unfurled and blew it straight. It was a green flag with a harp of gold and in Gaelic lettering across its centre were the words *Irish Republic* – a flag few of them had ever seen before. And while they continued to stare upwards the doors of the Post Office opened and two men came out, James Connolly and Patrick Pearse. Then Pearse read from the document he held, *The Proclamation of the Irish Republic*.

When he finished reading a half-hearted cheer went up and the crowd became interested, expectant – something might happen. But after shaking hands with Pearse, Connolly went back into the building and Pearse followed him. Still the crowd waited, but apart from a few men distributing leaflets and others fixing notices to walls it appeared as if the excitement was over. The crowd broke up and began to drift away.

Dolly, still unable to accept the fact that Jem had let her down, looked in the direction of Noblett's, but her view was blocked by the moving people. 'Maybe,' she said, 'they came late and we missed them.'

'I thought you didn't care,' Bid said, taking her arm and

154

steering her in the direction of the Bridge. 'I bet you it was all Kevin's fault. It's not the first time he's let me down. I don't know, it's been a waste of time all round. First them two not showing up and then that crowd of feckin eejits with their flags and speeches. Nothing to it at all and me thinking it would be great gas. What'll we do now with the rest of the day?'

They were back on the Bridge. The organ grinder was gone and so were the flirting soldiers. 'You can do what you like, I'm going home,' Dolly replied.

'Ah don't do that,' Bid entreated, 'it's early yet.' Then a smile lit up her face, and she said, 'I know, let's go up the Park. You've all the stuff for a picnic.' A breeze blew off the Liffey, she clutched at her hat before it lifted from her soft fair hair, and laughingly added, 'I bet we won't be on our own for long.'

By way of an answer, Dolly let go her arm and upended the velveteen bag over the river's wall, shaking and dislodging its contents. A shower of biscuits and bread fell towards the water where a flock of waiting gulls swooped on their unexpected feast.

'You didn't have to do that!' Bid protested. 'I only meant . . .'

'I know what you only meant,' Dolly interrupted. 'And you've got another think coming. I'm going up no Park looking for soldiers.'

'There was no call for any of that,' Bid remonstrated. 'Taking the head off me and wasting the food. You'll folly a crow forty miles for that bread one day. You're not the only one who was let down.' Dolly said nothing and Bid continued, 'The trouble with you is you're awful stuck up.' And when Dolly still made no answer, Bid went on, 'You think you're somebody because you work in the office, and sing on the Hall, so you do.'

Dolly still said nothing. She was thinking about Jem and

how she'd give him a piece of her mind. She wasn't that late, he could have waited – he always waited. He always came early. And drove her mad when he came to call for her, hanging round like a dog waiting to go for a walk. And now all of a sudden not prepared to wait five minutes. And as for Bid! The cheek of trying to inveigle me up the Park. I should have stopped going out with her this long time. Mad jealous, that's what she is. Jealous of me in the office and she still in the bakehouse roasting the fingers off herself packing oatcakes. Always running up to the nurse for ointment. That's what the dig was about me being stuck up. Mad jealous!

Towards the two girls now walking up Westmoreland Street came a Highlander with a swinging kilt and bouncing sporran. 'I bet his arse is blue with the cold,' Bid said, and Dolly, who at that very moment had made up her mind never to speak to Bid again laughed out loud as the soldier passed them by, causing him to look back at the fair and brown-haired girls bent double laughing, then straightening up, linking arms and walking on.

At the corner of Georges Street a man stopped them. 'You can't go that way,' he said, pointing up Dame Street. 'There's trouble in the Castle.'

'For your information, not that it's any of your business, we're not. We're going up Georges Street if you don't mind,' Dolly said. She had had enough of old men for one day.

'You can't go that way either. They've taken over Jacobs,' the man informed them smugly.

'The blessings of God on them, I hope they keep it,' Bid said.

Crossing the road away from the man, Dolly said, 'We'll go down here.' They turned into a narrow street, then into another and eventually came to Winetavern Street Bridge, climbed the hill and outside Christ's Church stood to say goodbye.

'I'll see you in the morning,' Dolly said.

'Not if what that oul shite said is right about Jacobs, you won't.'

'Well then, I'll see you through the week.' Dolly said goodbye and started walking home. Thinking as she went, about the turn the day had taken. Who'd have thought it when I got up. Him not showing up and then them lot in the Post Office! The man in the crowd was right 'Take over the country how, are ye?' Not that she had any time for British soldiers. Dirty freemaking lot by all accounts. But you had to hand it to them – they were real soldiers. Not a crowd of eejits in makey-up uniforms and guns and things since Adam was in the Highlanders. The same Volunteers were nothing but a crowd of yahoos with nothing better to do than destroy someone's day out. She dismissed them from her mind and thought instead of Jem, wondering again why he hadn't come? Never in the two years she'd been going out with him had he ever been a minute late, never mind not showing up at all. Well he'd better have a good excuse. The day was ruined. She'd be stuck for the rest of it with her mother, and Maggie no doubt would drop up. The two of them giving out yards, hinting it was her fault Jem hadn't come. They were mad about Jem, couldn't wait to see her and him settled. It was, Jem this and Jem that. A decent little fella. Never see the sign of drink on him. You could do worse. Going on about him all the time. It was enough to put you off of him.

Dolly was now nearing the little park by St Patrick's Cathedral. She saw a crowd of women and children gathered at the railings. There must be a wedding, she thought. She wasn't in the humour to watch a wedding and began pushing through the crowd. A woman she knew said, 'There y'are Dolly. How's your mother?'

'Grand thanks.'

'Are you not waiting to see the bride? She's gorgeous. They'll be out in a minute, there's the music starting up.'

Dolly decided she might as well wait and see. A group of

157

young officers formed two lines on either side of the church door. Their scarlet uniforms bright against the grey stone walls. The soldiers raised their swords to form an arch, then the bride and groom appeared. 'God, she *is* gorgeous,' Dolly exclaimed, her eyes taking in every detail of Alice's face and figure, her gown, wreath and veil. 'Who is she?'

'That's oul Delahunt's daughter. She's a picture, God bless her,' the woman said.

'Yes,' Dolly said and thought, she must be the girl me and Bid saw that night years ago, unless Delahunt has more than one daughter. 'I'll tell my mother you were asking for her,' she said and bade the old woman goodbye. On the way home she imagined how marvellous it would be to have a wedding like that. To have that dress and the arch of swords and music and that handsome fair fella for a husband. Though come to think of it, she didn't fancy him. She wasn't mad about fellas with fair hair. And in any case, she could never have that sort of a wedding, only Protestant gentry got married like that. But there'd be nothing to stop anyone having the same sort of a dress.

All the same, it was well for the bride and groom with all the excitement of the wedding and a party before them. Not like her day that was ruined. It was the outing she'd miss more than Jem. Lately he was getting in on her nerves more than ever. Always trying to dog maul her. She wouldn't mind only he was the most awkward man God had ever created. He couldn't give you a kiss without his nose getting in the way. Not that he had a big nose, it was only that he didn't know how to arrange his face when he kissed you.

Now that fella, that soldier, she bet he'd be a great kisser. He was the spit of the fella she was always imagining meeting. It was just her luck to meet him in the street and him to be a soldier. Only the draggins-up went out with English soldiers, that's what everyone said. He was beautiful. She wouldn't forget his face in a hurry.

158

She arrived at the house and entered the hall. The smell of boiling cabbage, pig's cheeks and corned beef assailed her nostrils and she thought with longing of the Hill of Howth and the gorse and broom.

Robbie saw the men march out of Abbey Street and charge the GPO. What was their game, he wondered? Who were they, in such a ragbag of uniforms? Students from the University, perhaps? A Bank Holiday prank. He walked on a bit then heard the commotion, looked back and saw the crowds gather outside the Post Office. Whatever it was it wasn't a joke. His soldier's training took over. He must get out of here and quick. A tram was lumbering by so he ran and jumped onto the running board. Once on, he realized he didn't know where the tram was going. He asked a woman sitting next to him. 'Rathmines,' she said. That would do. It wasn't far from Ranalagh. The conductor came down the stairs. 'Fares please.' He stood in front of Robbie. Robbie paid him and while the ticket was coming out of the machine, the conductor said, 'For all you know, this could be the last tram out of the city today. Them gougers are after starting trouble.'

'Who are they?' Robbie asked.

'The Volunteers. Feckin lotta gobshites. If I were you, son, I'd get back to barracks quick.'

His relations were aghast at the news. 'Glory be to God – are they mad or what?' one of the cousins said. 'Destroying the Post Office, did you ever hear anything like it?'

'It might be nothing. It could all blow over. Don't let it spoil our holiday anyway,' his mother said.

'And it might not. There's no knowing what it could lead to. I am going back tonight.'

There were gasps and pleas not to. 'What difference does it make to us?' his mother asked.

'I don't know, but it could. The boats and trains could be delayed, anything could happen, I can't take a chance.'

159

'Ah Robbie, that's not fair rushing Fanny away. Sure we've hardly seen her.'

'You don't have to come, Mother.'

'I'm sure it'll be all right,' the cousin who was doing all the talking said. 'If there was any hold-up sure, couldn't you explain what happened? They'd understand.'

'There's no excuses for arriving back late from leave. If you're late, you're Absent Without Leave. You can be shot for that.'

'Don't make jokes about such things Robbie,' his mother said.

'I'm not joking. Will you stay or what?'

'I'll come with you.'

Robbie swore under his breath. Why the hell did the Volunteers, as the conductor called them, have to start their performance today? He'd have enjoyed another few days in Dublin's fair city. He might even have bumped into that girl again. She was really something. He smiled ruefully as he pictured Dolly tossing her head, putting him in his place. Yes, he'd have liked to meet her again.

Chapter Eight

'Nobody makes a fry like you Ma,' Jem said, sitting down to his breakfast of rashers, sausages, black and white pudding and two eggs. He broke the white film on the egg yolk and dipped in a piece of fried bread. 'It's gorgeous,' he said with his mouth full, then asked, 'Have you seen that oul kettle anywhere, the one with the pot mended? I said I'd bring it for the tea.'

'I'm nearly sure I threw that out, but I'll have a look.' His mother couldn't find the kettle. Jem knew Dolly would be raging. They'd have to have minerals instead of tea. He could picture the annoyance on her face when he told her. Her expression changed from minute to minute according to her humour. You never knew when you had her, she was like quicksilver.

He smiled thinking of her humours and how he loved her despite them and wanted to marry her. There was nothing to stop him – he was earning a man's wages. But every time he brought up the talk of marrying she changed the subject. It wasn't easy loving someone as much as he loved her and having to be respectful at the same time. But you couldn't explain something like that to a girl. Anyway, sure you wouldn't know how to put that sort of thing into words.

He finished his breakfast and thought how if Dolly was his wife he wouldn't let the wind blow on her. He'd take her humours and all, never ask her to change, never try to break her spirit and every day of his life thank God for giving her to him.

'You'd better go if you're going,' his mother said. 'By the time you call for Kevin you'll be cutting it fine – you know what he's like for delaying you.'

Jem agreed she was right and that he had better get a move on. He left the house and walked down the street whistling. It was a beautiful day, he thought again and he felt glad to be alive. He nodded to shabby men leaning against corners and public house windows, their backs reflected in the plate glass decorated with gilt scrolls advertising whiskey. Now and then he had to step off the kerb so as not to impede the game being played by girls with black and brown, red and fair ringlets that bobbed in time to their singing of '*In and out go the dusty bluebells*', and he kicked back to their barefooted brothers the bundle of paper roughly shaped to resemble a football, its roundness secured with twine.

He walked on, heading towards the quays. Halfway there he saw an old woman on the other side of the street carrying a milk can and apparently talking to herself. He vaguely knew her and called, 'Hello.' She crossed over to him. 'Son,' she said, 'mind yourself if you're going that way.' She nodded towards the way she had come. 'They've all gone mad. They're pulling up the path, smashing bottles and everything.'

'Is that so?'

'Amn't I telling you there's ructions going on. Look at me head.' She pushed her face close and pulled back her black shawl. 'There, look, in the middle of me forehead. I was nearly split. And me minding me own business. Going down to me daughter's for a sup of milk and a stone met me between the eyes. Down there in Church Street. There's murder going on. Fellas in uniform plundering the homes of decent people. Black strangers every one of them.'

'That's terrible,' Jem said. He could see she had a bump

162

right enough. But she could have got that anywhere. Probably stocious the night before and fell over.

'Thanks for telling me, anyway. I'll have to go now. I'm in a hurry.' He left her and walked quickly to where Kevin lived. He took three flights of stairs two at a time. To his relief Kevin appeared to be ready and was sitting at the table with his brother Danny and Danny's wife, Josie.

'It's a rare oul day,' Danny said.

'Grand,' Jem agreed and then spoke to Josie, 'I bet you're glad of the holiday.'

'Delighted,' Josie replied and smiled shyly at him.

'You'll have a cup of tea?' Kevin's mother asked.

'I won't, thanks all the same, I'm only after standing from the table.'

'Just a sup in your hand, go on,' Mrs McEvoy pressed.

And not to offend the woman Jem accepted. Sipping the scalding mahogany-coloured tea, Jem motioned to Kevin that it was time to go. Kevin ignored him.

On the mantelpiece amongst a pile of broken candles, a skewer packed tightly with pawn tickets and a statue of the Virgin, her head imperfectly repaired so that she appeared to be looking at herself in the flyblown overmantel, stood a clock. Jem saw the hands move past twenty to twelve and knew that he would be late for his appointment with Dolly. With that on top of not bringing the kettle she would be lepping.

Kevin, as if aware of the thoughts passing through Jem's mind and deliberately wanting to delay him further, poured himself another cup of tea, tipped some of it into his saucer and slowly and noisily supped it.

'For God's sake will you hurry up, we're late as it is,' Jem said, putting down his cup of unfinished tea. 'Are you trying to ruin the day out or what?'

Kevin paused in his supping to reply, 'You're a right bloody eejit when it comes to mots, do you know that O'Brien? Let

163

them wait. Their tongues will be hanging out for us.' He winked knowingly at Jem and returned to his supping.

'Right then, I'm going without you. Thanks very much for the tea Mrs McEvoy,' Jem said and moved towards the door.

'All right, hold on, I'm coming.' Kevin got up and followed Jem out. In the street Jem related what the old woman had said about a disturbance in Church Street.

'More fool you for listening – she was probably full of red biddy,' Kevin said, then asked, 'How would you like to be like that, eh?'

'Like what?' Jem inquired, not understanding the question.

'Him back there – the brother, only just gone seventeen with a wife and a child on the way.'

'I wouldn't I don't suppose, it's terrible young. But sure what else could he do?'

'Listened to me, that's what. I told him to mind himself. I knew that wan would corner him. The shagging thick and look at him now.'

'Maybe it'll work out. Josie's all right. She's nice. There's something about her reminds me of Dolly. When's the child expected?'

'Josie like Dolly! It must be up the back. Them two's as different as chalk and cheese. Next month so I believe.'

They were nearing the corner of Church Street. 'Listen to that,' Jem said as the sounds of a commotion reached them. 'Maybe that oul wan was right.' And when they turned the corner they saw that she had been.

The street was full of people shouting and swearing and attempting to hinder a group of men dressed in green uniforms from erecting a barricade across the thoroughfare. Paving stones, planks of wood, battered perambulators and all descriptions of things were being heaved onto the mound while other uniformed men ransacked the surrounding houses for pieces of furniture to swell the growing pile.

One large woman danced like a dervish as she followed two

men manoeuvring a brass bedstead towards the barricade, screaming at them: 'You robbin' lotta country boss-arsed bastards! The curse of Hell on you for destroying me home. That's me bed. The bed I lay on the night I was married. The bed I was confined on and me lovely husband, the Light of Heaven to him, waked on. If he was alive he'd kick the shite outta you. Gimme back me bed!'

Her pleas and curses were ignored by the Volunteers and turning to her neighbours she asked of them, 'Isn't there a man amongst youse? Isn't there one of youse with a bit of spunk?' And, when no one answered nor came to her assistance, she screamed at them, 'You're nothing but a lotta oul Mary Ann bitches!'

'Move outta the way, Missus. We want no disturbances, you'll be compensated for your property,' a green-clad man told her.

She appealed to the crowd again. 'Did you hear that, did you? I'll be compensated! When the pig shites leather! You bloody robber! All I want is me bed and I'll die in the attempt to get it.'

With one powerful freckled arm she tugged at the bedstead and pushed the other through the rungs, catching hold of one of the men and pulling him close to the rails so that his face was pressed into the bars like an animal looking through a cage. A cheer went up from the crowd and they called encouragement. 'More power to you Mary! Go on, give it to him.'

Kevin stopped to watch. 'Jasus!' he said. 'I wouldn't like to tangle with her. Look at the arms on her.'

'Ah come on, we're late already,' Jem urged, attempting to steer him away.

The crowd, now emboldened by Mary's encounter with the Volunteers began to ransack the barricade and retrieve their possessions. They screamed and laughed, the men in green shouted orders and no one heard the sound of the horses' hooves except one woman whose cry of warning that the soldiers were coming was ignored.

Into the street rode a troop of Lancers with harness jingling and the sun glancing off lance and helmets. Proud and straight they sat, safe and secure they seemed, all the tradition of Army and Empire evident in their bearing, viewing disdainfully the men like threatened ants scurrying to finish their defences.

Above them the Lancers towered like Almighty Beings.

Time seemed suspended, bits and buckles stilled, voices silenced as each side surprisedly surveyed the other.

Then a man in green lost his nerve, raised his rifle and fired. Horses reared, screams filled the silence, commands rang out, gouts of blood gushed from the magnificent creatures that moments earlier had pranced into the street. The brass bedstead lay forgotten in the road.

Jem ran with Kevin and found shelter in an open door, from where, transfixed, he watched a Lancer fall from his horse, saw him roll into the gutter, saw the helmet which had reflected the sun, daubed with blood and a glutinous greyish substance. Looked in disbelief at the soldier's feebly picking fingers, then saw the hands stilled and the light go out of the man's eyes. 'Oh my God, he's dead! They killed him! Sacred Heart of Jesus have mercy on him. He's dead! Jesus have mercy on his soul.' Jem blessed himself.

'So will you be if you don't give over praying and get outta here,' Kevin said, pulling Jem by the arm. 'Folly me or we're done for. Come on will you, for Christ's sake,' he urged. Jem allowed himself to be led away and followed Kevin through backyards, over walls and through narrow lanes to Kevin's mother's rooms, where once they were safely installed Kevin announced: 'Well, that's our day out finished. You'll have the military down here in droves and anyone on the street will be fair game. Them Lancers were going back to barracks, bothering no one. What were them fuckers doing with their effin' barricades? Did you see them – they fired the first shot?'

166

Jem nodded his agreement, but said nothing for his mind was preoccupied with the dead soldier. Up there on his horse one minute and the next, dead in the gutter with his blood running down the shore. He closed his eyes and tried to think of something else. But the image persisted. He kept seeing the man in the shining helmet on the brown gleaming horse. Like a picture out of a story book, new and shining and perfect. And the next, crumpled on the ground. A young fella like himself – like Danny sitting across the table from him with the same sort of fair hair, he shuddered remembering how the Lancer's hair had looked.

There was a great commotion in the house as neighbours ran from one room to the next with the latest news of what had happened. A man who had been in Sackville Street brought word that the GPO had been commandeered by the Volunteers. Jem's heart constricted with fear. Dolly would have been in the thick of it. 'I'll have to go,' he said, rising from his chair, pushing away the whiskey which Kevin's mother had given him for the shock.

'You'll do no such a bloody thing,' Kevin said, barring the door. 'Do you want to get yourself arrested and maybe bring the military on top of us?'

'But I have to find out about Dolly. I have to know if she's all right,' Jem protested.

'Ah, she'll be all right. You wouldn't want to mind what that oul fella said about the Post Office, sure he's a terrible liar,' Mrs McEvoy assured him.

'Still and all I'd better go,' Jem insisted. 'Move away from the door, Kevin.'

Kevin continued to stand with his back to the door, his arms folded across his chest. 'You're not putting a foot over the threshold. My mother's right. That's a shaggin' oul liar. And if you put your hand on me again I'll lay you out.'

'Don't rise him Jem,' Mrs McEvoy entreated. 'We don't

want any trouble. I don't want Josie upset and she not far from her time. Sure you can go when it gets dark.'

Jem apologized and agreed he would stay. Kevin moved away from the door, put an arm round his shoulders and said, 'A bloody eejit, that's what you are O'Brien.'

'God bless us you gave me an awful fright,' Bridget said when the door opened and Dolly came into the room. 'I wasn't expecting you back for ages.' And as she saw the petulant expression on her daughter's face thought, that wan's in bad humour, something's happened to annoy her.

'Can you not open the window or bank down the fire, it's boiling in here,' Dolly said irritably. She removed her costume jacket and placed it on the back of a chair well away from the table where the remains of a meal lay.

Her mother, used to her fault-finding, ignored her requests and asked, 'What brought you back so soon? I thought you were going to Howth.'

'So did I, but the other fella didn't turn up, did he,' Dolly retorted.

'That's most peculiar,' her mother said, taking from the press a dish of corned beef. Dolly looked disdainfully at the dark pink meat with its selvage of yellow fat and exclaimed: 'Corned beef and cabbage, not that again!'

'Well, it's that or a bit of me arse with an onion,' her mother replied and began to cut the meat.

'I don't want it. I'll have a boiled egg. My stomach's in a knot after him not coming and then that mêlée in town. Where's me da?'

'Lying down with his belly full of porter.' Her mother nodded towards the other room. She stopped slicing the meat and began to clear the table, then asked, 'What mêlée was that then?'

Before Dolly could explain, from the other room came the sound of coughing.

168

'There now, you've woken him and me hoping for an hour's peace,' her mother complained.

'You're back early, alanna,' Dolly's father said as he came out of the bedroom in his stockinged feet, his braces hanging, his dry papery skin flushed from sleep and porter. He smoothed with a hand his tossed scant white hair and sat down.

'Is there a sup of tea going? I've a terrible thirst on me.'

'In a minute,' Bridget replied. 'I'm listening to Dolly. Go on with what you were saying about the mêlée in town.'

Dolly related what had happened outside the Post Office. Her father plied her with questions. Could she describe who was leading the Volunteers? How many were there? What did the public do? Was anyone hurt? Were there soldiers?

'That fella James Connolly. I don't know how many there was – I wasn't counting, was I?'

'The poor fools, the poor misguided fools – they'll be slaughtered,' Dolly's father said, getting up from his chair. 'But thank God anyway you weren't hurt, alanna.' He touched her hair as he passed by on his way back to the bedroom.

Bridget wet the tea her husband had asked for. She put the pot on the hob to draw and said to Dolly, 'He'll be like a hen on a hot griddle wanting to know the ins and outs of what happened. I wish . . .' But whatever it was she wished Dolly never knew, for before her mother could finish the sentence Johnny returned with his boots on, his braces adjusted and carrying his coat. Speechless for the moment Bridget watched him sit down and lace his boots, put on his jacket and head for the door. As his hand reached the latch she asked, 'And where are you going? The tea is made and the pubs shut.'

'Across town for a ramble and to see how the land lies.'

'A ramble across town! Are you out of your mind? Didn't you hear what Dolly said. There may be murder for all you know.' Her voice was mocking, angry, then the tone changed

169

and on a soft, pleading note she said, 'Ah don't go Johnny, it might be dangerous.'

Johnny looked back at his wife, surprise in his deep-set pale blue eyes at the concern in her voice. At how she had called his name like that. It was a long time since she had sounded it so. For an instant he saw a young girl with a laughing face and hair that tumbled round her bare shoulders. He looked again and the vision vanished and a voice he was more familiar with said, 'Ah well, please yourself.' He buttoned his coat and went.

And when he was gone Bridget continued talking while she ladled water from a pail into a small iron pot, put an egg in it and placed the saucepan on the fire.

'I might as well be talking to myself for all the attention he pays to anything I say. Anyway, I'm glad the oul anti-Christ's gone out. Since he's idle he has me demented, under me feet all the time.' She poked the coals near the pot.

'You can take that off – I don't want it,' Dolly said irritably, her face full of annoyance. She pulled her chair up to the fire.

Her mother knew she was still in bad humour, ready to fight with her nails. Well, she wasn't going to rise to her in order to vent her spleen. So without commenting on her change of mind Bridget took off the pot and began preparations for making apple cakes. Her neat figured body moving briskly about, collecting utensils and ingredients. 'You'll have to shift while I pull out the damper.' Dolly pushed back her chair and her mother asked: 'Are you going out this evening?'

'Where would I be going? Didn't I tell you what happened, that Jem O'Brien never showed up,' Dolly replied shortly as she moved back to the fire.

'That's right, so you did,' Bridget said and thought, you can be as impertinent as you like, I'm not rising to you. Though God knows you'd try the patience of a saint. Sitting there with a face like a fiddle. Raging with yourself and everyone else because you were let down. Not a word of concern in case anything happened to Jem. For all you know he could have been run over or killed, God forbidding all harm.

She began rubbing fat into the flour, her thoughts still with Dolly. She thinks of no one but herself. The sooner she settles down the better. Maybe Maggie's right, that I ruined her in her rearing. She smiled to herself, recalling Maggie's suggested remedy. 'What that wan wants is a kick in the arse and a houseful of children. Give her something to think about besides what she's going to wear to the next hooley. And she'd better grab Jem O'Brien while the going's good for there's no one else would put up with her.'

Poor vain Dolly, her mother pondered, rolling out the pastry. Poor Dolly with all your big ideas and unfortunate manner, I wonder what'll become of you. She felt sorry for her and guilty for maybe having spoiled her, let her have too much of her own way. 'You must be wallfalling with hunger. The minute I've done this I'll make you a nice pick.' Dolly didn't reply. Bridget put the dough on the baking plate, hummed a snatch of a tune for a minute then noticing that Dolly looked less bad-humoured said, 'All the same – wasn't it a pity you didn't meet Jem. He could've come for his tea. Wouldn't that have been grand with Maggie, Tom and the child here.'

'If I'd met him I wouldn't be here for me tea, would I?' Dolly retorted. And her mother's resolve not to rise evaporated. Wiping her floury hands on her apron she went and stood in front of her daughter.

'You impertinent little bitch, that's what you are! Since you came in you've been answering me like a dog. I'm not a bit sorry Jem left you standing and if you don't change your tune I wouldn't blame him if he threw you over.'

'Oh, is that so? Well, let me tell you I could have him tomorrow. I'd only have to snap my fingers and he'd marry me. But I don't want him. No matter what you, Maggie or anyone else thinks of him.'

171

'Don't you dare raise your voice to me. I'm warning you you're not too big yet for a slap across the face. Coming in here with tall orders as to what you'll eat and what you won't. You may be twenty years of age but you're not keeping the teeth in my head.'

Dolly began to laugh.

'What are you laughing at?' Bridget demanded to know.

'You,' Dolly replied. 'I'd have a hard job doing that. I never remember you with a tooth in your mouth.' She lowered her voice, her tone now conciliatory, her bad humour gone. 'I'd never marry him. His oul wan's a fish dealer. She'd have me out with a basket car shouting "fresh herrings" before you could say Jack Robinson. She's awful common.'

But Bridget was not to be placated so easily. 'A rossy, that's what you are. Passing remarks about your mother. And it's not Mrs O'Brien, a decent hard-working woman, one of the biggest forestallers in the market with pounds for our pennies, that's standing in your way. When did you ever let anyone do that? No, what ails you is your big ideas. It's a man made to measure you're looking for. Well, I hope it keeps fine for you!'

Dolly made no reply to her mother's accusation, but thought, little do you know how often I dream of meeting someone like that. So often that I know exactly what he looks like. How his voice sounds and what he'll say when I meet him. You're nearer the mark than you know – that's what I want – a man made to measure.

Sometimes, at the last minute, just before she fell asleep she saw him clearly and heard him speak. On fine mornings when she cut through the Park by the Cathedral on her way to work, when the sky was high and blue, with birds singing, she imagined meeting him. Occasionally, she glimpsed him in a passing tram or saw him ahead of her in a crowd. She knew him well.

He was tall, but not too tall, not lanky, well-made and not

172

footy. He had dark hair and eyes. Jem's eyes were dark but not like his. Jem's were gentle-looking, sad, with always the same expression. His weren't like that. His expression kept changing, one minute dancing with devilment, the next flashing with anger or filled with laughter. But they could be gentle, too, and look into hers with such love that her heart melted inside her. Come to think of it, not unlike that soldier.

His teeth were white and even with no spaces and his mouth lovely with soft full lips. But not girlish. On every one of his nails you could see half moons and he'd never bite them nor have torn quicks.

He lived in Rathmines or Rathgar, one of them places with a good address and a flight of granite steps up to the hall door with a brass lion's head for a knocker and a black footscraper on the top step. And he would never wear a muffler, not even to work. They would know each other as soon as they met. Love each other and live happily together forever.

While Dolly continued daydreaming Bridget sliced apples, arranged them on the plate, dotted them with cloves, sprinkled them with sugar, covered them with pastry and closed the tart. Now and then from far away the sound of rifle fire cracked, causing her to stop what she was doing and make a hasty sign of the Cross with floury fingers which left a white imprint on her forehead, and say 'God between us and all harm' – the way she did during a thunder storm, only now she added, 'And that oul lunatic of mine out in it.'

Dolly imagined her mother's response if she was to announce the thoughts going through her mind. She'd bless herself again or ask if Dolly was costive. And if she ever told Maggie! Maggie wasn't as polite as her mother. 'Is it your shite you've got?' she'd ask. And Bid? Well, *she* would laugh until she wet her knickers then lose no time telling everyone in the bakehouse that Dolly Devoy was suffering from delusions and didn't think Jem O'Brien was good enough for her. So she would tell no one and dream her dreams. They

173

were harmless. Only like letting on to someone she didn't know that she lived on the South Circular Road. She still went home to ninety-seven the same as she would still marry Jem one day.

She'd have a white silk dress like the one the girl wore coming out of St Patrick's. A dress that swished and rustled when she moved. And a wreath and veil, a wreath of tiny flowers like blossom on a privet hedge. On the day she got married the neighbours would stand to look after her and say to each other, 'Isn't she a picture?'

'Whisht,' Bridget said.

'I haven't opened my mouth,' said Dolly recalled from her dreams.

'That's them. I can hear them. I can hear the child.' Bridget smiled expectantly and Maggie's son Christie toddled into the room followed by his mother and father. The boy ran to Bridget who caught and hooshed him up in the air.

'A grand day Mrs Devoy. Did you hear about what's happened downtown?' Tom said.

'What are you doing in, I thought you were out in Howth? Where's me da?' demanded Maggie.

'He didn't turn up.'

'Gone down the town to see for himself, the bloody oul fool.'

They all spoke at once, asking questions, not waiting for replies before asking another. Eventually they calmed down and Dolly related again what she had seen in Sackville Street and how Jem hadn't turned up.

'That's very strange, not like him at all and as for that lot – taking over the Post Office – nothing but a crowd of feckin eejits.'

St Stephen's Green was commandeered without any opposition except an inquiry from the keeper as to what would happen to the ducks. They had to be fed twice a day. It was

174

agreed by the insurgents that feeding of the ducks would not be interfered with. Jacobs and the Mendicity were acquired with equal ease. The South Dublin Union was occupied and so was Boland's Mill. In the bakery a protest was made by a worker: 'There's thousands of loaves in them ovens – if you turf us out they'll be destroyed. I wouldn't give much for your chance of popularity if there isn't a bit of bread to be had in the city.' A handful of men were allowed to remain until the bread was baked.

It was done, the Post Office taken, the Republic proclaimed. Feverish with excitement and pride the men moved about protecting windows, using sacks of coal and dummies taken from a nearby waxworks when there was nothing else left. The women organized food and medical supplies. Lookouts were posted and snipers took up their positions; dispatches were sent off to the other outposts. Everything was ready; everyone was waiting for the Military. Fingers itched on triggers. In the street only a riotous crowd was in evidence.

Men, women and children screamed and laughed, jostled each other in their attempts to break the first window. Soon plate glass lay in showers and shards, the shops' window displays ready to hand, entry to the stores available. Women came out with furs draped over their black shawls, feathered, ribboned and flowered hats on their heads. Bottles of whiskey and boxes of sweets, tins of biscuits and flimsy lingerie were tossed around, dropped and left lying, for more of everything was readily available. Women decked in furs and ropes of pearls drank from whiskey bottles, shrieked with glee, drank again and lifting their torn and dirty skirts danced jigs.

'Fire over their heads, scatter them,' James Connolly ordered. The looters scattered until they realized the shots weren't aimed at them and then returned with gusto to continue availing themselves of things they had never imagined possessing.

175

'There's a troop of Lancers approaching from Parnell Street,' a lookout reported.

'Don't fire, not until they are abreast of the Post Office,' came the order.

This was it. This was what they had been waiting for – a chance to show the British Army how Irishmen could defend themselves. Fingers that had itched to fire in earnest couldn't wait for the Lancers to arrive outside the building. Shots rang out. Lancers and horses fell. 'There's four of them down, and horses too.'

'If you'd waited we'd have got more of them.'

'All the same we got some of them.'

The dead Lancers and their horses sprawled, where earlier in the morning the spring flowers had spilled from the dealers' baskets.

More customers than Bessie and Liam had bargained for crowded the eating house. People going to or returning from the Park, hearing the firing from Church Street and rumour of what was taking place downtown, came in. Some purchased food, others stood about looking bewildered. No one was exactly sure what was happening. More tea and minerals were sold than hot meals and Bessie thought despairingly that with the weather being so warm the meats would spoil. And the high hopes she had held early in the morning deserted her.

The apple cakes were cooling, the room filled with the delicious smell of cloves and cooked fruit. Christie had to be restrained from fingering the tarts. Maggie laid the table while Bridget wet the tea and bade her family 'sit over'. Halfway through the meal of cold meat, scallions and celery she turned to look at a photograph of Richard on the mantelpiece. 'God help him,' she said. 'I wonder where he is today and what he's doing? Wouldn't he have enjoyed the bit of corned beef.'

Everyone looked towards the picture and Maggie said,

'Please God he'll be all right, Mother. You might hear tomorrow. Letters from France sometimes take a long time arriving.'

'I might,' Bridget replied. 'And sure if I don't what can I do except keep praying for him night and morning? I often wonder what keeps people going who don't believe in prayer. Who do they turn to? Them and their wars, may God blast the lotta them and your father for encouraging my lovely son to go to England in the first place.'

'How was he to know there was going to be a war?' Dolly said.

Maggie in an attempt to change the conversation brought the talk back to Jem not having turned up, saying it was most peculiar.

'Not half as peculiar as what I'll do to him when he does,' Dolly said, spearing a piece of the earlier despised meat and eating it with relish. Tom, unaware that Maggie was trying to distract Bridget from thoughts of violence and war, spoke, 'You know, it's not only the Post Office the Volunteers have taken over, they're everywhere. It could be bad. And someone was telling me there was shooting round Church Street way. That's not a stone's throw away from Jem's.'

'Sacred Heart of Jesus I hope nothing happened to him! He could have been shot while I was making the apple cakes and listening to them doing it.'

'For God's sake Mother, stop it, will you! It's not like you to have someone dead and buried before you've seen them laid out. And anyway,' Dolly said, 'how could anything happen to him? He'd run a mile at the first sign of trouble.'

And while Bridget thought how easily Dolly put her mind at rest about Jem's safety, and everyone else was suddenly quiet the door opened and Johnny stood framed in its jamb.

'Jesus, Mary and Joseph!' Bridget exclaimed, staring in dismay as he staggered into the room and collapsed onto a chair. His right eye was red and puffy and the front of his

177

jacket soaking wet. 'What happened to you?' Bridget asked again.

'Savages! Animals! My own countrymen acting like savages. Trampling each other into the ground. Robbing anything they could lay their hands on. Up to their elbows in broken glass, pulling and hauling out of the shop windows.' Johnny sighed wearily, laid back in the chair and closed his eyes, wincing as his swollen lid descended.

'And I suppose you tried to interfere and got a puck in the eye for your trouble,' Bridget said unsympathetically as she brought a bowl of water and a face cloth. 'I warned you. You only got what you deserved. Here, let me bathe that or you'll have a black eye down to your navel. Interfering in what doesn't concern you.'

'I did no such thing. I was minding my own business. Watching everything – for it'll be a day to remember.'

'It's one you won't forget in a hurry, nor me neither. You've destroyed your suit. I'll be cut on that tomorrow,' Bridget retorted.

'How did you hurt your eye, tell us Da?' Dolly said.

'I was met in the face with a pig's cheek,' Johnny solemnly declared.

Maggie laughed. Her father ignored the laughter and continued slowly, 'I was standing outside a pork shop when along comes these two young fellas. One puts in the window with a bang of a stick, leaps in like a rabbit and starts throwing out the stuff. I couldn't believe my eyes! There were legs of pickled pork, rings of black pudding, bowls of dripping, all sorts, falling like snow. I was that startled I couldn't move and before I had time to shift a dreeping wet pig's cheek straight out of the brine barrel hit me in the face!'

'Oh Da!' Maggie laughed louder. 'You! A pig's cheek! And you not able to stomach one, not even with a nice bit of cabbage.' Everyone except Tom joined in the laughter, even the child who banged his spoon on the table with enjoyment.

178

Johnny's face grew red with shame and indignation. He bent his head further over the basin and continued bathing his eye, water from the face cloth dribbled down his chin onto his already wet coat. Tom brought a towel, removed the bowl and began patting dry his father-in-law's face. 'Tell me now,' he asked, 'what were the lads doing below in the Post Office? Was there much going on?'

Mollified by the attention and inquiry Johnny replied, 'Nothing much, Tom. A bit of singing, a few shots not aimed anywhere in particular. Plenty of trams upended, the work of gougers – there were plenty of them to be seen. And up by the Pillar poor dead horses. And then there were a few priests, God bless them, appealing to them that were robbing all before them. But sure they might as well have talked to the wall. And that was about it.'

Maggie, who while her father was talking to Tom had controlled her laughter, now imagined his predicament outside the pork shop, her upright honest father appalled by what he saw. His conscience struggling with his reticence to speak with strangers. And before he could make up his mind what to do, suddenly hit in the face with a flabby, wet, grinning, blind-eyed cheek. Laughter bubbled up in her again and exploded. Dolly and Bridget joined in.

Johnny looked disdainfully at his wife and daughters and rising from the chair said, 'Only fools laugh at nothing. But you'll laugh the other side of your face before this disturbance blows over.' Then, mustering what dignity he could, he left the room.

Photographs of the bride and groom had been taken as they left the Cathedral. Then there were pictures of the couple outside the Delahunts' house, alone and with their respective families, photographs with the entire wedding party. Now at the suggestion of Lady Delahunt, Alice and Stephen were posed in front of an arbour wreathed with wisteria in full

179

bloom. The guests were gathered to watch in groups beneath the trees, edging the beds ablaze with scarlet tulips, amber and yellow wallflowers, neat clumps of pale primulas.

Lady Delahunt stood near the photographer, issuing instructions: telling Alice to adjust her veil, to look up at Stephen, to stand still and to *smile* for Heaven's sake. Alice's face ached with the effort of smiling to order. Her eyes felt dry and heavy, forcing her to blink often, delaying the photographer. Her arm was linked through Stephen's. She longed for him to squeeze it reassuringly, to convey to her that soon it would all be over. That soon they would leave the feasting and speeches and toasts and be alone. That soon all her doubts and fears would be allayed. But Stephen stood as though on parade, stiff and staring straight ahead, not a muscle moving until a command from Lady Delahunt made his eyes regard Alice. At last the pose was right – the photographer ready. Then a young officer came running from the house, stood close to Sir Arthur and whispered something. 'Good God!' Sir Arthur exclaimed, so loudly that a number of the guests had their attention attracted. Lady Delahunt hurried to his side, and Alice and Stephen stopped posing and joined her. 'What is it, what's the matter?' Lady Delahunt demanded.

'Listen everyone,' Sir Arthur called, loudly enough to bring guests who had strayed from the group watching the photographs being taken, back to stand around him. 'Smithers here has just taken a call from a chap in the *Mail & Telegraph* office. For the benefit of those not familiar with Dublin, the newspaper office overlooks the Castle. The Sinn Feiners are attacking it. And they've taken over the GPO.'

The crowd gasped. The GPO was one thing. But the Castle! Their bastion for seven hundred years! 'It isn't possible!' 'It's unthinkable!' Angry, worried, alarmed voices began to talk. Sir Arthur raised a hand and commanded silence.

'Let's keep calm. Let's keep our heads. I suggest that Stephen and his fellow officers telephone one of the barracks and find out exactly what is going on and whether or not they should report back. And in the meantime nothing's to be gained by spoiling Alice's wedding. So back you go young lady, you and Stephen quickly, have the photograph taken, then make the call and then let's eat.' Before Stephen went to make his call Sir Arthur spoke to him out of the guests' hearing.

'At the moment the Castle's lines are cut and a group of rebels are in there. Other key positions are under siege. We don't want to alarm civilians more than necessary, so keep up a pretence that everything's in hand. But one thing . . .'

'Yes, sir?' Stephen said.

'You and Alice had better stay here tonight. It wouldn't be wise to make the journey to the west, don't you agree?'

During the meal everyone talked about what had happened. The audacity of the Sinn Feiners. The treachery of them. The dreadful inconvenience for guests from the country who had planned to return home and now might be delayed. What a shame it was that so many of the young men had had to report straight after their phone calls to barracks.

Officers on leave from England had been instructed to stay where they were until they received further orders. They added their voices to the conversation, wishing they were involved, hoping for instructions to go and seek out the Sinn Feiners.

Sir Arthur launched into an attack on James Connolly, 'He is nothing but a rabblerouser. Supposedly concerned for the working man! So much cant. The fellow is after his own advancement. Men like him don't give two figs for the working man. It's people like us who do. People like us who sink our capital and use our intelligence to provide them with a living.' His guests applauded him.

'I mean to say,' Sir Arthur continued, 'have you ever heard such rot – an independent Ireland run by a Bolshevik and a schoolteacher who writes poetry and speaks the lingo? Can

181

you imagine? A fine kettle of fish that would be. By tomorrow we'll have settled their hash, we'll have run them out of their verminous nests, what?'

'Maybe,' Bessie said to Liam, 'I should give a bit to the children. They've been here for hours and must be lost with hunger.'

'I suppose it'd be better than wasting it, only . . .'

'Only what?'

'Giving food to some and not all might cause ructions.'

'Surely no one would object to the children getting it?'

'Hunger's a powerful thing. There's them that would take the bit out of a child's mouth. Wait for a while. Maybe when it gets dark the worst of them might make a move.'

Some of them did, the respectable, sober ones. The others remained and more arrived, the majority men and most of them drunk. Arguments broke out as to the rights and wrongs of what the Volunteers had done. Two men started to box. Another brandished a chair, threatening to brain anyone who said a word against the British. He swung the chair above his head, let go and it flew towards the counter landing on the apple cakes, smashing the crockery. Bessie screamed. Liam went amongst the crowd but soon realized that on his own there wasn't much he could do. 'You'll have to get the police,' Bessie was shouting, pushing her way through, ducking the flailing arms. 'Go for a policeman.'

Liam caught hold of her. 'Go into the kitchen and lock the door.'

'Look at it! Look what they've done. Everything we've worked for – all ruined. Everything destroyed.'

Liam turned away from the sight of upended tables, broken crockery and the stained wall where a cup aimed at someone's head had landed, spilling tea. 'Do what I'm telling you and go in the kitchen. With the help of God it'll soon be over. They're beginning to flag. There's two of them out for the count.' Bessie looked to where he pointed at the men asleep, faces down on the table. 'The others won't last much longer. I'll sit it out. It's better than leaving you on your own. And sure anyway with things as they are in the city I might never find a policeman. Go on now.'

In the kitchen Bessie sat close to the range and shivered. All their work had been for nothing. All their saving and striving, all Liam's backbreaking work gone for nothing. Their hopes wrecked because people took the law into their own hands. First the men in the Post Office, then the hooligans looking for any excuse to career, to torment and scourge people like herself and Liam. Not caring that their hour's 'devarsion' put paid to years of hope. She prayed that Liam was right, that they'd become stupefied from the drink and sleep. That they'd collapse where they sat or fell and he could evict them.

She sat for a long time thinking. Now and then she heard Liam's voice cajoling and the sound of the door opening and closing. And slurred voices protesting but more quietly than before. And then at last Liam was in the kitchen and she started to cry. He held her close and told her it was all right. They would be over it in a day or two. He stroked her hair and said he loved her and that now they'd go to bed and to Hell with the broken chairs and if the mutton stew didn't keep they'd give it to the woman who came for pig feeding.

She felt the strength of him flowing into her and was comforted. It was grand to be young and have the faith to move mountains. He began to lead her to the stairs, and she let him until they were by the bottom step. Then she remembered the state of the room. She couldn't go to bed leaving the place like that. Every night of her life her mother had left the kitchen clean and tidy, the hearth swept in, not a crumb on the floor. And in the Big House her mother's training was reinforced – you never left till tomorrow what needed doing today.

'Go on up,' she said. 'I'll be after you in a minute.' He tried to persuade her to leave everything until morning. But she wouldn't be persuaded. 'All right so,' he said, 'I'm tired.' And she was sorry he went. She would have liked his help and company.

She swept up the broken crockery, righted the tables and thanked God that only one chair was damaged, but perhaps it could be mended. There was nothing to do about the stained wallpaper, a rub with a damp cloth would bring it down in shreds. Maybe she could hang a few pictures to hide the worst. And so, sweeping and cleaning and talking to herself she worked until some semblance of order was restored to the eating house.

'It might be wise for you to make a move now,' Mrs McEvoy said to Jem as it began to get dark. 'You'd be more than welcome to a shake-down only your mother will be out of her mind worrying about you.'

His mother! Suddenly Jem realized that so concerned had he been for Dolly, he hadn't given her a thought. What must she be thinking and him out since before twelve? He'd go home and put her mind at rest, then go to Dolly's.

'I thought you'd been killed, thank God you're safe,' his mother said and Jem could see that she had been crying. 'What happened? Did you get to Howth?' He told her he hadn't and that he hadn't seen Dolly either and that now he'd make his way to her place.

'You'll do no such thing. Not the fur of your foot will you put outside the door. Are you wanting to kill me altogether? Wasn't it enough that I sat for hours not knowing if you were dead or alive. All day I've been hearing the shots of rifles and one of the neighbours told me that there's Volunteers in the City Hall and across the road British soldiers on the roofs ready to take a shot at anyone passing. It's the same in Trinity, they're defending it for the British, them young officer cadets

184

and Australian soldiers giving them a hand. Whichever way you went you'd be endangering your life. And for what – for a young wan that wipes her feet on you! I'm telling you you're not going.'

Oh God, Jem thought, what am I going to do? If I go against me mother I'll never hear the end of it. And if I don't put in an appearance it might be the end of me and Dolly.

'Listen till I tell you,' his mother said, changing her tactic. 'I know you're worried about Dolly, but chances are she's all right. She'd have gone straight home when the trouble in town started. In the name of God and His Holy Mother don't do anything foolish like going out. Go up tomorrow after dinner. It might be all over by then.'

'All right then,' Jem agreed. His mother looked terrible. It wouldn't be right to put her through more worry and please God Dolly was safe and would understand when he explained everything to her.

'It's a pity Miss about your honeymoon, the west is lovely at this time of the year,' Bridey said as she put away Alice's wedding gown.

Alice agreed that it was a pity and thought how ill-luck seemed to have dogged her and Stephen since the summer of 1914. Her father rushing her home from Horsham before an engagement could be announced – then the war and her mother refusing to allow a weekend wedding. Once she had hoped to spend her honeymoon in Paris. She wondered what had become of the girl Nella had met in the restaurant with Stephen, if he ever thought of her. It was something she would never know. Paris would have been glorious. The west of Ireland would have been glorious. Anywhere preferable to spending her first night in her own house. Why on this of all days did the Sinn Feiners have to cause trouble?

It wasn't pleasant for Stephen, either. He couldn't be relishing the prospect of having to stay in Dublin. Poor Stephen.

He'd had such rotten luck since the war. Posted to Gallipoli instead of France – thousands of miles away. What a strange and terrible experience Gallipoli had been she thought, remembering Stephen's letters. Brilliant sunshine and the air full of the smell of wild thyme: soldiers landing, storming the cliffs and being mown down by the Turks' machine guns.

How gallantly the men had behaved. Fighting like tigers. The Irish regiments and Australians never giving up though their losses were dreadful. In spite of heat and disease they kept going.

Stephen was full of praise for them. Then he got ill. He was mortified about that. Said he felt the most awful skrimshanker being in a hospital ship with a foot infection. Sharing a ward with men who had lost limbs. A foot infection was painful, and like all skin complaints in such a climate and conditions, slow to heal. But hardly something to feel proud of. He was terribly depressed. Heaven only knew what would have happened to him if the Gallipoli campaign hadn't been abandoned and everyone shipped out. Thank God he was spared and whole, and they were finally married. From now on surely everything would go well for them. She would be a loving wife and they would live happily together once this wretched war was over.

'Still and all Miss,' Bridey said, bringing Alice's pink silk afternoon dress, 'it's nice that you won't miss the dancing this evening. You and the Captain will lead the floor and there'll not be a more handsome pair.'

Alice smiled her thanks for the compliment and Bridey continued, 'While you're having tea I'll get your things shifted into the master bedroom. Her Ladyship says it's there you'll spend the night.'

Stephen got very drunk. Several times he trod on Alice's feet and after he stumbled and nearly fell during a one-step, she suggested that they sit out the remainder of the dance. Eagerly he consented and no sooner had he unsteadily es-

186

corted her to her seat than he excused himself, 'Won't be long – I must find out what the latest is on the GPO situation.'

Later on Nella came and sat by her. 'You've been deserted, so I see. I've just passed the library – Smithers is practically chained to the telephone. The room is absolutely packed with men. Drunk, needless to say, fighting every war from the beginning of time. They love it. Glory in it from the moment they can stand and point anything. Of course, they've got an advantage – always a weapon to hand!'

'Oh Nella, you are dreadful!' Alice laughed.

'Oh God, I'm drunk.' Stephen collapsed across the bed. Alice solicitously stroked his face. He smiled at her then closed his eyes and began to snore. Unsuccessfully, she tried to waken him. He was sprawled over the bed leaving no room for her. In any case she couldn't leave him as he was. He had to be undressed. She got up from the bed and tugged the bell-pull. Bridey looked past her to the prostrate figure on the bed.

'Get Captain Whitehead's batman.'

'Well, the thing is Miss, I've just come from the kitchen and I'd say that fella's in the same shape as the Captain. Maybe I'd better get Higgins.'

Her father's man came, a quiet discreet person who made no comment on Stephen's condition but efficiently moved him into the dressing room, then closed the connecting door. Bridey talked while she undressed Alice. ''Tis the same with many a young man on their wedding night. Nerves, that's all it is. I do hear it said often in the kitchen and know of many a case the same at home. Tomorrow he'll be as right as rain.'

Searching for a book, for she knew sleep would be a long time coming, Alice chose one and leafed through it. Towards the centre she found the buttercup she had pressed. Looking at the faded flower she remembered the day in Horsham and the man who had given it to her. Was memory playing tricks, she wondered, or had he really been so handsome, so attractive? And had she been all of a dither when he held the flower under her chin? It was a long time ago, but yet she felt certain that her memory wasn't at fault. There was something so special about him, a kind of magic. And she felt sure that he wouldn't have fallen asleep on the first night of his honeymoon.

It was cold in the GPO. Men not on duty huddled in blankets on the floor and tried to sleep in the unfamiliar surroundings. By a window, two Volunteers watched Sackville Street. The crowds were long since gone. Darkness shrouded their earlier handiwork except where remnants of fires they had started still smouldered.

One of the men spoke, 'Wouldn't it be terrible if they ignored us?'

'Ignored us, who?'

'The Military. Supposing they let us keep the Post Office. Stay here till we starved or perished with the cold.'

'No fear of that.'

'I don't know, they've done nothing so far. Apart from the Lancers after dinner we haven't seen sight of them.'

'We caught them unawares. Tomorrow it'll be a different story. The lads cutting the wires in the Castle hamstrung them for the minute. God – wasn't it a pity we couldn't have taken the Castle, that would have been them finished. You'll see tomorrow – they'll be out in all their might.'

'I hope you're right. Imagine the let-down if we never saw a bit of action.'

Bridget, Dolly and Maggie sat by the fire, the two older women gossiping, talking about who was soon to be married, who was dying in consumption, the woman carrying on and her unfortunate husband out in France. Dolly gazed into the fire, seeing pictures in the coals that had parted and exposed their glowing depths.

188

She thought about Jem and wondered why she hadn't heard from him. And whether or not she would marry him. In the long run she supposed she would, unless someone, the man she often imagined, turned up. You had to get married, for what else was there except finishing up an old maid, working until you got bad on your feet from the heat in Jacobs! Living on the floor with your mother or, worse still, when she went, a relation. And on top of everything the disgrace and shame of not getting a man. Old maids were looked down on – no one respected a woman who didn't marry. No more than they respected a barren woman. A child crowned a woman, but only if she was married. To have one and be single, that was worse than anything, and a sin as well as a disgrace.

The heat from the fire was burning her face. She drew back her chair and continued her thoughts. She would definitely get married, but not for a while. To hear Maggie and her mother on about her settling down anyone would think she was ancient instead of twenty. Not like the oul wans in work – some of them would never see forty again except on a hall door. Doing Novenas and praying 'Blessed St Anne, send me a man'. She still had years in front of her. All the time in the world, and Jem could wait until it suited her.

She thought of all the concerts, the hooleys, the dances she still wanted to go to. All the costumes, blouses, hats and shoes there were to buy. How she loved the feel of new material, the smell of it. Seeing herself in the dresses and costumes for the first time, she loved that. But once you were married it was goodbye to things like that. So Jem was rushing her into nothing.

That was the best of him, he'd do whatever she wanted. Stand on his head if she asked. She smiled at the idea of him trying a handstand, his trouser legs wrinkling down over his knees, the tails of his coat falling over his face and his hair fanned out.

'You're very quiet,' Maggie said, her voice intruding on Dolly's musings.

'I was just thinking.'

'What were you thinking about?'

'Work, and what'll I do if it is true that Jacobs' has been taken over by the Volunteers,' Dolly lied.

Later in bed she resumed her thinking. Jem was awful nice. You could be yourself with him – like you were with your family. Too nice, though, that was half his trouble. You never felt excited at the prospect of seeing him. Like this morning, she was raging that he had let her down. But not raging that she wouldn't be seeing him, only that the day was spoiled. But it might be different if they were married, she might feel more for him.

They could live in England, that would stop any interferences from his oul wan. England would be great to live in. You only had to look at anyone who'd gone over and come back to see there was full and plenty there. In England they wore kid-gloves every day.

Her and Jem would have a house of their own. No one lived in tenements in England. She'd have Nottingham lace hangings on the windows – you could tell a house by its windows – and cream Holland blinds with deep lace edging and a tassel like an acorn. Every morning she would polish the letter-box and knocker. She'd keep it like a babby house. And when they'd come back to Dublin for a holiday what a dash she'd cut. Her father and mother and Maggie and Richard, they'd all be at the North Wall to meet them. Yes, she'd get married when the war was over or when she was twenty-five, she promised herself before falling asleep.

The journey back was pleasanter than Robbie had anticipated. His mother, after a tearful farewell, accepted her abrupt return philosophically. 'Maybe it's all for the best. Once or twice during the week I didn't feel very well and got afraid I might have been laid up in Dublin and be a burden on them. There's nowhere like your own home if you are sick.'

'But I thought you were better. You look so well, much better than when I first arrived from France,' Robbie said.

'That was the change and seeing Ireland again,' she laughed, 'though little I saw of it, but still I could feel it all around me. And do you know there were times when I believed I was a girl again, that I was whole and healthy, that's what had me looking well. I wonder if your father came in during the time we were away and what he thought of the note. He'd have got a drop finding me gone.'

'If he did it may change his ways,' Robbie said.

His mother sighed. 'I wish that were so, but I'm afraid he's too far gone ever to change. It's madness of a kind, maybe a second childhood, I don't know. It isn't that I wouldn't want it otherwise. There's times I let my mind believe there will be a miracle. That he'll walk in and everything will be normal again. Nothing silly like thinking it could be the same as when we were young, only being together, having each other for company, someone to touch or call out to in the night. I get so afraid.'

'Are you sure that doctor was right, that a tonic is all you need?'

Fanny looked at her son and was tempted to tell him the truth, that she had cancer, inoperable and would probably be dead by Christmas. To see the shock and grief on his lovely face, to have him hold her and tell her he loved her and not to worry, he would take care of her. The comfort she would get, the relief from trying to appear bright and cheerful, the lifting of the burden of secrecy. But it wouldn't be fair. He was too young and, although she knew that in one sense his youth, the pressure under which he lived at the Front, the surge of his own on-going life would diminish his grief, yet there would be moments when it would creep up on him, when it couldn't be assuaged by seeing her and realizing, she hoped, that she wasn't spending her remaining days in agony. Let him be, she thought, let him return to France believing all that ailed her was tiredness and growing old. 'I have great faith in him. Little turns, that's all they are. You'll see.' The crossing was nearly over. She gathered her things together. Robbie took the heavy bags and walked in front of her down the gangplank, calling back to her to walk carefully.

'How do you manage for money?' he asked when they were on their way to London.

'Manage, what do you mean?'

'Money. With Dad spending so much time away from the house, what's the arrangement?'

'When he does come in he leaves enough.'

'Have you tried talking to him, asking for an explanation?'

'In the beginning until I was blue in the face. I never got one, now I don't ask any more. You can get used to anything.'

'What about the doctor? Have you told him?'

'I have.'

'Well?'

'Eccentricity, that's what he calls it. Do you know what he said once? I was very annoyed, because the thought had never entered my mind. He said, "Mrs Brightwell, you weren't hoping to have him committed? He isn't violent. The fact that he sees to your financial affairs is an indication that his mind is sound – there could be no question of me being a party to anything like that. An eccentric – that's it, tiresome for you, but there, the world is full of such people."'

'And since you've been having your "little turns", hasn't he suggested having a talk with my father – you know, explaining that his help might be needed?'

'No,' Fanny replied.

'A fine doctor he sounds.' Looking across the carriage at his mother's face, Robbie was again filled with the terror he had experienced on the day he came home from France. She was more than tired. She mustn't be left on her own. He

192

would go and see the doctor and his father before he went back to the Front. And between now and arriving in London he would get the truth out of her.

The train was slowing down, stopping at Bangor. He hoped no one would join her carriage, then they could stretch out and sleep for an hour or two. But the door was being opened and a man, woman and three small children came in. They were a pleasant-looking family who greeted Robbie and his mother in English and then spoke in Welsh to each other. Robbie moved to sit beside his mother and the family took the other seat. His mother dozed and Robbie slipped an arm round her, making her head comfortable on his shoulder. The family travelled with them to Euston and, although his mother woke long before that looking refreshed, the opportunity for talking to her was lost.

And when they arrived home she seemed so well Robbie dismissed his earlier fears and decided that a visit to the doctor wasn't necessary.

'He's been in, the note is gone,' his mother told him, going to the mantelpiece where she had left it. 'I'd love to have seen his face when he read it.'

'What about your money – did he leave that?'

'He never fails – look, twenty pounds. He's not stingy, I'll say that for him. Here,' she gave him ten pounds. 'I've more than enough.'

He felt a softening of his heart towards his father. He would go and see him – who knows, he might work a miracle, bring him home. He left his visit to the woods until the day before he went back to France. He told his mother that there were one or two people in the village he wanted to say, 'So long' to and she smiled at him and guessed that the few people would be some girl. She was proud of him and loved him so much she didn't know how she could bear to live when he went away, and so the thought of her approaching death wasn't so terrible.

The hut like the house and everything he remembered from before he went to the war had shrunk, but not the massive oaks which grew close by. The hut smelled as it always had, a mixture of wood smells and the grease with which his father wiped the axe and saws – a lovely smell. There was a narrow bed neatly made and a few cooking utensils on a shelf but of his father there was no trace. He looked round for a sign of anything personal, a photograph of him, of the boys, his mother, letters. There were none.

He went outside and walked round the hut. There was a new addition at the back, a lean-to made of tin sheets and inside, a small primus. Whatever else his father was he wasn't taking chances on starting a fire. Again he looked round for personal items and again there were none. Where was he, he wondered and went back outside, calling him. For an hour or more he walked several ways along tracks he remembered covering with his father, stopping now and then to whistle and call, but there was no answer. Well, he had tried and wasn't going to waste any more time. To his mother's inquiries he said that he had enjoyed himself and now he was going to press his uniform and shave again, for tonight he was going to a dance in the village, but he wouldn't be home late.

She lay in bed listening for him, hearing the clock strike the hours until just after three when she heard him come in. And she wouldn't let herself cry, afraid that once she did she might not be able to stop or control it and she didn't want anything to spoil his last night.

Chapter Nine

Alice had slept badly, dozing and waking, hoping that Stephen at some time during the night would come and join her in the double bed. But each time she woke she was alone and from the dressing room came the sound of snoring. In the morning she couldn't face the dining room and her mother inquiring if she and Stephen had slept well and why he wasn't down to breakfast. So she went to a place in the garden, a seat by a wall just inside the kitchen garden where as a child she liked to sit and watch the old man who looked after the greenhouse, working.

She had been there no time when her father came looking for her. 'Ah, there you are. I wanted a word with you and Stephen. Why isn't he down? Why didn't you come in to breakfast?'

'I'm not hungry and Stephen isn't very well. His stomach is upset.'

'I see. Well, what I wanted to tell you was that the trip to Connemara had better be postponed for a couple of days.'

'Oh no! Please, Papa. It's not fair, Stephen will be furious.'

'Stephen's a soldier – he'll understand. He wouldn't take unnecessary risks.' Alice began an impassioned plea for their honeymoon plans to go ahead which was interrupted by the arrival of a manservant who was very agitated.

'Excuse me sir, I'm sorry for butting in but I think you'd better come quick. Mr Fox is in the library and I'd say he's having a fit. I said you weren't at home, it being so early, but he won't leave.'

'A fit?'

'Well, sir – he's only short of foaming at the mouth. Will I say you're coming?'

'Yes, all right, thank you.'

'Please Papa . . .'

'Leave it. Tell Stephen what I've said.' Sir Arthur left for the library.

There he found Mr Fox, an elderly neighbour pacing the room and talking to himself loudly.

'Ah, Charles, good morning. What brings you out so early?'

'Look here Delahunt, it's not good enough! I stayed over-night in town. I've just arrived back, and do you know the Post Office is *still* in the hands of the Sinn Feiners! Where's the army? Why haven't they been run out of the place? *Why isn't something being done about it?* You're an MP. I demand answers. We'll be a laughing-stock before the world. What's being done, eh?'

'For God's sake, sit down man, you'll have a stroke. Every-thing's being done. Sit down, have a brandy.'

Mr Fox accepted the drink but refused to sit, though his pacing was slowing down. 'You haven't answered my question: what is being done?'

'Look, please sit down, there's a good fellow. Drink the brandy and listen. Yesterday evening reinforcements arrived from the Curragh. There was a slight hitch when the Sinn Feiners attempted to take the Castle, for they cut the wires. But they were rooted out and the lines repaired. So everything's in hand. More troops are arriving at Kingstown today.'

Mr Fox sat and accepted another brandy. 'Even so, they've disrupted business. Thousands of pounds will be lost, to say nothing of the meal the foreign press will make of them holding us at bay even for a day.'

With blandishments and excuses Sir Arthur eventually calmed the old man, though inwardly fuming himself. For he knew Mr Fox's reaction would be shared by many. God knows he had been warning the authorities for years that what had happened yesterday was on its way. And they were still caught napping. Allowing themselves to be lulled into a false sense of security by Casement's arrest, the scuttling of the *Aud* and MacNeill's notice in the paper.

'Sorry to have bothered you so early and that, Arthur.' Mr Fox, fortified and calm, took his leave.

Alice went from the garden to find Stephen and talk with him. He would agree with her, tell her father there was no need for them to stay over in Dublin. He would sympathize with her, comfort her . . .

He was still asleep. She shook him gently. 'Darling, wake up.' He opened his eyes and stared blearily at her. His eyes were bloodshot and his breath still smelled of drink. She bent to kiss him. He turned his head away and mumbled that his teeth needed cleaning.

'You silly old thing,' she said and laughed, bent catching hold of his face and trying to turn it towards her. 'I don't mind, honestly. You can kiss me.'

He moved further away, his shoulder shrugging off her hand as if he couldn't bear her touch. But that couldn't be the reason. He probably was feeling rotten. The lie she'd told her father about his stomach being out of order was no doubt true. 'Shall I have something sent up?' she asked hesitantly.

'No, thank you. I'd like to sleep a little longer, that's all,' he said, without turning round. She felt like a servant being dismissed, but waited for a moment wondering if she should try again to get his attention. But his shoulders were hunched, his head bent as if he wished to burrow beneath the bedclothes to escape from her.

*

197

Dolly sat behind the lace hangings in the parlour watching for Jem's arrival and listening to the voices of her mother and the women from the house gathered around the hall door talking about yesterday's events and their consequences today. Jem, she thought, was bound to come soon and the minute she caught sight of him she'd be up from the window and make her father say she wasn't in. He had another think coming if he expected to find her ready and waiting after the fool he had made of her yesterday.

The women's conversation drifted in through the inches of sash window open at the top.

'I believe things are terrible across town. Shops smashed and burned and people laying dead.'

'Go way! Who killed them?'

'Stray bullets from them in the Post Office and then there's other fellas on the other side of the street firing across it and people get caught in the middle.'

'Bad luck to them anyway to start such a commotion without giving a thought to the likes of us. There's no delivery of bread, and how can you feed your family without bread?'

'And did you hear the worst of it – the pawn offices are all shut! What am I going to do for the rent?'

'Jacobs is shut – look at the loss of wages that'll be.'

Answer them better, Dolly said to herself, to be in minding their snotty-nosed children. And my mother's every bit as bad – out there with them, laughing and jeering and making a show of the place. It's a good job it's only Jem I'm expecting. Not that he's killing himself coming. But he'll get a drop when he does. He won't lay eyes on me before Friday, that's if I bother to go to the Dempseys' hooley.

From the haggard behind the dairy across the street she heard Mary Fleming's milk cows lowing. Their soft plaintive calling reminded Dolly of summer days long ago. And for a while she forgot her annoyance at Jem's absence and the gossiping women. Remembering instead running barefooted

198

through the tussocky grass where the cows grazed. She wondered if they were the same cows in the haggard today? Did cows live that long? Live until they fell down and died. She didn't know. And thought instead of how, long ago, the days were always warm, the sun shining and the field full of flowers and butterflies. Blue ones, and whitey, lemon-coloured ones with black spots on their wings, little red ones and the ones she liked best – brown and orange like her mother's combs. She made bowers for them. Scooping out handfuls of warm, sweet-smelling earth and lining the bottom with dock seeds. Running her hand up the plant to strip the seeds that looked like dried tea leaves. Padding the sides of the bower with daisies and buttercups and searching for a piece of broken glass to cover the bower. And then, when all was ready, tiptoeing through the long grass, hands outstretched to catch a butterfly when it came to rest. She could feel again the fluttering of wings as she carried the captive to its flower-strewn nest and slid it under the glass. But no matter how softly she lined the bower or how many flowers she strewed inside, the next morning the beautiful butterflies were always dead. Lying with their wings folded amongst the wilted flowers, staining her fingers with fine powder when she lifted them out.

The arrival of her father in the parlour brought Dolly back to the present.

'Alanna,' he said, 'isn't it a terrible thing with all that's going on and not a paper to be had? The tobacconist was telling me there's none printed, only the *Irish Times*. And sure – where around here would you get that?'

Johnny dabbed with a handkerchief at his eye which, despite all the bathing of the previous night, was black, yellow and purple.

'Did you hear what I said?' he asked when Dolly made no comment about the newspapers.

'I did. I heard you.'

199

'You could have answered, civility costs nothing,' he gently reproved her. 'Now, like a good child call your mother in from the door. I could do with my dinner.'

'I will if you'll tell Jem O'Brien when he comes that I'm not in.'

'Pollute my lips with a lie! Well, indeed I won't. Go now and call your mother.'

Dolly went to the hall door and gave her mother the message. 'Is that right about MacDonagh taking over Jacobs'?' one of the women asked.

'He can keep it for all I care,' Dolly replied rudely and followed her mother in.

'Stuck-up looking bitch!' the woman said when they were out of earshot.

Johnny was pacing the kitchen, still complaining about the lack of a newspaper. 'Nothing to go on, only rumours and oul wans' gossip. And one of them saying the Germans had landed! How is a man to know anything if he doesn't see it in black and white?'

Bridget, annoyed at being summoned, said sarcastically, 'Maybe you'd like them to print one specially for you.' Johnny said nothing and she continued: 'That's men for you, sitting on their arse reading the facts. Or down in the public house rehashing what the gobshites have written. That's men all over. But never a word about the women without wages, or children looking up in their mothers' faces crying with hunger. And when it's all over and the dead are counted, where will the men be? Down in the public house consoling themselves and saying why it went wrong and how it could be put right.'

Dolly stood before the mirror checking on her appearance. Her mother now turned her annoyance on her. 'And what happened to your hands all of a sudden? Did you lose the use of them? Wasn't the stew in the pot only wanting lifting? Get away from in front of the glass so I can get to the fire and the pair of you can wait a bit longer for your dinner. For whatever

200

else is rumour it's a fact the bread hasn't been delivered and I'm going to bake a bit.'

Dolly and Johnny waited without further complaint while Bridget made the brown squares. And afterwards, when they were having dinner Dolly coaxed her mother to tell Jem when he came that she was out. 'Go on, will you, please. In any case, I'm going out when Bid calls.'

Bridget said, 'Yes, all right.'

But the dinner was over, the table cleared and the delft washed and there was still no sign of Jem. Johnny went into the parlour to lie down and not long afterwards, Bid arrived.

'Not a word about either of them,' she said when Dolly asked if there was any news of Jem or Kevin. 'But wait till you hear the latest. Them fellas in the Post Office are hand in glove with the Germans, everyone says so. And what do you think of them commandeering the Green, and me thinking of all the fellas I could click there while I was feeding the ducks. We'll have to go across town – I believe it's terrible. Everything's destroyed and the Liffey's choked with bodies.'

'You'll do no such thing, not unless you want the arse blown off yourself, Dolly Devoy. You saw what happened to your father.'

'Ah Mother, for God's sake,' Dolly protested. Then Johnny, having decided he didn't feel like sleeping, re-appeared. They changed the conversation.

'Your eye looks awful sore, Mr Devoy. You'd want to mind it,' Bid said, her voice full of concern.

Johnny, who considered Bid a forward little girl with too much to say, ignored her and proceeded to lecture Dolly on the dangers of going across town.

'Of course I wouldn't go, Da,' she agreed, winking at Bid behind her father's back. 'We were only talking about that before you came in. You'd want to be mad, looking for trouble. We wouldn't have the nerve, would we Bid?'

'Indeed we wouldn't,' Bid said. And between them they

convinced Johnny they wouldn't put a foot near the town. But there was a girl in Terenure, very bad, a nice girl from work who had gone into rapid consumption and wasn't expected to last. Tomorrow would be the right day to visit her. And on Thursday there was a special novena in a chapel as far away from the trouble as Terenure.

Bridget, while she wrapped the cooked soda bread in damp tea towels, watched Johnny swallowing the story, nodding his head in agreement as the girls outlined their plans for the following days. And thought, let them go, I'd have done the same at their age. And danger or not, sure I can't keep Dolly tied to the leg of a chair all her life.

Dolly and Bid sat on the bed-settee and talked to each other in whispers, Bid confiding that she thought Kevin was going off her. He'd become very cool lately, but she didn't care, there was plenty more fish in the sea. And Dolly telling her that Jem was in for a shock when he arrived and found she wasn't in. And that nothing terrible could have happened to him or she'd have heard. Anyway, nothing terrible ever happened to someone you knew. So there was no excuse for him not coming. No matter how much trouble there was in town, sure weren't there a hundred and one ways to come over and see her without going anywhere near it?

Jem could hear the firing as he left his house. It terrified him. Never until yesterday had he seen or heard a gun being fired. His natural inclination was to turn back but he was desperate to see Dolly. To ask her forgiveness for not meeting her on Monday. To explain why. To say he was sorry for not coming last night as well. He needed to tell her about the Lancer he had seen die. How the man's face wouldn't leave his mind. Tell her of the fear that was haunting him since he had witnessed the shooting. He needed her to touch him, to laugh, make everything all right again.

Last night he had tried talking to his mother. Attempted to

202

explain his horror, his incredulity that in seconds a man could cease to exist. 'Stop thinking about it and say three Hail Marys for his soul. Isn't he better off? Isn't he with his Maker this minute in Heaven?' his mother had replied.

And he had wanted to shout: 'No, he's not better off! He was alive, he was beautiful, up there on his horse with the sun shining on him. All decked-out. Happy. How's he better off? Maybe he loved a girl. Maybe like me he wanted to marry her. Now he's dead. That's not better off.'

But he couldn't talk like that to his mother, she was old and holy. And in very bad humour because he had suggested setting out first thing in the morning to see Dolly. And they had had words. He wouldn't annoy her any more. She wouldn't understand. But Dolly would. She'd understand it wasn't only the dead Lancer. He was afraid for himself, for her. Having seen death come so suddenly he was afraid. She would know what to say. He wanted to hear her laugh. She had a lovely laugh, 'like a peal of joybells' was how his mother had begrudgingly described it. He would brave whatever it was that was going on to be with her.

He walked up Capel Street, crossed the bridge and up Parliament Street and onto Cork Hill where the battle was taking place between soldiers and the Volunteers, who were in City Hall. Bullets showered the street. There was a crowd dodging in and out of doorways ignoring orders from soldiers to leave the area. He made his way amongst them, praying for God to protect them all. He saw men and women fall. When it wasn't possible to proceed without almost certainly being shot he sheltered in a shop door, until after a long time there was a lull in the battle and he made his escape. As he approached ninety-seven his heart beat as fast as it had during the firing.

'Shhh, that's him. I know his knock,' Dolly whispered when the gentle tap sounded on the door. 'Tell him I'm not in,

Mother, please.' Her father closed his eyes pretending sleep. Bridget went to the door.

'Quick into the parlour,' Dolly said, still whispering. Bid followed her and they sat on the bed with fists stuffed against their mouths to stifle their laughter, and listening to Bridget telling the lies.

'I hope to God she doesn't offer him a cup of tea.'

'She's bound to. Then we'll be in here all night.' Bid took her hands from her mouth, laughing out loud until Dolly pushed her down on the bed and held a pillow over her face.

'Are you sure you won't have one? You know you're more than welcome,' Bridget was saying and Jem could be heard replying, 'No, honest to God, thanks all the same. You won't forget to tell Dolly what I said.' And Bridget's voice reassuring him she wouldn't. Then the sound of her going to the door with him and calling, 'Goodbye, son, and mind yourself. May God forgive the pair of you,' she said, coming into the parlour. 'He'd want to have been deaf not to hear the spluttering and laughing.'

'What did he have to say?' Dolly asked.

'That he'd see you at the hooley and explain all about yesterday. I'm sure he heard you. The poor unfortunate boy, coming all this way and to get such a let-down.'

'Didn't he say anything else?'

'That he was sorry about yesterday. And could you make your own way to the hooley in case like yesterday he'd be delayed.'

'Make my own way! The cheek of him! I've got a good mind not to go at all. He killed himself coming, didn't he? Nearly five o'clock! I could have been dead and buried for all he knew or cared.'

Jem thought as he left the house, I must have been imagining it. God knows Dolly has queer ways, but she'd never hide in the parlour laughing and letting on she wasn't in. Yet, as he hurried to get home before the curfew the thought persisted that he had heard the sound of laughter.

After Bid left, Dolly began sewing a blouse she was making for the hooley and as she gathered the fine material to fit the cuffs, she felt a sense of guilt for what she had done. Jem might have heard them laughing. That was terrible if he did. Letting on she wasn't in was nothing. She could have been out – he'd never have known the difference. But if he'd heard them, that was very hurtful. She wouldn't have wished that for the world. She stroked each pleat of the silk with the eye of the needle to ensure an even gathering and continued to think about Jem. Her mind searched for a justification. If he'd come early enough she would have seen him, even though she'd asked her father to say she was out. But she wasn't going to let Bid think any man could walk on her. Anyway – it was his own fault, leaving it till such an hour before he showed up.

By the time she had completed the cuffs Dolly's conscience was clear and she was having second thoughts about marrying Jem, even after the war or when she was twenty-five. Reasoning that there should be more to marriage than just feeling comfortable with him. She felt comfortable with her mother and father – but she didn't have to get into bed with them. But getting into bed was what you had to do when you got married. Taking off your clothes and laying down beside him. You'd have to fancy him an awful lot to do that. Jem might snore like her father, snort and snuffle in his sleep and drive her demented.

Come to think of it, Jem did nothing except get on her nerves. He was as exciting as being with her mother, but at least her mother could get her rag – have a row with her. And wasn't it funny how after a row you felt better, your bad humour gone. But not Jem, he wouldn't row with anyone.

She knew exactly what he would say and do. Twenty years from now he'd be saying and doing the same thing.

She folded her sewing and put it away and thought about going across town tomorrow. Herself and Bid would have a great time. And you'd never know who you might meet. For all she knew, tomorrow could be the very day when she met the man she was waiting for.

The city was being bombarded, buildings set alight, the number of civilian deaths rising. Remorselessly, the army made up for lost time. In their commandeered posts the Volunteers fought back. Since Sunday no one had slept properly, eaten sufficiently or had time to wash properly. The women served what food was available and bandaged the wounded. Courage and exhilaration lent them strength and endurance. They were fighting for Ireland! They would fight to the last. They were fighting for their dream, their hopes, for all who had struggled before them, who had been exiled, executed, died from starvation. Fighting for all who had kept the spark alive. It burned brightly in their hearts. This land would be theirs again. A free land, an Independent Ireland for their children and their children's children. It was a grand time to be alive.

On Wednesday Dolly and Bid with the lies tripping off their tongues once again assured Johnny they weren't going near the town. Hadn't they told him about their friend who was dying with consumption, and couldn't he see the things they were taking to her – here they held up their brown-paper wrapped parcels hanging by string loops from their fingers, and afterwards they were going to make their novena . . . As soon as they were out of Johnny's sight they collapsed laughing, discarded the bundles of paper and began walking to Sackville Street, towards their real destination.

'I didn't tell you the latest – there's a boat with guns firing from it in the Liffey and my father says it's doing desperate

206

damage, sending shells flying everywhere. You're lucky living on the southside, I don't suppose them shells could reach here. I wouldn't like to be Josie and Danny living up by Amiens' Street station.'

'And her expecting a baby!' Dolly said.

'Jesus! Will you look at it!' Bid exclaimed as Sackville Street came into view. Dolly stared in disbelief at the once beautiful wide street through which they had walked in the Easter sunshine: the street with which she was so familiar she seldom noticed it. Today it demanded her attention. Buildings with their fronts or sides missing exposed their insides to her eye. Piles of rubble lay heaped on the paths, spilling into the road. Empty cartons, paper, cardboard, bottles discarded by the looters littered the pavements and clogged the gutters. Amongst the rubbish a bedraggled purple feather boa stirred by the wind made slow sinuous movements like a snake mortally injured.

'I can't believe it,' Dolly kept repeating. 'Will you look at it.'

'I know,' Bid said. 'You couldn't credit it happening in your own place. It's like being in a bad dream and you think you'll wake up in a minute and everything will be the way it was.'

Smoke and dust hovered in the air. There were strange smells. Smells of blood, of burning debris, of things old and rotten, of creatures that had burrowed in walls, floors and ceilings – insects and animals blown from their secure cracks and crevices. Bewildered, Dolly and Bid walked on.

Bessie from her window saw soldiers and equipment going down the quays. Infantry and artillerymen, machine and field guns and she thought with pity of the men against whom the army and its guns would be used. On Monday they had caused her annoyance. She had partly blamed them for the disturbance and damage in the eating house. But now she thought sadly how they were poor men, inexperienced in the ways of war with only brave hearts to spur them on and stand between them and the might of the British Army. And she recalled with regret the basins of food she had thrown out. How they'd have relished that. Cooped up as they were since Sunday, and whatever else they got, it wouldn't be lovely mutton stew. She wondered about their mothers, wives and sweethearts. How must they be feeling today, knowing that the fighting was now in earnest?

At Kingstown harbour troops disembarked. Yesterday, they had been hastily summoned back to barracks. Ordered from public houses, from fairgrounds, from their families and friends and quickly entrained for they knew not where. France seemed the obvious destination – until during the train journey someone noticed that the train was travelling north. The men joked about being sent to Russia, smoked and laughed, played cards and remained unaware of where they were going until the boat docked in Ireland. Then they joked again about Paddys and Micks and Irish colleens.

After disembarking, they were divided into two columns. One would take the inland route and so avoid the city where it was known an ambush was likely: the other group would march to Dublin via a route parallel to the coast. Both groups were greeted by women who showered them with well wishes and thanks for their arrival and plied them with food, sweets, chocolates, fruit and biscuits. The young men congratulated themselves on being in Ireland and went their separate ways.

On towards the city marched the second column, passing through Blackrock, Booterstown, and Merrion Road. Leaving behind the seaside villages on went the soldiers at their fast infantry pace. The sun shone on them, their stomachs were full of food. It was good to forget the motion of the tossing ship, to feel the ground firm beneath your feet, it was good to be alive.

They were entering the suburbs, roads of red-bricked, substantial houses with gardens and tree-lined paths. The shadows of the newly-opened leaves were dancing on the paths. There was a smell of things growing and the laurel-leaved hedges shone brightly green. The road was overlooked by dozens of windows. On some, the sun shone dazzlingly.

From the windows, they were being watched. By small boys, who admiringly shaped their shoulders and imitated the soldiers marching, stamping their feet on the nursery floors. Servants came up the area steps to get a better view. The young men winked at them. Behind the lace hangings stood the women of the houses, the look in their eyes expressing whether or not they were pleased at the troops' arrival. The Volunteers watched and waited, peering down their rifles.

A shot was fired. A soldier fell and the one behind him stumbled over the body. More shots were fired. Falling dead, or seeking cover from the rain of bullets, the young soldiers hit the ground. '*Seek cover!*' they were ordered and they sought it behind walls, in shrubberies, wriggling on their bellies over gravelled paths, kneeling behind gateposts and hedges. Their officers and NCOs scanned the façades of the houses, trying to pinpoint where the rapid, accurate firing was coming from. Believing they had located the house, an order was given to charge. With fixed bayonets the soldiers obeyed and were mown down before they got very far. The survivors regrouped and the dead and wounded were taken from the street. Again and again the soldiers charged, presenting an easy target for the spitting rifles. For hours the battle raged, hopelessly it seemed for the infantrymen until reinforcements arrived and the house was rushed, the door broken down and grenades used.

Dolly and Bid walked down the street, stopping to look over at the Post Office and the coils of barbed wire outside it. 'It's funny all the same to think of them in there, and there's girls as well. I'd be afraid of my life, wouldn't you, Dolly?'

209

Dolly said she wasn't sure, that maybe it would be exciting. That you'd be bound to feel very important.

'I could think of better ways of being excited – they must all be out of their minds. Come on, anyway, we'd better turn back.'

They walked towards the Bridge. Today there was no organ grinder, nor any lounging soldiers. But a crowd still thronged the street and Monday's air of festivity was replaced by an excited awareness of danger. Soldiers began firing in the direction of the Post Office and in the Liffey the gunboat *Helga* prepared to fire. Sailors rammed a shell into the gun's breech, inserted the charge, closed the breech and elevated the gun. The right angle was found and the order 'Fire!' given. The shell whined through the air. 'My Jesus,' a woman screamed, clapping her hands over her ears. 'It's the end of the world.' The shell fell short of its target. Momentarily deafened and slightly stunned, the sightseers stood silent, terrified. Then realizing they were still alive colour returned to their cheeks, defiance and curiosity to their minds. First a young boy, then men and women leant over the Bridge. Some climbed the parapet, the more agile clambered up the lampposts to get a better view of the gunboat, to shout and jeer.

Through a megaphone orders were shouted to clear the Bridge, to clear the street. The crowd ran. Dolly ran with them, feeling an exhilaration that reminded her of childhood games. She found shelter in a shop door and stood panting, almost expecting a playmate to run through and call, 'Relievo'.

Bid joined her, bright-eyed, her cheeks flushed, breasts heaving from the unaccustomed exertion.

'That's a fine pair of dairies. Give us a goozer,' a man who was also sheltering said, leering at Bid.

'You dirty blackguard.' Dolly stared contemptuously at him. Unabashed the man returned her stare. Then put a hand to his nose and waggled his fingers.

210

'Ride on that till you get a pony,' he said, before running back into the street.

'A right bowsie,' Dolly said and Bid agreed. The sound of gunfire and shelling had stopped. Cautiously they left the shop doorway. It began to rain, a cold drizzle that got heavier. Their hats flopped and their skirts clung to their legs. Ambulances drove slowly past, stopping at intervals to pick up the dead and wounded. Two barefooted boys sat astride a dead horse urging it to 'gee up' with blows from a pearl-handled umbrella.

Early the next morning before it was light Josie McEvoy woke. She lay still for a moment wondering what it was that had woken her. From the nearby streets came the crack of rifle fire. Flames from the burning city lit up the sky, and now and then one flared and brightened the room. For a while she watched the flickering shadows on the walls then closed her eyes and tried to sleep again. She was almost gone when the pain began. It surged through her belly, taking her breath. Beside her Danny snored softly. It's only cramps, she thought, something I ate. There was a lull in the firing. The pain ebbed and Josie grateful for the ease, turned on the lumpy flock mattress seeking a comfortable position. Then the pain began again. Gripping each side of her spine it spread vice-like, encircling her, making her cry out: 'Holy Mary Mother of Jesus.' Her hands went to her belly and felt not the familiar bumpy form of the baby but a solid mound shifting and pushing upwards beneath her spread-eagled fingers. The pain became unbearable. She screamed, jerked her knees and screamed again. Beneath her hands the mound shifted, softened and subsided, the pain receding.

'Danny, Danny!' she cried as the next contraction began. 'Danny, wake up!'

Startled and confused-looking, Josie's screams ringing in

211

his ears, Danny sat up in the bed. 'What ails you? What's wrong?'

'Get up,' she gasped. 'The child's coming. Get up. Get me mother and . . .' The pain engulfed and silenced her.

Danny jumped out of bed, stumbled across the room, found the matches and lit the lamp. The wick flared and by its long ragged flame he saw the contorted face of his wife. 'Sweet Mother of Jesus,' she moaned. 'Sweet Mother of Jesus, help me.'

'Hold on now. Hold on. I'm going. Can I get you anything? Wait now, I won't be a minute. It'll be all right. I'll call one of the neighbours.' Danny babbled helplessly as he pulled on his trousers and pushed his bare feet into his boots.

The firing began again and in a moment's relief between contractions Josie saw the pale frightened face beaded with sweat and thought, God love him having to go out in it. Then all fear and sympathy for her husband was wiped from her mind as the child began its descent into the birth canal. 'Get me mother quick and the doctors from the Rotunda.'

Danny went from the room and ran down the stairs, pausing only to knock on a door and shout that Josie's pains had started. Through alleys and back lanes he went, keeping his head down, hugging the walls. Several times he stumbled over things, bodies or booty discarded by the looters. He dared not look.

He reached his mother-in-law's, pounded on the door and shouted the news. From within, the woman urged him to hurry and to mind himself. Back in the street, he ran the last few yards to the hospital, left his message and walked out. Now the excitement and fear which had speeded his flight drained away and with it, his strength. He felt exhausted and leant against the hospital railings. After resting for a minute he searched his trouser pockets for his matches and a butt. He bent to strike the loose match against the granite base of the railing and only then noticed that his bootlaces were

212

undone. Jasus! he thought, I could have broken my effin' neck. He lit the butt and holding it between finger and thumb inhaled the gutter then bent and tied his laces, straightened and crossed the road.

From a rooftop a soldier saw the figure illuminated as a searchlight swept the street. The soldier raised his rifle. As Danny's foot in his tightly-laced boot mounted the kerb the bullet entered his brain. He fell face down, his hands thrown out as if to break his fall.

His son was born before the doctor and medical student arrived from the Rotunda, the grandmother and a neighbour doing what was needed, and wondering now and then what was keeping Danny.

When it was no longer possible to believe that he was only delayed Kevin and Jem O'Brien set out to look for him. The city was full of people on similar searches. 'Try the market,' a man advised Kevin and Jem. 'They're being brought in there in droves. But with the help of God, your brother won't be one of them.'

The army threw a cordon around the city. In a diminishing circle the troops moved towards their main target, the Post Office, the heart of the rebellion. Squeezing out, as they advanced, the rebel strongholds: machine gunning, shelling, showering hand-grenades on the positions. Soldiers stormed houses in the vicinity of the posts, seeking entrance, shooting anyone who got in their way.

From the Shelbourne Hotel an onslaught was launched on St Stephen's Green. The ducks sought refuge on their little islands. The dead were left behind. In the Post Office the situation was evaluated. There now seemed no hope of anyone coming to the Volunteers' aid. Perhaps there never had been. But they still had fight in them. There were wounded in the building, though so far no one inside had been killed. News of the men who had lost their lives in other actions reached

213

them. They had made the sacrifice, done what was expected of them. But no one had anticipated the number of civilian dead. That was hard to accept. That hadn't figured in their plans for an Independent Ireland. It weighed on their conscience, making the strain harder to bear.

Jem and Kevin took the man's advice and went to the market. A place where in normal times black-shawled dealers sold secondhand clothes spread out on tables and in heaps on the floor, today the scene was different. There were no shawled women, no cheeky bargaining. No holding up of trousers for inspection, nor ribald comments about knickers and flannel drawers. Only men and women apprehensively bending over bodies laid out on the floor and demented cries as they identified their dead. Among the genuine seekers moved the ghouls – like vultures, they strained their necks, devouring with their eyes.

Beside one body a young girl tried to comfort an older woman. The woman's agonized voice cried out: 'Jesus, it's my son! It's Paddy. Holy Mother of Jesus have mercy on his soul. Look at my child. Look at what they've done to him.'

'For God's sake, Mother, come out of here,' the girl entreated. After the first glance she had averted her eyes from the body. 'Come on out, sure that's not our Paddy.' The woman stood heedless of her pleas. She held in her hand a foot of the body encased in a shabby boot, her fingers caressing a small leather patch, new and shiny against the worn surface of the boot. 'Yesterday,' she said, 'I gave him ninepence to pay for that. That's where his boots always went, even when he was a child. Oh my child,' she cried, 'my little child.'

Jem followed Kevin from corpse to corpse, forcing himself forward, compelling himself to look. Trying to ignore the unfamiliar sweet and sickly odour mingling with the smell of overripe fruit from the adjoining market. Jem saw Danny first and drew Kevin's attention. 'Oh Mother of Jasus, it's him!'

214

Kevin went forward. Afraid to go any nearer, afraid to look at Danny, Jem hesitated. Kevin was kneeling by his brother, smoothing back the matted bloody hair.

'The bastards! The fuckin' murderin' bastards.' Jem moved and knelt beside him and put an arm around him. Beneath it he felt Kevin's shoulders heaving. He didn't know what to say. He stayed kneeling until Kevin's crying and swearing stopped. 'We'll have to get him home,' Kevin said, wiping his sleeve across his face.

'I'll ask the fella on the door.' Jem stood up. 'You'll want an undertaker. His head'll have to be fixed. You wouldn't want Josie or your mother to see him like that.'

Josie screamed and screamed. Her mother slapped her face. 'Stop it this minute, do you hear! You've a child to feed. You'll send your milk astray.'

'Oh Mother, Mother I sent him out to his death! Oh Mother, I loved him. I'll never see him again.'

'My poor child.' Her mother held her. 'Cry now all you like.' She rocked her in her arms. 'Cry love, only don't scream any more, sure you won't.'

Danny's mother sat holding the baby, now and then touching his cheek, wiping away her tears that fell on it.

On Thursday afternoon Dolly and Bid again went into town to see the desolation. This time they went no further than the middle of Westmoreland Street, for at its junction with Dolier Street a machine gun was mounted on top of a tobacconist's and bullets were falling like hail into Sackville Street. They watched for a while. Then someone shouted that it was all up with them in the College of Surgeons – it was surrounded. 'Let's go up and see what's happening! The Countess is in there – we might see her.'

'You and the Countess!' Bid said, laughing at Dolly. 'You're mad about the gentry – but all right, we'll go.'

215

Word of the imminent surrender at the College spread. 'Eh, did you hear the latest, they're givin' in at the College of Surgeons.' People headed off in that direction. Dolly and Bid hurried up Grafton Street. In the narrow streets lined with tenement houses close to the College, women sat on the steps giving suck. Around them children in torn frocks and ganseys, without boots or shoes, played. 'What's up?' the women shouted to people running down the streets. 'They're givin' in. The Countess is surrendering,' came back the answer. Babies screamed as nipples were wrenched from their mouths, and blue-tinged milk ran down their chins. Breasts were thrust inside pinnies and blouses as the mothers and children and their husbands who had been propping up the corner joined the throng running to where the College of Surgeons stood.

Facing the College the plane trees outside St Stephen's Green waved their catkin heads inviting the wind to carry away their pollen. Inside the Green, on lawns and flowerbeds blood spilled in yesterday's battle had already been absorbed by the hungry earth. The ducks had left their islands, and paddled up to the pond's edge, quacking expectantly. The man meant to feed them hadn't turned up. As if to show their annoyance the ducks dipped their heads and displayed their bottoms before swimming back to their reed-covered sanctuary.

Bid and Dolly stood jammed in the mass gathered at the corner of York Street watching the side entrance of the College. 'The military beat the shite outta them in the Green yesterday. Them and their Rebellion! They're holed up in there now. And that feckin' wan worse than any man. But she's finished now, I'm telling you.'

Dolly listened to the comments of the bystander – they weren't worth answering. Defeated or not, the Countess would bow to no one.

'There she is! Will you look at her,' someone shouted. All eyes focused on the door. 'Look at her hat! Be Jasus she's more plumes on that than an ostrich has on its arse. The dirty strap – wearing a man's breeches. Eh, empty fork, give us a lend of your trousers.'

Dolly stared awestruck at the Countess in her plumed hat, green jacket with orange flashes and men's trousers. She marvelled at her assurance, her apparent unawareness of the heckling crowd, the armed soldiers. How high she held her head. How cutting, the look she gave to the English officer.

The officer was pointing to a waiting car. The Countess was obviously refusing to be driven into captivity. The crowd became silent, watching. Then, with an exasperated shrug, the officer stood back. The Countess smiled at her victory, removed from its holster her revolver, raised it to her lips and kissed it reverently before handing it over. Then the men who had fought under her fell in behind, and she marched them away.

Dolly stared after the column. 'That's breeding for you. She bowed to no one.'

'A feckin' lunatic if you ask me,' Bid said. 'If I had all that wan has I'd find better things to do with my time than dressing up like a lump of a jack and kissing guns.'

'Still and all you have to admire her. Imagine being like that. Imagine being a woman like that.'

It had been a queer week one way and another, Dolly thought after leaving Bid and beginning her journey home. With no work it was like being on your holidays and yet it wasn't, because there was nothing to do in the evenings. The evenings were terrible long. Jem mightn't be the best company in the world but he was better than nothing. This was the longest she had ever gone without seeing him. Easter Sunday was the last time and today was Thursday.

I hope to God he didn't hear me laughing in the parlour. But anyway it was his own fault, he should have come sooner. She'd have to stick to the story about being out; persuade him down at the hooley tomorrow night. It was just as well Bid wouldn't be there. She might burst out laughing and let the cat out of the bag. Bid was always laughing and jeering – like earlier on, making a jeer of the Countess.

She began to think about the Countess. Imagine being someone like that. Not that I'd like to be that tall. Fellas didn't like tall women, not really. And if you couldn't afford the right things to wear you'd be an awful eyesore. Not of course that the Countess cared what anyone thought of her; the quality didn't. She was supposed to have a beautiful place in the west, and went backwards and forwards to London to balls and everything – and did hunting. And she had a cottage up in the mountains, somewhere up there. She raised her eyes and looked at them, clearly visible as they were from many parts of the city. Her mind moving away from the Countess, Dolly thought instead of the first week in August, when she was going to a holiday home in the mountains run by Jacobs.

It was supposed to be a grand place, so someone had told her. Still, it would be strange sleeping away from home. Them fellas in the Post Office were a long time out of their own beds – they must be finding that strange too. And the women holed up with them as well. They must be mad. You wouldn't be able to understand them at all. And the same with Jacobs, there were women in there as well and the place closed until further notice. Even if the trouble only lasted a week it would take another before it was ready to be worked in again. Though there was more to worry about than the loss of two weeks' work. The Countess could lose her life now that she had been arrested. Worrying wouldn't alter the outcome of that, either. And she had other things to be thinking about. Like what to sing at the hooley and how she'd give Jem O'Brien such a telling off that he wouldn't make a fool of her again in a hurry.

*

218

That night, Danny's body was brought home and waked in a closet off the main room which had once been a butler's pantry. Josie, propped in the bed, nursed the baby and received the visitors and their sympathy. She broke down completely at the sight of Jem, holding his hand, her tears falling on it while she sobbed her gratitude for all he had done to assist her in her affliction. Making him go red in the face and not know which way to look. A constant stream of friends and neighbours came, some staying all night. Towards morning, when those who had watched with the family were preparing to leave, a shell fell not far from the house. The centuries-old foundation shuddered, the worm-eaten floors trembled and the candles tottered and tipped, igniting the coffin's stiff white shiny lining. The smell of burning filled the room. The neighbours doused the flames with water and stout, even using the Holy water from the little dish beside the coffin.

'Thank God anyway,' an old woman said as she bent over Danny and blew at a charred fragment which had settled on his face. 'Thank God he didn't feel a thing,' and she blew again at a stubborn blackened flake lodged in the white cocoon of wadding encasing his head.

'The week has flown – Friday tomorrow,' Alice said when she and Stephen went to bed. 'Soon you'll be gone.'

He reached for her and began to kiss and caress her. She responded eagerly, then passionately. Stephen moved away, his mouth, his hands becoming still. 'I'm sorry about all the other nights,' he said.

'Don't talk,' Alice whispered. 'I love you. Kiss me again.' She brought his face back to hers until their lips met and his hands began again their exploration. 'I love you, I love you,' she repeated as he lay on her. And she waited and nothing happened. And she became aware of his weight – suddenly it was suffocatingly heavy and her thighs ached. Then he said he was sorry and rolled off. She wanted to scream and shout

219

and hurt him. Instead she cried quietly. If Stephen heard the crying he ignored it and when she stopped, he said he would sleep again in the dressing room so as not to disturb her.

'Oh don't, please. I want you to stay. We'll go to sleep and maybe we'll waken and everything will be all right. If you go what will Bridey think? And she'll tell the other servants. And I'll feel them looking at me and pitying me because my husband doesn't love me.'

'That isn't true. I do love you. Only I'm still feeling rotten. You can mention that to Bridey. If you'll be patient with me for a little longer it will work out.'

Alice felt sorry for him and said so and that she would be patient. She kissed him on the cheek. He got out of bed and arranged the covers around her and said 'Good-night.' When he was gone she cried again and thought how there were only two nights left of his leave and she prayed that he would be well enough for them to have a proper honeymoon before he went.

Chapter Ten

No one had come to their assistance. No German troops had landed. The people of Dublin hadn't risen to support them. Only in a few rural areas had the fight been taken up and quickly suppressed. Now the Post Office was hemmed in. North and south of the Liffey, in the streets behind it, on strategic points overlooking it, troops with machine guns and field guns started firing. Shells whined, whistled and exploded, bullets spattered ceaselessly.

All over the city the din was heard. Dolly getting ready for the hooley complained that it gave her a headache. Bessie said prayers for the men being attacked. 'Bad cess to them and their rebellion,' Mrs Dempsey muttered to herself as she put the finishing touches to her buffet supper. To have all that shooting today of all days and she giving the hooley for Jack to celebrate him being home from the Front. And, as he said himself, with his poor face like chalk and him shaking as if he had a rigour, it was like being back in France.

She had given him a good sup of whiskey and hot water. With the help of God he would sleep for an hour if the noise let him and be grand for the party.

In the Post Office James Connolly, now wounded and the wound gone septic so that he had a fever, considered the situation. No matter how bravely they fought it was only a matter of time, hours maybe, until the volunteers would have to abandon the Post Office. So far the shells had fallen short, the surrounding, protruding buildings spoiling the gunners' line of sight. But they'd soon overcome that – blow them up or set fire to them. One way or the other they'd be demolished – and what then? There was still a chance, maybe. If they had to evacuate they'd go into Moore Street and the streets leading off it, and continue with the fight.

As the afternoon wore on Mrs Dempsey continued talking to herself. Martial law or no martial law I wasn't putting off the bit of a night. For after all it wasn't every day of the week your only son came back from France safe and sound except for his arm. And wasn't that a blessing in disguise? She had asked God to send him home. He'd heard and answered her. There was no fear of the army wanting Jackie back with only one arm. She'd make an act of thanksgiving to Our Lady of Good Counsel who had interceded for her.

She hoped everyone would turn up. With the bloody oul curfew they mightn't want to risk it. Though she'd got word to them that they were to come early and stay the night. She took a last look at the supper, plates of sandwiches and sweet cake, three dozen of stout lined up on the chiffonier and minerals for the girls. And now she had better rouse Jackie, for if they were coming they'd begin to arrive any minute. Jackie looked better she thought, though now and then the sound of exploding shells made his face twitch.

'Someone's arrived anyway,' she said delightedly when the first knock came on the hall door and she ran downstairs to open it.

'Good, it's yourself,' she greeted Jem. 'I'm glad you're the first to come. He's a bit down in the mouth with all the shooting and that. Maybe you can cheer him up.'

Jesus, the change in him, Jem thought as he entered the room and saw Jackie. His eyes went to the empty sleeve pinned across Jackie's chest. Quickly, he averted them and

222

walked towards the chair. He's got very fat, blown-out looking and his face is the colour of a candle. It's all the weeks he was in the hospital, I suppose. He wasn't a bit like the Jackie he remembered – thin and wiry, always a bit sunburned-looking from working in the open air. Even his eyes looked half-dead. 'You're looking great,' he lied, the lump in his throat hurting. Jackie held out his hand and Jem enclosed it in both of his. He wanted to take him in his arms, comfort him, tell him it would be all right. Instead he said again, 'You're looking great, honest to God.'

'You're not looking bad yourself. How's Dolly keeping? I used to think about the two of you when I was over there. I thought you might have been married by now.'

'The divil a fear of that Jack – you know me. Dolly's gameball, she's coming later on. You heard about Danny?'

'Lord have mercy on him. It's hard to believe. Poor Danny at home in Dublin. There's no minding things like that in France – but here in Dublin!'

'Aye, well,' Jem said, becoming conscious of his hands, they felt clumsy and awkward. He withdrew them from Jackie and put them in his pocket.

Mrs Dempsey was running up and down the stairs letting people in. The room was filling up and young men crowded around Jackie, asking how he was, telling him how well he looked. Mrs Dempsey, in between trips to the hall door, joined them and said, 'I'm sure you must all be parched with the thirst. Jem, would you ever do me a favour and open the drinks?'

And Jem, glad of an excuse to leave Jackie, for he didn't know what else to say to him, hurried to do her bidding. For what *could* you say to him, he asked himself as he pulled corks and opened lemonade. What can I talk to him about? What used I to talk to him about – mots, handball, pitch and toss, work. Ask him how he's fixed for a start? God help him, who'd give him a start – a labourer with one arm! He paused in his bottle opening and looked at the press on the wall where before the war Jackie had kept his melodeon. He was good on the melodeon. Jem wondered if it was still there or had Mrs Dempsey got rid of it.

He poured a bottle of stout for himself and took a long drink, telling himself that unless he got drunk he might as well go home. He was a great addition to anyone's party! Fitter for him to have gone again to Danny's wake. For with the image of the dead Lancer and the things he had seen in the market he was not company for any celebration. Not that he supposed Jackie was in humour to celebrate, either. But his poor oul wan thought she was doing the right thing and into the bargain believed *he* could put heart into her son!

Jem finished opening the drinks and called that the bar was open. A group of acquaintances and friends came to the table, reaching for the drinks, telling him he'd make a great grocer's porter. Clapping him on the back, asking where was Dolly? Saying how sorry they were about Danny and how they'd go over to see him on Saturday or Sunday. Lowering their voices to comment on how bad Jackie looked and how they thought the poor bugger was finished.

Jem only half-listened; his mind was still preoccupied with all he had seen since Easter Monday. Before that, he had never given much thought to death. It was something that happened to old people, or them in decline that had been wasting for years. But dying in the whole of your health – that was terrible. He wondered if Kevin felt the same and wanted to ask him. But you never knew with Kevin. Even if he felt anything he'd never admit it. Dolly was the only one who would have understood him. Only she wasn't in when he needed to talk to her. Or if she was, he thought remembering the laughter, she wouldn't see him.

Snatches of the conversation going on around him drifted into his hearing.

'Did you hear about the fella in Capel Street?'

'No, what was that?'

'Well, this oul fella was out after curfew, on his way to a wake, when up comes an army lorry and out jumps a sergeant and two soldiers and shoves your man up against a wall. The aunt was telling me. She saw the whole thing from the window. She said you could see the oul fella was dropping. And what do you think happened?'

'They took him to the wake,' a voice replied cynically.

'How did you know that?' the first speaker asked incredulously.

'Ah – for Jasus' sake get sense, will you! That one has hair on it. There's more oul fellas going to wakes in army lorries than barrels in Guinness',' the cynic said.

Then someone else spoke in a voice full of admiration for the Volunteers, 'All the same, you have to hand it to our fellas. Look at the fight they put up today in the Four Courts. Look at the odds they were up against.'

The man who had dismissed the curfew story spoke again. 'A lot of lousers – that's what they are. Playing soldiers – destroying the city. And hand in glove with the Germans. Playing soldiers – that's what they're doing. Ask him over there, ask Jackie what he thinks of them – he's seen the real thing. Ask him about Roger Casement going round the prisoner of war camps in Germany trying to drum up support for the Volunteers – wanting Irishmen to become traitors.'

'Traitors! What the shaggin' hell are you talking about? Traitors to who? Sure they shouldn't have been in the British Army in the first place.' Voices were raised, became angry.

Mrs Dempsey hurried over, her pleasant face looking worried. 'Ah, now boys, let's have no disagreements. Sure it's not worth it. Not tonight, you'll spoil it for Jackie.' Then, taking Jem aside she appealed to him, 'See if you can smooth things over, there could be murder in a minute. And when you've succeeded run down to the hall door and see if there's any sign of Dolly. She's terrible late.'

225

Jem had a word with the men and they lowered their voices. He put down his drink and was about to go and look for Dolly when the door opened and she was coming into the room, her presence lighting it as if someone had lit an extra lamp. How lovely she looks, Jem thought as he watched her greeting Jackie. Bending to kiss the side of his face, never glancing to where his arm should have been, making him smile, look at her with pleasure.

Dolly's eyes in the moment she had entered the room flicked around quickly and saw Jem. Just as quickly she averted them, took longer than was necessary greeting Jackie, then saying 'Hello' to this one and that, determined that he should come to her. And he did, pushing through the groups of people, believing that Dolly hadn't seen him. 'Dolly,' he said, moving close, touching her arm, 'I was worried about you. I was just going down to see if you were coming when you walked in the door.'

'Like you were on Monday when you left me standing like an eejit outside Noblett's. You must have been awful worried!' She shrugged off his arm and continued to berate him. Not wanting him to have the opportunity to accuse her of being in the parlour on Tuesday and laughing at him. 'Awful worried you were. I could have been dead and buried for all you knew. Not sight nor sound of you since Easter Sunday.'

'But I came up on Tuesday. I gave your mother a message,' Jem protested.

'What message? I don't know what you're talking about – I got no message,' Dolly lied, knowing that Jem would never question her mother. And if she convinced him she never got a message – he couldn't accuse her of being in.

'She must have forgot. But I did come, honest to God. Ask your mother, she'll tell you.'

'Well, she mentioned no message. So what happened on Monday? Go on, tell me, I'm waiting for an explanation and an apology.'

Jem began to make excuses. Explaining how impossible it had been to get into town. 'There was a fella got shot and . . .'

'What fella? Do I know him?'

'I don't know who he was, a soldier, a Lancer.'

'That had nothing to do with you. The Lancers were shot by the Pillar.'

'This was in Church Street, another thing altogether.'

'How was I to know where it was? The Lord have mercy on him anyway,' Dolly said and thought that by now she must have convinced Jem of her annoyance. His mind would be taken off her and Bid laughing at him when he came to the house. He'd be so eager to please her there'd be no mention of that, even if he had heard. So for the first time since coming into the room she smiled at him and linked her arm through his. They moved to where it wasn't so crowded and he told her about Danny.

'Oh God no! Not poor little Danny. I can't believe it. Not poor little Danny McEvoy!' She was genuinely upset and began to cry. 'And there was me giving out to you. I wouldn't have said a word if I'd known. Fancy me not hearing. I'm sorry, you must have gone through a lot.'

Jem put an arm around her and drew her close. 'Don't cry, Dolly. Don't be upsetting yourself, he didn't suffer. Here, let me wipe your eyes.'

She let him dab gently at each eye. 'Keep the hankie,' he said, and thought how kind she really was, how beneath all her contrary ways she was soft-hearted. He'd never make her cry nor do anything to break her spirit. When she had stopped crying he brought her back to the main part of the room and got her a bottle of mineral.

Mrs Dempsey passed around the plates of ham sandwiches and sweet cake and cups of tea then announced that when everyone was finished eating, her niece Becky would play the piano and the night could get going. And when Becky, a plain-faced girl was seated at the piano, Dolly said, 'It's no wonder she never gets a fella, sitting all night with her back to the room.'

'How else can she sit if she's playing?' Jem asked.

'You – you never know how to take a joke. That's half your trouble – you're too serious.'

'It seems to have gone quieter, listen,' Bessie said. She was in bed waiting for Liam to get in.

'Yes, it has.' He went to go to the window.

'Don't,' Bessie said, 'you could be shot. There's a lot of people been shot like that, being near the window. Come to bed . . . It must be nearly finished now. I hope so. At least it'll put an end to the killing,' she went on when Liam was lying beside her.

'Don't be too sure about that.'

'What do you mean?' she asked.

'Well, you don't think the British are going to let them just walk out of the Post Office and go about their business.'

'I don't suppose so. They'll go into gaol maybe for a bit.'

'I wonder!'

'Oh now – don't start putting morbid thoughts into my mind otherwise I'll be awake all night thinking things and you snoring your brains away. I won't think about it. I'll pray for them and then I'll think about pleasant things. About how lucky we were to get off so lightly. Sure you'd never know there was a disturbance here at all – the place looks as good as new.'

Liam was already asleep. Bessie tried blocking unpleasant thoughts from her mind. But nevertheless they came. What would happen when the fighting was over? How were the poor fellas feeling, knowing that at any minute they'd have to surrender. Not that they had anything to be ashamed of. A handful of them to hold the British Army at bay for nearly a week. Indeed they could be proud.

*

228

'To Stephen.' Sir Arthur proposed a toast. 'To Stephen,' the dinner guests replied. Lady Delahunt looked at Alice. The poor child didn't appear well. But then of course her husband was leaving the following day. The war was such a strain on young people, all the comings and goings. It was a pity their honeymoon plans had had to be changed. But on his next leave they could have a second one in Connemara, even further afield. Perhaps the war would finish soon. One always had to look to the bright side.

Sir Arthur was proposing another toast to the gallant men who in less than a week had squashed the Rebellion. Afterwards, he talked to the guest sitting next to him, telling him it was all over bar the shouting. Incendiary bombs had set the Post Office ablaze. They'd be out of there in no time. And when they were he hoped there'd be no shilly-shallying by the authorities. The Sinn Feiners had to be made an example of. This sort of thing must never be allowed to happen again.

Becky began to play *Alexander's Ragtime Band*. And one of the men standing near by asked, 'You don't mind, do you Jem? I know you're not a dancing man.'

'He can't put a foot under him,' Dolly said and went into the man's arms.

Jem watched them dancing. He saw Dolly's eyes darting this way and that seeking admirers, and her lips moving as she talked animatedly, making her partner believe he was the only man in the room. And he found himself thinking that she wasn't really kind or soft-hearted. Maybe she didn't realize it, but she was cruel. At least to him. She didn't have to say that about him not being able to put a foot under him, not the way she did with a smile on her face. She was definitely cruel.

The one-step finished, the couples drew apart. Dolly's partner made a mock bow towards her, then moved close again and whispered something. Dolly laughed. The pianist began to play the *Gold and Silver Waltz*. Jem looked hopefully in

229

Dolly's direction – he could waltz a little. Then his heart sank as she held out her arms and waltzed away with the other man. He watched her looking up into the man's face, following his steps, never putting a foot wrong, reversing expertly and clapping enthusiastically when the music stopped.

Jem was filled with a raging jealousy towards the man who now held one of Dolly's hands, swinging it backwards and forwards, talking to her, making her laugh. Then he reasoned with himself that the man wasn't to blame. It was all Dolly's fault, for wasn't she leading him on? She was full of herself. Look at her now. Patting her hair that was perfect, smoothing and stroking the silk of her skirt, the stuff of her blouse, drawing attention to herself. He let his mind dwell on her faults. She was full of affectation. In a minute she'll be up there singing, but not until she's been coaxed and coaxed. Pretending she has a cold, that her throat is bad, that she couldn't possibly sing tonight. And all the time she was only waiting for the opportunity and would have swallied two raw eggs before putting her foot outside the door to make sure her voice was right.

The music began again and Dolly waltzing past, smiled at Jem. He felt his heart melt with love for her. I don't mean one of those things I've been thinking. It's only because I love you so much. I want you for myself. I don't want anyone else to lay a finger on you. I don't want you to sing for them. If you were mine I'd ask for nothing else on earth. If I could lay down beside you at night and know that when I opened my eyes in the morning you'd be there I'd be the happiest man God ever created.

After three more waltzes, Becky closed the piano and everybody clapped and said, 'More, more.' Dolly came back to Jem and began talking as if she had never left his side. The girls went in and out of the bedroom where Mrs Dempsey had arranged a convenience for them and the men went down to the yard to relieve themselves. Jem drank another bottle of stout, and Dolly said he was drinking an awful lot.

When everyone was back again in the room Mrs Dempsey

230

called for Dolly to sing. Other voices joined in, urging her to do so. Dolly made the excuses Jem had foreseen. Someone then called for a bit of encouragement and everyone clapped and shouted, 'Come on now, Dolly, don't disappoint us. Give us *For All Eternity*.' And Mrs Dempsey requested the best of order.

Jem joined in the clapping and exhortations and felt proud that Dolly was his girl. When there had been sufficient applause and cajoling Dolly, still clearing her throat, went to the piano and waited for Becky to give her a note. Then she sang, her voice filling the room with a sweet sadness. She sang, conscious that every eye in the room watched her, that there wasn't a sound except her voice. Her hands were stretched in front of her, palm upwards. Carefully she enunciated each word for she was proud of her diction. She finished and waited for the applause, afterwards saying, 'Sure, I wasn't very good tonight, I've a bit of a cold.' Her ears strained to catch the praises.

'What a voice! Did you ever hear the likes and what pronunciation. That girl is wasted in Jacobs. That voice should be trained.' Dolly's night was made.

In the Post Office, fires roared like beasts about to devour their prey. Tongues lividly red, were licking. With water buckets passed along a chain of hands the Volunteers sought to appease and curb their appetites. Blinded by smoke and fumes, coughing and choking, deafened by the roaring flames and falling masonry the Volunteers kept up their efforts, urged on by James Connolly who was more sick than on the previous day. The insatiable fire kept on devouring, its tongues licking the roof, melting, dissolving and eventually dislodging it in parts. It was out of control. Orders were given to evacuate. The wounded would be moved first. Connolly, it was suggested, should be moved with them, for he desperately needed treatment. He refused. He was staying with the men he had led out on Easter Monday until the last.

Tunnels to shops in Henry Street existed. Through them, the wounded would be moved to shops, until it was possible to get them to hospital. With them would go the women in attendance. The British soldiers held prisoner in the basements were remembered and released. The ammunition was shifted to a safer place. And now they must all abandon the Post Office, attempt to get through Moore Street and establish an HQ in Williams and Woods factory in Great Britain Street. The first party made a run for it. The army was waiting: the Volunteers were mown down. Those who escaped being killed or wounded went into the warren of narrow lanes, into shops and houses, there to carry on the fight. James Connolly was moved from the Post Office by stretcher, a young Volunteer shielding his leader's body with his own.

By the time it was dark only the carcass of the Post Office remained. All else had been consumed, including the staff and flag which had flown so triumphantly from it on Easter Monday morning.

When the stout and minerals ran out Mrs Dempsey made pots of strong tea and served thick cuts of bread and butter. 'Eat it,' she said, 'it will soak up the drink.' Other singers were called, there was more dancing and games of Spin the Bottle. And blushing, laughing girls protesting that they didn't want to, went to the landing with the lucky man at whom the bottle was pointed. Jackie wasn't left on his own for a minute and his mother was delighted that the evening was such a success.

The young men and women were all paired off, all except Becky who, true to Dolly's prophecy, hadn't got a fella and who, as daylight dawned, busied herself tidying the sheet music. The girls were sleepy and languorously laid tossed heads on their partners' shoulders. Jem sat with an arm around Dolly longing for morning when, if only for a while, he could be alone with her. Jackie's nonexistent fingers throbbed and he craved for sleep.

'Give it another half hour to be on the safe side,' Mrs Dempsey said when the couples showed signs of wanting to leave. 'Sure, what's your hurry?'

When the hour of curfew was safely past they drifted away calling back as they went, 'Thanks very much for a lovely night. God bless and safe home. Good-night Jackie, I'll say a prayer for you.'

Dolly and Jem walked along the narrow, clay-coloured towpath by the side of the canal. On either side of the path grew long rank grass, stinging nettles and wild flowers. The water was glassy green and down by its edges a small animal returning to its burrow made a scurrying sound. Birds were already singing and their nestlings chirruped for food. The morning smelt new and fresh.

From under the next bridge a thin grey horse emerged, plodding wearily. From its neck a taut rope stretched back into the distance. Dolly and Jem looked across the water at the patiently plodding horse and then at the long narrow canal boat sliding into view. From the direction of the city came the crack of rifle fire and Jem was reminded of Easter Monday. His arm tightened around Dolly's waist, his fingers making circling motions on the firm warm flesh he felt beneath the satin of her skirt. The boatman saluted them as the barge went by. They climbed up the bank and with arms entwined sauntered down the street towards Dolly's house.

Even at midday the hall in ninety-seven got little light and at this hour of the morning was very dark. 'Cough when you go in just in case there's anyone there,' Dolly said as they entered. Jem coughed. 'Not that loud, anyone would think you were dying,' Dolly whispered.

There were no other lovers in the hall and Dolly crept past her mother's room, Jem followed her into the far hall where they settled themselves against the cellar door. Somewhere high up in the house a child cried. Jem put his arms around

Dolly and kissed her. She closed her eyes and moved into him. All of a sudden she felt very affectionate towards him and while he kissed her she stroked his hair and fondled his ear. Her lips parted under his and his tongue went into her mouth. His hands moved down her back, clutching her buttocks, straining her to him. He slid a hand up over her hip, up to her breast, his palm enclosing it. His thumb found her nipple and gently circled it.

In the pit of her stomach there was a lovely warm feeling that spread, melting through her. The child high up in the house cried again and Dolly thought of purity and mortal sin. Jem's fingers continued to caress her breast, her heart raced and she felt warm all over. His fingers had shifted, were edging underneath the neck of her camisole. They were on her bare flesh. And she wanted him to go on touching, exploring, making the delightful sensation last. Then a voice in her head reminded her again of sin and pregnancy.

She struggled to break out of Jem's embrace. The more she struggled the tighter he held her, his mouth and teeth hurting her, pressing her against the wall, his knee forcing its way between her legs. The child's cry became piercing. There was a sound of footsteps and a door opening. Jem lifted his face and looked towards the stairs. Dolly seized the opportunity to wrench herself free. As she pushed him from her she heard the sound of tearing cloth and in disbelief stared down at the torn neck of her camisole. She raised her hand and brought it hard and flat across Jem's face. 'Get out,' she hissed. 'Get out before I call my father.'

She was hot and breathless, filled with a wild excitement, wanting Jem to take her in his arms again, yet afraid that he would. That if he did she would have no power to stop him, that she would ignore the voice of her guardian angel and let Jem do what he wanted.

Jem stood fingering his face. 'I'm awful sorry, Dolly. Honest to God I'm terrible sorry.' He reached out to touch her.

234

'Don't you lay a finger on me. The cheek of you! Get out and don't ever darken this door again,' she said, pretending more indignation than she felt.

She pushed past him, clutching her jacket over the torn bodice and praying, 'Please God, don't let my mother wake up and come into the room. Don't let her see me like this.'

She went very quietly into the room. It was dark except for the dim red glow of the lamp burning in front of the Sacred Heart. Her bed-chair was pulled out from the wall, made up for her. She undressed, pushed the torn camisole down behind a press, then knelt and said her prayers.

In bed she thought about Jem. He must have gone out of his mind. She had warned him about the stout – he wasn't used to drink. Still, that was no excuse for what he was trying on. What did he think she was? The nerve of him, no respect. Then she remembered how her breast had tingled and the lovely warm feeling in the pit of her stomach. It was the most gorgeous feeling. She tried to liken it to some other pleasurable experience. But could think of nothing at all, nothing at all that was like it.

She was warm and drowsy, the bed comfortable and the flickering lamp making patterns on the wall. She stared at them, willing her eyes to stay open. She didn't want to go to sleep. She wanted to think about getting married. It might be nice, after all. It wouldn't be a sin then. Every night lying in a high feather bed with frilled pillowcases and a starched valance and Jem holding her in his arms.

She'd have to remember not to struggle. The way he carried on when she did! He wasn't like the same man. Who'd have thought it of Jem O'Brien? Anyway, it wouldn't be a sin any more. She placed a hand on her breast, letting her fingers touch her nipple, remembering what Jem had done to it. Then, suddenly, as if the nipple was red-hot her fingers recoiled and quickly she joined her hands and whispered an aspiration for God to forgive her impurity.

Chapter Eleven

'Throw yourself down on the bed for an hour,' Jem's mother said when he came in. He had hoped she would be sleeping. He didn't feel like conversation. His mind was full of what had happened between him and Dolly. Half of it reliving the thrill of touching her bare flesh, the other half tormented with guilt and the need to go to Confession. What he had attempted was a mortal sin. If he was to die suddenly he'd go to Hell, and after the week that was in it, dying suddenly wasn't the distant possibility it once was.

'Well, if you don't lay down will I cook something for you?'

'No thanks,' Jem replied, hoping he wasn't letting his irritation show.

'You'll kill yourself not eating nor sleeping and me into the bargain sitting up all night worrying about you and listening to the shooting.'

'They're making a last stand in Moore Street.'

'A crowd of gougers destroying the city and the cause of killing innocent people! There's that many dead, twenty-one on Monday alone, that Danny's burial will be delayed. I went over again last night. Poor Josie is demented with grief. It wouldn't have done you any harm to have missed the hooley and put in an appearance.'

'I was there on Thursday.'

'All the same, they'll think bad of you. I noticed Kevin didn't go to any hooley.'

'For God's sake Mother, he's Danny's brother – you'd hardly expect him.'

'It's that Dolly wan, she has you for a doormat. You mark my words. A convenience, that's all she wants you for.'

Jem's patience was nearing its end. He had to go out or he'd have a row with his mother.

'Don't go far,' she called after him.

He walked around the block thinking about Dolly, Confession and priests. There was no lull in the sound of firing. It kept reminding him of what a slender hold one had on life. How urgent it was for him to confess and be once more in a State of Grace. He thought how easy it would be if all you had to do was confess to God without a priest as a go-between. Sometimes he wished he wasn't a Catholic. You were always afraid of Confession. Even years ago, making his first one. The nuns drilling it into you that if you deliberately held back a sin you'd be committing a sacrilege and Hell was the price of that. Yet after you'd plucked up the courage and admitted your sins and got Absolution you felt great. A new person. That's what the nuns said Grace did for you.

But all the same, if you were a Protestant your sins were between you and God. Only Protestants didn't go to Heaven. No one went to Heaven except Catholics. He wondered where they went. It was the sort of question you'd have to ask a priest. For how, with only the Catechism, could you figure anything out for yourself? But a priest would eat the face off of you for thinking such things, never mind asking them. And in any case you'd never have the chance to ask a priest anything. For apart from Mass or a Retreat you never saw them. Well – you'd see them at weddings and funerals and coming to anoint the dying, but that was it.

And you never felt comfortable with them. Not even when you were a child in school. He remembered the priest coming into the classroom. Everyone standing up and saying 'Good morning, Father.' Sometimes the priest would ask one or

237

other of the children their names. Once or twice he had asked his. And he was shaking with nerves when he answered.

Down the country it was different, so he'd been told. There, everyone knew the priest and he them. Though that mightn't make it easier to talk to them. You'd never know. In Dublin it was only with them that were head buck cats in the Sodalities – rich publicans and them that gave big donations, statues or brass plates for the chapel benches that the priest had much truck with. Still, he supposed, to be fair there were thousands of people in the Dublin poor Parishes, the priest couldn't get round them all.

Ah, what good was it moidering his brain when it was Confession he should be thinking of. How he'd answer the priest's probing questions once he mentioned trying it on with Dolly. 'And where exactly did you touch her? Was it above or below the waist? On her skin or through her clothes?' Kevin had told him the drill. Told him how once he was confessing to going too far with Bid the priest let out such a roar it could be heard all over the chapel.

Jem began to sweat at the prospect of what lay in front of him. Oh God, I wish I wasn't a Catholic. No, I didn't mean that, that's another sin. I wish it was last Sunday. Easter Sunday and me in a State of Grace. My mind easy, no thoughts of death and damnation. Only thinking of the outing to Howth. Only thinking about Dolly. God, she's gorgeous! Remembering the feel of her bare skin and the roundness of her breasts he felt weak with desire. He must stop thinking like that. That's all he'd done lately. And in the queerest places. Bad thoughts filling his mind. At Danny's wake, even in the market surrounded by dead bodies thinking bad thoughts. He had better get himself home, have a strip-wash in cold water and then head off for Confession.

Moore Street was cut off at either end. Relentlessly the troops strafed it. Anything that moved was fired at. The Volunteers

238

watched in horror as people attempted to leave the area. Saw one man and his family carrying a white flag mown down by bullets. They knew no quarter would be given to anyone while they continued to hold out. And they knew too that no amount of courage now could give them victory. Patrick Pearse decided that to prolong their fight would mean the death of more civilians and there had been too much slaughter already. They would surrender. Under white flags, messengers were dispatched to the British post. Some were shot but one, a woman, got through and returned with word that if the surrender was unconditional it would be accepted. The Easter Rebellion was over.

Jem dipped his fingers in the font of Holy water and blessed himself, wondering as he did so why the water always felt flat and tepid. He went into the dimness of the church, his eyes taking a minute to get accustomed to the light. He knew there was a new priest who had come to the parish a week ago. He looked towards his box and saw there was a big crowd waiting on the nearby benches. He must be an easy mark. He'd try him and hope to get off lightly. After genuflecting to the altar he made his way to the benches and joined the seated queue. As people went in and out of the small shuttered cubicles on either side of the confessional he shuffled along the bench on his knees.

He prepared for the Sacrament of Penance. Examining his conscience. It was a week since he had last confessed. How many sins had he committed since then? In his thoughts he had been impatient with his mother. Uncharitable about Dolly in his mind. Then there was the other thing! If it wasn't for that he could have gone the month – the other sins were only venial. An Act of Contrition would have wiped them out. But not that one. Which should he tell first? In his mind he rehearsed the order of telling – the serious one first.

He said the first half of the Confiteor, his head bowed.

239

When the prayer was finished he raised his head and saw that there were only two people in front of him now. Behind his joined hands his heart raced. He swallowed the lump in his throat and began to pray fervently. A hand touched him and a voice whispered, 'It's your turn.'

Quaking, he entered the narrow, dimly-lit cubicle, knelt on the wooden ledge before the grille and heard the murmur of voices – the priest's and the penitent in the other box. Above the grille, barely discernible, hung a crucifix. Raising his eyes to it Jem prayed, 'Sacred Heart of Jesus, help me to be truly sorry for my sins.'

The slide of the grille brought his gaze from the cross. Through the gauze wire he saw the priest's outline, his hand raised in blessing and heard the Latin intonation begin. He waited for it to finish then confessed.

'Bless me Father, for I have sinned. It's a week since my last Confession.' His sins came out in the wrong order. 'I was impatient with me mother. And I had uncharitable thoughts about someone else.' He stopped.

'Yes, my son. Is there anything else?' the priest asked.

'Well, Father I . . . do you see, there's this girl. I've been going with her this long time. I love her and want to get married. Only last night – like I – well I attempted . . .' He couldn't find the right words.

'I can't hear you. Speak up.'

'I tried to have my way with her, you know. I don't know what came over me, Father.'

'Am I to take it you didn't succeed?'

'No, Father. I got carried away for a minute, that's all.'

'And the girl – would you say now she's a forward sort of a girl?'

'Oh, no. Not at all,' Jem replied without hesitation.

'So it was all your fault?'

'Yes, Father, all my fault,' Jem admitted.

The priest said nothing for a while and Jem waited in

240

trepidation for what he was sure was coming. The questioning. The lacerating tongue-lashing. The picture painted of Hell. The walls began to close in on him. His palms sweated. Then the priest cleared his throat and spoke. 'Now you tell me you want to marry this girl, isn't that right?'

'It is, Father.'

'Have you asked her to marry you?'

'In a roundabout way. I've given many a hint that she never took up.'

'Well now, this is what you're to do. Go and see her. Apologize for the disrespect you've shown her. Remember the Mother of God – women are to be respected. Tell the girl out straight, no hints, plainspeaking, that you want to marry her. And if she refuses, tell her you won't see her again. If she agrees, make plans to be married as soon as you can. And while you're waiting to be married avoid being alone in secluded places. Otherwise you'll both be entering an occasion of sin. And you don't want to play into the hands of the Devil. Do you understand all that?'

'I do, Father.'

'And be patient with your mother who reared you. Have you anything else to tell? Sins from your past life that you've forgotten at other Confessions?'

Jem recited a litany of missed morning and night prayers, cursing and the stealing of a shilling from his mother's purse, and his impure thoughts. 'For these and all my sins I am sorry,' he concluded.

'For your penance say six Hail Marys, six Our Fathers and pray to the Blessed Virgin to keep you pure. Now make a good Act of Contrition.'

'Oh my God, I am heartily sorry for having offended Thee,' Jem prayed aloud while the priest spoke in Latin absolving his sins, then made the Sign of the Cross.

'In the name of the Father and of the Son and of the Holy Ghost, Amen. God bless you.'

Jem left the box as light as a bird; the burden of his sins was lifted, his soul spotless, his heart filled with eagerness and hope.

On the way home he met a man who told him the Rebellion was over, though De Valera was still holding out in Boland's Mill. But one way or the other it was finished. Jem wondered what would happen to them all, them that had been implicated. Prison for a year, or two maybe, for the leaders. But thank God anyway there'd be no more killing. Life could go back to what it was before. Well – for the majority, for poor Danny and the Lancer it was too late. Then he told himself not to be thinking such morbid things. Life was ahead of him and Dolly. They were lucky, the Rebellion hadn't affected them.

The crowds were back in the city, looking at the latest damage, poking amongst the ruins for anything valuable or worth keeping as a souvenir. And lining the routes along which the Volunteers were marched to prison, laughing and jeering as they passed by.

Dolly sat at home wondering when Jem would make his next move. She doubted if he would show up before Sunday after the way she had sent him packing. The cheek of him attempting that! It was the drink of course, he wasn't used to it. But still and all a fella had to show respect. She let herself remember the pleasure she had felt but when her mind dwelt too long on it, forced herself to think of something else. Engaging her father in conversation when she found the effort of controlling her thoughts difficult. Johnny, delighted of an audience, was only too pleased to answer her questions.

'I wonder what they'll do to them, Da? They wouldn't kill them, sure they wouldn't.'

Bridget coming into the room inquired who Dolly was

worried about being killed. 'The fellas in the Post Office and the others that were mixed up in it.'

'They might,' Johnny said. 'For the sake of example they might. The English are great believers in example.'

'God between us and all harm,' Bridget said and blessed herself, 'they couldn't do that.'

'And who is to stop them?' Johnny asked. 'Aren't they the law of the land?'

'I know, but all the same the people would be up in arms if they did the like of that.'

'They wouldn't shoot the Countess, surely?' Dolly said and all thoughts of the previous night fled from her mind as she contemplated the Countess being shot.

'Alanna, I'm only giving my opinion for what it's worth. Maybe they'll be wise and merciful. We'll know more about it when there's papers published again.'

'It was a sorry sight to see them being marched off to gaol,' Liam said when he came back from town. 'Do you know, there were people spitting on them. Calling them names. There was one oul fella I'd have throttled if I'd had my way.'

'What was he doing?' Bessie asked.

'Running up and down the path, out into the road, making punches at them, calling them bastards. *Cross-born bastards*. Shouting at them: "That you may swing for what you've done."'

'And if the truth was known he was probably one of the first in there when the looting began.'

'No doubt,' Liam said. 'The sort of gouger that runs with the hare and the hounds. I was delighted when a British soldier shoved him out of the way and threatened him with arrest if he didn't clear off.'

'How did they look, the Volunteers?'

'God help them, the best they could. Marching up straight, putting a brave face on it. Some of them were only boys. I

243

never gave them much thought before. But today I felt my heart go out to them. And I was thinking of all the others down the years who've risen, Irishmen, Protestants too, and I was wondering how powerfully they must have felt to risk their lives for what they believed in. It must be great all the same to believe in something as strongly as that.'

'Musha then, I'm not so sure,' Bessie said. 'A lot of consolation it would be to me that you had believed strongly in a cause if this minute you were in gaol. I'd never in a million years be convinced that a bit of land was worth dying or killing for.'

'Ah,' Liam said, 'it's more than owning a bit of land. It's about freedom. Being ruled by your own. Having a say in your affairs. I don't know – it's only lately I've given it much thought. In my head I'm trying to make sense of my feelings.'

'Your own mightn't be any better to live under.'

'They might not. But they'd be your own, that's the difference.'

'You've lost me now,' Bessie said, coming to him and putting an arm round him. 'It's the great thinker you're becoming. Sit over now for your tea.'

When they were at the table Liam said one thing was sure and certain – there'd be plenty of labouring to make good the damaged and destroyed buildings.

'That's the way of the world. Someone always benefits from another's misfortune. I hope to God the authorities won't be too severe on them,' Bessie replied.

By tomorrow she'll have cooled down, Jem thought as he lay in bed. I'll go up after dinner, buy a bag of sweets on the way if the shop has them, and I'll tell her how sorry I am. Please God she won't hold what happened against me. I'll promise to respect her from now on. He fell asleep.

In the morning he didn't feel well. His throat was sore. He told his mother who said, 'Is it any wonder and you out all

244

Friday night. Are you well enough for Mass?' Knowing he would have to be dying before his mother would encourage him to stay away, he said he was. During Mass he had pains running up the side of his neck and into his ear and had difficulty swallowing the Host.

'I only hope it's not quinsy you're getting. Here, let me feel your head. It's like a furnace,' his mother said, taking her hand from his forehead. 'You've got a dose now of a septic throat. I'll make you a salt gargle and warm a bit of St Blaize's flannel to wrap round your neck. If that doesn't work you'll be laid up for a fortnight.'

Jem lay down, hoping that an hour's sleep might right him and then he'd go to see Dolly. But when he woke he felt worse. His head and limbs were aching and his throat was so sore it hurt to swallow his spittle. He got up and the room spun round. With the best will he knew he'd never make it to Dolly's. He went back to bed telling himself that tomorrow he'd be better and go then.

Dolly sat at home fuming as hour after hour passed with no sign of Jem. 'What ails you?' Maggie asked when she came to the house. 'It's such a lovely day I thought you'd have been down the town seeing the sights.'

'Jem and I had a tiff after the hooley. I was expecting him today but he never came.'

'Oh!' Maggie said.

'What do you mean – oh?' Dolly said.

'Nothing, only that's twice now he's let you down. Maybe he's throwing his eye elsewhere.'

'He is not. Last week there was a good reason and . . .'

'All the same I'd watch him,' Maggie said, deliberately goading Dolly.

'I hate you sometimes,' Dolly said, her temper rising and almost making her cry.

245

'Stop it, the pair of you. Honest to God you're like two children,' Bridget said.

No more was said about Jem. Maggie told them she'd heard that the Volunteers had been kept out in the open all night.

'Go way,' Bridget said.

'Made to stand outside the Rotunda all night long.'

'How do you know that's true?' Johnny asked.

'Someone was telling me.'

'If it's true it's a disgrace. Keeping men standing in the open all night never solved anything. Cruelty, that's all it is. But sure there's no knowing what's fact and what isn't until the papers are out again. They should be tomorrow.'

The next day Johnny took a penny from Bridget's purse and went out for a paper.

'Look at that now,' he said when he returned, 'it's a combined issue for the last week.'

Abandoning his usual chair by the fire he made himself comfortable at the table and said he didn't want to be disturbed. Bridget made a face at Dolly and they smiled. Johnny smoothed the paper, put on his glasses and began the task of catching up with the week's news. 'There's your answer,' he said after turning a few pages. 'They've shot three of them.'

'Lord Jesus have mercy on their souls. Who were they?' Bridget asked.

'Pearse, Clarke and MacDonagh, God rest them.'

'MacDonagh was the one who took over Jacobs',' Dolly said, 'and the other one, Patrick Pearse, I saw him on Easter Monday. And he's dead, I can't believe it.'

'May God comfort their people,' Bridget said.

'There's little or nothing about the happenings during the week. Indeed, if you weren't a careful reader like myself you could miss what there is. A bit about the seizing of the Post Office, news of Roger Casement's arrest, food supplies getting back to normal, and Jacobs have an announcement that little damage was caused and they'll be reopening as soon as possible. All the rest is war news, lists of casualties, and advertisements.' He turned another page. 'Here's the numbers killed and wounded on Easter Monday – twenty-one dead and thirty-six injured.'

At a base camp in France, Richard read the English paper's version of the Rebellion. He hoped his family hadn't been injured, it might be days before he got word. With the GPO having been seized, mail from Ireland had been delayed. It was terrible to be so far from home and not know what was really going on. Poor Pearse, dead, Pearse the idealist. He remembered the times he had heard him speak. How the man had inspired him with a love for Ireland and what he had believed was a hatred for England. How moved he had been, how desperately he had longed to join the Volunteers and avenge the wrongs. And would have done if it hadn't been for his father. How easily he was swayed. How few principles he had really. Swayed by impassioned speeches to take up one cause and in no time to take up another. Never his own man, dancing to whatever tune was played. Guilt-ridden when the others in the office began to go, ashamed before Emily, considering his Civil pay, but mostly hoping to impress her. And all the time she had someone else. What a fool he must have appeared. No, that wasn't true, only in his own estimation would he appear a fool. Emily wouldn't have thought so of him. If only he had his time over again. He would have stood out against his father – he would have joined the Volunteers. For if he was sure of nothing else he had no doubt that if he were to die, he didn't want to die for England.

'You look like a cow holding a shilling trying to stitch on them stripes – give it here,' Dusty said. Robbie handed over his tunic with the partly-sewn sergeant's stripes dangling from more than eighteen inches of thread.

'Too bloody long that,' Dusty said, snapping the cotton

with his teeth, 'and them stripes is crooked. Give us your hussif.'

Robbie passed his cotton case of thread, needles and buttons across. From it Dusty took a pair of scissors and unpicked the crooked stripes, threaded a suitable length of cotton in the needle, aligned the chevrons and began stitching. Watching him sewing Robbie thought of the many kindnesses he had received from Dusty, how though his manner had changed since Lil's desertion his willingness to help had never altered. Morose and silent he might be but to anyone in a jam, be it from a clumsiness in stitching on stripes or suffering loss or pain, Dusty offered his help and inarticulate sympathy.

'Sorry about that mate,' he had said the day Robbie got the letter from the priest at home telling him his mother had died in her sleep six weeks after they had come back from Dublin. Dusty hadn't said anything else, just sat quietly listening while Robbie read out the remainder of the letter. His father, the priest wrote, had been told of his wife's death. His reaction was strange to say the least. After arranging with the priest to pay the funeral expenses he had refused to come to the funeral or to see his wife before she was buried. The priest believed he was in need of medical attention and suggested that Robbie should apply for Compassionate Leave. It wasn't humane to leave the old man living as he lived. He would, if Robbie so wished, write to his CO to add weight to the application. However, without Robbie's say-so he did not want to be involved in anything that would lead to his father being committed to an aslyum. If he could not come home for whatever reason he would have his father visited to ensure his wants were seen to, but he hoped to see him in Southwater before long.

'Sod him,' Robbie remembered saying at the time. 'Let him die alone in his hut, the old bastard, it's what he deserves. He didn't help her when she needed him.' He cried, thinking about his mother dying on her own, spending her nights

248

frightened and alone. And he was sorry for all the things he saw now as neglect of her. How he could have written more often, stayed in on his last night at home, worked harder at finding out what ailed her. Dusty had squeezed his shoulder and offered his cigarettes, had passed no judgement on his decision to let his father fend for himself, was just there.

Dusty held up the tunic on which one set of stripes was now in place. 'Have a dekko.'

'That's fine, straight as a die,' Robbie said, then asked, 'Do you believe in Hell, Dusty?'

'Don't think about it,' Dusty replied.

'I used to, now I'm not so sure. At least not the Hell they taught us about. Hell's not fire and roasting, it's here, the trenches and that out there. Mud and swamps, horses and men falling off the duckboards, sucked down and down. Their lungs filled with slime choking the life out of them. Jesus! How does anyone stay sane?'

'You get the fire and roasting as well,' Dusty said. 'And you'd better not let the Captain hear you rabbiting on like that – he'd bust you, not good for the men, that sort of thing, that's what he'd say.'

'I only talk like this to you. You know what I mean. You must feel the same, when you look at what used to be trees and see the bark scorched off those that are left. When you see their twisted shapes, the gaping holes in their trunks. And what were once fields with grass or crops growing now only greyness and churned mud, mud everywhere. Don't you see all that, Dusty?'

'I only look to see where I'm firing,' Dusty said, making double stitches at the end of his sewing, snipping the thread and patting the stripes flat. 'I keep my mind on what I'm doing and have to do. I don't think about nothing else.'

'Maybe you're right. And Hell or no Hell I suppose we've been lucky to survive this long.'

249

'Don't you go spitting in the wind,' Dusty warned, handing back the jacket.

'Thanks,' Robbie said and reminded by Dusty's superstition of another occasion asked, 'Do you remember that bloke – Ginger Daniels I think his name was? The first night he came up the line you had a go at him about the third light, remember? Well, I dreamed about him last night.'

'Cocky little bugger, he got gassed, didn't he?'

'That's him.'

'I never dream. He died, that bloke.'

'That's what I dreamed about. Funny how you remember some.'

The salt gargles, hot compresses and St Blaize's flannel proved of little use to Jem. To drink was painful and eating impossible. His temperature was high for days and part of the time he was delirious. Once when he woke from a fevered sleep there was a neighbour in the bedroom with his mother. 'I'd get the doctor if I was you,' he heard the woman say. 'God between us and all harm it could be diphtheria, they die with that.'

'Well, for your information it's not.'

'You're very positive. I only hope you're right.'

'I'm right. I've had plenty of experience of diphtheria – didn't I bury three children with it? There's a foul smell with it, a smell you wouldn't forget in a hurry and I'm getting no doctor.'

Jem listened, feeling too sick to care what ailed him, or whether he lived or died. He closed his eyes and fell asleep. When next he woke his mind was more lucid and his first thought was of Dolly and how he had hoped by this weekend to be well enough to go and see her. Knowing that he wouldn't be, he turned his head to the wall and cried.

Chapter Twelve

For her return to work Dolly chose a blouse and skirt she normally kept for best, but today she felt was a special occasion. She had washed her hair and given it a final rinse with vinegar so that this morning it was soft and glossy. She took a long time brushing and combing it and when she was sure that the parting was dead centre, plaited it into two coils which she placed carefully over each ear, securing them with pins. She was all set for her meeting with Jem and knew she looked her best.

As she walked through the narrow streets leading to the biscuit factory she thought about the last two weeks. How she hadn't seen Jem since the night of the hooley nor heard a word from him. If his mother didn't make it obvious how much she disliked her she would have gone over. But you'd never know what reception you'd get from that oul wan. One thing was certain, the reception she'd give him. She'd let on to be very cool. That fella needed teaching a lesson.

She turned into Bishop's Street at the end of which the factory loomed, its huge red-bricked buildings dwarfing the surrounding houses and church. Despite the two weeks' closure the air was still saturated with the smells of sweet cake, chocolate and biscuits. A smell that tantalized if you were hungry and nauseated if your stomach was out of order. The heat from the great ovens spilled into the narrow street, reminding Dolly of the discomfort inside. But, still, as she often said, Jacobs was a great place to work. Where else would you get a swimming pool, recreation hall, gymnasium and a wedding cake or the money instead when you got married. A great place, even if you were sacked on the spot for fecking a Marietta.

She reported to the time office, collected her check and climbed the stone stairs to the cloakroom. It was filled with girls and unmarried women wearing blue smocks, washing their hands, tucking stray wisps of hair beneath blue caps and heatedly talking about the executions.

'The curse of God on them! Taking out them poor unfortunates and shooting them one after the other.'

'You want to live where I do, up near Kilmainham and listen to it. My mother gets us all up, kneeling down saying the Rosary. And a fella was telling my father they're in an open grave, not a shovelful of earth to cover them.'

'It's not human, you'd cover a dog. Why would they do that?'

'To save time and money, though more likely out of cruelty. To make them waiting to be shot suffer more.'

Dolly changed into her white coat and related how she had seen the Countess surrender, and how she was praying that she wouldn't be executed.

'I wouldn't put it past them. The English are capable of anything.'

Dolly looked this way and that in the mirror, touched her cheeks with a powder leaf and bit her lips to make them rosy. There was no sign of Bid. Dolly hoped she was coming in, she might know something about Jem. She watched the door. Then at the last minute, just as the factory hooter sounded Bid arrived, her coat half-off and struggling into her smock on the way down the stairs.

'You killed yourself coming to see me,' Dolly said.

'So did you. Anyway, I didn't feel like going out. Isn't it terrible about all them fellas being shot. And there were we on Easter Monday making a laugh of them. Thinking it was all a

252

bit of gas. How did the hooley go?' They were down the stairs.

'I've got lots to tell you. I'll see you at dinner-time.' She went to her office and Bid to the bakehouse.

During the morning, Dolly was kept busy laying trays for the manager's coffee, answering the phone and conducting new applicants to and from the doctor. Directing the successful ones to the main office, consoling the ones who had failed on health grounds and keeping clear of the ones with dirty heads. A couple of times her business took her past the mixing loft but she saw no sign of Jem.

At dinner-time she told Bid about the hooley and that she hadn't seen Jem since. 'Have you?' she asked. 'Or has Kevin mentioned him?'

'That fella, I haven't laid eyes on him either.'

'Didn't you go to the wake?'

'I couldn't bring myself to. I couldn't face poor Josie. And didn't want Kevin to think I was running after him. But you should make inquiries about Jem, there must be something up.'

'And let everyone know he hasn't got in touch? I will not.'

'You and your pride, it'll be the killing of you. He could be at death's door.'

'You'd hear that soon enough. And anyway, look who's talking – you wouldn't go to the wake for that very reason.'

'It's not the same thing at all. Jem wouldn't think any the less of you for wanting to find out. Kevin would.'

'Well I won't, especially after what happened.' Dolly told Bid about the scene in the hall.

'Jem O'Brien, Jasus, he found out it wasn't for stirring his tea! Did you let him?'

'I did not! What do you think I am?'

'I'm only codding you. God though, isn't life queer all the same. There we were on Easter Monday setting out for a grand day, and I suppose everyone else was doing the same. The Volunteers thinking they were going to be heroes. Do you remember the way they looked? Proud and all that. Terrible all the same the way things change in a minute. And that oul fella, the one who kept on about the horse running in the Park, I wonder what happened to him? And the soldier . . . wasn't *he* gorgeous. He could have been killed and all.'

'You're very cheerful I must say,' Dolly said and hoped Bid was wrong. She might never lay eyes on the soldier again, but she hoped he wasn't dead. He was too beautiful to be dead. During the afternoon she thought about him, surprised that his face was still so clear in her mind after such a brief glimpse. Then she realized she had his face and the man she daydreamed about mixed up, not able now to know which was which.

She knew it was unlikely but still hoped that Jem might be outside waiting for her when it was time to go home. He wasn't and she went home in bad humour which was dispelled when she arrived and her mother told her there was word from Richard. 'Only a field card, but thank God anyway.' She took the card from the mantelpiece where it was propped against the clock. 'All the way from France, imagine!' She gave it to Dolly.

'Do you want me to read it out loud?'

'Of course I do. Your father read it to me this morning, but that was hours ago. Read it.'

'*Dear Ma and Da,*

Sorry for not writing sooner. It's not that you are far from my thoughts. I don't have much time. I'm well thank God, and hope you are, too. Give everyone my love and tell Dolly not to get too cushy in the bed. Thanks for the parcel. In the next one send some Harrison's pomade and a tin of Keatings' powder. I'll write again the minute I can.

Your loving son,
Richard'

254

'Just think,' Bridget said, taking the card from Dolly and holding it close to her eyes, peering at the unintelligible symbols, 'he held that and was all right then and anything could have happened to him since. But please God nothing has. And when I've put on the coddle I'll run up to Francis Street for the Carrolls cigarettes. He loves them, and I'll get a quarter of bull's eyes, they're his favourites. And first thing in the morning I'll do the parcel. God help him as if he hadn't enough to put up with without being ate alive with fleas and lice.'

'Shut up Mother, you're making me itchy,' Dolly said and scratched her head.

'Pity about you, hand me over that pot.' Dolly gave her the iron saucepan and watched her prepare the coddle. Trimming the fat from the bacon pieces, washing and coring a pig's kidney, cutting a few thick pork sausages from a hank, dicing an onion, putting everything in the pot, adding water and pepper. Telling Dolly she wouldn't salt it for the bacon pieces might be petred. She put it to simmer on the hob and soon the savoury smell of the coddle filled the room. Dolly felt hungry and her bad humour returned as she considered how long it was with no word from Jem.

'What will she think of me?' Jem wondered. If only he had written a line sooner, before he got too bad to post it himself. God forgive him, but he wouldn't trust his mother where Dolly was concerned. Or if Kevin had dropped in he could have sent word through Bid. Now it was too late for notes. Nothing would do but himself in person, an apology and explanation.

'Another week off work for you unless you want to go into rapid consumption,' his mother said. She was stall-feeding him. 'You need packing after that bout of starvation,' she'd say each time she forced food upon him.

Although the swellings in his neck and the sore throat were

255

better he had no appetite. But he knew he must eat to get back his strength for work on Monday. 'Fine friends and companions you have!' his mother said as she brought him calves' foot jelly. 'Not one of them darkened the door. And as for that young wan, I told you what she was. She must know you're sick. Someone in work would have told her.'

Bid had. 'Jem's very bad, a fella from the time office was telling me.'

'Paralysis in his hands, I suppose.'

'That's not funny.'

'It's not meant to be. He could have written. As far as I'm concerned he's finished. I want to know nothing about him. I wouldn't recognize him, not if he got on his bended knees.' She was angry, hurt and mystified. She didn't care what ailed him. And knew that if it wasn't for everyone being in a state about the executions that were still going on there'd be plenty of talk. No one had a mind for the usual tittle-tattle, being too concerned as to what would happen next. Would James Connolly be dragged out of the Castle hospital and be shot too? Would the Countess be reprieved? And a lot of them were terrified for friends and relations amongst the thousands being arrested and sent to English prisons.

'I've never seen you cry before. Don't, Nella.'

'It's vile, it's terrible! Oh God, I'm ashamed. I didn't think they'd do it. Not take a man out of hospital, carry him on a stretcher and prop him up to shoot him. I knew him. He was a good man. Oh Alice, isn't life terrible?'

'Have a cigarette. I'll ring for coffee.' Alice was disconcerted by Nella's grief and not knowing how to comfort her. Nella was her rock. Before she had arrived she had been considering confiding in her about the honeymoon, asking her advice. But now it would have to wait for some other time.

'What do you think will happen to Constance Markiewicz?'

256

'Before they shot Connolly I was hopeful, now I'm not so sure.'

'But they couldn't, she's a woman.'

'You wouldn't think so, but they are barbarians – who knows what they'll do!'

Nella had always made her think. She did so now. She considered with what satisfaction her father had hailed news of the executions, news of Connolly's death. How her mother had agreed with him. Were they barbarians?

'You know,' Nella was saying, 'when the war is over I shall clear out of here for good. I can't tolerate the double standards. The lip service to religion, to morality. What a rotten lousy crowd we are. Only money and power matter.' She had stopped crying. Alice was relieved.

'Where will you go?'

'France, Italy perhaps.'

'If it wasn't for men being killed I'd wish the war to last for ever. What would I do without you? I'd be lost.' Now Alice was crying and Nella telling her not to be a ninny. To pull herself together. And Alice was glad that, at least for the moment, Nella was her old self. Sometime in the future, before Stephen's next leave she would ask Nella's advice about her problem. And she must start thinking more, questioning all the things she took for granted. Not being such a ninny.

On the day Jem returned to work Dolly had had no reason to pass the mixing loft. So that at lunchtime when she and Bid sat eating their bread and butter neither knew he was back.

'I don't suppose you've any news about Jem?' Bid asked.

'Not a word.'

'You should inquire in the office.'

'And let everyone know I haven't heard – I will not.'

'Suit yourself,' Bid said, then ate the last of her bread ravenously, all the while eyeing a piece of cake which Dolly

257

had pushed to one side. She wiped her mouth. 'This feckin' war's getting in on me nerves. Do you know what's being used now instead of Angelica?'

'What?' Dolly asked.

'Bloody celery. Your cake looks gorgeous.'

'Take it,' Dolly said, pushing the cake across the table. 'I'm not hungry.'

As Bid reached for the tart a thought struck Dolly. Maybe Jem wasn't sick! Maybe there was a good reason for him not being able to see her. After all the years they had been together wasn't it queer that now it should happen. It could be. Why couldn't it? It would explain everything. And what a difference it would make to her. She became excited. The uninterested expression which had been in her eyes while Bid talked about Jem was replaced by an expectant, hopeful one as she said, 'Bid, do you know I was just wondering!'

'Wondering what?' Bid asked, licking the cake crumbs from her fingers. Then suddenly she began to laugh. 'No! You're not. You're not thinking that!' she said, in between kinks of laughter.

'Thinking what, and who are you laughing at?'

'You. Jasus, you're a caution Dolly Devoy! You're codding yourself.' She went into another spasm of laughter. The cake crumbs went against her breath, she coughed and spluttered, crumbs flew out of her mouth. 'You . . . you think Jem's been lifted. Amn't I right! Amn't I?'

Dolly, furious that Bid had guessed her thoughts vehemently denied them. 'Such a thing never entered my mind. Never. It's your imagination. You've a bad mind. But now that you've mentioned it – why couldn't it be true? Why couldn't Jem have been arrested? Wouldn't he be only one of many? He could have been mixed up in the whole thing. And that's why he didn't come on Easter Monday morning. Not everyone was in the Post Office or Jacobs'. There must have been others behind the scenes. He could have been one of them.'

Bid was hysterical, unable to control her laughter, tears in her eyes, her fat breasts bouncing up and down. Women sitting at another table wanted to know what the joke was, shouting across, 'Don't keep it to yourself.'

'Dolly thinks Jem O'Brien was out in Easter Week,' Bid called back.

'You're a mouthy bitch. And whether he was or not there's no call to be so little-making. That's all you can do, make a laugh and jeer of people.' She wanted to scrawb Bid's grinning face. If she didn't leave this minute she would cry with anger and shame. Making a great effort not to, she stood up and said, 'I'm worse for bothering with you. You're a common tinker.' She walked from the table with her head high, raging at Bid, at the laughing stock she had made of her in front of the others. Hating her, though she knew she was right. Jem hadn't been arrested nor mixed up in the Movement. But wouldn't it have been nice if he had? Not that she wished him imprisoned, even if it was a genuine excuse for his silence. The more she thought about the idea the more appealing it became and she dwelt on it. Weaving fantasies as she went about her work. Jem in gaol and how she would dress when she went to see him. The contempt with which she would treat his gaolers.

She pictured his trial. Saw him standing in the dock. Heard his speech. It would be like Robert Emmet's. People would learn it by heart and point to her ever after, saying, 'She married Jem O'Brien.' They'd get married the night before his execution. In the prison chapel. Like that poor girl did last week. She saw herself being led sobbing down the aisle. And Jem waiting for her at the altar where despite his terrible wounds he stood brave and proud. She felt a lump in her throat and her eyes filled with real tears.

Then there, at the top of the real stairs she was about to climb, Jem appeared. No figment of her imagination. Jem in his flour-dusted overalls. No wounds and no bandages. Jem

259

looking sheepish. She was furious, aggrieved, cheated. What did he come now for, spoiling everything the way he always did. Resentment at all she had gone through in the last few weeks flooded through her. All the neglect, her wounded pride, the wondering, the constant asking why he hadn't come, why he hadn't written. She hated him. She began climbing the stairs. Look at him. Look at the cut of him and me imagining him a hero. He had to spoil it. She wouldn't recognize him. She wouldn't open her mouth not if it killed her.

Slowly, Jem came down the stairs, delighted to see Dolly but embarrassed that he was so untidy. He hadn't meant to see her in this state, not until after work. He was going to wait for her outside after having a wash and combing his hair. He knew he looked a sight. Ineffectually, he brushed at the spattered flour and smiled hesitantly. The distance between them narrowed. She was a step below him. He opened his mouth to say something and put out his hand. But before he had time to make a sound she was past him.

Jem gaped up the stairs after her, too stupefied with shock to call out. She had passed him without a word, without a look of recognition, as if he were a stranger! He watched her turn on the landing and disappear. He couldn't believe it. He went slowly down the rest of the stairs telling himself he was to blame, too. Why hadn't he stopped her, run up after her? Why was he such a fool? Gradually the self-accusation gave way to resentment as he went over and over in his mind the scene on the stairs. He had made a move. She was close enough to see. She was on the same step. That wasn't right, she shouldn't have done that, passed him by. He had put up with a lot from her, but this was going too far. He'd always been too lenient with her. Maybe his mother was right and she did make a cat's paw of him. Well it was time she learned a lesson. He had his pride, too. He was a man. It was time she realized that.

In the days that followed Dolly was also resentful and indignant. To pass her like that after she had made up her mind to marry him and all! The cheek of him. Well, now she would show him what she was made of. He'd have to crawl to her before she'd make it up with him. Whenever she saw him in the factory she tossed her head and looked the other way. If there were other men about she made a point of being extra friendly to them, knowing well that he was watching. She warned her mother that if he came to the house on no account was she to say she was at home, whether she was or not. And she threatened Bid, with whom she was friends again, that if she even mentioned Jem's name, this time she would fall out with her for good.

It was an exciting game which she enjoyed playing. Never knowing the minute Jem would appear and force a confrontation, come to the house and demand to see her, be waiting outside after work, grab hold of her arm and not let go until she agreed to talk. Each time he was near, her heart thumped with anticipation – maybe now he'd make a move. And when he took the tossing of her head and the disdainful expression at their face value she consoled herself that maybe tomorrow it would happen or maybe tomorrow morning there would be a letter telling her how sorry he was. How he regretted everything and would she please forgive him. There were such thrills and excitements. There had never been anything like it before; in a way it was like the night in the hall. It was a great game all right, so long as it didn't go on too long . . .

A week, Jem reckoned, was long enough to teach Dolly a lesson. But as one week followed another and still she looked the other way he began to despair. Maybe she had finished with him altogether. Maybe she was doing a line with someone else. He missed her so much and since the incident on the stairs, hardly crossed the door after work. It was ages since he had seen Kevin, and after a lot of thought one night, he decided to go and see him. Ask his advice about patching things up between himself and Dolly. Kevin knew a lot about women and their contrary ways. He'd let on they had had a row. Say nothing about the business in the hall. Kevin would latch on to that like a shot. Tell him you

261

should never leave a job half-done. That mots were always dying for it, and only said 'no' to egg you on. Jem had heard him say the same many times about other girls. And no one was going to say such things about Dolly.

'You've just missed him,' Kevin's mother said when he called. 'He's gone round to Josie's. If you hurry you'll catch him.'

Jem hurried to Josie's but didn't catch Kevin. 'He's left, but come in for a minute,' Josie said. And he followed her into the room, noticing that she had become stout since the birth of the child. And thinking that it suited her. She no longer looked like a little girl. Her brown hair was loose about her and the front of her frock disarranged.

'I was feeding the child,' she said and adjusted the dress. She smiled and Jem was reminded of Dolly. Their eyes were the same colour and she had the same way of tilting her head.

He looked at the baby and said he was a fine child. 'God bless him and spare him, he is.'

Josie began to cry. 'Poor Danny never lived to see him. My poor Danny, the Lord have mercy on him. I do miss him that much. It's terrible lonely on your own.'

'Ah don't cry, don't be upsetting yourself, Josie.' But Jem's words didn't console Josie who cried more loudly and he didn't know what to do. He should go – he shouldn't be here alone with a young widow – get her talked about. But he couldn't leave, not while she was so upset. Awkwardly he put an arm round her shoulders and patted her back, the way he had seen people comfort a crying child.

In between sobs Josie said, 'I'm sorry. I didn't mean to break down. Only seeing you brought it all back. If only I hadn't sent him out to be killed. My mother and the neighbour managed all right. There was no need for him to go.'

The crying stopped and Jem moved slightly away from Josie. 'Sure that wasn't your fault. You weren't to know what would happen. It was the Rebellion's fault if anyone's,' he said and made an excuse to leave, inventing an appointment with Dolly.

262

'Don't let me delay you. You're awful kind. And if you and Dolly are ever passing, drop up. I'd love to see you.'

The following week when Jem had still made no headway with Dolly he found an excuse for calling on Josie. And gradually the visits became regular. He brought her sweets and once a rattle for the baby. Josie was very understanding when he told her about the trouble between himself and Dolly. She advised him not to delay too long before making a move. She was sure Dolly would jump at the opportunity, for wasn't he a fine-looking man that any girl would be glad of?

Bid told Dolly that Jem had been seen coming out of Josie's late at night, and that there was a lot of talk.

'Let him,' Dolly retorted. 'She's one of his own – a fish-dealer like his mother.'

But she didn't believe a word of it. Jem wouldn't throw her over for a common wan like Josie. Bid was a mischief-maker. Venting her spite because she couldn't get Kevin back.

After her holiday in August she'd only have to snap her fingers and Jem would come running. Another few weeks wouldn't kill her. Then she'd let him know she had decided to marry him. The wedding could be before next Lent. That would give her time to join a big money club for the wedding dress and everything.

In the meantime there was the holiday to prepare for. She learned the words of *Roses in Picardy*, it was all the rage. And there was bound to be singing in the Holiday Home. She bought a big straw hat and the makings of two light dresses, and one evening when her mother was out fished the torn camisole from behind the drawer and repaired it. Thinking while she did so of Jem and the morning after the hooley.

And the way time flew! Who'd have thought that they'd have been bad friends so long. July and them not recognizing each other still. But it definitely wasn't true what Bid was saying about him and Josie. He wouldn't have thrown her over for someone like Josie. Maybe he dropped in once or twice – but that could be to make her jealous. What a hope he had. Her jealous of Josie! Mind you, she had better not let this state of affairs carry on too long. As soon as she came back from her holidays she'd patch things up with him. He'd jump at the chance, for it was one thing for him to see her every day even if they didn't speak but let her be away altogether and it would be a different story. She finished her mending and considered what things had to be done before she went away. Well, first she had to get the stuff to Miss Murtagh or she'd have not a new stitch to wear.

Miss Murtagh was saying the Rosary when Dolly arrived with her summer material. 'Every night I say an extra round of my beads for all the brave men who gave their blood for Ireland, Lord have mercy on them. But their sacrifice wasn't in vain. Mocked and jeered they were by their own and destroyed like mad dogs by the British. But they won't be forgotten. It took their deaths to change the heart of the people, but changed it is. England put a nail in her own coffin when she had them executed.'

Dolly agreed with her then changed the subject by asking, 'How's business?'

'Never better, thanks be to God and it's you I have to thank. With all your recommendations, haven't I the half of Jacobs' coming to me. And what about yourself? Are you still doing a line with Jem?'

'Sort of, we had a falling out.' Dolly told Miss Murtagh they had had words, and that now there was a coolness between them and even talk of another girl, adding hastily that she didn't believe it for a minute.

'Take your time about settling down, enjoy yourself while you're young. Time doesn't be long about passing. Tell me how is Richard, does he write often?'

'Not as often as my mother would like.'

'I pray for him as well. I do be awake half the night praying.'

264

'I was thinking I'd try a new style for the frocks. Wait'll I show you.' Dolly took from her bag a paper cutting. And together she and Miss Murtagh began studying the newspaper clipping.

Every so often the realization of how much older she was than Liam came upon Bessie, and for no apparent reason. He never referred to the difference in their ages even in fun. Yet suddenly the thought and with it a doubt of his continued love of her would come into her mind and she would need his reassurance that everything was all right between them. Nowadays she didn't seek the reassurance by a direct question, but couched her worry in an oblique way. Like now when she was lying with him in bed, casually asking if he ever missed living in the country.

'Sometimes I do. Sometimes I feel stifled in the city. And now and then I think of my mother and father and wish things were different.'

That was it! Her fears were confirmed. He regretted what he had done! He regretted marrying her! He was going off her, wishing himself single again. 'Different, in what way different?' she asked, dreading his answer, sorry she had raised the subject. Why did she have to probe the way you would at an aching tooth. Inflicting more pain on herself. 'That there'd been no bitterness. That they had answered my letters. Wouldn't it have been grand if they weren't all against us at the time. We'd never have come to Dublin. Of an evening we could ramble down to see them. You'd have liked that too seeing your own people. Knowing how they were instead of only hearing by chance that Michael had gone off to America without as much as a word to you.'

'I know only too well what you mean,' Bessie said. 'Not a day passes that I don't think about my mother and father and Michael too. And I do wonder about the rest of them. I thought we were very close.' Relief flooded through her. Liam's regrets weren't to do with her. They were the same as her own, grief for the loss of their families.

265

'Do you know I was surprised your parents didn't relent, they seemed easy going enough.'

'They'd find it hard to forgive me making a show of them. All the talk there'd have been. In their own way they're as proud and bitter as your mother and father.'

'I suppose you're right,' Liam said.

'But one of these days I'll go down and surprise them.' Bessie didn't add that she hoped by then there would be a child in her arms. Bitter though both families might be it would be another story when she came bringing their grandchild.

'Aye, one day maybe,' Liam said. For a while then neither of them spoke until Liam went on, 'Before we started talking I was thinking of the rare amount of business we're doing and the reason why.'

'And what is it?' asked Bessie, stretching like a cat, feeling as happy and contented as a cat, one that was warm and comfortable and knew it was loved.

'The crowds going up and down to look at Kilmainham Gaol. Isn't it terrible that we're prospering because fourteen men were shot in there.'

'We've been doing well for a long time. It was slack the week of the Rebellion, that's all.'

'Not as well as now. People come up the quays who never did before. Up to gawp at the gaol.'

'Not just to gawp, they come to say a prayer.'

'They could do that at home. Up for a queer sort of thrill standing so close to where men died. They'd have gone to the executions if they were public.'

'You're very bad-minded.'

'It's the truth. You know Thomas Street, where Catherine's Church is?'

'I do,' said Bessie.

'Outside there Robert Emmet was beheaded and the street was thronged with sightseers.'

'Sure that was over a hundred years ago. People change.'

266

Liam laughed. 'You know all about running an eating house but when it comes to people you're a right eejit.'

'Indeed! Isn't that a nice thing to say to your wife.' She turned away from him, pretending annoyance.

'Ah, don't be like that now, sure I'm only pulling your leg. Isn't it your softness and kindness I love the most about you.'

'It's a mother you're looking for.'

'It's you I'm looking for. Turn round to me this minute.'

'I won't then.'

'Oh won't you?' He caught hold of her. She pretended to struggle. Turning her head away from him when he tried to kiss her. 'Letting on now that you're the strong, cold-hearted woman. An eejit that's what you are,' he said imprisoning her. 'Say it, go on say what you are. Say it, go on.'

'An eejit that's . . .' She couldn't continue for laughing.

'All right, I'll let you off this time, but no more laughing nor talking.' He kissed her.

'The Somme' – after the first week in July the words were on everyone's lips. The big push that was going to send the Germans running and end the war. Then the telegrams began arriving, they came in their hundreds. The casualty lists in the paper grew longer every day. And everyone had a relation, a friend or friend of a friend who had been killed since the first of July. Dolly heard the women in work talking about the men killed and at home heard her mother speculating that Richard was on the Somme. And her father replying that no one knew where he nor anyone else was. Wasn't he forever explaining that a soldier wasn't allowed to disclose his whereabouts. Weren't all letters addressed from and sent to a Field Post Office that might as well be on the moon for all the information they gave about the location.

'Well, the girls in work say it's on the Somme the fellas are being killed,' Dolly said.

'Guessing, that's all they're doing.'

'Not about them being dead,' Dolly said.

'Don't be impertinent, alanna. I'm only explaining a fact.'

Dolly said extra prayers night and morning for Richard's safety and went willingly, when she had nothing else planned, to the chapel with her mother to make a novena for Richard. But all the same she was glad it was getting nearer the time of her holidays. All the talk of death was depressing.

Unknown to each other and serving in different regiments, Stephen and Richard were on the Somme, so too were Dusty and Robbie. Each with their private griefs on which the fighting gave them little time to dwell. But during occasional lulls or while they slept, their sorrows demanded attention.

Robbie grieved for his mother. For the fact that he would never see her again. Never have an answer to the many things about herself, her childhood, her runaway match, all sorts of things that she alone could have answered, that he had intended asking some time, but never found time to. Sometimes he felt sorry that he hadn't taken the priest's advice and tried to get home and help his father. It was too late for that as well. Another letter had come from the priest telling him that his father had killed himself, had lain dead in the hut for several days having cut his throat. Robbie was sorry that anyone should die in such a way, but felt neither grief nor loss.

Richard wrote love letters to Emily, put them in an envelope, addressed them and tucked them away in his tunic pocket. Smiling when a mate said, 'Oh aye, writing to her again.' When it was dark Richard tore the letters into shreds and walked them underfoot and remembered Emily – Emily with the sweet laughing mouth and merry eyes, laughing with him, teasing him, dancing with him. He saw again her curly dark hair tied up with a red ribbon, and he remembered falling in love with her and believing that she loved him.

On the night before he went to the army she agreed to meet

him. Walking along the Embankment he hesitantly told her that he loved her and asked her would she wait for him. She was saying something, but so pleased and excited was he that finally he had plucked up courage to say what he had felt for months, that he wasn't listening properly. Then she had caught hold of his arm. 'Richard, listen. Stop a minute. Let's go over here.' She guided him to the railings. 'I'm sorry Richard, I didn't know you felt like that. I like you very much. We've been friends – I thought that's all it was. I didn't lead you on, did I? And really, apart from the office we haven't seen much of each other. So I didn't think it was necessary to tell you I have a sweetheart.'

He looked down at the river, feeling sick, cold and ashamed. 'We're getting married when he comes on leave. Oh Richard, I'm so very sorry.' She touched his cheek. 'You're cold,' she said, 'your face feels like ice. Let's walk on. Let's find a café and have some tea.'

He said that was a good idea. They resumed walking. He said he was sorry, too, that he wouldn't have spoken had he known about her sweetheart. And that, no, she had never led him on. He said no more about how much he loved her or that he didn't know how to tell the difference between friendliness and love. That he had never been either friendly or in love before.

Emily linked his arm and asked him would he like her to write to him? 'No, no, thank you. I'm a terrible letter writer, I'd never answer them. I'm fine really, don't worry about me. I just got carried away back there. Did what I thought was expected – the soldier bidding farewell and all that.' He laughed to show how all right he was.

'Well, I'm glad you're not hurt or anything. I'd be sad if you were. This looks all right.'

In the café he watched her smiling mouth and merry eyes, memorizing them. When they parted she kissed his cheek. 'Goodbye and God bless you. I'll always remember what good times we had and that you were my friend.'

'Goodbye,' he had replied and hurried away, afraid that if he didn't he would cry.

He hoped her sweetheart had come back to marry her. He hoped they would live happily together. Tomorrow if there was time he would write her another letter.

In Dusty's spare moments he thought of Lil. Lighting one cigarette from the stub of another he could hear her voice talking to him. And he wondered if maybe she talked to him when he couldn't hear, when the whine of shells and the rattle of machine gun fire drowned every other sound. And he knew that if she did talk to him then and he didn't answer her she would think he didn't care for her. And he did, he loved her so much and was going to save her from Eric who kept her locked up even though Lil was very sick. And silently he spoke to her, telling her he would come. It wouldn't be long now. She told him over and over how much she loved him. How it wasn't her fault running away with Eric. He had made her do it, and now she was very sick, too sick to write to him. And Dusty promised that he would come soon.

Sometimes on the Somme Stephen dreamed of Émile. Émile was alive, they had never parted. The boy's eyes shone with love and his slender hands reached for Stephen. 'Oh Émile, I had this terrible dream. I dreamed we had parted. That I married a girl. That one day a letter came from your brother. He wrote that you were dead. And it's not true. Oh thank God it wasn't true. Thank God it was only a dreadful nightmare.' And he reached to take Émile's outstretched hands and his own hands touched nothing. And around him a mist shrouded everything, enveloped Émile so that he was no longer visible. 'Where are you, Émile? I can't find you. Where are you?' he called, walking, groping through the mist. His voice made no sound nor his footsteps either. Everywhere there was silence and the grey mist enveloped everything. He knew then he was dreaming and that the other time was real. Émile was dead and in a moment, he would waken from sleep.

And when he did he prayed to die. Prayed for the war to continue until he was killed. Then his mind cleared and his eyes became accustomed to where he was. He saw the men huddled in water-logged trenches, snatching sleep during a brief ceasefire. Suddenly the darkness was illuminated, the sky blazed with light, he heard the whine of shells, the sound of their impact. The ground shuddered, walls of earth rose upwards taking in their midst men and parts of men. Then Stephen prayed for God to ignore his earlier demented supplications.

The girls going to Jacobs' Holiday Home with Dolly caught the brake that would take them to Rathfarnham. They wore summer frocks and flower-trimmed hats and carried bags and parcels and laughed a lot from excitement and nervousness, for most of them had never been away from home before. Once the brake left the city they began singing, and then screaming with delighted fear as with a flick of his whip the driver set the horse at a good pace through the narrow country lanes.

The Holiday Home was built of grey stone. It was flat-fronted with long windows on either side of the door and a row of them above. Dolly thought it was a beautiful house. A stout, pleasant-looking woman introduced herself as the matron and told the girls what they must and must not do during their stay. The beds must be made every morning and the dormitory left tidy. No food was to be taken upstairs. And if they wanted advice about anything they should ask her. She showed them to the dormitory and told them to unpack.

Dolly looked at the six narrow beds arranged down two sides of the room. It would be funny sleeping here, getting undressed and saying your prayers in front of so many people. She wasn't sure if she would like it. No one else said anything about the strangeness of being away from home but busied themselves with putting away their clothes. Afterwards they

271

went down for a tea of home-made soda bread spread thickly with yellow farmer's butter, jam in pots with paper covers and sweet scones.

After the first night Dolly forgot her homesickness. The weather was glorious and most of her time was spent outdoors, sometimes walking with the other girls, sometimes on her own. She liked being alone admiring the scenery and thinking her thoughts, about Jem and how she would bring them together again. Wondering what it was like being in prison like the Countess. She must hate it and miss Dublin and the mountains. Penal servitude for life! Every day until she died in prison. Still, she supposed it was better than being executed and that's what the Countess had been sentenced to in the beginning. Then Dolly would remind herself not to think sad thoughts and turn her mind to pleasanter ones. Planning the hooley she would coax Maggie to give soon after she came back from her holidays. Maggie wouldn't need much coaxing, any excuse for a bit of a night. She would write a note to Jem asking him to come. Telling him that Maggie said a hooley without him wouldn't be the same. He'd jump at the chance, and before the night was over they'd be back together again.

If it wasn't for her in-laws' letters calling her their dearest daughter-in-law and inviting her to Horsham, Alice felt she could easily forget she was married. For though Stephen wrote often he never mentioned love, or wishing for an end to the war, not even a hope that he might get leave. His letters were pleasant and affectionate; but a stranger reading them would not have known they were from a man to his wife. Which of course she realized that in one sense she wasn't. What a failure she was. She didn't consider herself beautiful or clever, but even the plainest women's marriages worked, for there were children. So why shouldn't hers? There must be a way to make herself desirable to Stephen. It was no good feeling sorry for herself. If there was some secret she had to know. And after

272

thinking a lot about who she could ask for advice decided to go to her mother who would at least be discreet.

On the afternoon Alice came for her advice Lady Delahunt was in the drawing room working on her tapestry, thinking about Alice, hoping she was pregnant. Most of her friends' daughters had just produced or were about to. Everywhere you went the talk was of babies. She was beginning to feel left out. A grandchild would be lovely. And besides, it would once and for all still her doubts about Stephen.

So when Alice came in with an expression on her face which her mother recognized as awkward and embarrassed her heart jumped for joy.

'I was just thinking about you, come in and sit down.' Lady Delahunt pushed the tapestry frame to one side and patted the sofa.

'Well,' Alice began, 'I'm not really sure how to . . .'

'There's no need to feel shy with me, for heaven's sake. I'm your mother and in any case I think I can guess what you want to tell me.'

'How could you?' Alice asked.

'Oh come along now, don't be coy.' Her mother patted her knee. 'You've been married since April – what else could it be but wonderful news?'

'But Mama, it's nothing like that.' Alice guessed by the rapturous look on her mother's face what she was thinking. 'Not that at all. Something quite different – the very opposite.'

'You're not losing it! You haven't started to miscarry? Don't tell me that.'

'I'm not. There is no baby. There couldn't be. That's what I've come to talk about. To ask your advice. Stephen didn't . . . I mean we never . . . It wasn't right.'

'I don't know what you mean.' Her mother drew back the embroidery frame and stabbed the needle in and out through the canvas. 'I don't understand what you are talking about.'

'But you must. I have to know where I went wrong. The war

273

might end – Stephen could get leave. I want it to be right this time.'

'Ring the bell, I'm very thirsty. We'll have tea.' Alice pulled the bell-pull.

'What should I do, Mama? It never happened. On the first night Stephen was too drunk and after that . . .'

'Stop it, the maid is coming.'

After the tea was served Alice spoke again. 'I couldn't ask anyone else.'

'I should hope not indeed. Have a sandwich.'

'I'm not hungry,' Alice said. 'Talk to me about it, please, Mama.'

'Women don't talk about such things. At least I never did. I left all that side of things to your father. Perhaps you were too bossy, argumentative. You've become rather forceful lately.'

'Don't be ridiculous! We were in bed, not debating. And I didn't mind too much about the first night. But after that he only attempted it once and then he . . .'

'That's enough! I want to hear no more about your private life. It's a sacred bond between you and your husband. Finish your tea and have a brisk walk in the garden, you look pale. And don't you dare talk any of this nonsense to Nella. Apart from the laugh she would have at your expense it would be most disloyal to Stephen.'

What a *fool* I was to think she could help. And what a fool she is. Dying for me to have a child and not prepared even to listen to my predicament. For the time being there was nothing else she could do. Only hope and pray and wait for Stephen's next leave. Perhaps it would sort itself out.

Chapter Thirteen

It was all over Jacobs – Josie McEvoy was in the way and Jem O'Brien was the father!

'Could you believe it! Only four months after what happened to poor Danny. Lord have mercy on him. Sure he's not cold in the clay and that dirty bitch carrying on!' an oatcake-maker said.

'Maybe she was unhinged – with shock and that,' a more charitable person suggested.

'Shock me arse! The only unhinging was Jem O'Brien's trousers. But who's going to break the news to Dolly Devoy, that's what I'd like to know,' the first woman said.

'I will,' said Bid. 'After all, I'm her friend.'

'You look great – the holiday did you good. But wait'll you hear what happened,' Bid greeted Dolly the day she came back to work.

'What?' Dolly asked, smiling and realizing she had missed Bid.

'Well – you know I warned you about Jem and Josie?'

'Yes,' Dolly replied unsuspectingly.

'And you didn't believe me. Well, it was the truth and the wholly all of it is . . .'

Two women were approaching and Bid moved closer to Dolly and whispered the rest of her news.

Dolly recoiled as if stung. 'I don't believe you. That's not funny, so it's not! I don't believe you.'

'As true as I'm standing here. It's all over the place. He's leaving Jacobs! Going into the corporation – the bucket and brush brigade. They're getting married. Well, you know what her oul fella's like. He'd cleave the head off Jem for him molesting his daughter and her only after burying her husband. She wasn't long looking for a bit of comfort.'

Dolly felt hatred for Bid surge through her. Standing there prattling as if all that had happened was no more important than how many biscuits she had packed yesterday. She noticed things about her that she hadn't before – the sweat beading her upper lip – a hair growing out of a mole on her cheek, the beginnings of a double chin. She hated her. She was a fat, horrible bitch, a grinning, stupid *bitch*, she could *kill* her. Bid's hand reached out in a conciliatory gesture, but Dolly backed away. 'Don't touch me. And let him marry her, I don't care. She's one of his own – the draggings-up of the northside like yourself.' She walked away and left Bid staring after her.

Not if it killed her would she let anyone know how she felt: the hurt, the disbelief, the wakening up in the morning and it coming over you what had happened. To no one would she breathe a word. Not to her mother who showed her sympathy by making tasty things to tempt her appetite. Nor her father who searched his newspaper for items that might interest her. And above all not to Bid. She knew her. From the teeth out her sympathy would be. Delighted that Jem had thrown her over, consoling herself that Kevin wasn't the only louser. Bid was no better than the wans in work who told her, 'You're better off without the likes of him,' and behind her back she knew well what was being said: 'The price of her. She asked for it. Lost the run of herself after going into the office.'

Well, let them. She'd put up a front they'd find hard to crack. Act from morning till night. She'd talk about it to no one and let no one talk to her.

Maggie was the exception to her rule. One night she said to Dolly, 'Not that it's any of my business but I'd say it was you that threw Jem over.'

'He's the one getting married.'

'I know, but you pushed him into Josie's arms and, from what I hear about her, she was waiting to catch him or any other man. You let the coolness last too long. Did you ever love him?'

'He was my fella – we'd have got married the same as everyone.'

'You're not everyone. You've always had ideas. I don't think you ever knew what you really wanted. Maybe the money should have been spent on you instead of Richard – to give you an education.'

'And have me finishing up a Mary Hick of a teacher.'

Maggie laughed. 'I couldn't imagine you a teacher. You could have been a singer though, had your voice trained.'

'I used to think about that myself. But I knew it was no go. If I'd been a boy they might have made the sacrifice. Anyway, what's all this got to do with Jem O'Brien?'

'Nothing, except I was trying to show you that maybe it's your pride more than your heart that's hurt. For your sake I hope so, for whoever's fault it was, Jem's getting married and that's the end of him and you.'

'I won't marry her! You can shout and rave all you like – I'm not getting married.'

'You'll change your tune when her father comes to the door, he's not a man to be trifled with.'

'Let him come – I still won't marry Josie.'

Jem's mother sat down appearing to have given up and in a voice that sounded despairing, defeated she said, 'I wouldn't have believed it. A boy that never in his life gave me an impertinent answer, defying me, disgracing a poor unfortunate girl. A decent hard-working girl that would make a grand wife. Making a holy show of her and her family. May God forgive you.'

'I'm sorry, Mother.'

'Sorry! Oh, that's grand. Sorry will give your child a name, and comfort Josie and the McEvoys. Well let me tell you, I'm not finished yet.' The fight was back in her voice, she was on her feet again. 'I'll settle your hash for you. I'm up now to the presbytery to talk to the Canon. Let's see now how brave you'll be when he comes.'

'I won't see him. I won't go to see him.'

'You won't have to. I told you I'm bringing him here.' She got ready and went out. Jem didn't believe her. She was gone for a message, to talk to a neighbour. His mother wouldn't bring the priest on him. And when later she returned and didn't pursue the subject of him marrying Josie, he knew he was right. They had their tea without talking to each other, had left the table and Jem was trying to read the paper, but not able to concentrate for the state his mind was in. Torn between not wanting to marry Josie because then Dolly would be lost to him forever, and the obligation he owed Josie and the child.

'See who's at the door,' his mother said.

'I didn't hear a knock.'

'Well I did, answer it.'

Jem nearly collapsed when he opened the door and the Canon was there. He stood speechless until his mother, having given him time to receive the shock, came behind him and said, 'Good evening, Canon, come in and thanks very much for coming.'

The Canon took off his hat. 'Not a bit of trouble Mrs McEvoy.'

A priest in the house and no one dying – Jem's legs felt as if they would buckle under him. His mother was opening the parlour door showing the Canon in, telling Jem to go with

278

him, asking the Canon would he have a drop of something, the Canon refusing.

They were alone in the cold parlour, amongst the china dogs and the brass fender, the photographs of his father, the whatnots and leatherette chairs. The Canon was stout and smiled permanently. 'Sit down,' he said, waving Jem to a seat in his mother's parlour. 'Now what's all this your mother has been telling me?'

Reduced to the status of a child Jem inarticulately explained about Dolly, Josie and her pregnancy.

'So you don't want to marry the girl, is that it?'

'It wouldn't be right, Canon – I don't love her.'

'Oh I see, you don't love her, that's the problem. You love the other one, isn't that a great pity.'

Lulled by the smiling face, the soft voice and the way the questions were phrased into a belief that they were sympathetic and understanding, Jem eagerly pleaded his case. 'That's right, Canon. You see it wouldn't work, the marriage. I'd pay for the child, of course. No question about that. But not get married. There'd be no love between us. We wouldn't be happy. It'd be a cat and dog existence.'

The Canon sat back in the chair and joined his hands as if about to pray, then placed the hands so that his fingers were under his chin. From behind his spectacles his eyes smiled at Jem. Jem wanted to look away but couldn't. He wished the Canon would say something, not keep him fixed in his staring smile. He shifted his feet and cleared his throat. It was worse than going to Confession, at least there you were in the dark.

After what seemed ages the Canon spoke, 'When were you last at Confession?'

'The week after Easter.'

'Not since you got the girl pregnant?'

'No, not since.'

'Well, aren't you the brave man. Afraid of nothing. Not bothered about bringing an illegitimate child into the world,

279

or disgracing a decent girl and her family. And not afraid of God or Damnation. Hell is waiting for you. If you dropped this minute that's where you would go. *Isn't it?*'

Jem was speechless, terrified, his head nodding like a puppet on a string. The Canon stood up. 'Let me hear no more talk of love and what you want. Get yourself to Confession and three weeks today you and the girl will be married.'

Jem got to his feet, his intention to show the Canon to the door. 'Stay where you are, I want to talk to your mother.' Jem sat, burying his face in his hands. He stayed until he heard his mother bidding the Canon 'Good night,' then heard her going back into the kitchen. He went in.

'Well,' she said, 'thanks be to God that's settled. You won't regret it.'

'I won't stay here. Oh – I'll get married but we'll go away.'

'Are you mad? Where would you go?'

'To America. I'll write to my father's brother. He told me there'd always be an opening for me in his bakery.'

'We'll see,' his mother said, not taking the threat seriously but Jem was never more serious in his life. He would marry and be kind to her. After all, what had happened was as much his doing as hers. But he'd have to get out of Jacobs! He couldn't bear seeing Dolly day in and day out knowing what she must be thinking of him and knowing that he had lost her.

For the time being he would take the job in the corporation, then as soon as possible put the seas between him and Dublin. That way he might make a go of it with Josie, but never would the marriage succeed while he could turn the corner on any street and see Dolly. See the face that he adored . . . he couldn't bear that.

From Bid, Dolly learned that Jem was leaving Jacobs at the end of September and being married the same week. The finality of him having set a date for the wedding brought home to Dolly that it wasn't a game any more. Married, he might as well be dead. And she thought of how she missed the very things about him that had once irritated her. Not hearing his knock on the door, the way his hair got untidy, him waiting for her at the edge of a dance floor.

On the evening before Jem was being married Dolly walked home from work thinking about him, telling herself that Maggie was right. She had never loved him, it was just wounded pride. What she needed was a change, but where in Dublin would she get a change?

Dolly had reached Patrick's Park before she realized she was being followed. Turning round to look back she saw Jem and started walking quickly on. He called out, 'Wait Dolly, I have to talk to you.' He caught up with her.

'There's nothing to talk about.' She increased her pace almost to a run.

'Only a minute, please. You know about tomorrow.'

'It's nothing to do with me, leave me alone, go away.' She was surprised at how nice he looked, how well. He wasn't losing any sleep over her. The least he could have done was look down in the mouth. Then another thought struck her, supposing they were seen together – the talk it would cause. The scandalmongers putting her on the market cross. Her surprise, the thrill she had experienced when she turned and saw him changed to anger.

'You're making a show of me. Say whatever it is, I'm in a hurry and I'm not going out of the Park with you.'

'I'm sorry, awful sorry. I'm more than that. It's not easy to say these things to your face in broad daylight. That night in the hall it wasn't disrespect. It was because I loved you. We should have got married months ago. You know I never looked at another girl.'

'You did more than look the minute you found one!'

'There's nothing I can say about that. Nothing I can do about tomorrow. Josie's having my child.'

281

'Will you shut up! Shut up and go. I don't want to hear about you, her or the child.'

'Not till you hear me out. I have to marry her. But it's not for love. I'll never love anyone except you. You believe me, don't you?'

'What difference does it make? Anyway, she's your own kind. She'll sell fish for you. A fish-dealer like your oul wan! Now I'm going and if you folly me I'll call a policeman.'

She left him. She was dying to look back to see if he waited watching her, but she wouldn't give him that satisfaction. And she wouldn't cry either. The cheek of him thinking he could get round her. The cheek of him! She swallowed the lump in her throat and walked quicker. A change – to get out of Dublin, that's what she wanted. She was well away from the Park now – even if he had waited she was out of his sight. Walking more slowly she thought of places to go for a change. But there wasn't anywhere.

A few weeks after her meeting with Jem, a solution for a change presented itself to Dolly. A call came for girls to volunteer to work in Jacobs' Liverpool branch making oat-cakes for the troops. The firm would pay higher wages than Dublin and find lodgings. Dolly, who before working in the office had been an oatcake-maker, decided to volunteer. England would be a new start. She had always wanted to go to England, this was her opportunity. She would put down her name, but first because she was under age she would have to get her parents' consent.

'England! Definitely not. Isn't it enough that one of you is already torn out of this home?'

'It's Liverpool, Ma, not France.'

'I don't care where it is, you're not going and that's that.'

Dolly appealed to her father. 'Da – it's not fair. Tell her it's not fair. All the girls are going – go on Da – tell her.'

'Leave it,' Johnny said. 'Leave it for the time being.' And

she did, believing that it would only be a matter of time before she wore her mother down.

Every morning Bridget watched from behind the curtains for the postman, and when she saw him come into the hall, listened hoping that today he would call her name. But for a week now he in turn called everyone else's except hers. Then on a Saturday morning in late October when she heard him shout, 'Devoy, a letter for Devoy,' she was through the door and had claimed the letter almost before the postman had finished his shout.

She recognized the markings – the Field Post Office stamp – it was from Richard. 'Oh thank God,' she said over and over again, holding the letter to her breast. Then began to fume with impatience. Dolly and Johnny were in work and Maggie and Tom down the country at a funeral and, because she was ashamed of not being able to read, she wouldn't ask a neighbour.

When at last Dolly came home at the dinner-hour and read the letter, Bridget was overjoyed. Richard seemed in great form. The powders, he said, had done the trick and he hadn't scratched in weeks. Page after page Dolly read, every one filled with good-humoured news that made Bridget smile. But then the tone of the letter changed and he wrote about home and how much he loved and missed them all. How lately he would sit in the trench and imagine himself back. Picture the room, see the fire burning and the kettle singing and the table laid and all of them sitting round it. And then other times he would imagine he was walking through the street, meeting people he hadn't seen for a long time, people he had hardly given a thought to since going to France. And he'd see them and talk to them. And he'd think of the mountains and walking along the canal and through Stephen's Green. And how this minute as he wrote he wished he was walking into the hall, opening the door and knowing he was home.

Dolly was reading this part of the letter slowly, stopping

now and then to look at her mother who was crying, not making a sound, the tears falling down her face.

'God – I must say he's very cheerful I don't think. Anyone to hear him would think he was never . . .'

'Don't you say it, don't utter it not even in a joke,' Bridget warned. 'Go on – finish it.'

Dolly read on, then stopped again. 'Listen to this. I'm telling you that fella's gone mad or something, he's writing about that girl now. "*I hear occasionally from Emily* – remember I told you I danced with her before I was called up. If I ever come home could I bring her to see you?" And that's it except for sending us all his love. He's in his second childhood – if he ever comes home! Sure where else would he go?'

'Give it to me,' Bridget said. 'Eat your dinner and go out if you're going.' After Dolly went Bridget sat by the fire holding the letter next to her heart, staring into the fire trying to banish the presentiment that had come before her when the tone of the letter changed. Richard knew he wasn't coming back. He was saying 'goodbye'. Please God don't let me believe it. Let it be no more than the thought of a foolish old woman. Let me not try to see beyond this day. Let my presentiment be wrong.

But despite her prayers she couldn't shake off the feeling that this letter was Richard's last. Her heart felt like a stone. She had neither the will nor energy to move from where she sat. The fire died down and the room darkened and still she sat holding the letter and staring into the dead fire. Then a loud rapping on the door roused her and she knew who would be there when on shaking legs she reached and opened the door.

'For Devoy,' the young boy in the Post Office uniform said, holding out the telegram.

'Devoy,' Bridget repeated, 'that's right, that's me,' and she took the telegram and said, 'Thanks.'

She went back into the room and sat holding the telegram

and Richard's letter, looking from one to the other, moaning softly. Not long afterwards the door opened and a neighbour came in. 'I heard the telegram boy. I didn't want you to be on your own.'

Bridget didn't answer. 'I'll make you a drop of tea,' the woman said. 'Sometimes the telegrams only say they're prisoners like, don't you know. I wouldn't want to raise your hopes, but sometimes that's all they say. It's not always bad news. Will I open it for you?'

'God bless you Kate, you're kind. I know what's in it. I want to hold it for a while longer. While I'm holding it I keep hoping that maybe I'm wrong and that I don't know what's in it. So don't open it yet for a minute.'

The neighbour went quietly about making the tea. When it was poured, she said taking a Baby Power from her apron pocket, 'There's a drain in this. I'll put it in your tea, it'll do you good.' She poured in the whiskey and put the cup by Bridget.

'I had that this morning,' Bridget said, holding out the letter. 'And do you know he was grand when he wrote that. Grand,' she repeated. 'He held that envelope in his hand, and stuck it down and posted it, and was grand. And he's dead now. Open the telegram, and tell me I'm right.' And while the woman tore open the envelope and took out the sheet of paper, Bridget prayed, 'Only sweet Jesus let me be wrong, don't make Richard be dead.'

'I was right, wasn't I?' she said when she saw the woman's face go pale.

'You were right Bridget, and I'm awful sorry. I'll stay with you until Mr Devoy or Dolly comes, and what about Maggie?'

'She's down the country, she won't be back for an hour or so. Stay with me, Kate.'

Kate stayed until first Dolly and then her father came home. Maggie and Tom were sent for and the family cried together and attempted to console each other. Word went through the house and the neighbours came and offered their sympathy. They recalled what a lovely child Richard had been, what a grand young man, and a good son, and a marvellous scholar, and what a terrible thing this war was doing to people.

Later on, Johnny went with the men to the public house. And everyone said how sorry they were for his trouble, and plied him with whiskey and porter, some passing money over the counter and others giving the nod to the barman to put it on the slate. The edge of Johnny's suffering was momentarily dulled and he found some consolation in agreeing with those who said, 'You can be proud of him, anyway. He died a hero on the battlefield.'

Johnny got very drunk and the men escorted him home. The women of the house were there with Bridget, Maggie and Dolly, drinking tea and sometimes talking about Richard, but not all the time. Bridget's mind was constantly on him, and Dolly remembered that now he would never need the chair-bed back.

Towards morning, Maggie persuaded her mother to lie down, telling her it wasn't the same as a wake, and that she'd have to close her eyes if only for half an hour. Bridget slept and when she woke for an instant forgot that Richard was dead. Then, remembering, she cried quietly.

The lamp in the other room was out so she knew that everyone was gone. She lay for a minute listening to the sound of Johnny breathing, and thought of his suffering and how they no longer knew how to comfort each other. And how when he woke with the drink gone he'd be the broken-hearted man. And worse, though he'd never admit it to her, he would blame himself. For without his encouragement to better himself Richard would never have been a soldier. Up to now no Irishman had been made to go and she knew Richard would never have volunteered – not for the British Army. God blast it and all the armies.

She was still in her clothes; all she had to put on were her

286

shoes. She went into the other room, careful not to make a sound for fear of disturbing Dolly sleeping on the chair-bed. The fire was still in; she put the kettle over it and when it boiled wet tea in a cup, drank half of it and went out to get six o'clock Mass.

Walking through the streets to the chapel she thought of the many times Richard had walked this way with her. She remembered the feel of his little fat hand that had fitted so snugly into hers, and the first time she had given him a hiding for mitching school. And she thought of her last glimpse of him departing after a seventy-two hour leave, before going to France. Richard in his uniform, the khaki that didn't suit him, made him look sallow. And it didn't fit him – his poor neck was rubbed raw from the rough, tightly-fitting tunic collar. He'd laughed when she commented on it and told her to stop mollycoddling him. My poor lovely son. I hope you didn't suffer. I hope you died quickly and I hope you weren't afraid. I didn't bring you into the world to go far away and be killed for something that had nothing to do with you. God comfort me and all poor mothers and fathers everywhere.

Dolly bought a mourning outfit and was glad that black suited her. She found it hard to realize that Richard was dead, that she would never see him again. She was so used to him being away that she sometimes forgot all about him being killed until she arrived home many nights and found her mother sitting by the fire, her face wet with tears.

Sometimes, too, Bridget found it hard to realize that Richard was dead. Without a body to grieve over it was easy to delude herself that after all he might be a prisoner. Even the letter of sympathy from the King and Queen did not convince her, like the telegram that was only a bit of paper.

Then a packet arrived with an identity disc on which Richard's name and army number were stamped. The disc, Johnny explained, would have been one of a pair that all soldiers wore. One would have been buried with Richard and this one

287

sent to them. Bridget thought about the brown scapulars she had given him when he first went to London, and wondered had he ever worn them. She held the disc, turning it this way and that between her fingers, then put it to her face and let it lay for a moment against her flesh before giving it to Johnny to put with his mementoes of Richard. She would delude herself no longer.

For a while reminders of Richard's life in the army continued to arrive – his few belongings, monies owed him by the Paymaster and a bundle of letters written to him by various people. She made Dolly go through them searching for one from the girl called Emily but there wasn't one.

Dolly bought a mother of pearl rosary for Bid who was going as an oatcake maker to Liverpool and gave it to her on the night they said 'goodbye'.

'Ah you shouldn't,' Bid said, when she saw the gift.

'Say a prayer for me on them,' Dolly said and her eyes filled with tears. 'I wish I was coming with you.'

'So do I. Didn't we have great times.' Bid was laughing and crying. 'Remember the morning of the Rebellion when you threw the sandwiches into the Liffey. And you were in bad humour all the way home. God, who'd have thought of all the changes that were coming. Poor Richard and Danny McEvoy and Jem and Josie finishing up together. You're making me cry, Dolly Devoy and me supposed to be delighted about going to England.' Bid wiped her eyes and blew her nose then said. 'Commere, could you never get round your mother to let you go.'

'Not now. I couldn't fight with her now. Herself and me father are broken hearted.'

'I suppose you couldn't all right. But I don't envy you. You'll be in black for a year and no dances nor hooleys. Nothing to do except go to the chapel. You'll finish up a religious maniac or a nun. Don't mind me, I'm only joking, but you won't forget to write and I'll do the same, honest to God.' Dolly promised that without fail she would write.

Bid wrote regularly for the first month. England was a great place, plenty of fellas and no one to give a rambling damn what you did. Dolly should work on her mother. Leave no stone unturned to get over, it was worth it. Then the letters came less frequently and eventually stopped. Dolly missed them for, as Bid had forecast, her life now was very tedious, her evenings spent between visiting Maggie or accompanying Bridget to the chapel. She consoled herself by daydreaming about the man with the dancing eyes. He was out there somewhere waiting for her. Maybe tomorrow she would meet him.

Bessie and Liam's business continued to prosper; it no longer depended on passing trade, for clerks from the nearby auctioneering room used it regularly, couples had made it their place of an evening and at weekends the same families returned and were on friendly terms with Bessie. And as she often said to Liam, every one of their customers was a nice class of person. No one came with the sign of drink taken and there had never been a disturbance, not since the Rebellion.

'You've worked miracles in no time and us only in it barely three years,' Liam would say.

'We're coining it. It won't be long till I've enough saved for the small hotel my heart is set on.'

'Go easy now with your plans – the hotel could take a while yet.'

'Disheartening me again, I never knew such a man. A year or two is nothing, haven't we all the time in the world? So long as God spares us our health and you've the bit of work, we'll do it for sure.'

After these conversations Bessie would tell herself she was right – they had all the time in the world. God had been very good, showering them with blessings. They had prospered. Only seldom did she and Liam have a falling out. She loved him, more if that was possible than the day she married him. And he loved her. They had their health. They had everything except the one thing that would crown her happiness. Though she had faith in God's purpose there was no harm reminding Him of how she longed for the gift of a child. Morning and night she prayed for it, sometimes making her prayers informal, talking to God, explaining that she wasn't a girl any more so He'd understand her impatience. Often after praying in such a fashion she would tell herself she was a fool, for didn't God know very well what age she was. He knew the minute she was born and the minute she would die. God knew everything – hadn't she learned that from her catechism. So she'd leave everything in His hands. And if His Will wasn't for her to have a child then she would accept that as one of the crosses she had to bear.

One evening in January, Liam was late home from work. Bessie kept watching the clock, raging that the bit of pork steak she had bought for his dinner was drying like an old stick. When he still didn't come she began to worry – something must have happened to him. He'd been run over, fallen under the hooves of a horse and was this very minute dead in a hospital. She worked herself into such a state that when Liam did arrive her relief showed itself as anger. 'Where have you been till this hour?' she demanded to know.

'I called in to a meeting.'

'A meeting! Who do you know that was meeting?'

'Will you calm down. Anyone to hear you would think I'd come in footless.'

'I was sick with worry in case you'd met with an accident, which thank God you didn't. Tell me about your meeting and while you're doing it sit over for the dinner that's ruined. I've a drop of soup first. Well, go on.'

'I heard about it in work – the fellas are always talking about

Sinn Fein and the coming by-elections. Everyone speculating about their chances, especially the candidates that are still in the English gaols.'

'Is that so, you live and learn,' Bessie replied, ladling out the soup. 'Since when were you interested in politics?'

'You know well I never bothered my head with them. But you couldn't live through what's happened here since last year and not start thinking.'

'Thinking about what?' Bessie asked, a new fear clutching at her heart. Liam wasn't going to join anything! Surely to God he wouldn't do a thing like that. No more than herself Liam didn't come from a family that concerned itself with movements.

'About the Rebellion. About the courage that took – a handful of men taking on the British Army. But I suppose that was something that I might have forgotten about – but what happened afterwards – I'll never forget that, and I'm not the only one. There's thousands and thousands like me, men that never gave it a second thought until the executions. Now they're proud of being Irish and want the country to ourselves. Did you know that's what Sinn Fein means – Ourselves Alone.'

'No, I did not. And what's more, I don't want to. Not that I'd belittle what was done in Easter Week, nor forget to say a prayer for the poor unfortunates that were killed. But I don't want to know any more about it. Movements are not for us. We're trying to make a living, to get on in the world. We've no quarrel with England. For the likes of us what difference does it make who's in the Castle? Liam love, you wouldn't do anything foolish like joining something you'd regret?'

'Do you know I never met anyone like you for jumping to conclusions. First you have me killed because I'm an hour late coming home and now you have me joined up in something.'

'Don't laugh at me,' Bessie said. 'I'm in earnest. Don't

make light of my worries. Nothing good ever came out of anything that's to do with joining things.'

'I'm sorry, and I'm joining nothing. But you can't stop me thinking nor voting for who I believe should have a seat. And anyway, if you'd listen I'd explain that no one is looking for trouble. Don't you see what's happening now is a peaceful thing. It's men trying to win elections and change things that way instead of with guns and killings. Do you want me to tell you or are you going to stand there all night with soup spilling out of that spoon?'

'All right then, tell me,' Bessie said, putting the spoon in the tureen and sitting down.

He told her how the people awakened and enraged by the Volunteers' courage and the brutal executions were beginning to unite. All the different organizations were banding together. Men were being put up for by-elections – men of Sinn Fein were going to stand against the Parliamentary Party. De Valera who had held Boland's Mill during Easter Week and who would have been executed except for being born in America – he was standing. And the Countess who was in prison – she was up, so was Count Plunkett whose son was executed, he was standing, too.

'Lord have mercy on them all.' Bessie made the Sign of the Cross. Then said, 'For someone who only called into one meeting you know an awful lot.'

'I listen to the talk and read the papers and journals.'

You do too, she thought, for you know it all and explain it well. And here I am living with you, thinking I know you and I don't. You're not the boy from up the country who nearly died of shame because a solicitor made a fool of him. But despite her annoyance she felt proud of his knowledge, of his confident way of holding forth. No one could make a fool of him now. But mixed with her pride was still a fear he might join an organization.

'The people have lost faith in Redmond and his promises

292

of Home Rule. Home Rule isn't enough. We'll be satisfied with nothing less than an Independent Ireland.'

'That's what I'm afraid of, Liam – more killings, more executions and you mixed up in it.'

'You're a terrible woman and you don't listen. There'll be no shooting, no killing, haven't I told you?'

'Well, we'll see. And please God you'll be right. That's all I want for us, for everyone, that we'll live in peace.'

Chapter Fourteen

One by one the by-elections were fought. De Valera and
Count Plunkett, the father of Joseph who had been executed
hours after marrying in Kilmainham Gaol, were elected; so
was the Countess Markiewicz, thereby becoming the first
woman Member of Parliament. None of the members elected
for Sinn Fein took their seats in Westminster. In the same
year, 1917, the Third Battle of Ypres began. For Robbie,
Stephen and Dusty serving there it was their third year in
action.

Sometimes in periods of snatched sleep, sleep which came
without difficulty beneath lorries, curled in a nest of sandbags,
in trenches, Stephen relived the nightmare of the Somme. In
his dreams he saw the faces of the dead, his friends, his
men, trampled in the mud, limbless, headless, hanging like tat-
tered scarecrows on the wire. He dreamed they came to
point accusingly, saying, 'You wanted to die. We didn't.
We had everything to live for. We didn't think that shell,
that bullet had our number on it. Why?' And Stephen
said he was very sorry and didn't know why he had been
spared.

Awakening from the nightmare he asked himself the same
question. There was no answer only that he was alive, there
was a new battle and the men who lived needed him. The
young men still came out, not in such vast numbers any more,
but still they came. Young men, scarcely more than boys,
those from the country with fresh pink cheeks, healthy-looking

with bright eyes, and the stunted ones . . . pallid and under-nourished, cocky and cheerful from the industrial cities. Miners, labourers, ploughmen and public schoolboys, they all came. And looked to him for leadership. They needed his example; he gave them courage and hope. He was an old soldier.

The days passed and the seasons. The sun shone and the rain fell, winds rose and died. Spring and summer came again. In cornfields, scarlet poppies grew.

But whatever the weather the endless digging went on. Digging in and firing across the blasted earth at the enemy dug in on the other side. All day rifles spat death to and fro. Sometimes yards of earth were gained and Stephen with his men advanced across the dearly-paid for earth and dug in again. Sometimes the enemy paid their price and moved forward. Backwards and forwards went the war, and the fresh-faced boys and the pallid ones became indistinguishable. Weariness and fear etched the same lines in their flesh and their eyes, once bright, now looked dead.

In the brief intervals when they were withdrawn behind the lines, he thought about Alice. Alice who wrote him long cheerful letters, full of affection and hopes for his safety, and for their future.

What was to become of her – of them? He couldn't forever put off going to Dublin, continue taking his leaves in Paris. The war must end sometime. And what then? Not what Alice hoped for, not what his wife was entitled to expect. After the honeymoon he had deluded himself that next time all would be well. His subsequent visits to Paris left him in no doubt as to where his sexual preference lay. Poor, sweet, trusting Alice, he had ruined her life.

'Dolly! I'm delighted to see you. Where were you this long time?'

'I had a touch of the 'flu and got run down.' Dolly exagger-

295

ated the state of her health as an excuse for not visiting Miss Murtagh.

'There's a lot of it about. I'm working with a woman whose . . .'

'Since when are you working and where?'

'Things went slack with the dressmaking so I answered an advertisement for a seamstress in a gentleman's house in Foxrock. It's only temporary. A lot of their servants have been laid up with the 'flu.'

'Go way! What were you going to say about the woman in work?'

'Poor Bessie, she's very nice. Her husband got pneumonia out of the 'flu, it left his chest weak and he lost the labouring he was doing. He wouldn't be able for it now anyway, but he's well enough to manage the little eating house they have while Bessie does the bit of temporary work. Do you ever hear anything of Jem these days?'

'Very seldom. They had a little boy. Someone saw him in town sweeping the street. Can you imagine me married to anyone like that?'

'Indeed I cannot. You had a lucky escape.'

Dolly didn't want to talk about Jem. She had convinced herself that they had never been meant for each other. Habit was all that had kept them together. In a way she should be grateful to Josie for taking him before she had done anything foolish like marrying him. She was meant for better things – her 'man made to measure' as her mother called him. Since seeing that gorgeous soldier on Easter Monday 1916 she had his real face and the other one still mixed up in her mind. But she'd be in no doubt the minute she met him.

'Is the house in Foxrock beautiful?'

'A mansion. Carpets that you'd sink in. And you've never seen anything like the furniture and ornaments. I used to think my family were well-off but sure they were only in the ha'penny place compared to these people. Protestant, of course.'

'Who are they?'

'The Delahunts – he's an MP, then there's the wife and their daughter Miss Alice. She's a lovely girl. I've done a few alterations for her. Her husband's in France and she's dying for him to get leave. Buying all before her for when he comes.'

'It'd be like a second honeymoon,' Dolly said.

'It would, I suppose – be like a second honeymoon.'

While Miss Murtagh made tea Dolly let her mind dwell enviously on Alice who had everything, making comparisons with her own life. Going to dances, always hoping to click the right fella, living in ninety-seven, working in Jacobs' and not having a real friend any more. Ethel was all right but a drim and drue compared to Bid. Dolly didn't allow herself to dwell too long on the shortcomings in her life, for there was always hope – the future – and she could get a glimpse of it this minute. It was her real reason for visiting Miss Murtagh. She waited until the dressmaker had almost finished her second cup of tea and said, 'Do the cup for me.'

'You know I don't like doing it. It's a sin really, anything to do with fortune-telling is. I wish I'd never told you I could do them.'

'Well you did, so there. And anyway it's not a sin for I don't believe in it, it's only a bit of gas, go on.'

'This once and never again.'

'All right.'

'Drink your tea to the bottom, leave only a drain, then swirl that around.' Dolly did as Miss Murtagh told her. 'Now carefully drain out the drop and give me the cup.'

Miss Murtagh peered for a long time into the cup, turning it this way and that. 'I can see a dark man . . . You'll meet him in the space of two. Look – there he is!' She held the cup out to Dolly who also peered but saw only a group of tea leaves where Miss Murtagh was pointing. 'He'll come over the sea. He's a foreigner and wears a uniform.'

'Anything else?' Dolly prompted.

'He'll bring you great happiness and there's money around him. He's wealthy.' She turned the cup around again and studied another group of leaves. 'And you'll be getting letters. I can't see when they'll come or if they're from a man or woman, but the letters are there all right.'

'Anything else?' Dolly asked.

'No, nothing else.'

'What's the space of two?'

'That could be weeks, days, months or years.'

'Oh,' Dolly said. 'You're sure it could be years?'

'The tea leaves don't lie.'

'Two years is an awful long time.'

'But it might only be two months, don't forget that.'

'You're right.' Dolly was full of good humour on leaving. A dark stranger and money and letters. She had everything to look forward to.

Dusty and Robbie had also survived the Somme, Dusty only just. Shortly before leaving that Front he was buried alive when a shell exploded in his vicinity. He was a goner, Robbie thought as he and the others dug him out. 'Someone was praying for you,' he said, delighted to find Dusty alive. The man's face was waxen and covered with cold perspiration.

'He's suffering from shock,' the medical orderly said, feeling his pulse.

Robbie repeated what he had said about someone praying. Dusty spat earth from his mouth, grinned and replied, 'Looks like it!'

A week later he was back from hospital and shortly afterwards was offered a stripe which he refused.

'You should have taken it, it was extra money,' Robbie told him.

'Sod the money – it's not worth the responsibility. Listen to that bastard, I'd like to stick a grenade up his arse. Clear him out.'

'It would do that all right,' Robbie laughed before agreeing with Dusty that the removal of the German machine gunner in his concrete pillbox was eminently necessary. 'I don't know what our bloody artillery are doing, a dozen times fire has been requested on that position.'

'Them bleeding gunners, on a soft option they are. Shelled us, blew me up they did, got their map reference wrong that day – our own bloody artillery!'

Occasionally that happened – the artillery made a cock-up, but not that time. Dusty wouldn't be convinced of the truth. Robbie had tried it. He didn't bother arguing any more.

'We've had some lucky escapes, you and me.'

'Don't spit in the wind,' Dusty said, lighting a cigarette. Robbie watched his hand shaking, saw the difficulty he had holding the match steady and thought he had seen healthier-looking corpses. 'Watch out,' Dusty went on, 'here comes Charlie.' Robbie straightened his shoulders, stood to attention and saluted Captain Charles.

'Good morning, Sergeant.' He returned Robbie's salute by touching his stick to the brim of his cap. 'I wanted a word.'

'Yes, Sir,' Robbie said and followed the officer out of Dusty's hearing.

'I've been asked to recommend likely NCOs for commissions. I'd like to put your name forward. Would you consider it?'

Robbie considered it. Infantry officers got knocked off quicker than anyone else, that's why he was being considered. But he fancied the idea. A pip! A Sam Brown! A flashy service dress! What a dash he'd cut in that if he did survive to go on leave. And why not take the chance? In any case, he was going to sign on a regular engagement. No ties, the old man gone, nothing to go back to – the house and business gone in bankruptcy.

'Sir,' he said, 'I'd like to be put forward.'

'Good. I'll arrange to have you relieved one day this week. Come up to Company Office and we'll do the paper work.'

His particulars went forward and he waited. 'Might take a while,' the Adjutant had warned him. He didn't mind waiting; if he wasn't killed he had all the time in the world.

From his concrete pillbox, the German machine gunner continued to harass and slaughter the men and stop any advancement. Captain Charles had an idea. On a suitable dark night, a party consisting of a Sergeant and two men would go out and get the bastard.

'I'd like to have a go, Sir,' Robbie said.

'Good man, I hoped you would. Detail two other men – I'll leave the choice to you. Carry on, Sergeant.'

Robbie detailed Dusty and Perkins. Perkins was enthusiastic, while Dusty observed the formality of accepting Robbie's order but said no more about the proposed raid. After briefing him, Robbie had doubts about his choice. Maybe Dusty wasn't up to it any more – look at the way he had the shakes sometimes. He thought about it for a while longer then decided that he *had* made the right decision. Dusty was just fine in action – it might be the only time he was, but action they were going into, and Dusty was a good man to have beside you.

The next day, the Captain outlined a plan and asked for suggestions. Perkins and Dusty offered none. Robbie proposed that during the daylight hours they should study the ground between their trenches and the pillbox and pick out certain objects on the routes they were taking, tangible things that would help them keep in the right direction in the dark. It was agreed that the raid would take place on the first moonless night . . .

They went up the ladder and out of the trench. Their orders were that on reaching the ground they would separate, each one approaching the pillbox from a different angle. Each man carried a wire-cutter and had two hand-grenades. Whoever reached the German position first would lob in the grenades and get away as quickly as possible.

Once through the wire they wriggled on elbows and bellies across no man's land, Robbie going in what he hoped was a straight line, feeling for the objects picked to keep him right – here a tree stump, further on an ammunition box. Dusty had gone away to the left and Perkins to the right. When close to the pillbox they would turn to come in under the machine gunner's post.

Slowly, inch by inch, Robbie went forward, plagued by a tickle in his throat, an urge to cough, and then to sneeze. He suppressed them and went on. He was getting closer to his objective. Close enough now to hear the sound of German being spoken and to smell tobacco and cigarettes unlike English brands. He was going to be there first. He was thrilled. Then his eyes, which were becoming accustomed to the darkness, saw a form ahead of him, to his left but now turning right, moving like an animal familiar with its terrain. It was Dusty – he'd beaten him to it. The man was kneeling, drawing out the first grenade's pin, getting to his feet, hurling the bomb into the pillbox, then the second one. There was a flash, shouts, curses and then the explosion. Someone screamed. Robbie turned and began making his way back. He had reached the tree stump when the shelling began. Shelling from behind their own lines. Christ, he thought, as he flattened himself into the earth, they're ours, the stupid bastards are shelling *us*. The shells are falling short, the stupid bastards: tonight of all nights to go for the pillbox and then get it wrong. It would be just his luck to be blown to bits by his own bloody side. Robbie burrowed further into the earth, seeking its protection, cursing the gunners. When the shelling stopped he made his way back to the trench.

301

'You're the first,' Captain Charles, who was waiting, said. 'Drink some of this.' He held out his hip-flask and Robbie drank the rum which burned his throat then sent its magic warmth coursing through his blood, relaxing him, releasing the tension which had spurred him through the raid and his fear while the shells fell.

Perkins climbed down the ladder and was offered the flask. 'I saw it go up, well done. Which one of you got it?' the Captain asked.

'Private Miller, Sir,' Robbie replied. 'He should be back by now.' They waited for Dusty. The flask was passed round again.

'He's a long time coming in,' Perkins said.

'Too long. He's been hit – I'm going back,' Robbie said and without waiting for the officer's comment, was up the ladder. He was grateful for the spirit coursing through him, taking the edge off his fear, the horror of worming his way out again, searching through no man's land.

'Dusty,' he whispered. 'Can you hear me? Are you there?' Again and again his searching hands encountered objects, hard, cold, lifeless things, metal and wood, stones, soft yielding masses, sometimes with sharp, splintered bones protruding. Oh Jesus, where was Dusty. Would he never find him? Was there anything left of him to find?

The air was becoming colder. Dawn was approaching, he'd have to abandon his search. Dejectedly he crawled back to the trench.

'No luck, Sergeant?'

'No luck, Sir.'

'Pity about that, he was a brave man.'

With the machine guns silenced, the next day's attack was successful. The Germans retreated. No man's land was in British hands. A thorough search was made for Dusty, but there was no trace of him – nothing, not even a badge, a boot, or any of his equipment. Poor sod, poor old Dusty, blown up,

302

scattered like dust before the wind, Robbie thought. He'll be reported missing, believed killed in action.

Alice was ecstatic. Stephen was coming over. He had just telephoned. 'I'm on leave, stopped for a night in Horsham. I'll be in Dublin tomorrow, darling.' She whispered into the receiver, 'I love you.' The line was bad, crackling, but she was sure he said, 'I do, too.'

Everything would be marvellous. He loved her. It was going to be wonderful. They'd have a week together, a whole week! And she would insist, no matter what her mother said, that there were to be no parties, no guests, nothing that would tire or irritate Stephen and give him an excuse to drink too much. She informed her mother of her wishes and was delighted that there was no disagreement.

'Perhaps you should go away for a few days,' Lady Delahunt suggested. 'After all, it is a second honeymoon.'

'I don't think so, he will have done enough travelling. Just a nice quiet rest, that'll be fine.'

Afterwards, Alice went to her room to sit quietly for a while savouring the prospect of Stephen's visit. She planned what she would wear for his arrival and what she would wear to bed. She took out the nightgowns she had bought, not ribbon-threaded virginal white this time, but pale pinks, and ivory-coloured satins lavish with lace. Garments that instead of falling in fullness, clung and followed the lines of her body. She held an ivory-coloured one up to her body and looked at herself in the glass. It was beautiful, Stephen couldn't help but love her in it. The neckline was low, meant to display her breasts. What a pity, she thought, there was so little to display. Why did she have to have silly little pointed breasts like a schoolgirl's? It had been so easy to improve the other parts of her. Following the advice in magazines her hands were soft, her skin velvety and supple, her nails like pink-tinged pearls from constant buffing. Maybe she should have sent for the

303

'bust improver'. Improvement by as much as four inches, the advertisement had claimed: there were pictures, before and after using it and testimonies from satisfied customers. No use thinking about it now . . . she would wear the nightgown's matching jacket to cover her little breasts. Everything would be absolutely marvellous. She hugged herself as she thought about the next night.

Alice counted the hours and minutes until Stephen arrived. She was surprised that he looked so much older and thinner, but it suited him: he was handsome and distinguished-looking. His delight at seeing her was evident. He kissed her warmly and held her close for a long time. She loved him, he was so wonderful and of course he loved her, she must never doubt that again.

It was a pity they had to eat, had to go through the formalities of sitting after dinner with her parents while her father discussed the war with Stephen. She was impatient to have him all to herself. And she was grateful to her mother for remarking much earlier than usual that she was tired and was going to bed, and to her surprised delight her father who never retired early, said he also felt like turning in. The way was clear now for her and Stephen to do likewise.

Perfumed, with her hair loose and dressed in the ivory nightgown and matching jacket, she lay in bed waiting for Stephen to join her. From the adjoining dressing room she could hear him moving about, the sounds of drawers opening and closing, him clearing his throat – she hoped he wasn't catching a cold. But what was keeping him? He had finished his bath ages ago, what could he be doing? She wondered if men always took so long about their bedtime preparations. She knew nothing about men, nothing about Stephen, really.

'Sorry I took so long,' Stephen said when at last he came into the room. 'I'm not used to lashings of hot water and soft, warm, clean towels. All these comforts of home are too nice to hurry.'

304

Fibber, Alice thought, your bath finished ages ago, you're nervous just like me. He got into bed and lay beside her. She waited for him to do something, to kiss her, put an arm round her, say she looked nice, that he liked her perfume. When he remained silent and still she asked, 'Shall I turn off the light?'

In the dark she took off the little satin jacket and flung it to the end of the bed.

'That's a lovely smell,' Stephen said.

'It's my perfume. I bought it especially for you.' Encouraged by his complimenting her scent she moved closer to him. He turned round facing her, and his fingers stroked her cheek.

'Your skin feels so soft.' He traced the outline of her face.

She put her arm around him and wriggled close to him. 'I love you,' she whispered. 'I've wanted this night so much.' He stopped touching her face and kissed her. His mouth was on hers for a long time. She was getting excited and yet felt that something wasn't completely right, something was missing. His mouth was just pressing on hers, still, as if you had laid your lips along your arm. Kissing must be more than this. Something magical should be happening, but it wasn't. Perhaps the fault was hers. For a start she shouldn't be so cold-blooded, analysing what the kiss felt like. She shouldn't be thinking at all. Stephen took his mouth away from hers and she heard his sigh and interpreted it as one of exasperation. She was failing him, being unresponsive. Oh why hadn't her mother talked to her? Why hadn't she asked Nella what women were supposed to do?

Stephen moved from her and lay on his back. 'Are you annoyed with me?' she whispered. When he didn't answer she repeated the question, adding, 'I'm sorry. I know I'm not good at kissing. But I could learn. You could teach me.' He turned away from her. She got angry, there was no need for him to do that. 'You shouldn't have done that, that's a horrible thing to do. You could at least talk to me. You've no right . . .' She touched him, put a hand on his shoulder, it was shuddering. He was crying! 'My God, you're crying. Stephen, don't, don't cry. What's the matter? Is it the war? Are you thinking about the war? Turn round, please.' She tugged and pulled at him until he was again facing her.

She kissed his face and tasted his tears and cried herself with pity for whatever ailed him. 'It'll be better if you talk about it.' He didn't and then she told him that perhaps it was better not to. He was exhausted, he should try to sleep and tomorrow everything would be all right.

'Alice, I'm sorry, terribly sorry. I . . .'

'Hush now,' she said, 'there's nothing to be sorry for. Rest and sleep. Don't think about anything. I love you.' She was overwhelmed with tenderness for him. It was heartbreaking to hear a man cry. Poor Stephen, he must be greatly troubled about something. The war, most likely. He had been in action for so long – three years – it was more than one man should have to bear.

'Oh God, Alice, you don't understand. I have to tell you something and don't know how to.'

'You could tell me anything, I'd understand. There's nothing so terrible that you couldn't tell me.'

Stephen moved out of her embrace. 'I want a cigarette.'

'You put them on the bedside table,' Alice said and waited for whatever it was he had to tell while he lit the cigarette and then lay back on the pillows.

'I'm not the person you think I am. I never should have married.'

'That's silly. I don't know what it is you've done or imagine you've done, but whatever it is it has nothing to do with us being married.' She felt sorry for the state he was in, sorry and protective but also enjoying a feeling of satisfaction, of being capable, a real woman able to understand and comfort her husband. 'Is it something to do with the war? I know it must be ghastly. Being a man and having to be brave all the time, that's ghastly, too. I'll understand whatever . . .'

'I had a lover. A man. He died and I thought it was all over, that it had just been a passing thing. That married to you I'd be normal. But I'm not, there have been others. I know now I can't ever love a woman as a husband should.'

'I'd understand about you being afraid, not wanting to go back.'

'Alice, you're not listening. I can't ever love you, not like that. Do you understand what I'm saying? Are you listening?'

She was listening. She had heard. But she didn't understand any of what he said. He was deranged. It happened to a lot of men at the Front. She knew, Nella had told her. Their nerves snapped, they walked away from the Front and just kept walking. They did strange things, thought strange things. They were slightly mad. Stephen was slightly mad.

'She met him.'

'Who?' Alice asked.

'Nella, once in Paris. His name was Émile. Ask her – she'll tell you it's true.'

The exotic Parisienne! Émile, and Nella had met him. She remembered it all now. Stephen telling her about the meeting with Nella, and her friend's reaction when she heard about the engagement. Nella's laughing up her sleeve whenever she spoke about Stephen. So then it *was* true. Stephen wasn't deranged – he had loved a man, he still loved men. She had to get away from him, she couldn't lie beside him.

She got up and shivered. The jacket of her nightdress was tangled somewhere in the bedclothes – her morning gown, where was that? In the dark she couldn't find it and she didn't want the light on – she didn't want to see Stephen's face. On the back of a chair she felt the fine cashmere shawl, part of her new trousseau; she put it round her shoulders and went to the window. The curtains hadn't been closed and she looked out at the night. From the bed, Stephen continued to talk. 'I never meant to hurt you. You were so beautiful, so sweet and gentle and I wanted to be normal, I thought I could make you

307

happy. But it didn't work and after our honeymoon I prayed to be killed in France. You'd think that prayer would have been an easy one to answer.'

Alice stared out into the darkness, trying to convince herself she was in a dreadful nightmare. Soon she would waken, everything would be all right. But Stephen kept talking, apologizing for himself, for what he had done to her. He talked away her delusion that she was dreaming.

'Come back to bed, or you'll catch a chill. I'll go into the dressing room.'

'That might be your prayer answered in another way,' she said bitterly. 'I might get pneumonia and die. And why shouldn't I feel bitter! I am bitter and angry. I feel old too, used and deceived. Tonight when we came to bed I was a young hopeful girl, delighted that my husband was home. You've changed all that.'

'I know. I'm sorry. It was despicable of me to marry you. I wish I could undo it.'

Oh God, undo it! She hadn't thought further than this moment, trying to come to terms with what he had told her. There was the future – what was she to do about that? Undo it, how could they? And if they didn't she had no future.

Stephen got out of bed and came to where she stood. 'Listen, Alice, and please believe me. One of the reasons I told you tonight was to let you know that there's nothing wrong with you. That to a normal man you'd be the most desirable woman.'

'How would you know? And what are you going to do about this situation?'

'I thought that for the time being we could carry on as usual. I'm only here for the week and after that, well, we'll have to think of a way to sort things out.'

'You mean we'll keep up appearances. I'll laugh and be happy and you'll be attentive and everyone will smile on the young lovers except the servants who'll know we aren't sleeping together. Mama will begin counting the days again, waiting for the announcement that I'm pregnant and from Horsham will come discreetly-veiled inquiries about my health.' Alice laughed – a harsh, hysterical sound.

'Are you all right? You're not going to break down or anything?' Stephen asked concernedly.

'No, I'm not going to break down or anything. I'm tired, go in the other room, I want to sleep.'

She lay in bed wanting to cry, to scream and shout. Rail against what had happened to her. It wasn't fair, oh it wasn't fair. Why her? It wasn't fair. She had loved him, wanted to please him. Had done everything she knew how to please him and all the while he was like that. Why was he? What made him? Did anyone else know? Nella must have, perhaps even her parents did? Maybe everyone knew except herself. She had to find out, she had to ask. Not her mother, *she'd* never tell her the truth. But Nella would. Now she owed Stephen no loyalty, she owed him nothing, there was no longer a need for silence. Nella would tell her, and if it was common knowledge, she would kill herself. There was nothing else for it. To keep up the pretence of being husband and wife would be difficult enough but to know you were the laughing stock of Dublin – that she couldn't bear.

Then she thought of men who were lovers of men and was filled with revulsion. Remembering Stephen's fumbling attempts to make love to her in the knowledge that he had been intimate with a man nauseated her and made her feel unclean. She had to wash, bathe, scrub every inch of herself, clean her teeth, use the mouthwash. She rang for her maid.

'I want a bath. Prepare it for me, please.'

'Are you sure, ma'am?' a sleepy Bridey asked, her eyes going round the room, seeing the closed dressing room door. 'It's the middle of the night.'

'I know the time. I've a chill, a bath will do me good. Make

309

sure it's very hot and I'll see to myself. You can go when you've run it.'

'Very well, ma'am.'

In the bath Alice scrubbed at her flesh until it tingled and afterwards wore a nightie belonging to the time when she was single. Everything she had bought for Stephen's homecoming and the underwear worn on her honeymoon must be thrown out. Not the cashmere shawl, he had not touched that, it was never meant to allure him. Cleansed, she lay in bed planning how she would broach the subject to Nella, deciding that she would leave the asking until Stephen went back. In the meantime she would pretend to be unwell, which would excuse her from going out of the house during his leave. She wouldn't ever be seen in public with him until she felt certain that no one in Dublin knew what he was really like.

'You actually met Émile?'

'I met a man in Paris with Stephen, I don't remember his name.'

'Oh Nella, how could you do this to me?'

'Alice, will you sit down and tell me calmly what you are on about. You came barging in here babbling about a Frenchman and Stephen, saying you are destroyed, your marriage ruined. Now be a good girl, sit and tell Nella.'

Alice told her what Stephen had said. Nella shrugged. 'I'm not surprised, devastated for you, of course, but not surprised.'

'Then you knew! Why didn't you tell me? Why did you let me marry him? Oh Nella, you were supposed to be my friend and you said nothing.'

'I suspected, that's not the same as knowing. I heard in Paris that he was running around with a rum lot and then of course I met him. But even so that's not the same thing as seeing people in bed together. And in any case I did sort of warn you and I did tell . . .'

'You did tell what, who?' Alice had got up from her chair and was agitatedly walking up and down.

'You,' Nella lied. She wasn't going to say 'your mother'. Alice had enough to put up with. To know that her mother had been aware of the possibility that Stephen had homosexual tendencies, would be the last straw for her. 'I did tell you to come to London when I did the nursing thing, remember. Without having absolute proof I couldn't do more. I hoped either that I was wrong or that Stephen just went through a phase, as some men do. And when all seemed well between you, well – what was I to think? You must see that.'

'I don't know what I see or think. I suppose there was nothing much else you could have done. I expect I wouldn't have believed you, anyway. But what do I do now?'

'Hope he gets killed – what else can you do?'

'Oh God, what an appalling mess. Does everyone know about Stephen?' Alice asked, before taking a chair.

'I doubt it. He has none of the mannerisms people associate with that sort of thing, which of course just goes to show how little we know about anyone. Some of the most masculine-looking men are that way. No, I'd say no one in Dublin has any idea.'

'But you said you'd heard rumours.'

'That was in France. A completely different set up, different crowd, all arty types, Americans, French, not Stephen's normal crowd, no army types. No, I'd bet on it that no one suspects a thing.'

'Well, that's something I suppose. But what about the rest of my life, children, for example?'

'You could take a lover. A lot of women do, even when the husband isn't "musical" as they say.' Alice seemed to ponder Nella's advice. 'I must say, whatever else Stephen's sordid confession has done it has made you grow up. Last week at the mention of a married woman taking a lover you'd have had a fit.'

311

Alice sighed and admitted that Nella was right, she did feel very grown up – old in fact, disillusioned.

'You're bound to, but the situation will improve, about you feeling ancient, I mean.'

'Women who take lovers – what do they do about babies?'

'Well in cases where the husband can perform it's an easy matter, for as they say, "it's a wise child knows its father", and vice versa. In your case it would be difficult, to say the least. But who knows, you might be able to come to an agreement; you keep his secret and if you get pregnant he buys champagne all round. Seems fair to me.'

'Oh Nella, when the war finishes, don't ever go away. I'd die without you. You can always make me laugh. Look at me in the middle of all this and you have me laughing.'

'I'm glad to be of some help. And keep on laughing. Life is lousy really, so to laugh is our only defence.'

As the year drew near its end Dolly lost faith in Miss Murtagh's fortune-telling. She hadn't had a postcard never mind a letter, and as for the tall dark stranger coming over the sea wearing a uniform, he was a long time coming . . . Nothing exciting had happened for ages. Miss Murtagh got in on her nerves these days, complaining about how much she missed working in Foxrock, how she missed the nice woman Bessie. And when Dolly reminded her that she knew the job was only temporary, saying that didn't stop you missing people. She was getting old and cranky.

The only bit of good news, not that she was really interested, was that Jem and his wife weren't hitting it off. Josie was supposed to have a roving eye. And there was talk of him planning to go to America after the war. Taking the Josie wan with him of course, though how that would stop her eye roving, she didn't know. If a woman was that way inclined, what difference would America make? Anyway, it was the price of him.

*

312

For a while after telling Nella about Stephen, Alice believed she could cope. Put the shame and bitterness from her mind, occupy herself and plan her future, but very soon she found her shopping expeditions, the sewing circle, the invitations she accepted and other pursuits were not enough to block the prospect of her future from her mind. Stephen was what he was: she had no marriage, divorce was out of the question and she would spend the rest of her life unloved and childless. Stephen's answer, when before he left she had asked what he saw as a solution, was to pray that he would be killed on the Front. And if he wasn't, he'd stay on in the army and serve abroad.

Much good that would do her, Alice thought wretchedly. She'd still be married, if only in name. And she wished he would be killed, telling herself that was the only way out, convincing herself when the thought of Stephen's parents crossed her mind, that for them too it was the best way. Once they recovered from their grief they could console themselves that he had died for his country, defending their way of life.

Then would come the guilt and remorse for wishing him dead and a black hopelessness filled her, so that when she woke in the mornings she didn't want to get up. What was there to rise for? She couldn't countenance the routine of living, washing, dressing, facing her parents, the servants. Only the knowledge that if she didn't put in an appearance her mother would come fussing, inquiring if she was ill, hoping she was pregnant, driving her further into despair, forced her to rise.

Nella, when she tried explaining how she felt, was impatient. Alice knew her so well, could read her face like a book, saw the glazed expression come into her eyes, and knew she was thinking: 'What a bore some people are. Why can't they sort out their lives, be positive.' Nella wasn't like that. If a place irked her she left it, the way she would leave Ireland after the war. If people became tiresome and demanding she dropped

313

them. She never asked for sympathy or advice for herself and she expected others to do likewise.

'What ails you is sex, or rather, the lack of it. You're still a virgin! It's bound to make you neurotic. You should read Freud. A lover, that's what you need, and to grow up. And for God's sake don't start crying. Be positive, find a man and then think about getting out of here after the war. Come with me to Europe. The war can't last forever, if for no other reason than they are bound to run out of cannon-fodder.'

Alice dried her eyes and made an effort to be cheerful. She promised herself that in future she would try to be positive, and that never again would she come crying to Nella or anyone else for advice. For however harsh Nella might seem she was right – you had to solve your own problems.

During the following weeks, Alice considered taking a lover. But how did you go about it? The men she met considered her a happily-married woman and she didn't have the knack or whatever it was to send out signals that she was available. Besides, she wasn't. No matter what Nella said she couldn't have just anyone for a lover, not just go to bed with someone because sex was supposed to be good for you. If she ever did it had to be someone she felt something for.

Chapter Fifteen

Stalemate – the guns on both sides silent, not a rifle fired in two days. The rain back again, dark, dank November weather: the men listless, bored, huddling in their waterproof capes, the capes glistening wetly. Robbie thought about last September, when there'd been a fine spell. Charlie had put him forward for a commission. It was a long time coming. It was dry on the night of the raid, he remembered . . .

'Sarge!' A man coming back from the latrine called, 'bloke just told me this front's closing down at the end of the month. Any truth in it, do you think?'

'Could be,' Robbie replied. 'They know what's happening in the bog before HQ does.'

'Be great, wouldn't it?' the soldier enthused.

'We'd only go somewhere else,' another man said. An argument began as to the merits of moving or staying.

'Cut it out, for Christ's sake you two,' someone shouted.

'Aye, cut it out. Let's have a sing-song. Cheer us up.'

Thank God for the Perkins of this war, Robbie thought. Always making the best of things. Loud, bawdy, no respect for officers, taking the piss, making you laugh – even at yourself.

Perkins was banging the spit and tobacco shreds out of his mouth organ, hitting it on the palm of his hand. 'Right now. *Take Me Back To Dear Old Blighty*.' The soldiers sang, thinly at first, then with increasing gusto. A repertoire of brisk, cheerful songs followed – *Keiler's Jam, Tipperary, Pack Up*

315

Your Troubles – and forks and spoons beat time on mess-tins.

Then love songs, sad, sentimental, sung with great feeling. They rested their voices, smoked, and afterwards a soldier known as Paddy was asked for an Irish song. 'Come on Pad, give us *Molly Malone*.' Paddy obliged. Robbie joined in: '*As she wheels her wheelbarrow, Through streets broad and narrow, Crying cockles and mussels alive, alivo*.' The last line was belted out.

They were too – the Dublin streets – broad and narrow. Robbie recalled his all too brief sight of them. That was another world – the sunshine and the lovely girls. In his mind's eye he saw it all again. Nelson's Pillar towering over the main street, the crowds, the sweetshop, the two girls arguing. His attempt at picking up the dark one. He would have succeeded if that old man hadn't pushed in.

'Eh up, here's the postman,' Perkins shouted. 'Like Father Fucking Christmas with that sack.'

Instead of beginning to give out the mail, the Post Corporal made for where Robbie stood. Ignoring the men clamouring for their letters, he said: 'He's back – Dusty's back. I just seen him.'

'Who's Dusty?' a soldier asked.

'The bloke who came on the raid with me and the Sarge,' Perkins said.

'What raid?'

'Look – piss off,' Perkins told him. 'It was before your time. Dusty got killed and the Sergeant's getting a gong. Now sod off, I want to hear what's going on.'

'I saw the Red Caps bringing him in. You want to see the state of him,' the Lance Corporal continued.

Robbie had never liked the foxy-faced man who always seemed to delight in bringing bad news up with the mail. Now he hated him and wouldn't give him the satisfaction of asking for more details of Dusty's return.

'All right – give out the mail.'

'Living rough, he's been. A Frog farmer found him in a

barn and turned him in. Up near Boulogne – he'd walked all
the way. Going home, he said, he was going to Newcastle.
That's what the Red Cap told me. He's still saying it.'

'Give out the mail and get going, that's an order.'

'All right Sarge, just thought you'd want to know,' the
Lance Corporal said.

'*Get going – that's an order*,' Robbie yelled in a voice that
threatened. The man gave out the mail. Robbie watched him,
hating him, knowing he was being unreasonable. He saw him
go and his arm form a salute. Captain Charles was coming up
the line. 'Sir,' Robbie stood to attention and saluted.

'He told you, I suppose.'

'Yes, Sir. I thought he was dead.'

'Everyone did. Might have been better.'

'How will it go?'

'He'll be court-martialled. They'll bring in a Major, Captain
and a Lieutenant to try him. The CO will defend and the
Adjutant prosecute.'

'Prosecute! You can't. He's mad. Been mad for years.'

'He seemed sane enough to me. First-class soldier.'

'How would you know, Sir, about his sanity? He's mad as
a bloody hatter. He's had the lot – gas, buried alive, been out
here three years.'

'We're all under a strain, Sergeant. We'd like to take off
for Boulogne. But we don't. I'll give him a good character,
of course.'

'A good character, is that all? They could find him Guilty,
shoot him. I've seen it happen. Bloke tried one day, verdict
the next, two hours before his execution. You've got to do
something – get a psychiatrist – get him a proper defence
counsel – soldiers on trial are supposed to have one now!'

'According to the book, but you know what it's like. What
I really came to tell you was that things are moving. You
should be commissioned shortly, nothing yet though about
the decoration.'

317

'Thank you, Sir.'

'Yes, well then, carry on Sergeant.'

Liam's health improved enough for him to look for a job when Bessie's temporary work with the Delahunts ended. She congratulated herself that he was in out of the wet and cold, in a shop that sold secondhand furniture, helping the owner cart in and out the articles bought and sold. Liam missed the fresh air, and his companions on the building site. He was determined that when the fine weather came back he'd go to labouring. But on the whole they were both contented. The bank balance was growing again, only sometimes Bessie felt lonely and one night told Liam so.

'It's a queer thing,' she said, 'here I am busy from morning till night, people in and out all day and yet there's times I feel terrible lonely.'

From behind his newspaper Liam made a sound which Bessie knew was meant to convey he was listening to her – though she was well aware he hadn't heard a word.

'There was a man "drownded" today – he jumped over the Liffey Wall.' Liam made the same noise. 'You fraud,' she said, throwing a pair of socks rolled into a ball from a pile of darning, hitting the newspaper.

'What's up? Why did you do that?' Liam asked, looking around the edge of the paper.

'Because you weren't listening to a word of mine.'

'I was.'

'What was I saying?'

'About the place being busy.'

'Ah,' she said, good-humouredly, ''tis easy to see the first flush is passed. There was a time when you hung on my every word, when I talked to you. Now we could be an old married couple sitting by the fire.'

'I'm sorry.' He put away the paper. 'Tell me so what I didn't hear.'

'I do wish I had a friend to gossip with, to sit with and have a cup of tea. The women around are nice enough, they bid you the time of day – but it goes no further than that.'

'They might think you're stand-offish.'

'Me?'

'You've property and a business. And you're up from the country. Dubliners are queer about Culchies as they call us.'

'You could be right, I never thought about that.'

'Join a Sodality, or the Third Order in Church Street. 'Tis only round the corner.'

'You're not serious?'

'I am – you'd meet the women.'

'And have my habit, waiting for me to die!'

'Who has their habits?'

'The women in the Third Order, blue habits, you bring them home.'

'What harm would that be and isn't blue a becoming colour on you?' He laughed at Bessie's shocked expression. 'I'm not serious! Stay home with me, I'll keep you company.'

'I know well you would – only it's talking I want. A friend I want – a nice woman with a husband you'd get on with. The two of you could go for a jar and we'd sit here pulling the pair of you to pieces.'

'I wouldn't say no to the jar,' Liam said and went back to his paper.

A friendly neighbour would be nice, but what ails me really is the want of a child, Bessie thought as she retrieved the socks and prepared to darn them.

Robbie and twelve men picked at random were detailed to report to HQ on the day of Dusty's court-martial. They would stay the night. If the verdict was guilty and the sentence death, Robbie would witness it and the twelve men perform the execution.

Not long after arriving Robbie saw two officers walking to

the mess-tent. One looked familiar. He asked the man he was talking to who they were.

'The Major is here to try Dusty, I don't know the other bloke.' The officers stopped outside the mess, and the Major turned so that Robbie saw his face. No wonder he looked familiar, it was Stephen Whitehead.

'Christ!' he exclaimed. 'I know him, I've got to talk to him, hang on.'

He marched quickly to where Stephen stood. Stephen looked in his direction, his face surprised, then delighted as recognition came.

'Rob . . .' he began. Robbie cut him short.

'Sergeant Brightwell, Sir!' He came to attention and saluted the two officers.

'Sergeant Brightwell, I'm delighted to see you. How are you?'

'Well, Sir.'

The other officer excused himself and left. 'Oh God, Robbie, it's so good to see you. I can't believe it. You – out here.'

'I thought it was you, Stephen. Where are you?'

'A few miles up the line. Down here for this court-martial.'

'I know. He's a mate of mine. A poor mad bastard. Look, just for a minute forget where we are, who we are. It's just me and you – two blokes who were kids together, and I want a favour. Go easy on him. He was the finest soldier. The bravest man, no deserter. Only someone who finally cracked. Do what you can for him.'

'Robbie, I can't discuss this man – you must realize that. I was sorry about your parents.'

'I don't *want* to discuss him: I'm telling you what he's like. Asking you to go easy on him – otherwise he might be shot.'

'I can't. I find court-martials and executions abhorrent. But they take place. Men are tried and someone must try them. I listen to the evidence and try to make a fair judgement. That's it – don't discuss it further.'

320

'Sir,' Robbie stepped back, saluted.

'Look after yourself.'

'You too, Sir.'

Dusty was found guilty of desertion in the face of the enemy. Sentence would be awarded in the morning. What would it be? The thought was in everyone's mind. The twelve men detailed to form a firing squad wondered which of them had the live ammunition.

'Desertion in the face of the enemy.' Robbie bitterly repeated the sentence, talking to himself. 'Dusty who had gone up to them, looked into the enemy's face and blown them up!'

He got drunk on wine bought from a soldier who made a business of supplying goods that couldn't be got through normal channels. At four a.m. he was woken by the guard. Stupefied from the cheap wine, his head pounding, he sat up.

'The Provost Marshall's here – Dusty's had it – he's to be shot at six o'clock.' Robbie got up and began dressing. He was putting on his sodden boots when Stephen came.

'I couldn't have done anything, you know that.'

'It doesn't matter now.' Robbie stamped his feet, working them into the boots.

'We found him Guilty on the facts presented. A plea was added because of mitigating circumstances. We had nothing to do with the death sentence. That's decided higher up.'

'I know, by bastards who've never been in action. Never known men like Dusty. Sitting on their arses playing God and soldiers.'

'That's the way things are, I'm afraid. Not much you can do about it. I'm sorry for your friend. Now I have to go. Goodbye Robbie, take care.' He held out his hand. Robbie took it.

'You too, Stephen. And thanks for coming.'

By five a.m. Robbie decided there was one thing he could do about it and went to inform Captain Charles.

321

'You have no choice in the matter, Sergeant. You will attend.'

'I won't, Sir.'

'It's an order.'

'I'm refusing it.'

'You're what?'

'I won't watch Private Miller being shot.'

'Brightwell, for Christ's sake, have you gone mad? You could be shot yourself – for inciting a mutiny. Lose your commission, the decoration.'

'Fuck them! I won't attend. I'm not watching a poor madman shot. Seeing his brains blown out at close range if the firing squad miss.'

Captain Charles liked Robbie, admired his qualities. He was a good soldier, would have made a fine officer. 'I know this is a hell of a strain but be reasonable man, for God's sake. No one likes what's happening, but it has to be done.' For a while longer he tried persuasion then gave up. 'Sergeant of the Guard!' The NCO came. 'This man is under arrest. Take him away.'

In the guardroom Robbie watched the hands of his watch move towards the hour, thinking how when you waited for something pleasant they crawled like snails; now they raced. He could hear the rain lashing down and men moving about, orders being shouted. And as the time came nearer, prayed as he had when a child, for Dusty, the words of the long-neglected prayers coming into his mind. He heard the volley, closed his eyes and hoped it had been accurate.

'Cap off. Quick march,' the RSM ordered, then marched Robbie before the CO. His charge was read.

'Have you anything to say for yourself, Sergeant Brightwell?'

Standing to attention, his eyes not meeting the Colonel's, Robbie said: 'Nothing, Sir.'

'Only your previous record as an outstanding soldier prevents me sending you to prison. Is that understood? You will be reduced to the ranks.'

'About turn. Quick march. Left, right, left, right,' the RSM roared. Outside he said, 'You crazy, stupid bastard, Brightwell! Get them stripes off before you go back up the line.'

'Conscription'll never succeed here. You should have seen the thousands signing the pledge against it.'

'Eat your dinner, Liam,' Bessie said, worried because lately Liam only picked at his food.

'Are you not interested in all that's going on?'

'Of course I am. I wouldn't want you off for a soldier. It's bad enough you attending the meetings but I'll put up with them if it means you'll stay here safe and sound.'

'Safe and sound – too many don't think beyond that.'

'It's all that concerns me.'

'That's women all over, wanting to keep the men by the fire.'

Bessie knew he said that half in a joke. Though she didn't care if he was serious. She wanted him safe by the fire, or in the bed with her, not endangering his life for any country. Nor swept along with the tide of the young men that nothing less than an Independent Ireland would satisfy. She prayed daily that he wouldn't, that their life would stay as it was and that she would conceive a child before she was too old.

In the summer of 1918 the Allies mounted a counter-attack against the Germans and gradually the enemy's advance was halted. Stephen's letters were written still with no mention of how he and Alice should live their future lives.

People talked optimistically about the war's end being in sight. Alice's mother said that maybe this time next year she and Stephen would be living in Horsham. She would miss

Alice so much but it would be lovely visiting them at Rudgewick Park. Then they must get a London house. Oh yes, it would be wonderful when the war was over. Sugar would be plentiful – no more of that sandy stuff.

Her mother was a fool, Alice thought. A silly pretentious old woman. A snob, greedy, but not wicked. Not someone who, knowing or even suspecting Stephen's homosexuality, would have arranged a marriage between them.

Her father was less hopeful that the world would be a better place after the war. Everything had changed, would change further still. Their lives and those of people like them would never be the same again. The Bolsheviks would take over the world. Look at what they had done in Russia – the Tsar and his family murdered. Between them and the Sinn Feiners few could rest easy any more.

Thinking about the end of the war, Stephen's return and the remainder of her life spent in pretence, for that was what she had decided must be, Alice sighed.

'I don't know,' her mother said, looking at her. 'You've never completely recovered from that illness, whatever it was.'

'I'm fine, Mama.'

'You're not. You mope about, pick at your food and look pale.'

'I'm all right.' Just leave me alone. Don't force me to think too much. Leave me to go on a bit at a time, Alice thought.

'I worry about you, though Doctor Summers assures me there's nothing wrong. I was wondering, Lady Basset runs a canteen, it's near the Park. She's always looking for volunteers. Nothing strenuous, serving tea and being pleasant to the soldiers, that sort of thing. It might do you good. Shall I tell her you are interested?'

Alice said, 'Yes, if you like.'

Chapter Sixteen

On the night the war ended Dolly was standing outside Amiens Street Station waiting to meet her friend Ethel. The street was crowded with people out celebrating the Armistice. It was cold and damp, Ethel was late and Dolly began to regret leaving the fire to stand shivering in the November night. She was half-listening to a conversation between two men standing near her.

'Well, this has put an end to all the furore about conscription, thank God,' one man said.

'That thing, though they made it law, never had a chance of getting off the ground. Sure we wouldn't have let it,' the other man said.

They were both drunk – in a minute the argument could come to blows, Dolly thought, and she moved a few feet away from them. Crossing over the road in front of the station she saw a woman who even in the dark couldn't be mistaken for anything else but a wan out on the game. Dolly watched. The woman came nearer. She could see the colour of her outfit shown up by the street lamp. Shiny bright purple and a hat with a feather as long as your arm. A soldier called out something in an English accent that Dolly couldn't understand. But the woman in purple who had now reached her side of the road did and shouted back, 'I might if you could afford it!' The soldier laughed. The voice – that was Bid Dunne's! But Bid was in England. Well, she wasn't, she was on the path walking towards Dolly. Bid was out on the town!

Oh Sacred Heart of Jesus don't let her see me. I'll die if she does. Everyone will think I'm the same if she stops and talks. Bid, how did you finish up like that? Bid was sauntering along the path, her thin costume skin-tight, the feather waving on her hat. In a minute she'll be on top of me. I have to avoid her, Dolly thought. She turned and ran up the station steps, praying as she went that Bid wasn't going there as well. She stood by the door not looking back for what seemed hours. Afraid as each time someone came near her that it would be Bid. When at last she looked around there was no sign of her.

Ethel came soon afterwards and on the way to the Armistice party Dolly told her about Bid.

'That was your pal, the one who went to England?'

'Yes, Bid Dunne. Remember I told you she was mad about a fella, Kevin McEvoy, years ago.'

'My mother was telling me last week about a girl from Jacobs that went to England and came to a bad end. I never thought much at the time, she's always telling me about girls coming to a bad end. Now that I come to think of it, I'm sure Dunne was the girl's name. Where did she live?' Dolly told her.

'That's her then. Isn't that a coincidence? There's terrible talk about her. Apparently she stayed no time in the Liverpool factory. Went into munitions. She was making shells and earning great money – three pounds ten a week. The woman who told my mother had a daughter living near Bid in Liverpool. There was talk of a child. Anyway, she's back now and according to the latest is in Monto. But the worst of all is that she has the bad disease. She was seen coming out of the Lock hospital the other day. And to think I didn't believe my mother. Isn't it a small world all the same. Did she see you?'

'No. She was crossing the road and I was just going to call her. Then a cab stopped in front of her. She must have got in. I never had the chance to shout or anything.'

'Just as well. You know what they say, "Show me your company and I'll tell you what you are".'

Dolly tried to put thoughts of Bid from her mind, but during the following weeks everywhere she went there were constant reminders. All over the city, on walls, hoardings and painted on gable ends in big letters were messages: *Rally to Sinn Fein. General Election December 14th. Come out and vote. Remember the Men of Sixteen.* How could she forget Bid or the men of Sixteen? Jem and Kevin McEvoy and Danny and the ones she had seen marching that day. Poor Bid, she should have stopped her, spoken to her. But maybe Bid would have been ashamed to be seen by her the way she was. Otherwise, wouldn't she have dropped a line to say she was back? She didn't want anyone to know about her. That was it.

'Dail Eireann,' Dolly said and before she could add, 'not that again,' her father asked, 'Do you know what it means? Do you know what's happening in the country?'

'Not really.'

'I didn't think so, for you spend too much time out gallivanting and never a glance at a newspaper. Will I explain, alanna?'

'If it doesn't take too long. I'm going out in a minute.'

Johnny knocked out his pipe, settled himself comfortably and delighted to have a listener, began to talk. 'Dail Eireann – the Assembly of Ireland, that's what it means in English – is our new government with seventy-three elected members, though half of them are still in gaol. Seventy-three, that's the number Sinn Fein got, beating the others into a cocked hat. In January they met for the first time in the Mansion House and declared an Irish Republic. And in February when De Valera got out of Lincoln Gaol they made him the President. Are you with me so far?'

Dolly said she was and her father continued. 'Well, Dail Eireann is going it alone. Ignoring the Castle, setting up its own departments and Ministers of one thing and another. Michael Collins, the big fella from Cork, is selling Republican Bonds to raise thousands that'll finance the government. There'll be Sinn Fein courts, councils and everything that was run by the British will be ignored and run by us. Passive resistance, they call it. So far the British think it's all a bit of a cod. Though maybe after Dan Breen's raid on the Soloheadbeg RIC barracks they'll think again. Myself, I don't think it'll work – once England sees that Sinn Fein mean business she'll crack down. What I believe will happen is . . .'

'Listen Da, thanks for telling me, but honest to God I have to get ready now.'

'Ah – go on then, I only hope I've given you some understanding of the situation.'

'Oh yes you have Da, but if there's any more to it you'll have to finish telling me another time. I have to get ready now.' And she thought as she went into the other room – understand – I do in my eye. All I understand is that everything and everyone has changed. Never a word from Bid and her back in Dublin although she wasn't sure what she'd do if she did get in touch. Jem O'Brien and his wife going to America and Kevin McEvoy living up in the north. Nothing was the same any more. And the dances were a cod. Full of eejits up from the country. Grocers' porters and shop assistants, drenched in sweat, not wearing a jacket and feckin oul ceildhe music, with them swinging the arms out of you and talking Irish. The changes were terrible! All the crowd married. Everyone who had been at the Dempseys' hooley during the Rebellion, even Jackie, one arm and all, the father of two children. Only herself and Becky left looking for a husband.

It was only on rare occasions and then only to herself that Dolly admitted she might have missed her chance. Now as she finished getting ready for the dance her mind dwelt on it. Fellas weren't easy to come by any more. Well, not fellas you'd look twice at, anyway. The decent ones were all dead, killed in the war, left cripples or married. There were plenty of awful-looking tickets and widowers, oul fellas who'd be better employed saying their prayers than out dancing.

She smiled at herself in the mirror, stripping her teeth. Her teeth were lovely. She teased her hair forward, it didn't suit her, she pushed it back. Licking a finger she smoothed her eyebrows, she liked their shape and colour, arched and a shade darker than her hair. She was ready and went back to the kitchen to wait for Ethel to call. Her father was dozing in his chair, her mother by the fire sewing. She sat opposite her, her mind still occupied with how things had changed over the years.

The wans in work, little bits of things, impertinent bitches, all engaged and saving up to be married. Getting on your nerves, always flashing their rings up in your face. And you wouldn't mind only half of them were bits of glass, or bought secondhand from the pawn. The way they took them off before washing their hands, and their screams if you as much as tipped near the side of the sink. 'Mind and don't knock me ring down.'

Bridget watching Dolly's face saw the lines of discontent marring her mouth and pictured her in the years to come finishing up an old maid. A bitter, fussy old maid, her looks gone and bad on her feet. That's what's in store for her, she told herself, unless she hurries up and gets a man. The crabby ways she's getting. Forever at her clothes, pressing and ironing and folding them like a draper's assistant. Poking and probing at every bit of food, sniffing the milk, losing her rag over a few crumbs on the table and washing her hands fifty times a day. It's a man and a houseful of children she needs.

Dolly, unaware of her mother's scrutiny, pursued her own thoughts. Even going across town of a Saturday, all the good was gone out of that. Not like it used to be with Bid. Ethel was all right, very respectable, but not like Bid. She hated bumping into someone who used to work in Jacobs years ago.

Full of sly digs and the face of policy on them when they said: 'God, Dolly! Dolly Devoy! It's great to see you. Are you not married yet? Nor doing ne'er a line?' And their eyes taking in every stitch you were wearing and only waiting to meet someone else and say, 'Do you know who I've just been talking to – Dolly Devoy – all dressed up as per usual and still looking for a man!'

Well, if she never got a man she didn't envy them. Didn't want to be one of them with their streels of children, not a decent flitter on their backs and their bellies tipping their chins year in, year out. She didn't envy them their men, mouldy drunk every night of the week and wanting you to dance attendance on them. Not if she never married. And if and when she did, she'd take a man to be proud of, a man they'd stand and look after.

The picture she kept in her mind of him was as clear as ever and she measured all other men against it. But as days and dances came and went and another year was over Dolly wondered often if she would ever meet him at all. Soon she would be twenty-four, then twenty-five before you knew it. The days and nights might drag but the years flew. Twenty-five was getting on. She used to think she'd be married by then. Definitely by then or when the war was over. The war was over this good while and she didn't even have a fella.

Neither did Ethel. Ethel wouldn't tell you her age but she must be gone thirty – what a hope she had of finding anyone. She was desperate for a fella, even going out with soldiers. Wanted the two of them to go up the quays looking to click soldiers. She has her glue if she thinks I'd lower myself. Only the lowest of the low did that. Everyone knew what soldiers were.

'Your brother was a soldier,' Ethel always threw up to her the way Bid used to.

'He had no choice. My father says only scum join the army, fellas that wouldn't be given a job anywhere else. They're

330

here today and gone tomorrow leaving bastards behind them, and they're Protestants, that's what he says.'

'Your father's an oul fella, they all say them things about religion and strangers. They're back in the penal days, expecting every soldier to kill or rape you. They're not like that, they're only fellas and sure thousands of them are Irish anyway, and a bloody sight more attractive than ordinary fellas with the uniforms and the lovely carriages of them. Uniforms are gorgeous.'

'I know all that – I'm not blind. The handsomest fella I ever saw was a soldier. But I'm still not going up the quays.'

'Well I must say, working in the canteen has done wonders for you!'

'It keeps my mind occupied,' Alice said.

'What's the situation with you and Stephen now that the war is over? You haven't said anything for ages and I didn't want to pry,' Nella said.

'He's staying on in the army, hoping to go abroad. The Gold Coast – that would be a legitimate excuse for me not joining him, he says.'

'Is that all?'

'I thought about a divorce.'

'And?'

'I wrote and suggested that he might consider arranging one.'

'You mean have him go to Brighton for a weekend, pay some woman to stay in the same room and a grubby little detective takes pictures of them entering the room and signing the register?'

'Yes, that sort of thing – that is how it's done, isn't it?'

'Oh yes – the chivalrous man lets his wife divorce him. What did he say?'

'Wouldn't hear of it – not yet, not while he's still in the army. He pointed out that everyone in the Regiment knew

331

he wasn't a womanizer. Rumours would circulate that it was a put-up job, that I had been unfaithful and he was doing the decent thing.'

'The bastard!' Nella said. 'It's his own skin he's considering. Afraid someone might put two and two together and come up with his secret.'

'I came to that conclusion myself. At first I felt sorry for him, because if it came out not only would he be cashiered, but as homosexuality is illegal, he might even face prison. If he'd been honest and said these were his real reasons for not arranging a divorce I'd have had sympathy for him. But of course he went on about my reputation being damaged, about the fuss my parents would create . . . it sickened me, all the lies.'

'Unfortunately there is some truth in what he says. Your reputation would be damaged and I'm not sure if you've changed enough to weather the cold-shouldering you'd be bound to receive. And of course your mama would have a fit.'

'I know, but still the lies sickened me. Talking about Mama, she's bound to find an excuse for popping in here. Let's go into the garden.'

Nella laughed. 'She'll want to check up on my smoking. All right – the garden it is. Shall we walk or sit?' she asked when they arrived.

'Sit,' Alice said, leading Nella to her favourite seat near the kitchen garden.

'Aren't lilacs horrid when they are dying! Move up, I don't want them dropping bits in my hair. As I was saying, your mama would have apoplexy. Families hate scandals. They preach morality and respectability when what they really mean is – don't be found out. And if you are, for God's sake, hush it up quick. So what is the position now with you and Stephen? How long ago did you have his letter? Have you replied – has he, and what's the outcome?'

'His latest suggestion is that I be patient for a little longer,

332

while he thinks things out.' Nella snorted derisively. 'Yes, I know,' Alice said. 'But at least now he knows that I've seen through his excuses, that I'm not going to be easily fobbed off. I've told him so. I've told him that he's only concerned with himself and keeping up appearances and I'm the one paying the price.'

'Good for you. So what's your next move? You must have some plans. It's ages since we talked like this, since you first told me about Stephen.'

'Two years,' Alice said.

'Good heavens, is it that long?'

'Yes. Do you remember when I first told you and I thought I'd grown up, could cope?'

'Yes, I do. I thought good for you. It's one of the reasons I haven't brought up the subject, since you seemed fine.'

'I wasn't. What Mama put about as my having influenza was really a breakdown. I thought I was mad.'

'You looked perfectly sane to me!'

Alice laughed. 'Dear Nella, I love you, you're my friend, but don't let's pretend. You didn't notice how I looked. You'd see my dress, my hair, nothing beyond that. I'm not blaming or criticizing you. You're always so occupied – getting on with your own life. And you're right. You make demands on no one. I think, I hope, I'm changing.'

Nella stood up, brushing at her skirt, touching her hair, then getting a cigarette and lighting it before speaking. 'I don't know what to say. You've given me an eye-opener. I never saw myself like that, selfish, insensitive. Perhaps you're right, perhaps that's me. So you can take me or leave me. I'm not going to change, but I'm glad you have. And I'm glad you don't intend waiting too long. Dress it up how you like – what you need is a man, love, sex. Only find it soon. Don't be lulled into thinking – tomorrow, next week, next month. Or one morning you'll wake up and be forty and lovers won't be so eager then.'

'We're not quarrelling – you're not annoyed with me?'

'Annoyed . . . no, disconcerted for a moment. No, we're not quarrelling. You had a right to say what you did.'

Alice touched Nella's hand, 'Come on, sit down. Tell me about your plans for going to Europe.'

'They're postponed.' Nella sat and continued, 'There's this gorgeous man . . .'

'Hand in glove with England, that's what America is,' was the comment of the Irish nation in May when the Sinn Fein delegation returned from the Peace Conference at Versailles. They had gone with such high hopes. President Wilson would put the stamp of approval on Ireland's newly-declared Independent State – hadn't he said as much? And they quoted him: 'Every people in the world should choose its own master.' They had chosen. The President would endorse it, and Britain be forced by American and world opinion to accede to it.

'That oul bags refused. Nothing but flowery speeches, all blather, like all politicians.'

'You'll see now how long passive resistance will last,' Johnny announced when he read the account of President Wilson's refusal. Dolly let on not to hear, she didn't want another lecture. 'Wait'll you see the harassment and pressure that'll be put on Sinn Fein now.'

In September when Dail Eireann went underground, Johnny again looked for an audience. And when Bridget and Dolly ignored his opening remarks, he expounded them nevertheless. 'Now you'll see the turn events will take. With a fella like Collins, the man's a genius, with him in charge of organization and intelligence – the days of passive resistance are gone by the wall. Did you see his picture in *Hue and Cry*, did you?'

'Yes we saw, didn't you show it to us. Now will you for God's sake shut up and stop giving me a headache,' Bridget said.

334

He was quiet for a while until Dolly made the mistake of saying that Michael Collins was a gorgeous-looking fella. 'Gorgeous-looking! Is that all you can say about him? The man's miraculous. He could organize anything. No one can touch him. Every policeman in the city is looking for him and he's riding a bike under their noses.'

'Games, that's what you think it is. Like little boys playing – "I'm the winner". Games – but the dead are real. There's no getting up and running home for them when the play is over. You're an oul booby like oul fellas everywhere. Too old for the games yourself but delighted watching the sport. And quick to change sides. I remember when you hadn't a good word to say for Sinn Fein, the Volunteers, the lot of them. When you couldn't wait to get Richard out of Ireland. Did you forget that, did you?' Bridget asked, her voice hoarse with bitterness and anger.

'No, I never forgot that,' Johnny said, and put away the paper.

20 November 1919

'*Dearest Alice,*

Bad news, I'm afraid. I'm being posted to Cork in the New Year. Typical of the Army, ask for Yorkshire and you get Surrey or in my case Cork instead of West Africa.

Still, in the circumstances and with me being considered a veteran, I suppose it's inevitable. Things really are in a bad way over there. Reading about the murders, attacks on police barracks – raids by the Army and Republican ambushes, I wish you'd go to Mama in Horsham. Ireland seems more dangerous than the trenches – at least there you knew who the enemy was.

Alice, I have to tell you how much I grieve for the appalling position I've put you in. I'd give anything that it might be otherwise. Please believe that and always remember that had it

335

*been possible for me to love a woman, there is no other I would
have chosen.*

> *My fondest love*
> *Stephen'*

At last he had mentioned it, Alice thought after reading the
letter. She was moved by the final line and for the first time
in months felt sorry for Stephen. Thinking that what ailed him
wasn't of his choosing. She remembered the nice things about
him, his kindness and gentleness and silly things like when he
had taught her to ride a bicycle, years ago, during her stay at
Horsham. Poor Stephen, condemned to such a way of life.
All the fears, the lies and subterfuge. For the time being she
would go ahead with the deception. He'd come up from Cork
sometimes and she'd play the good wife. But her sympathy
would not cloud her mind or interfere with her making something of her own life.

The evenings lengthened and grew warmer. Ethel began again
to coax Dolly to go walking with her.

'Say you will. We might click two nice fellas.'

'Soldiers you mean.'

'Soldiers won't eat you!'

'And what about the Black and Tans – look what they're
doing. Shooting innocent people, breaking down doors and
ransacking places.'

'They're nothing to do with soldiers. That feckin' oul Lloyd
George brought them in to help the police – they've nothing
to do with the army.'

'What do you think of their get-up?'

'Desperate – the black belts and caps are awful-looking with
khaki.'

'My father says they're called after a pack of hounds – the
Black and Tans, queer that.'

'You're only telling me all this to change the conversation. I know you, Dolly. Soldiers I was talking about. Are you going to come?'

'No,' Dolly said. 'Never.'

'One of these days you'll change your mind, wait'll you see.'

Liam heard the sound of a lorry stopping. He went to the window and looked through the lace curtains. 'It's the Tans – they've stopped a few doors down. Quick, put out the light. They're coming this way. No, they've gone in next door.'

In the dark Bessie walked to the door and bolted it. 'There's no one next door mixed up in anything.' She talked in a whisper.

'They'll have had a tip someone's hiding. Not that they need a reason to rob or murder or terrorize. That's why they're over here.' From the next house came the sound of women and children screaming.

'Sacred Heart of Jesus protect them. I hope they don't find the man if he's there,' Bessie said.

'Whether they do or not they'll leave their mark on the place.'

'Please God make them go. Let them find nothing. Let them not come near us.'

'Listen!' Liam said, 'they're out in the street. Don't make a sound, don't move. With the help of God they'll drive off.' They waited for the sound of the engine to start, scarcely breathing.

'*Open up.*' The door shuddered under the rifle blows. 'Come on, open up.'

'Don't; Liam. Don't open it,' Bessie pleaded. 'They'll kill us.'

'I have to – they'll only smash it down.' Liam drew back the bolt. He was pushed aside and the Tans came in, a Sergeant and three men. The men pointed their rifles at Liam. 'Over there, move, out of the way,' one of the men ordered.

337

'Who's here?' the Sergeant asked.

'Me and the wife, no one else.'

'Light the bleeding gas.' Bessie lit the mantle. The Sergeant, cock-nosed with gingery hair showing beneath the black cap went behind the counter searching, raking with his rifle the spare crockery for arms. The delft fell, smashing on the floor. 'Right, you, into the kitchen.' Liam went, followed by the three men. 'Give it a good going-over lads,' the Sergeant called after them.

They opened the presses, dragged out their contents, threw them on the floor, swept the dresser of its plates and tureens, their boots crunching on the broken delft. Their bayonets slashed through the sacks of flour, oatmeal and dried peas. 'Nothing here, Sarge,' they grinned, looking around at their handiwork.

'Is there gas up there?' with a nod in the direction of the stairs the Sergeant asked Bessie.

'Only an oil lamp.' Bessie's voice was little more than a whisper. 'It's down here. I was trimming the wick.'

'Light it, then up the stairs.' Carrying the paraffin lamp Bessie led the way, fear and hatred making her legs tremble and her heart pound. Please God, she prayed, I don't mind what they do, nothing, so long as they don't take Liam. She heard the other men come running up behind them. She led them from room to room. Watched as they searched the drawers and cupboards, wrenching out the drawers, throwing them on the floor, slitting the feather bed. The down escaped, rose in the air, hovered like snowflakes, fell and settled in the men's caps and shoulders as they ransacked and kicked in the door of a closet that wouldn't open easily. Fine feathers irritated her eyes mingling with her tears and she silently prayed. Dear Jesus, I offer it all up. They're only things – they don't matter, let them smash and break everything. But please make them spare Liam. And please God make him keep his mouth shut.

338

'Nothing,' the Sergeant said and gave the word to leave. Bessie lighted their way down. Liam was at the foot of the stairs. She knew by his face what he had endured while she was upstairs. Everyone knew the Tans didn't always stop at killing and smashing. 'It's all right, love,' she said, trying to reassure him.

'No, by Jesus, it's not all right! You murdering lot of bastards! Coming into innocent people's homes, terrorizing them, destroying their places!'

Bessie knew it was his relief from fear of what might have happened to her that gave him a foolish courage. A courage that could lose him his life. 'Shut up, love. Everything's all right. Don't say anything. Don't say a word.'

'Do what the little woman says, mate. Like keep your lip buttoned.' The Tan hit Liam across the mouth. 'Like that, see.'

'Come on,' the Sergeant called, walking towards the door. Liam wiped his hand across his mouth and looked at the blood. The others were following the Sergeant. Liam lunged after the man who had struck him. Bessie threw herself on him, dragging him back, pleading with him.

'Let them go – for God's sake, let them go – they'll take you in the lorry – let them go.' She held on to him tightly – her eyes never leaving the door until the last man was through. Then she relaxed her hold. 'Let me see what they did.' She turned him around. 'Your poor lip, it's in gores. Come into the kitchen, I'll bathe it and staunch the blood. It'll want a stitch, though. We'll go round to Jervis Street.' She began to lead Liam to the kitchen.

'Fucking Micks!' She recognized the voice of the Tan who had hit Liam. Jesus, he was coming back! She looked around to see – the door flew open. 'Fucking Micks!' she heard again, then there was a terrible noise in her head and she knew no more.

When she came to it was very cold and she could hear

voices. Voices telling her, 'It's all right. Lie still. You'll be all right. Don't move now.' And she noticed a strange thing – she could see the moon as if it was in the room with her – not like looking at it through the window. She was shivering and her head hurt and her legs, and she didn't know where she was. Then the voices were talking again. 'I saw them. They were just getting into the lorry. They had the engine on and all. And I thought thanks be to God they're off when one of them jumped out, ran back to the eating house and threw in something. It must have been a grenade. They'll be stone dead, I thought when I heard the explosion and saw the walls collapsing. Weren't they lucky to survive it.' Then Bessie began to remember and realized why she could see the moon without looking through the window. And she began to scream, 'Liam, Liam, where are you? What's happened to you?'

'He's all right. He's safe. He was knocked out that's all. Your legs were trapped for a while but you're clear now. Just hold on for a minute and everything will be grand.'

Then she was being lifted and carried into the parlour of a public house. Someone put a pillow under her head and covered her with a blanket. A man bent over her. 'I'm a doctor, let me have a look at you,' he said. His hands moved over her. 'Well,' he said, 'you and your husband had some-body's prayers. A bit of concussion. There's nothing broken. You'll be all right.'

Bessie caught hold of his hand. 'Where's my husband, where's Liam?'

'They have him in the snug. He's stretched out on a bench doing the women out of their seats. He's grand. The landlord'll put the pair of you up for the night.'

'His lip was cut, did you see that?'

'I put a stitch in it. It'll be fine.'

In the landlord's bed Bessie held Liam while he cried like a child and said, 'I could do nothing for you. I couldn't lift a

340

hand to protect you. That was the worst part of it. Standing by while they ordered you about, took you up the stairs not knowing what their intentions were.'

Bessie comforted him. 'Don't be blaming yourself. What could anyone do against four men with rifles? I didn't expect you to try anything. I kept praying you wouldn't, kept asking God not to let them goad you into doing something. But you were very brave all the same. You risked your life for me. I was proud of you making the stand.'

'A stand how are you! A lot of good it did. But something came over me at that minute. I didn't care, I'd gone beyond reason, beyond weighing up the odds. Do you know it was a terrible situation to be in – to stand by not able to protect your wife – it's something I'll never forget.'

'Hush now, it's all over and we were spared. We have each other, I love you and we'll overcome the setback.'

'What would I do without you, Bessie? I love you.' He tried to kiss her.

'Don't, your poor lip. It's twice its size. Leave the kissing for tonight. Sleep is what we need.'

But Liam wasn't sleepy and without kissing, made Bessie forget for a while the ordeal they had gone through.

Miraculously, some pieces of furniture and cooking utensils had survived the explosion. Bessie and Liam retrieved them the next morning and a neighbour stored them until they found somewhere new to live.

The publican's wife said: 'Rooms round here are hard to find since men came back from the war. Girls that lived on their mother's floor, want their own place now their husbands are home. But I'll ask.' The woman went into the snug and returning told Bessie there was a room going in Clanbrassil Street, number ninety-seven. 'Knock on any of the doors and someone will tell you where the landlord lives. I'd go straight away before it's gone. Please God you'll be lucky, and till you move in stay here.'

341

Bessie cut up through Thomas Court, taking what she believed was the quickest way to Clanbrassil Street. She found the house and knocked on Bridget's door. 'Good evening, ma'am, I'm sorry for disturbing you. I'm looking for a room, someone told me there's one vacant here.'

'Come in,' Bridget said, 'it's cold in the hall. Sit down for a minute. There's one vacant at the top of the house, though I wouldn't recommend it.'

'I'm desperate.' Bessie told her about the Black and Tans.

'God help you. The curs, the murdering curs. Have a cup of tea, it's wet. It's a back room, no size, but if you're desperate it'd do.' She poured the tea and gave Bessie bread and butter. 'Have that and then I'll bring you to the landlord. It's only round the corner in Lombard Street.'

On the way to the landlord's, Bridget told Bessie she'd say she knew her, that she had a good principle. 'As long as he feels sure of his rent you'll get the room.'

The room had been damp and dirty and Bessie was still in two minds about taking it. 'I don't know what to do,' she said to Bridget. 'If I turn it down I mightn't find another in a hurry and I can't impose on the publican's wife.'

'If you're that desperate take it for the time being. A bit of elbow grease and a couple of good fires will make a difference. And I'll tell you this, ninety-seven is a nice respectable house, with decent people living in it.'

'Well, ma'am, if you're anything to go by they are surely. I'll take it in the name of God.'

'If you're in a hurry to go home I'll tell the landlord and the room will be yours.'

Bessie thanked Bridget and went back to the public house to tell Liam they had a roof over their heads again. The publican's wife was waiting for her. 'Mrs Maguire, your husband's lying in the parlour. I made him lay down on the sofa.'

'Sacred Heart of Jesus! What ails him?'

'He's all right, a bit of weakness. They brought him home

342

from work,' the woman said, bringing Bessie into the parlour.

Liam was asleep. 'I wouldn't waken him, the rest will do him good,' the woman whispered as Bessie went to the sofa and bent over Liam. He opened his eyes and smiled at her.

'Are you all right, love?' she asked, trying to keep her voice steady for he looked terrible.

'Did I give you a fright?' He held her hand. 'I got dizzy for a minute, that's all. I'd have been grand if your man had left me alone. But sure he's a bulldriver. There was a wardrobe to go out on the cart. "Can you lift it or not?" says he. "Let me get back my breath and the head stop spinning," I said. And do you know what he did?'

'Don't keep working yourself up, lay back there,' Bessie said as Liam started to sit up.

'He went out to the corner, there's always a crowd of fellas there, and brought one of them in to shift the wardrobe – "and you," says he, "go home and don't bother coming back".'

'So you lost the bit of work?'

Liam sighed. 'I lost it, but to Hell's gates with him, I'll go back to labouring.'

'Please God you will. I got a room.' Bessie told him all about it and that now she'd find a young fella with a handcart to take up their things. She also told him about Bridget and what a kind woman she was. 'I'm sure she'll be a grand neighbour.'

And Bridget told Dolly about the woman who had taken the top back room. 'I'm sure you'll like her. She's been through a terrible ordeal.'

'Is that so?' Dolly said, not particularly interested.

'A lovely person. God, I forgot all about the letters. Two of them for you. Who'd be writing to you?'

'Letters, for me, where? Give me them.' For a minute she hoped Jem O'Brien had written. She looked quickly at the envelopes. There wasn't one from America. 'From Dublin,'

343

she said. She recognized Bid's handwriting and opened her letter first, taking out the single sheet and reading it.

'Who's it from?' her mother asked.

'Someone in work. She left to be married – you wouldn't know her,' she lied. She hadn't told her mother she had seen Bid on Armistice Night, nor would she tell her Bid wanted to meet her in town on Saturday.

She opened the other letter. 'It's from Miss Murtagh. She's giving out yards about me not going to see her. Listen to this: "*It's months since you were here. I hope nothing ails you. I haven't been too good myself. My sight's bad. I should go to the Eye and Ear – I can't see a stim in front of me. Threading a needle's very hard to do.*" You can say that again – she's nearly blind. That's how she made such a bags of the last frock.'

'God help her, she's getting old. One day you'll know what it's like.'

I'm getting old now, Dolly thought, putting away the letters and sitting down for her tea. I don't need reminding. Ethel's constantly doing that, telling me time is passing and I'm missing my chance. That I should try the quays, what did I have to lose?

While she ate Dolly wondered what to do about Bid. Should she risk meeting her, being seen with her? If Bid arrived in the get-up she'd worn on Armistice Night, she'd die. It might be wiser not to go. She couldn't make up her mind. Though she'd love to see her for old times' sake, and to find out if what Ethel said about a child and Monto was true.

'Give us the letters again, Ma.' Bridget handed them to Dolly. Suddenly she remembered Miss Murtagh and the fortune-telling! She was right – two letters! That's what she'd said – and in the space of two. It had come true, even if one of them was from herself. Maybe the other bit would as well. The dark man in uniform with the money round him. She felt on top of the world. And for old times' sake she decided to risk meeting Bid.

Chapter Seventeen

On Saturday she stood at the top of Grafton Street waiting
for her, sometimes looking down the street, sometimes over
to the Green, not sure from which direction Bid would come.
She was late, maybe she wouldn't turn up. Maybe that would
be for the best. She'd have an easy conscience and once and
for all could put Bid out of her mind, instead of feeling guilty
about the night she had let on not to see her. Dolly looked
across to the gate of the Green, then down towards the
Shelbourne – not a sign of her. Then someone touched her
back, she turned round and there was Bid. She was overcome
with delight, the years fell away, it was as if they'd never been
parted.

'Dolly! Dolly Devoy!' Bid went to embrace her, her face
looming near Dolly's, ready to kiss her. Dolly remembered
the bad disease and stepped back, attempting to conceal her
repugnance by pretending fright.

'You put the heart across me,' she clutched her bosom, 'I
wasn't expecting you to come up behind me.' Her eyes examined Bid's face looking for sores, a rash, but her skin was pink
and clear. And she looked reasonably respectable in the navy
blue costume. But she'd become a devil for feathers, another
long one on her hat now swaying and waving and she could
have done without that long string of a blue scarf around her
neck. Still, it was lovely to see her again. 'I'm delighted to see
you. After all these years! I can't believe it. Why didn't you
write?'

'Listen – I'm dying for a cup of tea. Let's go into the DBC and I'll give you all the news.' Bid linked her arm through Dolly's. Dolly could smell her scent and something else. Surely to God not drink, but that's what the smell was. She hesitated.

'Come on, I'm starving.' They began walking. 'Remember the night in Coppollo's after the concert and Jem O'Brien forgot his money?'

'Indeed I do,' Dolly squeezed Bid's arm affectionately. 'We had great times. You clicked that night with Kevin.'

'Don't mention that bastard's name.'

'Bid, keep your voice down. Don't be cursing, not here.' It was a mistake to come. I'm sure she's drunk – she'll make a show of us. 'Maybe a walk in the Green would be nice before we have a cup of tea,' Dolly suggested after thinking her thoughts.

'The tea first,' Bid insisted.

They found a table and sat down. A girl took their order and while they waited Dolly was studying Bid's face. It was flushed from more than excitement and every time she opened her mouth the smell of drink was terrible. 'Did you have something to drink?'

'A bottle of stout,' Bid said apologetically, then laughed. 'Jasus! Listen to me making excuses. It's easy to see I'm back in Dublin.'

'You've broken your Confirmation Pledge, do you know that?'

'Give over Dolly, we're not kids any more.' Bid's voice was no longer laughing nor apologetic.

She's drunk and the heat in here is making her worse. I knew it, I was mad to come. How am I going to get out of this without a scene? Dolly looked quickly around at the well-dressed respectable men and women drinking tea, eating scones, talking and laughing quietly. Supposing Bid kept on cursing. She was a show . . . her face the colour of a beetroot. It was more than one bottle of stout she had drunk. And that

346

feather on her hat, nearly knocking the eye of the man at the next table. She hoped the tea would come soon. Then she'd humour Bid, agree with all she said and get her out as soon as possible. Hoping her disapproval didn't show in her voice she asked, 'Will you be coming back to Jacobs?'

'I will in me arse! Eightpence-an-hour for a forty-seven hour week. There's no green in my eye. I can earn that in a jiffy.'

'It's good money for Dublin and with you being at the oatcake-making in Liverpool you'd have no bother getting back.'

'Do you think I'm mad or something – go back to that kip? If it wasn't for Jacobs I wouldn't be where I am today.'

'How do you say that?'

'Wasn't it through Jacobs I met him – that little lousy bastard that's the cause of all my trouble.'

'Don't talk so loud Bid, the girl's bringing the things.' They'd be asked to leave in a minute, Dolly was sure, the man at the next table was looking daggers at them. 'Keep your voice down, everyone's looking.'

'Let them look,' Bid said truculently. 'Let them look,' she repeated, but this time quietly, and as her voice subsided her body appeared to do so as well, her shoulders slumping, her breasts sagging and when she spoke again it was in a hoarse whisper. 'I never told you, I never told anyone. He made it up with me before I went to Liverpool. Three times we went out before I went away. I wanted to change my mind about going I was that delighted. But he coaxed me not to. He said he'd folly me over, we'd get married. He told me he was mad about me, and I believed him – I wanted to believe him. I loved him. God knows I've had plenty of fellas since, but if he walked in that door this minute I'd split him with the teapot and then I'd go with him wherever he took me.'

'Oh Bid – I knew you liked him, but I never knew you had it that bad. Well, what happened after you got to Liverpool?

347

You wrote and said you were having a grand time, plenty of fellas.'

'I only said that – you can't go away then write that you're not happy. What happened was that I was there no time when I knew I was up the pole.'

'Oh God!'

'And being the eejit that I am, I thought, well it's not the end of the world. Me and Kevin's getting married anyway, so what's the odds. I wrote and told him. Days went by and no word. I thought maybe the letter went astray, so I wrote again. And for a joke I said, maybe he'd rather we had the wedding at home and that if I didn't hear I'd be over. There was a letter by return post. I nearly died. I couldn't believe it.' Bid was crying, the tears running down her face.

'Oh Bid, don't cry. I've never seen you cry before. Don't cry.' Dolly's own eyes filled with tears.

'Do you know what killed me altogether – he said how was he to know he was the father. He made me out to be a prostitute. And he said, "Don't come home for I've enlisted and I'll be in France."'

'The dirty cur – that was lies – he joined no army. So what did you do?'

'I nearly went mad. I couldn't come home. My mother would have thrown me out. Then it would have been into one of them places for fallen women. And the prospects in Liverpool weren't much better. I wanted to do away with myself . . .'

'You should have told me. I'd have done something.'

'What?'

'No, I suppose you're right. But all the same I'd have written to you.'

'It wasn't letters I wanted.'

'So what did you do?'

'I stopped thinking about doing myself in, tightened my stays until I nearly burst and prayed it would go away. Then

348

one day I fainted. Afterwards a girl breasted me with the truth and said she knew someone who could get rid of it. But it would cost me five pounds and I needn't tell you I didn't have the colour of it. She said she'd lend it to me.' Now and then Bid dabbed at her eyes with the end of the long silk scarf. Dolly was thinking, surely to God she didn't get rid of it. You couldn't do that. That was a mortal sin. And she shouldn't be listening to Bid telling about it if she had. But a feeling of morbid curiosity as to what had happened made her prompt Bid to tell her all about it.

'I agreed to let the girl take me. It was somewhere in Bootle, but too dark when we set off to know where exactly. The woman was nice enough. "A soldier was it, love?" she asked. "Took pity on him going off to be killed . . . you girls never learn." I was going to say, no it was not, it was someone I'd known for years. You know I felt awful with maybe her thinking I'd done it with just anyone. I started to answer, but she said, "No names, no pack drill. I don't know you nor you me, that's the best way, love." She had a look at me and said I was further gone than she liked but she'd take the risk. Anyway, she filled me up with soapy water, carbolic soapy water. And I lay there and the smell reminded me of my mother doing the washing with the smell of the red soap being the same. And I kept thinking of that, letting on I was at home and not in some strange place with an oul wan I didn't know from Adam and my clothes up around my neck and my private exposed and the wan from work holding my legs.

'"Lay there for a few minutes," the woman said, and I did. When I got off the bed some of the soapy water and bits of blood ran down my legs.

'"Is it starting now?" I asked.

'"No, that's only the overflow what didn't go into your womb. It'll come later on – or tomorrow. Put on your knickers. And don't say a word about me or this. Into prison you'd go. Don't forget that now." The girl from work put me on a tram

349

and said if I wasn't in work in the morning she'd say I was sick.

'In the middle of the night I woke with terrible pains. I thought my end had come, but the pain was that bad I didn't care. There was a country wan sharing the room. She was a bit simple. Every time I roared she asked what ailed me and I let on it was cramps. She had to be in work by six and I was praying I could hold out until then. She was one of them real religious wans, you know. She might have got the priest or something. Anyway she went to work. The pains got worse. I kept calling for my mother and telling God I was sorry for what I'd done. Then it came and I lay there afraid to move or to look. But I put my hand down in the bed. Thank God, I thought, it's done. And before I knew it there was another pain and something else came out. My hand felt funny things, one of them like a lump of liver, that's what I thought it felt like. But there was something else like a pipe or a tube and I thought, Sacred Heart of Jesus with all the pushing my insides have come out. I'm dying.'

'Oh Bid, how did you go through all that on your own! I'd have died.'

'I began to pray. If I was going to die I didn't want to go to Hell. I kept making the Act of Contrition over and over again. One minute I was asking God to spare me and not let me go to Hell and at the same time thinking I'd have to get up in a minute and get ready for work and clean up the bed and do a lot of oatcakes to pay back the five pounds. It was getting light by this time. And nothing seems as bad when it isn't dark. I thought maybe I would live after all. I was feeling my strength come back. So I threw back the sheet and started to get up.'

Bid put her hands up to her face and bent her head so low it was touching the tea things. 'Oh Dolly, I thought what I'd gone through was the worst thing that could happen to anyone. Little did I know. When I looked down in the bed there was

350

a child in it – a baby. Small. Only the size of a gelatine doll. But a real child. I never knew it would be like that. I thought it would be just – I don't know, things, bits, but not a child. It had eyes and everything, a little girl. Oh Jesus, it was terrible. I'd killed my own child.'

For the time it had taken Bid to tell her story Dolly was so moved she had forgotten where they were. Now Bid's audible sobbing brought her back to the present and she glanced around the café quickly. Everyone, except a woman near the window, seemed intent on their own business. The woman by the window was staring in their direction – though maybe she was only trying to catch the waitress' eye. Still, she had better try to quieten Bid. 'Try and eat something. You went through an awful ordeal, God help you. But dwelling on it won't do you a bit of good. Stop crying and drink your tea.'

Bid ignored her entreaties and continued talking, her head still bent, her hands covering her face. 'I didn't know what to do with her. And all these things kept going through my mind. If anyone came I'd be arrested for killing her. And she hadn't been baptized. She'd go to Limbo. But maybe with her being dead anyway it was too late for baptism. I wiped her face. Then I thought God might make allowances so I got the bottle of Holy Water and sprinkled it on her forehead. A voice inside my head kept telling me I had to get rid of her, so I dressed myself and wrapped everything in the sheet. It was only a small bundle and fitted into my marketing bag. I was living near the docks . . . I walked down to a lonely part and threw the bag in. It didn't sink for a few minutes, then did and I walked back. I never worked in Jacobs' again. I couldn't face the girl who'd got me – you know – fixed up. Though after I went into munitions I sent her the five pounds.'

Bid began to wipe her eyes with the end of the scarf and a few sighs shuddered through her. Dolly was watching her plump hands busy with the scarf, the cheap rings flashing in the sunlight shining through the café window and thinking how those hands had cleaned the baby's face, felt all the horrible things in the bed, had sprinkled Holy Water over the child's head. And she thought her heart would break for Bid. Maybe she had committed a terrible sin, but she was desperate, demented, with no one to turn to. It was easy to condemn when you didn't know what people had gone through. And it must have broken her heart to have thrown the child away like that. God look down on her. Her heart and mind were filled with compassion for Bid. From now on she would try and help her. Be a friend to her. She had paid a terrible price for her sin. Dolly's eyes were still regarding Bid's hands when suddenly her friend let go the sodden scarf, reached for her handbag, undid it and drew out a Baby Power full of whiskey. In the instant, Dolly's feelings of love and pity underwent an abrupt change. What was Bid thinking of to do such a thing! Was she mad, drinking here? They'd be asked to leave. Disgraced. She had to get her out quick. But do it in a careful way. Coax her along. If she showed how she was really feeling Bid would create a scene. Imagine bringing whiskey into a place like this! 'Bid,' she said, 'there's people waiting for a table. I think we'd better get the bill.'

'Feck them. Let them wait,' Bid said and drank from the bottle again.

'Listen, I'll tell you what – we'll go over to the Green and you can finish your drink there. Come on, it's awful stuffy in here anyway.'

'It's lovely. I'm not moving.'

'Ah, come on. I'll carry that for you.'

Bid grinned at Dolly: 'Oh no, you won't. I know you. Confirmation Pledge how are you.' She lifted the bottle again and drained it. Then, as if all the time she had been waiting to leave, she rose unsteadily to her feet and began making her way to the door. Dolly got up and started to follow her.

'Excuse me, you haven't paid the bill.' Dolly nearly died of embarrassment. On top of everything else the girl thought she was ducking out of paying.

'Half a crown,' the girl said, tearing a receipt off her pad. Dolly fumbled in her purse. Bid had the door open, swinging it backwards and forwards – the empty whiskey bottle was still on the table. Pennies and ha'pennies came out of the purse. Then Dolly found two florins and gave them to the waitress. 'I'll get you your change,' the girl said. 'Keep it,' Dolly replied and pushed past her. It was an expensive tea but what matter, so long as she had Bid outside.

In the street she linked Bid's arm, telling her they would go over to the Green.

'I can't. I feel sick. Let go of my arm, you're hurting it.' Dolly let go and Bid leant against the wall.

'I feel terrible. I'm boiling.' Bid undid her scarf and pulled it away from her neck, exposing a necklet of mother of pearl beads.

'You kept them!' Dolly exclaimed. 'You kept the Rosary I gave you.'

'Well of course I kept them. Why wouldn't I?' Bid asked.

'I was just surprised seeing them, I suppose. I'd forgotten all about them.'

'I wear them all the time. I pray on my old ones.'

'You could pray on them, they're blessed.'

'I know that. Only they're so nice I was afraid of losing them, so around my neck they stay.'

Dolly felt the stirrings of pity again. Bid wasn't that bad. If she could only get her out of sight for half an hour . . . in one of the shady corners of the Green. Sit on a bench where no one might see her like this. She'd sober up. Then they could talk sense – make arrangements to see each other again. That's of course if she wasn't in Monto. But she probably wasn't. That could be just talk.

'Listen Bid, I'll tell you what we'll do. Open your eyes,

listen, will you.' She looked awful. She'd fall down in a minute, draw a crowd.

Bid opened her eyes and stared blankly at Dolly for a minute. Then recognition filled them and she smiled affectionately and said, 'Dolly, do you know why I really came? I want you to . . .' Her voice trailed off and the blank stare returned to her eyes.

Dolly took her arm again, urging her to move. 'You'll feel better sitting down, where it's cool. Look – the Green's only over the road. Come on.'

Bid started to laugh. 'The Green. That's all you've said since I met you. Go over to the Green and feed the ducks.' She laughed again and imitating a loud childlike voice recited, '*Oul Granny Grey. Let's go out to play. We won't go near the water to frighten the ducks away.* You've got ducks on the brain.'

'I never mentioned ducks,' Dolly said, trying hard to keep the annoyance out of her voice.

Bid began to say the rhyme again, louder this time. A few people stopped to look. Dolly was getting frantic. 'Who are you looking at?' Bid shouted and the people moved off.

Dolly thought, that's it. I've stood enough. 'If you don't stop it Bid Dunne I'm going to leave you. I'll walk off and leave you standing.'

'Oh no, don't do that. Don't leave me,' Bid pleaded. She reached for Dolly's arm and clung on to it. 'You can't do that. I need you. I didn't tell you the real reason I came. I have to go to Confession, only I'm afraid. I've tried a few times, got right up to the box and at the last minute didn't have the nerve to go in. But if you were there beside me I'd do it. I know I could if you were kneeling beside me. I'd go in, honest to God. We'll walk up to Adam and Eve's. You can ring the bell. A priest will hear your Confession any time.'

That's all she needed – a walk up the quays with Bid in the state she was. Maybe the chapel would be full of people and

354

Bid stocious. At the end of her tether, Dolly forgot her resolve to humour Bid and exploded, 'You're not in any state to go near a priest. You're drunk. Take hold of my arm and we'll cross here. Do what you're told. We're going into the Green to sit down. And don't open your mouth again. Do you hear me?'

'Yes,' Bid said meekly and allowed herself to be led across the street. Dolly began to congratulate herself. Maybe this was the way to handle her, after all. They got as far as the gates of the Green, then Bid stopped walking, wrenched her arm free and declared, 'I'm not going any further. Feed the fecking ducks, how are you. You thought you'd fooled me, well you hadn't. I know you, Dolly Devoy. You were always a stuck-up bitch. More fool me for thinking I could count on you. Get away from me. Go on. Clear off. I don't need you. I don't need anyone.'

Stung, Dolly retorted, 'That's the thanks I get. After all I've put up with to turn on me like that. You're nothing but a common . . .' tinker she was going to say but prostitute flashed into her mind. She hesitated.

'Go on, say it, I dare you,' Bid said, her voice belligerent.

'A tinker, that's what I was going to say.'

'Shag off,' Bid said, and turned and crossed the road, narrowly escaping going under a passing cab. The jarvey raised his whip and swore at her. Bid shouted an obscenity at him. Dolly watched, half-tempted to run after her, risk taking her to Confession. Then she saw Bid reach the other side, sway, almost fall, bump into a man and guessed from the way he recoiled that Bid had sworn at him as well. Bid was a drunkard. You couldn't help anyone once the drink took hold of them. She had gone to the bad all right, there was no helping her. And sure, who was to know if what she said about Kevin was true? He mightn't have been the father. When a woman drank she was anyone's. All the way home Dolly found one reason after another to console her feeling of guilt that she should have taken Bid to Confession. Finally telling herself that Bid wasn't a child, she didn't have to be led by the hand.

Occasionally during the following weeks Dolly thought about Bid. Wondering if she would hear from her again, if she had gone to Confession, hoping that she had gone back to England for good. Dolly almost convinced herself that she had gone until the evening her father said, 'Listen to this!' and read from the paper, '*This morning the body of a woman was taken from the Liffey. The woman, believed to be in her early twenties, had been in the water for several weeks. A number of cheap rings and a mother of pearl Rosary were found on the Deceased.* The poor unfortunate – desperate I suppose and did away with herself,' Johnny said.

Dolly sat very still, afraid to lift her head from the magazine she had been looking through when her father began to read the item of news. Wanting to ask her father to read it again but afraid that her voice, her face from which she was sure every drop of blood had drained, would cause her mother to ask what ailed her. Afraid she would say, 'I know who she is. I know why she did it. It was all my fault. She was desperate. She needed me, begged me to go with her to Confession. And I wouldn't. I was ashamed to be seen with her – it's all my fault. And now she'll be in Hell. Two mortal sins on her soul – what she did to the child and killing herself.'

'Of course she might have fallen in or been pushed, you'd never know. There's parts of the Liffey with no wall down there past Butt Bridge, on both sides.'

She might have fallen in. The words fell on Dolly like soothing water on a scald.

'Aye, she might. Anyway, we'll never know how it happened or who she was. After that length in the water her face mightn't be recognizable,' Johnny said and turned to another page of the newspaper.

356

You'd never know who she was. Dolly grasped at the straw. It mightn't be Bid at all. There were millions of women in their twenties. Even with rings. Rings were ten a penny. But the Rosary – what about that? Well, it never said it was around her neck and lots of people had mother of pearl Rosaries. The beads could have been in a purse, or in a handbag. But would they have found a handbag? If someone drowned themselves wouldn't they let go of a bag once they were in the water? But they might not. Oh, please God, don't let it be Bid. Not killing herself. Not dying in mortal sin and all through my fault.

'Dolly – are you deaf? I've been talking to you.'

'Sorry, Ma. I didn't hear you. I was miles away.'

'You look very pale. Are you all right?'

'I'm all right, a bit of a headache. I think I'll go out for some air, maybe ramble up to the chapel.'

'Do, it'll clear your head.'

In the chapel Dolly prayed for a long time. Asking God not to let it be Bid. But if it was, to take pity on her. Telling Him how sorry she was for not helping Bid and that she would pray for her always. She found great consolation from the time she spent praying and returned home with a less troubled mind. Days and then weeks passed without her thinking of Bid. But on one occasion when the thought of her returned she asked Ethel casually if her mother had ever heard any more about her friend.

'That's funny you should mention her now. Only yesterday my mother was saying she'd heard Bid had cleared off to England. The talk was that the bad disease got worse, that the hospital could do no more for her. Anyway, she vanished, so she must have gone to England. I don't blame her. You go mad with the bad disease and then do you know what they do to you?'

'No,' Dolly said.

'They smother you between two mattresses.'

'They do not. That's only if you get bitten by a mad dog and foam at the mouth.'

'Well, I knew they smothered you for something. So that's where Bid is – England.'

Dolly chose to believe Ethel's story. Bid was alive. But every night she continued to pray for her soul just in case.

'This is Bessie,' Bridget said introducing her to Dolly.

'I'm delighted to meet you,' Dolly said, 'my mother is always talking about you.'

Bessie apologized for intruding. 'I didn't think you'd be home yet. I was only bringing back the soup bowl. Your mother is very kind to me, God bless her.'

While Bessie talked, a memory stirred in Dolly's mind. She had seen this woman before. 'I know your face but I can't remember from where.'

'Maybe you dropped into the eating house. We had one on the quays.'

'Sit down Bessie, that wan won't rest till she puzzles out where she met you,' Bridget said pulling out a chair.

'God I do – that was you. In that lovely little place. I remember it well. It was spotless and you had lovely apple cake.'

'It was grand all right, until the night the Tans came,' Bessie said.

'And me mother told me about what they did and I never realized it was the same place me and this fella went to. Imagine that.' Dolly asked Bessie how she was settling in, half listening to her reply, thinking about the night in the eating house and Jem. Remembering the fair and the swinging boats. Forgetting her aggravation at him for not being more romantic. Remembering only all what was lovely about the evening.

Bessie said she was getting used to the room but missed the view of the Liffey. Then she excused herself. Liam would be home soon.

'Please God he'll have found something,' Bridget said. 'And don't forget come down anytime, I'm always in.'

'Is her husband not working?' Dolly asked after Bessie left.

'Not doing a tap. And I'm afraid he won't again. I think he's in consumption, he has all the appearances. I give her what advice will help without disheartening her, the poor creature. What good would telling her what ails him do, when there's no cure?'

'That's terrible sad. I liked her. Didn't you say she was older than him?'

'She is, but to see them you'd never think it, they're like a pair of lovebirds. It's a pleasure to have them in the house.'

On the way upstairs Bessie thought how attractive Dolly was and not a bit stuck-up like the woman on the landing had said. A lovely young girl. She hoped they would get on. But it was a pity she'd come home early tonight, for she had wanted to tell Bridget about the baby. She was dying to tell someone. Though maybe it was just as well she had said nothing: wanting wasn't the same as having and her monthlies having gone astray could be from another cause.

A couple of months later she knew without doubt she was pregnant. And she thought how strange were God's ways. She had wanted a child so much, prayed for one, imagined the day she would tell Liam – it would be the happiest day of their lives. Now the day was here and she didn't feel happy. Her mind was full of worry. Bridget might say she'd worked wonders with the room, but it wasn't a good place for the child to start life in. And Liam still hadn't found work – that was her biggest worry. It clouded her joy. The night she wanted to tell Bridget about the baby she hadn't dreamed he would be idle this long.

There was a big hole in the savings and no sign of compensation for the eating house. Mr Geoghan the solicitor had explained they weren't the only ones in the city to have had

359

their home and business destroyed by the Tans, nor in the country, either. These claims took time. She must be patient.

God gave with one hand and took with the other, Bessie thought, then told herself she was questioning His Will. That was wrong, a sin. At your age you should be on your knees thanking Him for the gift of a child. She continued talking to herself, counting her blessings. Things would change; God would open another door until she was able to face the future with hope. But she decided to postpone for the time being telling Liam of the child. He wasn't himself these days. Often dejected-looking and bitter about the Tans and not finding work.

She had taken Bridget's advice, bought codliver oil and made a flannel bodice for him to wear under his vest. He said the codliver oil repeated on him, was destroying his stomach, that's why he had no appetite. And more often than not he went out without the bodice. Please God it was all to do with the upset of losing their place. Liam was a big, strong healthy man, he'd be on the mend soon.

Bridget and Dolly were delighted when Bessie told them about the baby.

'When are you expecting, please God?' Bridget inquired.

'Round about Christmas,' Bessie said.

'You mind yourself now, no dragging and hauling up and down them stairs. I'll give you a hand.'

Dolly said Christmas must be a beautiful time to have a baby, and she felt sad watching her mother and Bessie with their excited faces and wondered if she would ever sit like this listening to her mother's advice about pregnancy.

'I'll tell you what,' she interrupted. 'I'll buy the christening gown. Miss Murtagh could make it, please God.'

'A little thin woman with glasses, a dressmaker?' Bessie asked.

'Do you know her?'

'I worked with her out in Foxrock.'

'God! Then you're the Bessie she told me about. And I never put two and two together, fancy that!'

'How is she keeping?'

'It's no good asking that,' Bridget said. 'Dolly hasn't been near her for ages and you ignored her letter, didn't you?'

'I kept meaning to go and see her. I will now I've a good excuse,' her daughter replied.

Bessie asked if she might go with her and Dolly said that would be grand.

'Shangri-la, Hong Kong, the road to Mandalay – that's what I was banking on,' Robbie said.

'Dublin's not to be sneezed at,' the soldier standing beside him on the boat's deck said. 'Dublin's all right. Got the best whorehouses in Europe – a place called Monto. I was stationed in Dublin before the war. Beautiful girls!'

'I know, I was there for a few days in 1916 at Easter, when they had the Rebellion.'

'Oh yeah, a rum do, that. Is that where you got the Military Medal?'

Robbie laughed. 'No, that was in another rum do – France.'

'I missed it all – spent the war in Catterick, with nothing but bloody sheep and lousy weather.'

'Maybe you'll make up for it now. There's plenty of action going on in Ireland these days.'

'You're like a hen on a hot griddle, in and out, up and down. What ails you?' Bridget asked.

'The weather. It's too hot for dances – and what else can you do with yourself of an evening? If I stay in you and Bessie and Maggie only talk about babies and confinements.'

'What else is there for women to talk about?' her mother said.

'It gets on my nerves.'

361

'Pity about you, at your age I had children myself. Anyway here's your confederate, I'd know the sound of her step a mile away.' Immediately afterwards Ethel knocked on the door. 'I'll leave you to it, I'm going up to Bessie's,' Bridget said and left Ethel and Dolly alone.

'I was wondering as it's such a fine evening if you wouldn't change your mind about rambling up the quays?'

'What have I got to lose?' Dolly replied.

'You will – that's marvellous! What's come over you all of a sudden?' Ethel was delighted.

'Whatever it is, let's go before it leaves and I change my mind . . .'

Strolling along the quays in the warm evening, the air smelling of the Liffey, a mixture of sea and mud and the fumes from Guinness', Ethel and Dolly stopped by the quay wall and leant over to look at the swans gliding by.

Two soldiers in gleaming leggings, smart uniforms and swagger-sticks under their arms came along and stood beside them.

'Hello – and what's two lovely girls like yourselves doing all on your own?' the shorter of the two asked. Robbie thought one of the girls was familiar – she reminded him of the girl on Easter Monday. But it was so long ago he couldn't be sure. Anyway, it was a bit of a weak line to play, so he let his mate from the boat do the talking.

'Going for a walk, not that it's any of your business,' Dolly answered tartly.

'Only asking, love,' the little fair man replied in mock apology. 'How about taking pity on two lonely soldiers far from home and showing us the sights?'

Dolly tossed her head indignantly and said, 'The nerve of some people!' She should walk away, but the dark fella intrigued her. She was sure she had seen him somewhere before. She puzzled her brain, trying to remember where. There was a fella once years ago, where was it, a fella just

362

like him, a soldier too. God it was annoying, her not being able to remember. It would come to her now in a minute if she stayed that long. Then suddenly it came to her – it was outside Noblett's on Easter Monday. He'd been very forward, but so handsome . . . exactly the sort of fella she dreamed about meeting. Her 'man made to measure' as her mother called him. She was sure it was him. So intrigued was she by Robbie's looks and the coincidence of meeting him again she agreed to walk as far as the Park.

He told her his name was Robbie. He's gorgeous, she thought, and what a lovely way of speaking. She wondered how old he was. 'How long have you been in the army?' – that would give her an idea of his age.

'Since 1914.'

'If my father knew I was walking along the quays with a soldier he'd kill me.'

'Don't tell him, then he won't know.'

'Ah listen – Dublin's a very small place. You'd never know who you'll meet, anyone could see us.' Dolly spoke slowly and carefully, paying attention to her pronunciation.

The family of swans which earlier she and Ethel had stopped to watch were now swimming in the other direction, soft brown cygnets and lost feathers trailing in their wake. The fair-haired soldier, whose name was Badgie, was walking in front of them with Ethel. He stopped and turned, asking, 'Would you like a feather for your hat, Miss? Go nice with that hat it would.' He leant over the wall, but the swans swam past. 'Too late, I've missed them. But for two lovely coleens I'd have done it – dived in, boots and all.'

'God you're a howl,' Ethel said, laughing and playfully pushing at Badgie. And Dolly thought, you can have him, a bloody little dannyman and fancies himself as a hardchaw. She was glad when they paired off again and she deliberately walked slowly so that the distance between them increased.

From time to time she laughed at something Robbie said,

tilting her head, consciously displaying her teeth. And she noticed how people passing by looked admiringly at herself and Robbie.

Now and then he took her arm, manoeuvring her past groups gathered on the pavements talking. He's very well-mannered, she thought. But hoped at the same time she'd meet no one she knew or her name would be up. He caught hold of her hand and swung it gently to and fro, told her where his barracks were and how much he liked Dublin. Then he asked her where she worked.

'In Jacobs, but in the office, you know.' She watched his face as she exaggerated the clerical side of her duties, not mentioning making tea for managers and doing messages. He's a picture, she told herself. And was sure that every woman passing looked enviously at her. It was a marvellous feeling.

'You know,' he said, as they neared the Park gates, 'my mother came from here.'

'Go away! From Ireland!'

'From Dublin. I have relations here. In Ranalagh, is that how you say it?'

'Ranalagh, that's right. I don't live far from there. Well, it's the South Circular Road, but it's not far.'

She was very impressed. Ranalagh was a beautiful place, big houses with flights of granite steps up to them, brass knockers and footscrapers. The sort of house Miss Murtagh had lived in when she was a child. She had never written to her. Well, she would now and tell her about Robbie. She put Miss Murtagh from her mind and thought how his relations must be very comfortable to live in Ranalagh. There was no harm in her telling a lie about where she lived. It didn't do to let people know all your business.

'So you see,' he said, breaking in on her thoughts, 'I'm not just any soldier.'

'No, I suppose so. Still and all my father's very strict,' Dolly

364

replied as they entered the Park and she remembered she had only intended going as far as the gates. Robbie let go her hand and slipped an arm around her waist. Recalling all she had heard about soldiers and their fast ways, she shrugged it off, and thought, he has another think coming if he believes I'm an easy mark.

Away in front she saw Ethel and Badgie turn the corner and walk in the direction of the Hollow, a grassy, treelined slope favoured by courting couples. Robbie took her hand again, squeezing it gently and attempted to pull her in the same direction.

'I'm not going down there,' Dolly exclaimed indignantly.

'Why, what's wrong with down there?'

'I'm not, that's all. I wouldn't be found dead down there.' Sacred Heart of Jesus, she thought as soon as the words were out of her mouth, maybe that's how I'll finish up – dead or worse. She felt a mixture of fear and excitement, a feeling similar to the one she had experienced years ago when she and Bid had gone running through the streets after the Rebellion. But feelings or not, she was going nowhere near the Hollow, not the first time anyway.

'Come on,' Robbie coaxed. 'We'll just sit on the grass and talk. It's quiet and peaceful down there. You must be tired, it's a long walk up the quays.'

'I'm not that tired, thanks very much. You seem to know a lot about the Hollow for someone not two minutes in Dublin.' She felt a stab of jealousy, wondering who else he had taken there. She had never met anyone like him before. Standing there looking at her with his beautiful brown eyes, not annoyed or flustered at her refusal. Just smiling a smile that made her want to go running down the grassy slope with him. But she would do no such thing. Her mind grappled with the situation. If she was too offhand, too cutting, he mightn't make another appointment. And although she had only known him for half an hour she was in no doubt that she wanted to see him again.

Then, floating on the evening air came the sound of children's voices. The Monument! The very thing – why didn't I think of it before? Dolly looked towards her left to where the sounds came from and saw the Wellington Memorial, its obelisk tinged pink by the setting sun and half a dozen boys running up and down its sloping granite steps. It was the excuse she was looking for. 'Let's go up the Monument – I haven't climbed up there for ages. Come on – I'll show you.' To her relief Robbie agreed and this time when they went towards the Monument and he slipped his arm around her waist, she let it remain.

'What's the time, Mister?' a boy in a long gansey and torn trousers running down the steps asked as he almost collided with Dolly and Robbie climbing up.

'Did you hear that, boys? Did you hear what the time is? We'll be kilt so we will,' the child shouted up to his companions who were racing around the platform.

Dolly and Robbie reached the top and stood looking down at the Park. The air was cooler now and smelt of the sleeping flowers in their beds below. The boys asked the time again and cadged a cigarette and, with their racing impeded by Dolly and Robbie and the encroaching darkness, ran whooping down the steps and off towards the Island Bridge Gate.

She was alone now with the stranger. She felt a shiver of fear, but it wasn't unpleasant. And anyway, as she told herself, she was ten times safer standing on the Monument than stretched out below in the Hollow.

Robbie with his arm about her waist walked her around the platform, pointing out the battle scenes depicted on the plinth, giving her pieces of information as he pointed. 'Did you know that the Duke of Wellington was born in Dublin?'

'No,' Dolly said, 'I didn't.'

'Or that he fought a duel because he was accused of favouring the Catholic religion?'

Wouldn't it be awful if he kept talking about Dukes and

366

things she knew nothing about – the evening would be wasted. She'd have to let on she was interested, though. So she said again, 'No, I didn't.'

'Well, he did,' Robbie told her, at the same time manoeuvring her against the wall beneath a scene from the Battle of Waterloo and kissing her, a long skilful kiss that left her breathless and dizzy.

'I'll have to be going, it's getting dark,' she whispered.

'I know,' he said, releasing her. 'Your father is very strict.'

She felt uneasy. He was imitating her accent, mocking her. She felt annoyance too, but only a little. For no one had ever made her feel with a kiss the way she felt now. More than anything she wanted to see him again. What would she do if he asked to see her home? She'd have to take him to the South Circular Road, stand outside one of the houses letting on that's where she lived until he left. She definitely couldn't take him to ninety-seven, especially not on a summer's evening. There'd be a travage of oul wans around the door taking the air, her mother included. Maybe she was worrying for nothing. He mightn't want to see her again. He had probably been trying her out. She hoped not.

'Right then, let's get you home if that's what you want. And tell your father I'm a Catholic, then he might let you see me again, eh?'

Everything was all right. He wasn't jeering her voice now. He was a Catholic. He wanted to see her again. Dolly was overjoyed. Now all she had to do was convince him she'd be fine going home on her own. Lightheartedly with her hand in his she skipped down the Monument steps, across the grass and onto the path. Talking nonstop all the way to the park gates, assuring him the tram would take her right to the front door. Agreeing to meet him the night after next in town. No, she couldn't tomorrow, honest to God, she had an appointment she couldn't break. Much as she wanted to see him again it didn't do to be too eager.

367

He put her onto the tram, gave the conductor a sixpence, telling him it was for Dolly's fare and to keep the change. The tram moved off and she watched him grow small under the gas lamp, grow smaller and smaller until she couldn't see him any more. Then she sat oblivious of all about her, reliving the evening, going over every word he had said, hoping she had made a good impression and praying that he wouldn't let her down for the appointment.

They were at Winetavern Street Bridge and the conductor was shaking her arm and telling her this was her stop before she remembered Ethel and wondered if she was still in the Hollow. She got off the tram and forgot about her, thinking instead that at last she had found him. He was all she had ever dreamed he would be. He had been worth waiting for. Please God, she prayed silently, let him come to meet me on Friday. Don't let me lose him now. Not when I've waited so long. Make him come.

Chapter Eighteen

'Nice girls, weren't they?' Robbie said to Badgie the next morning.

'All right. You seemed to get the best of the bargain – then you always do.'

'Are you seeing the other one again?'

'No, I didn't really fancy her. I'm going down town this evening, coming?'

'Not me, I'm fixed up for tomorrow night, saving my money. Tonight I'll stay in, first time for months. Later on I'll probably go over to the canteen.'

'Oh, so you *were* taken with what's her name.'

'Dolly – she's a nice girl. I liked her.'

'Best of luck. Don't forget your motto – love them and leave them.'

'I won't.'

As a matter of course Robbie's eyes went to the canteen counter, for sometimes the girls serving there were very pretty. Tonight there was a real corker, dainty, dark, a beauty. He joined the line of men waiting to be served. When his turn came Alice smiled and said 'Yes?' then to his amazement the inquiring smile changed to an expression of delighted incredulity and she went on, 'It can't be! But it is! We met . . . oh I'm sorry, you must think me crazy.' She became incoherent, flustered. 'You must think I'm mad – only you see, I know you. I mean – we've met before. It was a long time ago, but we did.'

'We did?' Robbie searched his mind. Where? When? How could he have forgotten someone like her?

'In Horsham, just before the war. I was staying . . .' Alice almost said . . . 'with my husband's family,' but checked herself. She didn't want this man to know she was married. Of course he might notice her ring but that couldn't be helped. 'Don't you remember? It was very early, a lovely morning. I've never forgotten it. You did a silly thing with a flower.'

Robbie couldn't remember the flower, the morning nor the girl, but he could tell that the memory was important to her.

'A flower – of course! And if I'd known you were here tonight I'd have brought you a bunch of them. I bet you can't remember what I said to you that morning.'

'I can, every word. You held the buttercup under my chin and asked if I liked butter.' Alice laughed and hoped he didn't notice her blushes. 'It sounds silly now, but it wasn't and I got such a surprise when I saw you standing here. I couldn't resist telling you we had met.'

With smiles and carefully chosen words Robbie convinced her that his memory of the morning was as precious and vivid as her own. A soldier nudged him. 'Come on mate, get a move on.' Alice stopped gazing into Robbie's eyes and remembered why she was in the canteen. 'I'd better serve you, what was it, you never said?' Robbie asked for tea. Her hands shook as she lifted the heavy brown enamel teapot and went on pouring, allowing the cup to overflow, her confusion and blushing increasing.

'Thanks,' Robbie said, accepting the cup in its pool of tea. 'I'll come back when you've served the others.'

'You look radiant tonight. Having Stephen back in Ireland speaks for itself, though I suppose the canteen helps, too. It's a pity this trouble hangs on. Poor Stephen, buried in the country for weeks on end – you must long for it all to be finished. When is he coming up again?'

370

'He never knows in advance, Mama. It depends on how things are down there. Do you mind if I go to bed? The canteen was very busy tonight.'

Her mother said of course she didn't and Alice bade her good-night. In her room she found the book in which she had pressed the buttercup. Looking at it, she relived again the morning in Horsham and then the moment when she had raised her eyes and seen Robbie across the counter. It was a miracle! He had been sent! Sent to compensate her for all she had suffered. She would not let him go. She would tell no one about him. And he mustn't know she was married. Before going to the canteen again she would take off her wedding ring. Alice lay in bed thinking and planning how and where she could meet him; wondering where in Dublin they could go without her being recognized.

In the weeks that followed her meeting with Robbie, Dolly was enchanted. All day she thought about him, about the shape of his face, his straight nose and the lovely square chin of him, his eyes that were big and brown, that she could look into forever and the smell of him – a mixture of soap, the tobacco he used and his own gorgeous body smell. She loved the feel of him, of his smooth golden skin, his lips, his teeth pressing against hers, the taste of his mouth. She even loved the feel of the rough khaki tunic against which she laid her face and heard his heart beating.

She sang as she went about her work. Laughed and joked with the young girls and thought that they weren't so bad after all. And they said to each other behind her back: 'There's a great change in Dolly Devoy – she must be in love.'

Her mother, too, noticed the change, was relieved and wondered who he was. Maggie knew about Robbie and had promised not to tell her mother, for Dolly was still afraid she might lose him, and the fewer people who knew about him, the less explaining she would have to do if she did.

She saw him whenever he asked. She wished it could be every night, but he had explained that wasn't possible – there were guard duties and other things the army made you do. On the nights he was free she rushed home from work, changed and was out of the door without breaking her fast, her mother's voice calling after her that she was going the right way about getting consumption – not eating was the quickest way to go into a decline.

Robbie couldn't dance. But Dolly didn't care. To be with him was enough. He brought her gifts – sweets and scent and a bunch of flowers. No one had ever given her flowers before. Once, after admiring a pair of gloves in a shop window, he had arrived at their next meeting with the gloves wrapped in tissue paper.

She lived in fear of something happening to him. Every day the Tans or Republicans were killing someone. Then her father, alarmed by the violence, forbade her to go out in the evenings. 'In future you'll come straight home from work and not put your foot outside the door again. D'ye hear me?'

'Of course I hear you. But I hope you know I'm twenty-four, not a child.'

'It'd be a lot of good telling that to the Tans. You'll do what you're told.'

Dolly decided to humour him. 'All right Da, but I've got to go out tonight. I've an appointment with the dressmaker. I'll only be an hour.'

'What dressmaker?' her mother asked.

'Never mind who the dressmaker is, make sure you're home in an hour or you'll find yourself in the back of a lorry driven up the mountains, destroyed and then thrown out with a bullet in your brains. That's the Tans' latest venture,' Johnny said.

She ran all the way to the tram, her mind grappling with this new development and how it would affect her and Robbie. She could defy her father, but that would mean constant rows. And these days he never looked well, he seemed to have

372

become an old man all of a sudden. Her mother said he had never got over Richard. Anyway, whatever it was, she didn't want to be always aggravating him.

If only she could bring Robbie home! She'd have to bring him to the house sometime, but not yet, not until she was sure of him. Even then it wouldn't be easy bringing home a soldier. All she could do for the time being was tell him how her father was afraid she would come to harm at the hands of the Tans and hope he'd understand . . .

'Your father's right,' Robbie said in the coffee shop to which he took her. 'They're a murdering lot of bastards. Jailbirds and scum the majority of them and the auxiliaries who are supposed to be their officers are no better. They all have too much money which they spend on drink.'

'That's exactly what my father says.'

'It's true. Do you know how they recruited them?'

'No, how?'

'An advertisement in the paper: ten bob a day for the Other Ranks and the officers get a quid. There's no love lost between them and the British soldier.'

'Is that a fact?' Dolly asked, gazing at him and regretting that they would have no time alone this evening.

'Yes, a fact. A lot of cruel sadistic sods, they are – mad. Kill for the sake of killing, and rob too. There's plenty of them lining their pockets over here. Do you know, the other night one of them lobbed a grenade at the end of their barrackroom wall. Could have blown the lot of them to Kingdom Come. Then another crowd took a horse up to their room and drove it frantic.'

Dolly looked at the clock, it was nearly time to go. 'Will I see you before the weekend?'

'What day is it?'

'Wednesday – are you losing your memory?' She smiled at him and touched his hand.

'I wasn't thinking straight. I've a duty tomorrow night and

373

Friday I'll be doing my kit – there's an inspection on Saturday. But in any case, how can you meet me – hasn't your father stopped you going out?'

'I could find a way, my father's very easy to fool. So long as I didn't stay out too long I'd let on I was seeing my sister or a friend, there'd be millions of excuses.'

'It'll have to be the weekend.'

'That'll be all right,' Dolly said, eager to fit in with his plans but disappointed that two whole nights must pass before she saw him again. 'So I'll see you Saturday after dinner and all day Sunday?'

'All day Sunday,' he winked at her.

He walked with her to the tram and held her hand until it was time to go. He tried to kiss her, but she pulled away and asked if he was mad, trying to do a thing like that with everyone looking.

'It's an absolute disgrace! I don't understand Stephen. What can he be thinking of, allowing you to work in the canteen during his leave?'

'Mama, I've told you it *isn't* leave – he's on a course, learning how to tackle all these ambushes and things and he doesn't mind me working – it's only for a few hours in the evenings.'

'Exactly – the evenings are when he's here. The very time when you should be by his side. Really, I have a good mind to speak to Lady Basset. I'm sure she's not aware of the situation – she wouldn't tolerate you working if she knew.'.

'Stephen doesn't mind, honestly. He understands that if I stopped going to the canteen now I'd probably never go back. And please don't mention it to Lady Basset. I wouldn't want her interfering, no matter how well meant.'

That was the last thing she wanted – attention drawn to herself. Once or twice she had noticed Lady Basset look disapprovingly in her direction when Robbie delayed at the counter. What was she to do? He spent several nights a week talking to her. How he managed to drink all those cups of tea! She was sure he had been about to make a move – then Stephen had arrived in Dublin unexpectedly and of course she had had to miss the canteen for a few evenings. When Robbie asked why she had been absent, she lied about not being well – she could see he hadn't believed her, but she could hardly tell him the truth. Now he didn't seem quite so interested in her. Oh God, it wasn't fair. Why did Stephen have to come up from the country? Why did she ever marry him? Why that morning in Horsham hadn't she realized that she loved Robbie and done something then – let him know, run away with him?

She was losing her mind, nothing surer, spinning fantasies about running away with Robbie years ago. Dreaming about him at night. Living from one glimpse of him to the next. Staring at him across the counter, thrilled when their hands touched as money or cups passed between them. And what did she have to go on? He had never said one word that a reasonable person could interpret as anything but pleasantries. But then she wasn't a reasonable person: she was in love with him. She wanted to be held by him, to have him kiss her. To lie in his arms.

Robbie cleaned his teeth, combed his hair and went to the canteen, thinking as he went that he would give it another try – though he had to admit the last few weeks had been a waste of time. Nights that he could have spent with Dolly were spent instead drinking tea by the gallon, listening to the out-of-tune piano, getting in a few minutes leaning on the counter when Alice wasn't busy, trying to soften her up. In the beginning he had seemed to be doing fine then, all of a sudden – after she had been off for those few days, a wall had seemed to come up. Of course she was married. He knew that, even though the wedding ring had disappeared. An old trick that, never fooled anyone. The pale circle of flesh showed where it had been. Maybe her husband was back – that's if he had ever been away. The trouble with Alice was he knew nothing about her – not even her other name. Once he had asked one of the other women, 'Alice – you know, the pretty dark girl – what's her other name?' The woman had smiled sweetly: 'Soldiers address her as "Miss". Did you want tea or lemonade?'

She was serving another soldier when he got to the canteen, talking and smiling at him. Robbie felt jealous – an emotion he had never experienced before where women were concerned. Hold on, he told himself, remember your rule – love them and leave them. She was just another girl, the world was full of them. But for all that he was delighted when the man left and Alice looking towards the door saw him and he knew that the smile she smiled at him was more than a polite recognition that he was there.

'I wondered if you'd come in tonight,' Alice said.

'So you think about me when I'm not here?' Robbie asked, and leaned on the counter.

Alice blushed. 'Well – I, yes, sometimes.'

'Only sometimes?'

'Often.'

'I think about you all the time. You don't know what it's like, only being able to see you behind this. Watching other blokes making up to you. Never being able to touch you, talk to you for more than a few minutes. I want to take you out. Will you come?'

'I'd love to – only . . .'

'Only what?'

'I don't know where we could meet, where we could go.'

'Anywhere. I know Dublin well. I can meet you wherever you say,' Robbie urged. 'Come on, say you will,' he coaxed.

'I can't, not yet. If you come again tomorrow I'll have thought of somewhere by then.'

'You're a funny girl, what's there to think of? I told you I know the city – I could name half a dozen meeting places.'

Alice didn't reply but looked furtively towards the end of the counter where an elderly white-haired woman was counting money out of the till, then back at Robbie. 'I think she's been watching me. We're not supposed to spend more time talking to one soldier than another. I'll let you know – the next time you come in I'll have arranged something.'

'Promise?' Robbie said, his voice artificially bright, thinking, some you win, some you lose. I hope I don't lose this one, but I won't press my luck.

'I promise.'

'Right then – I suppose I'd better have a tea in case she's still keeping tabs.'

He took the tea and sat at a table from where he watched Alice serving and being pleasant to other men and again he felt jealous. Before he finished his drink she went into the kitchen and though he remained for a long time she did not reappear.

That night, while Alice and Stephen sat with her parents, the men drinking a nightcap and the women hot chocolate, Alice racked her brains as to where she could meet Robbie. Her father was as usual talking about the situation in Ireland – dismissing the reports of the Black and Tans' lootings, killings and rampaging as calumny, her mother nodding in agreement and Stephen silent.

Alice finished her drink, yawned and said she must go to bed. Stephen said he was tired, too. Lady Delahunt made soothing noises and remarks about how difficult life was for young men and how she hoped all this horrible business would soon blow over and then he and Alice could begin to take up their life in England. Silently, Alice echoed her mother's wish. The sooner the trouble in Ireland came to an end the sooner would her road to freedom begin. But tonight she was not as despondent as previously, for she had Robbie to occupy her thoughts. And in her bedroom, while Stephen talked about the course he was attending and his return to the country the following week, Alice thought hard about a plan to enable her to see Robbie away from the canteen. After kissing her cheek Stephen went to sleep in the dressing room and Alice, as she did whenever he was home, rumpled the pillows on the side of the bed where, if their marriage was normal, he would have slept. Appearances must be kept up in front of the servants.

In bed she tried again to think of a place where she could spend time with Robbie and after some thought she decided that the only possible place was Nella's flat. Tomorrow she would go to see her and ask if she could use it.

'You wicked old thing! Do I know him?' was Nella's comment when Alice told her.

'He's in the army, he's English – that's all there is to tell, except that for the first time in my life I've fallen in love.'

'And I suppose now you're looking for a love-nest?'

'I've nowhere else to take him.'

'I can see that your Mama is hardly likely to welcome him. Tell me more about him. What's he like? What's his name? Do I know him?'

'He's a private soldier.'

'A private soldier! Where did you meet one of those?'

'In the canteen.'

'And no one knows? Don't tell me "sheep's head" hasn't noticed.'

Alice laughed at the nickname Nella had given Lady Basset because of her tight, white curly hair and long mournful face. 'Not even "sheep's head" – we've been very discreet. Actually, all we've done so far is to talk over the counter.'

'And now you want my flat to commit sin in. You must be very eager for him – no preliminaries – no socializing.'

'Be sensible, Nella. Where could I possibly socialize with him in Dublin?'

'No, I suppose not, not with a private without causing an uproar. I'll be delighted to let you have the flat, and enjoy your fling. It won't last, you know. I remember one I had with one of our gardeners. I was sure it was the real thing but his feet smelled . . . It'll be the same with thingy – Other Ranks and gardeners tend not to be very clean. Anyway, when are you planning this assignation? Hold on, let me get my diary. Would the week after next do?'

'Yes,' Alice said. 'The week after next will be fine.'

Bessie took the bank book from an old brown handbag that had belonged to Liam's aunt and looked at the balance. Ten pounds – only ten pounds! Where had it all gone, what had she spent it on? There must be a mistake – she couldn't have spent that much. Going back through the pages she did sums in her head, telling herself she would find an error – there had to be a mistake somewhere. When the mental arithmetic balanced with the final sum shown she got a pencil and paper and added each withdrawal, afterwards subtracting the answer from the amount in the bank before the eating house was destroyed and her cash withdrawals had begun. Again the figures balanced as she had known they would but in her heart she had hoped for a miracle, hoped to find a clerk's error . . . a few extra pounds owing to her. A little more for security, for the rent and food and firing. Enough for when the child came, please God, to pay the nurse her ten shillings, get the necessities to cover the baby and have something to slip in the envelope for the priest at the christening.

But ten pounds was all there was between her and destitution. When that was gone she would have to depend on charity if Liam didn't get work – apply to the Parish for a few shillings a week and ask for the 'St Vincent de Paul'. Have them coming into the room, eyeing its contents, estimating their value, suggesting what could be pawned or sold before she was entitled to a food docket . . . Not that there was anything in her room worth tuppence. Not a thing – unless you stripped the bed of its clothes, left Liam without his razors or made the greatest sacrifice of all and sold or pawned her wedding ring. Women did, women in the house, when they had to – took the sheets and the blankets, the flatirons, anything on which they could get the price of a meal and when all else was gone their wedding rings, and then they bought brass ones to wear instead. But please God, it would never come to that. She had the ten pounds, she would make it go a long way, manage every ha'penny with care and long before it was all spent Liam was bound to find work. The weather was fine, they'd want labourers at this time of the year. She mustn't lose hope. And tonight when he came home she would tell him about the child.

She hoped that not having told him sooner was a wise decision. According to Bridget you should tell your husband immediately so that he left you alone during the early months. It was very dangerous to have relations with your husband then. It could cause you to lose the child, or worse maybe, have it born an imbecile. But not having told him she couldn't refuse him, though every time afterwards she waited for the miscarrying to start. But thanks be to God she hadn't lost the baby and she prayed that it wouldn't be born deformed or foolish. Anyway, tonight she would tell him – she'd have to, for she was getting the size of a house.

Now she needed another piece of paper to work out her budget. In the brown bag there was a letter from the solicitor, the one Mr Geoghan had sent to Liam telling him of his inheritance. She read through it quickly, a sad smile playing over her face as she remembered the high hopes of those days. Then, because there was no other paper available she turned over the letter, smoothed its creases and began her calculations. Two shillings a week for rent, another two for coal and paraffin oil. Four shillings for bread, tea ninepence, sugar another eightpence and milk? She hesitated before adding milk, then decided she'd use condensed, it was cheaper and sweetened so she'd save on sugar. Cabbage, potatoes, onions and yellow turnips – a shilling's worth would see her in for the week. A quarter of butter and a quarter of dripping – the porkshop at the corner sold lovely dripping. Margarine she wouldn't buy – it was cheap but tasted like axle-grease. Shell cocoa was nourishing and only cost fourpence a pound. Meat was the dear item, even the cheapest cuts. She didn't mind going without it herself, but you couldn't expect a man to tramp the streets on bread and dripping – meat would have to be bought. And on Fridays a few fresh herrings and mackerel.

One day a week she would make a blind stew. That was a queer name. She'd never heard of it until coming to Dublin. The first time Bridget mentioned it she had asked what it was. 'Plenty of carrots, onions, potatoes, yellow or white turnips, whatever vegetables you have, boiled together with pepper and salt.'

'Why is it called a blind stew?' Bessie asked.

'Because it's a letting-on stew, I suppose. Half of Dublin's reared on them and fine men and women they are too. Will I show you how?'

'No thanks, I was just wondering, that's all,' Bessie said. She didn't want Bridget to know her circumstances. Bridget was kind enough already, always offering her things to eat, passing on Johnny's newspaper, making an excuse that papers made the place untidy and she could use it for the fire. Bridget would want to help her but if you considered Johnny's regular drinking and Dolly's style it was little enough her friend had to spare. And anyway, she was still too proud to tell even Bridget how badly off she was.

She went back to her reckoning up. Sixteen shillings, the final total came to. If nothing out of the ordinary cropped up the way it did last week, like the globe of the lamp breaking and another cough bottle for Liam – if she could keep to the sixteen shillings they'd get a few more weeks in. Beyond that she mustn't think.

Then she heard Liam's step on the stairs. He came up slowly these days. It was a long climb to the top of the house, but there was a time when four flights wouldn't have taken a feather out of him. Again Bessie felt a foreboding that more ailed him than not having a job or brooding over the Tans' attack. Quickly as it came she put the thought from her mind, returned the bank book and her budget to the handbag and was all smiles when Liam came in.

By the dejected expression on his face she knew he hadn't found work but waited for him to tell her. 'I've been over to the North Strand, then up to Glasnevin – someone said they were taking on gravediggers, but there was nothing doing. A fellow there said I might be lucky in the grease works at Harold's Cross so I went there, but it was the same story – nothing there either.'

'Never mind love, maybe you'll be lucky tomorrow,' Bessie said, going to help him off with his jacket. 'Sit down now and I'll undo your boots and then I'll wet a cup of tea – you must be jaded with walking from one end of the city to the other.'

'It's a fair oul walk when there's nothing to show for it,' Liam said.

Bessie knelt and began to open his laces. 'Don't let it dishearten you – tomorrow's a new day.'

'That's what we've been saying for months.'

'I know, but all the same it's true.'

'Sometimes I get the feeling I'll never work again. I do think to myself I'm a young man with years and years in front of me and maybe I'll spend every one of them walking the streets of Dublin looking for a start and not getting one. Day after day coming home to you, knowing that all the while I've been out you've been hoping and praying.'

'For God's sake don't be talking like that. If you lose hope we might as well lie down and die. We're luckier than most –

382

we still have a few pounds – we're far from beaten.' And though one part of her felt that Liam wasn't in the right humour to be told that she was having a child, that on top of all his worries there would soon be another mouth to feed, something inside her said – tell him, shake him out of himself, let him know he has to go on trying . . . more now than ever before.

'Liam,' she said, getting up from her knees, 'Liam, listen. I've something to tell you. I'm going to have a child before the end of the year.'

'A child! Bessie, that's grand news.' His eyes showed their delight, his expression that of a small boy anticipating a special treat. 'When is it to be?'

'Before Christmas, maybe Christmas itself. Wouldn't that be a wonderful thing to have a baby on Christmas Day?'

'Aye,' he said and Bessie watching his face saw the expectation leave his eyes and a look of fear replace it. 'Aye,' he repeated. 'Christmas is a grand time for a child to be born – only how will we manage? In the bad weather I might never get work.'

'Indeed you will – if not at the building, at something. And anyway, Christmas is a long way off – anything could happen by then. Mr Geoghan might have the compensation even.'

'I suppose you're right.'

'Of course I'm right, you'll see. And now we'd better have the tea before it's stewed.'

'Stewed!' Liam said and laughed. 'You haven't wet it yet.' And Bessie laughed with him and was glad he had taken the news of the baby so well and looked more himself. But while they were drinking the tea he began to talk about the country and his father's farm. Her hope that she had put the fight back into him died and she experienced a fear that hadn't touched her for a long time. Was Liam regretting marrying her? Was he thinking that if he hadn't run off to Dublin he would still be a carefree young man living in a comfortable home, surrounded by the people he had known all his life, walking his own fields instead of saddled with a wife and child.

'I didn't know you missed it – that you ever gave it a thought,' she said.

'I never used to. But now sometimes when I'm walking through the streets I see a face that reminds me of someone there. Today up by Harold's Cross I saw a farmer in his cart going back from the market – or I'll pass a dairy yard and smell the cattle – things like that, you know. I suppose it's having so much time on my hands.'

'Did you ever wish you were back?' Bessie asked and waited in dread for the answer.

'Wish I was back! Have you lost your mind, what would I wish that for?'

'Then you're not sorry we ran away?'

'Ah, Bessie, is that what's worrying you? You haven't asked me that this long time.' He left his chair and came to her – stooping and kissing her. 'I'm sorry – I'm very cranky these days but it's not you I'm cranky with. I never regretted for a minute what we did. I love you. Without you I'd be nothing. I don't know how you put up with me. If anyone should have regrets, it's you. Ah love, stop crying. Commere, stand up, let me dry your eyes. I'll make it all up to you. One day I'll deck you in diamonds the way I promised.'

'There'll be two of us to deck in diamonds don't forget,' Bessie said, taking his hand and putting it on her belly.

The delighted expression came back into his eyes. 'Two of you, so there will. I forgot about the child. But hold on – for all you know it might be a boy.'

'It might,' Bessie said. 'It could well be – think of the money you'll be saved if it is.' She reached and kissed him. 'Now then,' she said, 'sit down by the fire and I'll have your dinner ready in no time.'

That night, while Liam slept, Bessie lay beside him thinking back over the day. Understanding exactly what Liam had

384

meant about certain sights and smells reminding you of the country. Many a time she was transported in the same way. She saw again the place and the people, her mother and father's faces. Lord have mercy on them. To think they were both dead and gone and she never knew. And wouldn't have only for bumping into a man from home one day on the quays. 'I was very sorry to hear about your trouble, Bessie,' he had said. 'And what trouble is that?' she had like a fool asked him. The man was taken aback and looked at her as if she had two heads. 'Your poor mother and father going so sudden and within a week of each other. My brother wrote and told me. Surely to God you knew, Bessie?'

'I did not,' she replied and held onto the man's arm for fear she would faint. 'Will you come back with me to the house, I'm dropping. Come back and tell me.'

The man went with her and told her what he knew. Her mother and father died a year ago and an aunt came from America a while after and took the younger sister back with her. 'And Michael, is there any word of him?'

'Not that I've heard.'

Everyone belonging to her gone, what was there for her ever to go back for? But Liam should if only for a few days. Anyway he should write. In the long run what did pride bring but separation and regrets when it was too late. Long ago she should have gone herself to see her parents. Liam must make it up with his mother and father. For now there was the child to think of. The farm should come to the child. Land was precious. A man with land was his own master. But what was the use of thinking. Liam was stubborn – he'd never get in touch with them. The Maguires were hard people, with not much give in them.

The child moved inside her – a definite movement unlike the feathery flutterings which was all she had felt so far. Did you know I was thinking about you? she silently asked, placing her hand where the movement had been. You'll never know your father's people, you'll never see the lovely place he came from. It's a grand place and by rights it should be yours – but if it's left to your father to get in touch you'll never see the sky over it.

She stopped talking to the child and returned to her thoughts. Considering how she had changed, remembering her previous contempt for those who valued owning land. Wondering had it been contempt or only sour grapes because her family had never been owners. Whatever her true feelings had been in the past she was in no doubt as to what they were now. She wanted the farm to come to the child. Liam had to do something about it. And if he refused to get in touch with his parents then she would, even if she went behind his back. One way or the other the Maguires would know that she was carrying their grandchild.

Chapter Nineteen

Robbie unfolded the note which Alice had slipped across the counter and read:

'We can meet at this address next Wednesday. If you are free, any time after half-past seven would be fine. And if you can come could you please wear mufti. I hope you can make it. Alice.'

He looked again at the address. He knew the place – a turn off Fitzwilliam Square – big beautiful houses. He had walked a few skivvies home who worked in them. And Wednesday was all right – but he hadn't any plain clothes. He had better straighten that part out. So he watched until Alice wasn't serving and went back to the counter. 'I haven't any civvies,' he said.

She looked disconcerted but only for a moment. 'It doesn't matter. Will you be able to come?'

'Try keeping me away.'

Lady Basset was in her usual place by the till. Glancing towards her Alice whispered, 'I'm sure she's watching us. You'd better have a tea or something.'

As she passed over the cup, Robbie touched her hand. 'Till Wednesday,' he said.

'Till Wednesday,' she repeated softly as he went away.

*

387

When Alice arrived at the flat on the evening of her appointment with Robbie, Nella was just about to leave. 'Everything arranged?' she asked.

'Everything, except that he hasn't any civilian clothes. Supposing he's seen?'

'What are you worried about – him being shot by the Sinn Feiners or someone knowing you have a lover from the ranks?'

'The mufti was your idea in the first place.'

'So it was – but if he hasn't any, why worry? Anyway – there's a dustcoat someone left behind – tell him to wear it when he leaves. In the early evening he could be calling for numerous reasons – but there's only one reason a man stays all night.'

'Who said anything about all night?'

'Alice, you're blushing! And I thought you'd grown up. If he's not staying the night why all the lies to your Mama about you and me going down to Wicklow?'

'It's just that you make it sound so awful – so premeditated. Anyway, he may not want to stay the night.'

'He will. I have to fly now. Enjoy yourself and help yourself to anything you want. Bye, see you soon.'

Alice looked at her watch. Robbie would be here in half an hour. That's if he came. Maybe he'd changed his mind. Maybe he was only being polite when he said yes. Oh please, God, make him come. I couldn't bear it if he didn't. Make him think I'm lovely. Let him love me.

Agitatedly, she moved about the room, touching things, rearranging chairs – that one should be closer to the sofa. She'd seat him there and herself on the chair. She must remember to offer him a drink. She didn't know if he smoked. She put an ashtray near the sofa. And she mustn't forget to draw the curtains. Ten minutes gone already! He might come early! She must look a sight. She was sweating and her heart battering.

I should have worn something cooler. But that would have

made Mama suspicious. You don't travel to Wicklow in a cool dress, not in the evening. Perhaps there's something of Nella's I could borrow. She went into the bedroom. Laid out on the bed was a brilliant blue dress. Alice held it up to her and looked in the mirror. It's beautiful but I couldn't wear it. It wouldn't be decent – the neck's so low. 'What you're doing is hardly decent,' a voice inside her head said. She argued with it: 'I know, but all the same I couldn't receive Robbie in a dress like that.' 'Why not?' asked the voice. 'Don't you want him to think you're gorgeous? And look what the colour does for you . . . and the way it's cut would flatter your bust.' 'It's too long, I couldn't,' Alice said but her voice lacked conviction. 'Not if you lift it and tie the sash beneath your breasts.' 'I couldn't. It is lovely, but the sash is the only fastening. It's satin and satin slips. It could easily come undone, but I suppose there is no harm in trying it on.'

She took off her dress and put on the blue one. Her face and figure were transformed. Her colouring was emphasized, her features softened and her eyes glowed. 'It's unbelievable,' she said out loud. 'I look beautiful – I really do.'

Robbie took a tram to College Green. Looking up at the clock above Trinity he saw that it was not yet seven. Walking at his usual pace he would arrive much too soon. He had to kill time, so he decided to stroll along Grafton Street. There were always beautiful girls walking through Grafton Street – he could study form. It crossed his mind that he might bump into Dolly. What would he say? Tonight he was supposed to be on guard duty. He could tell her it had been changed at the last moment. She knew nothing about the army, she'd swallow it. But she might expect him to stay with her. On the other hand, he mightn't meet her – so why worry?

He safely negotiated Grafton Street, turned left at St Stephen's Green, walked on in the direction of Baggot Street which would lead to Fitzwilliam Square and the address Alice had given him. Anyone seeing me approaching the place will think I'm meeting one of the skivvies. Little do they know it's the mistress herself.

Robbie found the house and was halfway up the steps when he heard a tapping sound like someone knocking on a window pane. He looked towards the drawing room, but there was no one at the window. The tapping continued. Now he placed where it was coming from and looked down into the area. There, through what he thought was the kitchen window, Alice's face was framed. She stopped tapping and pointed to the flight of narrow steps which led down from a gate let into the iron railings on the main steps. By the time he arrived below she had the door open. 'I should have told you it was the basement flat. The house is let out in flats. Come in.'

'It's very nice,' he said, following her in and looking around. 'Is this where you live?'

'No, it belongs to a friend. Let me take your cap and stick, and sit down. Would you like a drink, some tea, coffee or a sherry, anything?' She spoke quickly and nervously, delighted that he had come yet afraid of what she had set in motion. Not sure how to conduct herself in such a situation, wanting desperately to please him. Wanting him to take hold of her, to kiss her, but terrified of doing anything that might make her seem forward. He would be aware how unusual it was to be invited to the flat where she was alone. Nice women didn't do such things. He was looking at her, smiling. She thought how handsome he was. It wasn't just the arrangement of his features or the colour of his eyes, it wasn't just good looks. There was something about him, an air that seemed to flow from him, reach out and envelop her. The room was filled by his presence. She wanted to touch him, to be held by him. She could eat him.

'I'll have a sherry,' Robbie answered. While she poured the drinks he said, 'The dress is beautiful on you.'

'I'm glad you like it.' Suddenly her nervousness was gone.

She felt happy and excited. He sat on the sofa and she beside him but not too close. Robbie sipped his drink and talked about Dublin, his impressions of the Irish – all favourable. He loved the friendliness of the people, their wit and their generosity.

'You know them well for someone who's only been here a short time.'

'I make friends quickly.'

'Come to think of it – so you do. You made friends with me on very short notice.' She was surprised at the ease with which she was talking to him – flirting with him. Robbie looked blank. 'You've forgotten already. Horsham, remember.'

'I hadn't forgotten,' he lied. 'I was just wondering how someone so gorgeous isn't married.'

'Because no one has asked me.'

He looked at Alice's face, she returned his gaze and her lips parted. He reached and kissed them. Not much of a kisser for a married woman, he thought, as he felt her mouth close under his. He took her in his arms and kissed her again. Using his lips with expertise, he gradually and gently parted her lips and tentatively his tongue probed her mouth. Bloody queer bloke of a husband – she's never been kissed like this before – but she learns fast, he thought after the next one.

He couldn't make her out. She was passionate but inexperienced. He could do what he liked with her. But all the same, better not rush things. The most willing ones often changed their minds at the last minute. And besides, it would be nice to have her on a bed. Nice for her, too – give her something to remember him by. He couldn't see this lasting, not him becoming a regular at the flat. Funny thing that it should bother him, the thought of not seeing much more of her. There was something about her he liked very much – something more than the sex.

He took his arms from around her. She opened her eyes.

391

Her face was flushed, and the sash of her gown had slipped so the neck gaped, showing her breasts above the lacy camisole. Robbie's fingers itched to touch them. But he restrained himself, knowing that his self-control had limits. He leant back on the settee, took cigarettes from his tunic pocket and lit one.

'That jacket must be terribly warm, you could take it off,' Alice said, fiddling with the sash but making no attempt to adjust it. Say something nice, her eyes pleaded. Tell me that you love me, that you liked kissing me.

But instead Robbie asked, 'That summer you were in Horsham – who were you staying with?'

'Just friends of my parents. They were on holiday from India and had rented a house, but they didn't stay long. Why?'

'I wondered if I'd know them. In a place like Horsham you know most people. What was the house called?'

'I was trying to think of that the other night, but I can't remember. Still, it was ages ago and we only stayed a few days.' She supposed his question was normal – just curiosity about someone he might have heard of. But she mustn't tell him anything. He must never know about Stephen: what would he think of her being a married woman and allowing him to come here like this? He'd think she was a loose woman and probably never want to see her again. Maybe he had already decided that. He was probably making conversation to avoid kissing her again. She had been too forward, frightened him off. She shouldn't have let him kiss her like that. Men didn't expect women to be forward – but she couldn't play games. She had to respond as she felt.

'I was wondering what time your friend is coming back,' Robbie said and got up from the couch. He was going to leave. He'd go now and she would never see him again. He was looking around the room, probably wondering where she had put his cap and stick. She would lose him. 'Your friend, when . . . What's the matter? What have I done? Eh, come

392

on, don't look like that. Don't cry.' She was standing too, her hands pulling the neck of the gown together. He was beside her, his arms around her. 'Your friend . . . ?'

'She's not, not until the morning. I thought, I wanted you to stay. But it's all right. I expect you have to be back in barracks. I'll get your things.'

'Alice, Alice.' He cupped her face in his hands. 'Look at me. You wanted me to stay. I hoped you would – I banked on it. I got someone else to sign me in tonight. If you keep crying I'm going. That's better . . . you look beautiful when you smile.' He kissed her. His hand found and fondled her breast. 'Will we go into the bedroom,' he whispered.

And Alice said in a voice barely audible, 'Yes' – and took his hand to lead him there.

Still kissing her, Robbie lowered Alice onto Nella's wide, soft, silk-sheeted bed. The cloth of his tunic was rough against her flesh, the tunic buttons dug into her breastbone, but it was a pleasurable discomfort, hardly noticeable amongst the exquisite sensations she was experiencing. Then she felt real pain and cried aloud. At the same time, Robbie became aware that the entry he sought was blocked and realized that Alice was a virgin. She hadn't lied! She wasn't a married woman! The realization filled him with a sense of tenderness so great it overcame his desire. Lying still, he talked to her, telling her he loved her. She was beautiful. Promising he wouldn't hurt her. He would be very gentle, she must trust him. Then slowly and skilfully he broke her maidenhead. A wave carried Alice with him into an ecstasy that bordered on delirium. The wave mounted bearing her away and away, higher and higher so that she felt she must die on its crest and she cried out for the joy she felt. Now the wave subsided and flowed calmly, bringing her back from the faraway place to lie exhausted, her face, her body, wet with tears and sweat in the shelter of Robbie's arms. She called his name in wonder. He kissed her salt tears. 'I love you,' he said. 'I love you,' she responded.

393

He lay beside her, touching her hair, stroking her face. 'I didn't know,' he said. 'I thought you were a married woman. I didn't hurt you, did I?'

'A little, but it was nothing. I forgot about it. I forgot about everything. Oh Robbie – it was the most wonderful thing. The most marvellous thing. It can't be like that for everyone, can it? It couldn't be. Everyone would be so happy, wouldn't they. No one could be sad. No matter what happened if you had that you could never be unhappy again.'

They lay for a while without talking until Robbie said he was hungry and Alice said of course he must be and she would make him something to eat. She sat up and saw the blood on the bed and on Robbie's trousers. She felt ashamed and embarrassed. She didn't want Robbie to see it but she had to draw his attention, otherwise his uniform would be ruined. 'Look,' she said, 'your trousers. I'm sorry. You'll have to do something, sponge them. I'm really sorry.'

'Oh Alice, you're such a funny, innocent girl. Don't apologize for that. It's beautiful. But all the same I'd better sponge it – the Sergeant-Major wouldn't appreciate its beauty on parade.

'Your friend has friends,' he said when he came back from the bathroom wearing a man's dressing-gown. Alice laughed and said she believed so.

Together they made sandwiches and coffee which they took to the bedroom and picnicked in bed. Afterwards they made love, slept, woke, made love again. Wakening and loving and sleeping until when dawn was breaking Robbie said it was time for him to go. Reluctantly, Alice kissed him goodbye, so sleepy she forgot until the last minute about the dustcoat.

'But why do you want me to wear that?'

'In case there's any Sinn Feiners about. And my friend – well, she doesn't want a soldier to be seen leaving here,' Alice said, saying too much and putting all the blame on Nella.

'Oh, I see. Maybe she wouldn't mind if it was an officer.'

'I don't really know.' She was sorry to lie. She loved him. But for a long time yet she would have to be cautious.

'What am I supposed to do about this?' Robbie held up his peaked cap.

'You could hide it under there, I suppose.' She took his hat, and put it inside the coat. 'Hold it under your arm. No one will notice.'

'I feel a bloody fool dressed like this.'

'You look all right,' Alice assured him, 'honestly. Will you come again next Wednesday?'

'Next Wednesday and Thursday, Friday and Saturday.'

'I wish you could,' Alice said.

'One day. Now I'm off. A kiss to last me the week.'

When he was gone she lay in bed thinking how she had never known such happiness. Never imagined it was possible to feel for someone as she felt for Robbie. Robbie – Robbie what? She didn't know his second name, he didn't know hers. Which name would she tell him when he asked? Neither. She would invent one. Men gossiped like women. He might mention her name to one of his friends. Word of her could spread through a barracks, from one man to another, to a batman, to an officer. The army was as much of a village as Ireland. Before you could say Jack Robinson, Stephen would be posted back to Dublin. So much deception, so many lies! But she would lie and deceive, do whatever was necessary to protect her love and Robbie's.

He had two beautiful girls. Robbie lay on the barrackroom bed and thought about Alice and Dolly. Around him on the other beds soldiers sat cleaning their kit, singing, whistling, joking and smoking. There were smells of polish, Brasso, cigarette smoke and the sweat of men. There were sounds of brushes working on leather, of spitting on boots to work in the polish and the clink of buttons being gathered into button-sticks.

Robbie thought of his luck – having two girls mad about him. Well, not luck really. He had a way with women. His looks helped, but it wasn't just that. He liked women – all women, lovely soft, sweet-smelling women. He loved them and left them. Or he always had until now. But Alice and Dolly? He loved them but he didn't want to lose them. Not yet. Not while he remained in Ireland. So long as they didn't get serious. No talk about marriage – at the first hint of that he was gone. Marriage was years away. He wanted to see the world.

Alice was something special. Though she kept everything close to her chest, never spoke about her family, where she lived, who the friend was who lent her the flat. She was very reserved – except in bed.

And Dolly. Now there was a girl. No experience either, and not as willing to learn as Alice. Of course she was a Catholic – that held them back in the beginning. Supposing he was thinking of marriage . . . how could he choose between them?

The shootings, lootings and burning of properties, homes and business premises continued. For every atrocity committed by the Black and Tans, the IRA retaliated with equal ferocity. Dolly's father kept the ban on her being out late in the evenings. And Alice worried about Robbie in his inadequate disguise making his way back to barracks. She pleaded with him to take great care, making him promise to keep on the dustcoat and his cap hidden until he was almost back at the barracks. Reminding him when he dismissed her fears that only last week a soldier was killed when the bread lorry he was with was ambushed.

Dolly consoled herself that although she saw Robbie less often than previously and then only for short periods of time, the weather was still lovely and there was always Saturday and Sunday, which they spent in the Park in a place of their own, far away from strolling soldiers, noisy boys and families going to the Zoological Gardens.

She bought a thermos flask and at weekends filled it without her mother knowing and purchased cooked ham and bread on her way to meet Robbie, and they picnicked under the trees. Throughout the summer and into the autumn they feasted under the chestnut trees. Lying there one Sunday afternoon with Robbie stretched beside her smoking, her fingers idly combing the grass, she thought how beautiful his eyes were. How she felt herself melting whenever she looked into them. She had never known anyone with eyes the colour of his. Brown, but not just brown. How would you describe them? Her idly-searching fingers closed on something – a chestnut bursting from its spiky pod. She picked it up and eased it from its fleshy packing. She looked at the gleaming fruit. Chestnut, that was the colour – the exact colour of Robbie's eyes. She held the nut close to his face. He opened his eyes and smiled at her. 'What are you doing?'

'Wanting to match this to your eyes – they're the same colour.'

'I know,' he said complacently and pulled her to him.

'How do you know?' She struggled playfully.

'My mother told me.' He lifted her hand and bit her fingers gently one after the other.

'I'm sure she did!' Dolly said, her heart racing, quivers of pleasure speeding through her. Robbie gave her back her hand and sat up.

Brushing grass and leaves from his tunic he reached for the nut Dolly had discarded and caressing the hard shiny surface said, 'One day when I was sick, my mother sat on the bed and told me my eyes were like new shining chestnuts.'

'That was a queer thing to say. How did she come to do that?' Dolly asked and lay down again beside Robbie.

'She was marvellous, made ordinary things seem magical.'

Dolly looked up at the leaves shivering in the little wind

397

and prayed, 'Please God, don't let him leave me. I love him so much. Let me keep him.' Robbie's hand covered her breast, his fingers circling, caressing, while he told her about his mother. Her runaway match, how he took her to Dublin when she was dying.

'When did she die?'

'After, when I was in France. Do you know I'm sure I saw you then, that Easter in Dublin. You and another girl near Nelson's Pillar.'

'I thought that was the day we met but wasn't sure. And do you know the funny thing – someone, a woman who did the cups told me I'd meet you. It's as if it was all planned – meant to be.'

'Of course it was,' Robbie said.

'Lord have mercy on your mother.' She must have been great all the same. All the magic about him. A mother who had eloped, who remarked on the colour of your eyes. A mother like that would have been wonderful, she thought, comparing her with Bridget's rough and ready kindness.

She sat up and began smoothing her hair, checking it for pieces of grass or leaves. 'Have a look at my back. I don't want to advertise where I've been.' Robbie's fingers began their search for grass but soon slid around to find her breasts. She sat very still for a while then turned into his arms and together they sank back into the grass.

'When are we going to meet this fella of yours?' Maggie asked Dolly a few weeks later.

'As soon as I get up the courage to ask me Da.'

'You'll want to hurry up. The days are drawing in – you'll freeze the arse off of yourself courting in the Park.'

'I wish you didn't always have to curse. You're awful, real common sometimes. But you're right – I'll have to ask him to the house. I'll tell me mother first and then maybe you and her can put in a word for me.'

Bridget listened and agreed. And the next day told Dolly it was all right with her father. She could bring Robbie home the following Sunday. 'Mind you,' Bridget added, 'that's no guarantee he'll get a warm reception from your father.'

'It's a start anyway,' Dolly said. 'And I'm sure when he meets him and knows he's a Catholic and his people came from here, he'll take to him.' She spent the remainder of the week wondering and worrying what Robbie would think of ninety-seven.

Several times Bessie suggested that she and Dolly go to see Miss Murtagh. Dolly kept promising that she would but whenever Bessie tried pinning her to a definite time Dolly had some excuse.

'Don't mind that one and her promises,' Bridget said one night after Dolly had again fobbed Bessie off with an excuse. 'Go yourself.'

'Well, you see I only knew Miss Murtagh slightly and now I've left it so long about visiting, without Dolly I'd feel awkward. And to tell you the truth I don't like going far in my condition.'

'Ashamed of your belly! Poor woman. That's the fault of the church – preaching modesty, though for the life of me I never understood the sense behind it. Aren't we carrying God's gift of life? I think them things were made up by some cranky old priest that hadn't much regard for any woman except the Blessed Virgin.'

'I can't help me thoughts, though it's not to everyone I'd voice them.'

'What will you do about Miss Murtagh?'

'I'll wait till after the child, please God. It would be a good excuse for going.'

Chapter Twenty

The factory sounded its long mournful wail and simultaneously all over the city the Angelus rang out. It was six o'clock and time to go home. Dolly ran to the cloakroom, took off her white coat, tidied her hair, put on her outdoor things and calling 'Good-night' to the other girls, ran down the stairs. She wanted to get home quickly. She still had a lot to do in preparation for Robbie's visit.

She hurried through the narrow streets forced now and then to step off the pavements to avoid bumping into gossiping women who stood holding loaves, blood-soaked papers of meat and tilly-cans of milk. Telling herself that when she got married she'd never leave her messages until the last minute. Emerging from one of the narrow streets she entered Patrick's Park, a short-cut home. It was a fine evening with no sign of rain, but the air was cold with the first hint of winter. Soon it would be dark, she thought and wondered if the old men sitting on the benches had any homes to go to, or did they all use the lodging houses near by.

Over to her left she saw the Cathedral towering above the tenement houses and red-bricked flats surrounding the Park. And into her mind came the memory of Easter Monday 1916 when on her way home she had stopped to watch the wedding. The girl's face was as clear as a picture. She was beautiful. She couldn't remember what her husband had looked like, only that he was a soldier. Well, an officer. But a soldier all the same. That was in the days when I wouldn't be seen dead with a soldier and she smiled to herself as she left the Park and hurried up the street making her plans for all she would do that night.

She would take all the delft from the dresser, wash and rearrange it. Her mother had it a show. The table and chairs wanted a good polishing. She'd do them, clean the mirror and give the pictures a rub. At least inside she'd have everything like a new pin. If only, just for once, she wished the hall door could be shut. But she reminded herself there wasn't much chance of that – there'd be the usual crowd gathered around it. Unless it rained. Please God, she prayed, make it lash rain. Then she remembered the leaking lavatory roof and how often men used it and prayed for Sunday to be fine.

Tonight she would do all the big cleaning and after work tomorrow have the afternoon free to go across town. That blouse might still be in Kellet's. She had had her eye on it for ages. Nineteen and eleven – still it was a beauty, though Miss Murtagh could have made it for half that. Poor Miss Murtagh, she wondered how she was. One of these days definitely, she would go and see her. Maybe even bring Robbie. Thank God this week was her number in the money club. Though after buying the blouse and shop cakes with cream, there wouldn't be much of the thirty shillings left. And she'd buy a brack as well and an ounce of tobacco for her father, keep him in good humour. If all went well and he took to Robbie he could become a regular visitor.

'Is that you?' her mother asked when Dolly eventually arrived and pushed through the door.

'Who did you think it was? Has me father said any more about the visit?' Then Dolly noticed her mother's face. 'What's up? You've been crying!'

'Your father's at death's door up in the Union.'

'Sacred Heart of Jesus!' Dolly exclaimed. 'What ails him? He was all right this morning.'

'He wasn't all right this long time. Sudden pneumonia –

double, and he's very bad.' She took a plate from off a pot of boiling water. 'It's only a bit of fish and potatoes. I had no mind for cooking. He took bad about twelve and I sent over to the dispensary. The minute the doctor saw him he said he was a hospital case. I only hope I did right having him shifted. The doctor said he wouldn't last the night at home. But they say shifting anyone with pneumonia kills them.'

'Will he be all right?' Dolly asked. She pushed the food around her plate, eating little.

'God knows. He was that bad he said nothing about going into the Union. And you know the dread and fear he had of ever finishing in the Union.'

'He could get better, couldn't he?'

Bridget ignored the question and continued, 'My heart nearly burst when I saw him choking and gasping for breath. His poor chest seemed to have fallen in. And I wasn't able to give him any ease.' She began to cry and say over and over, 'Poor Johnny, your days are numbered.'

Dolly was shocked and concerned and tried comforting her mother, but still at the back of her mind were her plans for Sunday. She waited until her mother had stopped crying before hesitantly saying, 'I was just wondering what to do about Robbie coming for his tea?'

'Cancel it.'

'Ah mother, I can't do that. I couldn't get word to him.'

'You'll have to.'

Dolly knew there was no use arguing for the time being and instead offered to give the room a good going-over.

'You can forget that as well. I don't want you pulling the place about.' Then she relented and said, 'Anyway, leave it until Tom and Maggie come back from the hospital and see how your father is.'

Dolly fumed as she watched the hands of the clock, in her mind accusing Tom of deliberately delaying their return to thwart her. She thought of all there was to do. It wasn't fair

– she wanted everything to be lovely for Robbie's visit. And her father couldn't be that bad. Her mother was exaggerating. If he was that sick why hadn't she gone to see him? Bridget, as if she guessed the thought in Dolly's mind, said, 'I should have gone myself only I didn't want you arriving home from work and no one to tell you what was wrong.'

It was nearly nine o'clock before Tom and Maggie came.

'Well, tell me, how is he?' Bridget asked.

'He's holding his own, Mrs Devoy,' Tom told her and Maggie added that he wasn't grand but he was no worse. Dolly waited until all the inquiries were exhausted then broached the subject of Robbie's visit, appealing to Maggie to persuade her mother that he should come. Bridget considered it, agreed then remembered that if Robbie came on Sunday she couldn't visit Johnny. Dolly couldn't have him to the house with no one else there.

'Look, I'll tell you what,' Maggie said. 'Me, you and Dolly'll go tomorrow and Tom will come with me on Sunday. That's the best thing. The nuns don't like too many around the bed.' Bridget, who felt too tired to do any more arguing, reluctantly agreed. Soon the girls coaxed her to go to bed. And between them washed the delft, polished the furniture and arranged the dresser to Dolly's liking.

They're killing themselves answering the letter, Bessie thought as days and then weeks passed and no word came from her in-laws. Then when she had almost given up hope a letter arrived. Written by Mrs Maguire and addressed to Liam, it said:

'It's not before time you dropped a line. The world's a hard enough place without not knowing whether your only son is alive or dead. Thank God you came to your senses before it's too late. Much good would a letter have been when me and your father were mouldering in the clay. That's the only thing

403

anyone is sure of and the older you get the nearer it comes.

Since word came I haven't been off of my knees giving thanks to the Blessed Virgin for answering my prayers that a foolish child would see the error of his ways and know the love of parents is always waiting for a spark to rekindle it. And now I've started a novena for the baby to be born safe and well.'

The witch! The bloody oul witch! Not a mention of me that wrote the letter. A novena that the child might be born safe and well and not a mention of the mother who is carrying him. But that's pride for you, Bessie thought. Mrs Maguire will take a long time yet to say 'All is forgiven and forgotten.' Whatever might be at work in her heart she couldn't let it show. But it's a start anyway. I'll answer it a bit nearer Christmas. Maybe by then I'll have told Liam about the letters. Or maybe it would be better to wait until the child is born, please God.

She got the old brown bag from under the mattress and put away the letter. She was tempted to look at the bank book but didn't, telling herself: you know to the last farthing how much is in it. Less than you thought when you worked out your fine budget. But isn't that how it always is – on paper it's easy but it never works out the same when the money is in your hand. She put back the bag and smoothed the disturbed bedclothes, thinking as she did so that they weren't warm enough now that the weather had turned cold. The room was so draughty. The wind came in under the door and through the broken pane of glass which she had stuffed with cardboard and rags. It wanted a piece of board tacked across it – Liam was forever promising and forever forgetting. God help him, he was always that tired and disheartened when he came in at night after his fruitless searching for work.

On Sunday when Robbie arrived and was introduced to Bridget she was very impressed. He was all that Dolly had

404

said, a handsome, smart fella. Robbie shook hands with her and she noticed that it was a good firm handshake.

'Sit down. Make yourself at home. I've heard so much about you I feel I've known you for years.'

He apologized for coming at what he said must be an inconvenient time. She said not to worry about it, sure how was he to know. She liked the way he gave his time to Christie who was there while Maggie and Tom visited Johnny. Taking off his bandolier and letting Christie play with it. Answering his questions about guns and soldiers. Telling him stories that made his eyes shine while his sticky fingers opened and shut the bandolier's pouches and left imprints on the gleaming leather. In the presence of the laughing, charming stranger Bridget temporarily forgot her worry and her guilt at not having visited Johnny.

Dolly was delighted it was all going so well. And there had only been two women at the hall door – two of the most respectable women in the house wearing clean pinnies. She had noticed the look of admiration they gave Robbie and was pleased with the way he had saluted them.

She hovered around the table, smoothing the cloth, altering the position of a cup and saucer, putting the jug and sugar basin closer together. Watching him drinking the tea Bridget had given him, she thought of how he'd smiled when her mother had said, 'It's only a cup in your hand,' and had then laid before him sandwiches and bread and butter. She was relieved that her mother seemed to like him – though looking at his dark head bent to drink and his beautiful hand holding the best china, knew that whether they liked him or not she would folly him to the ends of the earth.

Robbie finished the tea and searched his trouser pockets looking for cigarettes, then stood up and with the flat of his hands patted his tunic pockets. 'I was sure I had a packet,' he said.

'You'll get them across the road in Fitz's,' Dolly informed

him, disappointed that he would leave, if only for a while, so soon after arriving.

He retrieved his bandolier, rubbed off the mark Christie had made, put it on, then moved to the overmantel where he took his time arranging his cap.

'It's straight across the street, you can't miss it,' Bridget said, watching him preening before the mirror.

'Right. I won't be five minutes.' He touched the child's head in passing and placed a hand on Dolly's shoulder repeating that he wouldn't be long. At the door he turned back and asked Bridget, 'I forgot to ask, Mrs Devoy – would you like me to fetch you something?'

'Well, if it's no trouble I wouldn't say no to a bottle of stout.'

'What did you want to do that for? Letting him know you drink!' Dolly shouted at her mother when the door closed.

'Drink how are you! A bottle of stout I asked for, not a bottle of whiskey.'

'All the same, you shouldn't.' Dolly had lowered her voice. 'But anyway, what do you think of him?'

Christie had moved to sit on the fender, resting his head against his grandmother's knee. She ran her fingers through his hair massaging his scalp and hesitated a moment before answering Dolly's question.

'Go on, tell me,' Dolly urged.

'He's gorgeous. All that you said he was. I think he's the one you've been waiting for, all right. But he's full of himself.'

'What do you mean – full of himself?'

'Don't start shouting again.' Bridget's fingers stopped caressing the child's head and he cried, 'Don't stop doing it, Grannie! Do it again. Itchy me head, I like it.'

'You be quiet Christie and let your granny talk. Full of himself, that's what I mean.'

'You!' Dolly said, her voice raised again, 'you're awful – you get in on me nerves, do you know that? Always fault-finding.'

406

'For God's sake, will you talk easy – he might walk back any minute. There's someone coming, listen, I can hear them.'

From the passage came the sounds of laughter, voices, then Maggie, followed by Tom and Robbie, came into the room. Robbie had his arms full of bottles of stout. Everyone began talking at once – Bridget wanting to know how Johnny was, Dolly asking how they had all arrived together and Christie clamouring for his mother's attention. 'What did you bring me, Mammy?' he asked running to her, looking up at her face. 'What did you bring me?'

'See to the child, we'll get no peace till you do,' Bridget told Maggie. Dolly found three tumblers and poured the stout while Maggie told her son to put out his hands and shut his eyes till he saw what God had sent him. Into his outstretched palms she put a gaudy, pink-wrapped packet and a yellow fizzbag with a liquorice stump sticking out of it. He whooped with joy and ran back to Bridget who was waiting patiently for news of her husband. 'Your father, how was he?'

'He wasn't well, ma.'

'Did he say anything about me not being there? I hope you let on I wasn't well.'

'Of course I did. Not that he paid much attention with the way he was.'

'Was his breathing any easier?'

Attempting to comfort his mother-in-law, Tom lied and said it was. 'I wouldn't have said so,' Maggie contradicted. 'It sounded like a fan bellows.'

Robbie handed Bridget a glass of stout. She drank a mouthful before remorsefully saying, 'I shouldn't have let them shift him. It'll be the cause of killing him.'

'Have another drink of the stout,' Robbie urged kindly.

'Go on, do, Mother,' Dolly coaxed, her earlier disapproval of Bridget's drinking abandoned, fearful that if something didn't happen her mother would begin to cry and remember that if it wasn't for Robbie's visit she would have been with

Johnny this afternoon. Dolly fussed around her, asking if she wanted this or that. Christie found a whistle in the lucky bag and blew a deafening blast. Dolly snatched it from him and threw it up on the mantlepiece. 'Your granny has a headache, suck your fizz bag.'

'Would you like me to slip over to the pub and get you a whiskey?' Robbie asked.

Bridget thanked him, but refused. Christie screamed for his whistle and Maggie gave it to him and told him to go out the back. 'Let him deafen the neighbours. I don't give a shite whose eardrums he bursts so long as it isn't mine.'

Dolly wanted the ground to open and swallow her up. Fancy Maggie cursing in front of Robbie. What would he think of them? Robbie laughed uproariously and Bridget smiled for the first time since they came back from the hospital and drank some more of her stout.

Dolly breathed a sigh of relief. It was going to be all right. In a few minutes she'd suggest making tea. But first she asked Maggie how she, Tom and Robbie had arrived at the same time.

'Your sister recognized me. I was . . .' Robbie began and Maggie joined in, 'That's right. We were coming up the lane and I saw this soldier coming out of Fitz's and I said to Tom, "I wouldn't be surprised if that's our Dolly's fella. He fits the description to a tee." So I asked him was he going to ninety-seven.'

Dolly said wasn't that a coincidence and everyone agreed it was. Her mother said it was time for tea. Dolly reached through the kitchen window to the meat-safe where she had kept the fresh cream cake overnight. Christie was called in from the yard and ogled the cake, reaching with grubby fingers to touch it and being rapped across the knuckles each time.

During and after the meal they talked about Johnny's illness. Tom said he'd known plenty to get over pneumonia. His own father had had it after the Spanish 'flu and was now hale and hearty. Robbie said that as a child he too had had it. And Dolly wondered if it was then his mother had said the thing about his eyes. Maggie said if her father got through the crisis he'd be all right.

The visit was a great success. Dolly was delighted with the way everything went. No one mentioned the Tans or Michael Collins or the British Army. And Robbie followed Tom in and out to the yard, laughing and talking. Maybe fellas weren't as particular as girls, didn't pay attention to things like that. All her worries had been for nothing.

When it was time to go, Maggie and Tom said they would walk on slowly. He would catch them up and they'd put him on the right road. Robbie kissed her in the dark hall and held her close. But she couldn't stay too long and have her mother shouting for her to come in. If only, she thought, when she returned to the room, my father wasn't sick the night would have been perfect. But it was lovely anyhow.

'Sleep 'ithin with me tonight, it's not worth pulling out the chair-bed,' Bridget said and Dolly agreed, adding, 'Tell me now what you didn't finish saying because they came in. About Robbie, you know,' she asked her mother.

'He's nice and very good-natured.'

'I know you – saying one thing and thinking another.'

'It's the truth I'm telling you. He's a handsome man, but full of himself.'

'He is not. He only looked in the glass to put on his cap.'

'And every time he stood up or went anywhere near it. He's very vain. It's a bad fault in a man.'

'You!' Dolly said exasperatedly, flouncing to the clothes press for her nightdress. 'And I was worrying about the reception my father would have given him. But he wouldn't have reefed him to pieces behind his back.'

'Dolly, child, I'm not finding fault with him for the sake of it. If he'd come here on another errand I'd have had nothing but admiration for him. But he came because you asked him.

Because you're mad about him. And I'm warning you, that's all. He's vain from his head to his heels. He's any woman's fancy and he knows it. Any girl who married him will cry many a tear over him.'

Dolly sniffed contemptuously and glared at her mother.

'Sniff all you like and give your derisive looks only don't annoy me any more with talk. I've enough on my mind with your father lying dying above in the Union.'

'Who said anything about me father dying? Tom nor Maggie never said that. You're only making that up.' Dolly tried to hide her alarm by bullying her mother.

'Your father's dying and more shame on me for not cancelling your man's visit and being at his bedside. Now go into bed. I'll be in in a minute when I've swept the hearth.'

After saying her prayers Dolly got into bed and lay thinking. Sometimes her father got in on her nerves, but she didn't want him to die. He wasn't going to die. That was her mother trying to frighten her. He looked all right last night when she saw him.

And her mother had her glue if she thought she was going to be put off Robbie by all the talk about mirrors and being vain. What would she know about fellas? Talk – that's all it was. I'll get round her tomorrow. And then I'll have to find some way of Robbie and me being here on our own. It wouldn't be easy, but she'd have to try. For cold though it was in the Park at least they had privacy. And Robbie would soon get fed up if their courting was curtailed to a quick kiss in the hall.

'That's the third time this week you haven't eaten your breakfast. I hope you're not sickening for something.'

'I'm all right, Bridie, just not hungry,' Alice lied and hoped she could control the mounting nausea until the maid had left the room.

'Will I get you something else, milk maybe?'

'No, nothing, thank you. I'm tired. I'll sleep for a while longer.' She closed her eyes and waited until Bridie went. Then, rising quickly, she ran to the bathroom and was sick. She rinsed the sour taste from her mouth, bathed her face with cold water and felt better. Fearing that Bridie might return she went back to the bedroom and locked the door. Then, as she had for several mornings lately, took off her nightdress and studied her body in the long mirror.

Surely, she thought, there should be some sign of change. Shouldn't her shape have altered – or her face look different? She moved closer to the mirror, examining her face. No pallor. No dark rings. Her eyes were bright, her complexion perfect. She stepped back, her eyes returning to her body, her hands cupping her breasts. They felt heavier, rounder. But that might be her imagination. So might the blue veining which seemed more prominent. Her hands left her breasts and moved over her belly. She smiled. In there was Robbie's child. She hugged herself and wished that the arms around her were his. But soon they would be. Soon they would be together for always, their lives no longer ruled by his nights off-duty and Nella's flat being available. Soon she would tell him about the baby. But not yet. First she had to have every detail of the plan for their life together perfect.

She put on her nightdress, unlocked the door and got into bed stretching languorously and wishing Robbie lay beside her. A sound in the passage made her close her eyes. It might be Mama, Bridie having told her about the uneaten food. Mama come to fuss. If she pretended sleep she might not disturb her. The footsteps passed the door and went away.

Alice thought about the plan. She had her godmother's legacy – a fortune which would set them up in Canada or New Zealand. They could farm, or grow apples. She pictured rows of apple trees crowned with blossoms.

One night very soon they would slip away. Take a boat to England and then another to Canada or New Zealand,

411

whichever country Robbie preferred, and then their glorious life together would begin. It was a pity it had to start off with lies. But she couldn't tell him about Stephen, not yet. Asking him to desert was one thing, he was bound to see the advantages of a life where he was his own master, but a bigamous marriage, that he might not be so keen to go through with. But he believed her to be single and she could explain that a marriage in Ireland or England would be impossible. Without revealing who her father was, she would let Robbie know he was influential and opposed to her marrying a Catholic private soldier. Robbie understood the ways of the world and how the army worked. A word from her father in the right place and Robbie would find himself on the next boat to some ghastly place. Then, unbidden, into her mind came a disturbing thought: supposing Robbie wouldn't agree to desert? This disturbing thought was followed by another and another. So quickly did they come and so many of them that her vision of a blossom-decked orchard was blackened out beneath a cloud of doubts and questions which swarmed in her head like a cloud of locusts.

Robbie might refuse to leave the army! Might not want to marry her – after all, he had never mentioned marriage. And what about Stephen? And if he *did* desert and marry her she would be committing bigamy. And if he didn't, the baby would be illegitimate! It would be illegitimate anyway, but no one would know. Oh my God, what have I done? Why didn't I take Nella's advice and use the sponge and vinegar.

She got up and paced the room, terrified at the predicament she found herself in. Talking to herself, asking God to help her, to direct her. Robbie does love me. Don't let me doubt it. It was all so wonderful, so beautiful. Only someone who loved you could make it like that. Only someone who loved you could make you feel the way he had. No one could pretend, say or do the things he had unless he felt deeply for you. Gradually a calmness filled her and she knew everything would be all right. It was foolish of her to have thought otherwise. She would tell Robbie about the baby and he'd agree to all her plans. And once they were married, she'd confess about her marriage to Stephen. Robbie would understand why she hadn't done so before. She'd make him see that she was afraid of losing him, that was why the lie was necessary. At peace with herself, Alice went back to bed.

Hopeful again, she resumed her plans for their departure. A list – she must make a list. Things to do. Dates of sailings to Canada and New Zealand. She must transfer her money. Buy suitable clothes – Robbie would have to have some, too. She smiled, remembering the night in the canteen when he had explained he had no civilian clothes. There was so much preparation. Really, she should get up and begin. She was happy and excited at the prospect of all the activity in front of her. She could store everything in Nella's flat. Of course, she would have to be let into the secret, but that couldn't be helped and anyway Nella was a staunch friend and not likely to become moralistic about her leaving Stephen, or about the baby.

When would the baby be born? How did one work that out . . . Isn't it silly – here I am expecting one and I don't know when. Alice thought back to the first time Robbie had come to the flat – that was a date she would never forget. Then to her first missed period. How long before that had she conceived? Some time in the preceding three weeks. So the baby was due in April. April would be a lovely time to give birth.

She supposed Bridie must have noticed that she had missed two periods. The servants were probably already speculating about her pregnancy. Funny how she hadn't thought of that sooner. Bridie took care of her clothes – she was bound to have noticed. That was why she was so concerned when she refused breakfast. Yes, they would all be waiting for the announcement. Waiting to tell her how they were all praying for her, secretly hoping she would have a son for Stephen.

413

Though never voicing their wishes, for fear, as they did, of flying in the face of God. They would be so delighted for Stephen. 'The kindest, gentlest man that God ever created,' was how Bridie often described him.

He is too, Alice thought, kind and gentle, but is also what he is. He would be hurt by her leaving without telling him, or saying goodbye, but he'd survive. She wondered if he would resign his commission. Probably – he wasn't a career soldier, wouldn't have signed on had he remained single.

Tongues would wag in Dublin once the news broke that she had run away – deserted her husband. Desertion! There it was, back in her mind again. Would Robbie do it? Men had such loyalty – to things, regiments, institutions. But if a man was forced to choose between them and the woman he loved, surely he'd place the woman first. Of course he would. She felt confident again.

Maggie was sitting in the main office when Dolly arrived not knowing why she had been summoned there. Maggie was crying and Dolly knew without anything being said that her father was dead. Someone handed her a glass of water and led her to a chair. The manager came and said he was very sorry and for Dolly to convey his sympathy to her mother. Then he gave her an envelope. 'It will help you to buy black,' he said, and Dolly knew it would contain a five pound note, a customary gift from Jacobs to an employee suffering a bereavement.

'When did it happen?' she asked Maggie when they were outside in the street.

'Three this morning. They came to tell me mother not long after you went to work. And do you know, a funny thing – the clock, mine, stopped dead on the hour.'

Dolly began to cry and Maggie said, 'I keep telling myself he's better off out of his suffering. But it's hard all the same.'

'How will I let Robbie know?'

'Send a young fella out of the house with a note to the barracks.'

'Isn't it sad all the same – they never met. Me worrying about how Dad'd receive him and now he's dead without ever seeing him.'

Bridget was sitting by the fire crying and consoling herself out loud. 'Well, thank God I never let the policy lapse. Look at all the unfortunates that do and are buried as paupers.'

Maggie asked if she'd made up her mind about the arrangements and without waiting for an answer urged her mother not to bring the body home. 'Leave him where he is and give him the last night in the chapel.' Dolly said she thought that was the best thing, too.

'It's not what your father would have wanted,' Bridget said.

'That's all very well but you've no way for a corpse here even if it is me father, Lord have mercy on him.'

'If he'd died at home, where he should have, he'd have been waked here.'

'Thank God that he didn't then,' Maggie replied. 'And you'd better hurry and make your mind up, because Tom'll have to let the undertakers know and have it right for the paper.'

'It's your father's home and he should be buried from it,' Bridget protested. 'I don't know what to do for the best.' She felt numb and confused and thought how once she would have put Maggie in her place, but now she seemed the stronger one. It was getting old. Your children took you over.

'The funeral will pass the house, you know that. And there isn't really the room here, Ma. Nowadays lots of people don't bring the bodies home,' Maggie argued. And Bridget gave in.

Tom made the arrangements with the undertaker and brought back a white card bordered with black. And because he had the best hand, wrote on it Johnny's name and RIP under it. It was tacked on the hall door where anyone reading it would know because the card wasn't draped in black crêpe that John Devoy wasn't waking at home.

Robbie came at teatime and ordered a cab to take the five of them to the dead house where Johnny as yet uncoffined lay on a marble slab, his head fitting neatly into the cold, hollowed pillow. Dolly, who had seldom seen her father lying down, was surprised at the length of him. She cried when she touched his stiff fingers and thought of all his kindness and how he called her 'Alanna'. And she was sorry that she had helped Maggie overrule her mother about bringing him home. She was sure he wouldn't be happy lying amongst strangers. They went again the following night to take their last of him. Dolly thought he looked more himself without the white cloth tying up his chin.

Bridget kissed his forehead and caressed the cold yellow fingers entwined in beads and took her leave of him. Allowing Tom to link her out of the mortuary, praying silently for God to give her strength to bear this latest cross. Not such a heavy one, she consoled herself. Not like losing Richard. Johnny like herself was old. Sometimes he could be cantankerous, though she remembered when he wasn't. And she thought of a summer's night long ago lying on the banks of the Dodder with the light fading, the sound of water and the smell of the wild woodbine that entangled the hedge under which they lay. And wondered, as she hadn't done for years, was that the night her first child was conceived? A little girl with china-blue eyes so like Johnny's that her mother had said, 'You'd think they'd been lifted out of his head.' Johnny would be with her now in Heaven and Richard too, and their other babies that had died.

Afterwards, on that long-ago summer's night, she remembered how Johnny had pulled a strand of the honeysuckle and wound it wreath-like in her hair. Then, suddenly realizing how dark it was getting and afraid of her father's anger they had like the children they were, ran hand in hand all the way home.

'Are you all right?' Tom asked, recalling Bridget to the present.

'I'm all right, son. I was just thinking how the years fly. But I'm all right.'

Dolly lingered until the last minute by the coffin. 'My poor father,' she whispered to Robbie who stood ill at ease, moving back from the coffin to let people look at Johnny. Amazed when he realized they were mostly strangers. Horrified to see them move on, viewing other bodies and repelled by their comments.

'God love him, he must have suffered. That woman's like a skeleton. Ah well sure, she's only gone a step before us. He's a lovely corpse.'

On the way home Dolly thought again how her father and Robbie had never met. Now they never would. She'd never have to worry about the reception Robbie would get. She felt glad, then guilty that she should be thinking so at such a time and tried to put herself in a frame of mind more appropriate for the occasion. But random thoughts filled her head – what she would wear to the funeral, how Maggie's hat didn't become her . . . And worse than anything else she suddenly felt hungry and wondered what Bessie, who was looking after things, would have made for the supper.

Robbie held her hand. She leant against him and looked suitably sad. It was a good job people couldn't see into your mind, she thought. She wondered what Maggie and her mother were thinking about. Not food, that was for sure. She must be a most unnatural being.

'I won't be able to come to the chapel tomorrow night.'

'Why?' she asked, her expression genuinely saddened at the statement.

'It's Wednesday – I'm on picket duty.'

'Could you not change it, just for once?'

417

'You know if I could you wouldn't have to ask,' Robbie said.

'I suppose so,' Dolly said. 'You've been very good coming the two nights. All the same, I wish you could come tomorrow.'

Robbie squeezed her hand. 'I'm sorry. Don't cry again, you've been very brave. Here, take this.' He gave her his handkerchief and she dabbed at her eyes. She heard her mother say to Maggie, 'Poor Dolly, she's taking it very bad. He loved her, and though she didn't always show it, she loved him.'

So I did. But it's not for him I'm crying. I wanted Robbie with me tomorrow night, linking me up the chapel, Dolly thought and sobbed loudly.

Johnny was buried more than a week before Dolly realized she had missed her period. It'll come in the morning, she told herself and when it didn't she spent the day running to and from the lavatory to see if she had started. One of the older women in work noticing her frequent visits advised her to drink barley water, and told her to wrap a piece of flannel around her loins. 'That and barley water is the boy for a chill on the kidneys!'

It might be that, Dolly consoled herself and got her mother to boil barley, strain it and she drank it by the gallon. And if it wasn't a chill on her kidneys it could be the weather, it had got very chilly. Or it could be the shock to her system of her father dying suddenly. But when the weeks passed and no period came she could no longer comfort herself with such excuses. Yet she couldn't believe she was pregnant. It couldn't have happened to her – not pregnant. That was the worst thing in the world that could happen to anyone not married. It couldn't happen to her. Then she remembered the times in the Park and a sick, hopeless feeling claimed her. She prayed: 'Holy Mary, Mother of God, don't let it be true. I'll go to

418

Confession and I'll never do it again. Sacred Heart of Jesus don't let me be pregnant.' But supposing I am – what's to become of me? Maybe he won't marry me. For all I know he could be married in England. Oh, God help me. I'd never be able to tell him. I'd die of shame. I couldn't tell anyone. What'll I do?

Dolly longed to confide in someone. She should tell Maggie, but maybe it was something else and if she told Maggie, her sister would know what she'd been doing. And putting it into words might make it come true . . . but she had to talk to someone or she'd go mad. Robbie remarked that something about her had changed – she didn't laugh so easily. She said she was grieving about her father. Sometimes, she desperately wanted to blurt out the truth but was terrified in case of his reaction. On the nights she didn't see him she went to the chapel and spent hours praying. Once, she overheard her mother say to Maggie, 'You know – I'm worried about Dolly. She always minded her duties but since your father died she's never out of the chapel. The knees must be worn off of her. I hope she's not going funny. Grief can have a queer effect on some people. Grangegorman's full of people with religious madness.'

That's where I'll finish up if I don't do something about it, Dolly thought, and that night in the chapel asked God to direct her. It was several more weeks before He appeared to answer her prayers. While she was kneeling before the statue of the Sacred Heart, into her mind came the face of Miss Murtagh. And she believed she heard a voice telling her, 'Go and see her.'

She went home and changed the clothes she had worn to work and the chapel. 'Where are you going now?' Bridget asked.

'I thought I'd ramble over to Miss Murtagh's.'

'Not before time. For all you know, she could be dead and buried.'

'You're not very cheerful. Anyway, she couldn't. Maggie would have read it in the deaths.'

'Not if it was in the *Mail*,' her mother said.

For the first time in months Dolly felt calmer. And was glad she hadn't confided in Maggie or Bessie. Bessie had enough trouble with Liam's health not improving. No, she had made the right decision. And wouldn't Miss Murtagh be surprised at the coincidence of Bessie living in ninety-seven. She'd ask her advice about stuff for the Christening robe.

She pictured Miss Murtagh's kind, worn face, her room – the familiar smell of it. They'd sit and talk and for a while she could pretend it was years ago, before the Rebellion, and she had come for a frock. Herself and Bid. Poor Bid, the hasty way she had judged her, blaming her for drinking. Well, she hadn't been drunk the first time in the Park, not at any other time. It was easy to pass judgement when trouble wasn't at your own door.

After a while, Miss Murtagh would tell her all the news. She was bound to talk about the Tans. Dolly smiled, remembering how Miss Murtagh always knew to the last what was going on. Then she would tell the dressmaker what she knew of Bid, some of it, anyway. It would be a relief to talk about Bid. And then she would move on to speak of a girl in work who was pregnant and too afraid to tell the father. Miss Murtagh would say she didn't know what the world was coming to. She said that about everything, but beneath it all she was kind and sensible, too. She'd say what Dolly wanted to hear: that though it was a bad start to a marriage many a one like it worked well. And the sooner the girl told him the better. So long as there had been no hunker-sliding on her part with other fellas, for that was a terrible thing for a girl to do. And Dolly would say, 'She's definitely not that sort of a girl. Not at all.' 'Well then,' Miss Murtagh would say, 'advise her from me to tell him immediately.'

Dolly stopped at a sweetshop and bought a quarter of toasted marshmallows and a quarter of the peppermints Miss Murtagh liked.

The yellow curtains with the card hanging between them looked very shabby. The card was yellowed too, and curling at the edges. Dolly's repeated knocking and calling went unanswered. The dressmaker's eyesight had probably improved. She must have gone out, maybe slipped around to the chapel for half an hour. Or maybe she was asleep, tired from sewing and had dropped off. She knocked again. A door in the hall opened. A woman came out and asked, 'Were you looking for someone?'

'Miss Murtagh, but she isn't in. She's round the chapel I suppose?'

'She was – a week ago tonight – waking. She died and not a soul only me and a woman from up in the house to folly her to her long rest.'

'Was it in the paper?' Dolly said, the first thing that came into her head.

'Sure, who'd put it in the paper? She didn't have one belonging to her, nor friends either. A decent creature. Do you know she had the funeral paid for, months before she died, so the hearse-driver told me. Went in and made all the arrangements. Did you know her?'

'Oh no,' Dolly said. 'Someone in work said she sewed. I wanted her to make a frock, that's all. Good-night, ma'am.'

She cried quietly to herself on the way home, yet she felt strangely comforted for having gone. God had answered her prayers, not in the way she had expected, but still she was consoled. All the thinking she had done on the walk over there, the way she had talked to Miss Murtagh in her mind and listened to her advice had shown her what she should do. And that was answering her prayer, wasn't it? Tomorrow night her mother was going out, so she would ask Maggie to come up and make a clean breast of it.

But the following evening while she waited for Maggie, her calmness deserted her. So that when her sister arrived, Dolly had worked herself into bad humour, picked a row with Maggie over being a few minutes late then broke down, cried and announced, 'I'm in the way.'

'You!' Maggie said incredulously.

'Yes, me, and don't you try to be funny about it, either.'

'I'm sorry. It was a surprise, that's all. How far gone are you? Does me mother know?'

'I can't bring myself to tell her. Two months, I think.' Dolly paced the room while she answered.

'Sit down for God's sake, you're making me dizzy.'

'I can't, me nerves are bad.'

'It's not your nerves you want to be worrying about. How did Robbie take it?'

Dolly sat down and began drumming her fingers on the table. 'I'm too ashamed to tell him.'

'Ashamed me arse. You're carrying his child. You didn't get that through holding his hand. Ashamed indeed!'

'It's all very well for you to talk, you don't know how I feel.'

'That's you and your affectation. I hope you'll feel the same when you give birth to a bastard.'

After a while Dolly wiped her eyes. 'I suppose you're right, I'll have to tell him. Only, will you tell me mother? I can't face that. Not after all she says about women making a catspaw of themselves and having to get married.'

'She says lots of things you don't want to be minding. You know one thing, she'll stick by you, so will I.'

'Maybe he won't want to marry me. Maybe he'll say the child isn't his. Fellas are supposed to hate you for trapping them. And they've no respect for you, because – you know – you let them.'

'For Christ's sake Dolly, half the women in Dublin have to get married. In any case, you have to tell him and I'll tell me

422

mother. For there's one thing sure and certain there's two things you can't hide – that and sore eyes.'

For the first time since Maggie arrived Dolly smiled. 'No matter how much you may annoy me, I can always rely on you to make me laugh. You're right – I can't hide it. But on second thoughts don't tell me mother till after I've told Robbie.'

She delayed taking Maggie's advice for another while. But tonight she was going to tell Robbie. She dare not put it off any longer. Soon someone was bound to notice and then it would spread like wildfire around Jacobs. Once she knew they were getting married she could brazen it out, defy anyone to look crooked at her. If anyone commented on the suddenness of the wedding she'd say he was being posted back over the other side. Then let them think what they liked. No one need know her business. Thank God Ethel had moved down the country.

She looked at the clock. It was after seven. Her mother would be out soon. For weeks she had gone over in her mind how she would tell him. But one thing was sure and certain – there'd be no pleading. No whinging. For no matter how much she loved him there'd be no follying him to make him marry her, not if she had to write 'bastard' on the child's back and sing in the street for a cut of bread.

As soon as Bridget left, reminding Dolly not to let the boil go from under the Christmas pudding, Dolly loosened her stays, fluffed her hair around her and sat down to wait, straining her ears for the sound of Robbie's whistling. It was beautiful, sweet and clear like a bird's. And then he arrived, with no whistling, no warning, just the familiar tap of his swaggerstick on the door before he pushed it open and announced, 'Hello, I'm here.'

'God – you gave me a fright. I didn't hear you coming.' Her heart almost burst with joy at the sight of him. She forgot her fears and hurried to greet him. 'Come in,' she said. 'Come in, you must be perished with the cold. Sit over to the fire.'

'Your mother not in?' He raised his eyebrows.

'She's become more lenient since me father died or maybe she's still stupefied with grief. Anyway, she raised no objection to me being on my own with you.'

He slipped an arm around her, kissed her and pinching her waist, laughingly said, 'You'd better lay off the biscuits.'

Colour scorched her face. She disengaged herself, moved away and busied herself with the fire.

He took off his cap and sat on the sofa she had drawn near the fire. 'Sit down.' He patted the hard shiny surface of the couch. She sat beside him feeling awkward and nervous, wanting to tell him, not knowing how, her carefully-rehearsed words forgotten.

'I think I'd better turn up the lamp, look how dark it's getting.'

'Leave it,' he said, putting his arm around her, pulling her close. 'It's nice with the light like this and the fire. Better than the Park, eh?'

'Yes,' she agreed, the warmth of the fire and the nearness of him melting her.

The room was very quiet. Only the rolling boil from under the pot where the Christmas pudding lay in its layers of linen made any sound. Robbie kissed her. His hands moved along her back, stroking, stilling her fear. With the ease of familiarity his fingers found the row of tiny covered buttons and began to release them from their loops.

'Don't do that!' She jerked away angrily. 'Don't dogmaul me,' she said, reaching behind her back to fasten the buttons.

'Why, for Christ's sake?'

'And don't curse either.'

'What's come over you? I was only . . .'

'I know what you were only doing. Well, I'm not letting you.'

424

She left the couch and stood with her back to the fire watching Robbie light a cigarette and puff angrily at it. 'What's the matter with you? Now every time I touch you you give me the cold shoulder. Why, for Christ's sake?'

'Because I promised I wouldn't.'

'What do you mean – promised? Who did you promise – the priest?'

She was going to cry in a minute, then he'd think she was pleading. She swallowed the lump in her throat that seemed as if it would choke her, squeezed her eyes against the tears she wouldn't shed, before answering him. 'No, not the priest. I haven't been to Confession for ages, God forgive me. Not since you know when.'

'Who did you promise then?' He got up and walked towards her, brushing close as he bent to throw the butt in the ashes.

'Mind the pudding,' she cried.

'To hell with the pudding,' he said sulkily and repeated the question.

'Myself maybe. Never mind, anyway. I promised and that's that. D'ye want a cup of tea?'

'No, I don't. The Irish – they live by the teapot and the frying pan.'

She loved him when he was ratty. 'Look who's talking,' she said banteringly. 'Not long ago you were boasting about being half-Irish, now you haven't a good word to say for us.'

His bad humour never lasted. He laughed at himself and while the smile was still on his face she told him and saw the shocked expression wipe the laughter out of his eyes.

'You can't!' he said. 'We haven't – not since – not for a long time. Not since your father died.'

'I am,' she said, confident now that it was out. 'And it's since before my father died, the Lord have mercy on him.'

'Are you sure?'

'Sure of what? That I'm having a child, or that it's yours? I hope you're not insinuating that.'

'No, I'm not.' He walked wearily back to the couch. Not attempting to comfort her, to take her in his arms, the way she had sometimes imagined it might be when she told him. Her mother, she thought, and all the oul wans who warned you to keep your hand on your ha'penny were right. He wasn't jumping for joy.

Robbie was too stunned even to smoke. He'd been careful, the same as he had been with Alice. Some fellas got away with it for years. But now he was done for. Trapped. All the things he wanted to do. The places he wanted to go. And Alice. If he married Dolly, what about her? Jesus, what a predicament. Loving two women and one in the family way. He'd go and see his CO. Get out of Ireland. He was marrying no one.

'Well – what are you going to do about it?'

'I don't know.'

'Well, you'd better think.'

'It's a shock. I wasn't expecting it.'

'How do you think I feel.' She sat beside him, longing for him to touch her, to tell her he loved her and was glad about the child . . .

Instead, he moved away and said, 'I suppose you want to get married. It wouldn't be easy. I'm not supposed to get married until I'm twenty-five and I'm not yet.'

'It's a pity you didn't think about that in the Park.' She always felt uncomfortable when he referred to their age difference. 'I know how old you are – what's that got to do with it?'

'I'm not on the strength till then, not entitled to a marriage allowance or married quarters.'

'I wouldn't live in a quarter if I got it for nothing – dog boxes with bricks on the walls instead of plaster. So don't let that worry you.'

'But if we haven't a quarter I can't live out of barracks and how would we manage for money?' Robbie argued.

426

He's finding excuses. He's backing out. Sacred Heart of Jesus he's not going to marry me. Oh, if only I had my time over again. Well, I'm not going to beg nor plead. But at the same time he needn't think I'm a fool. He's not going to blind me with a pack of lies. 'So you couldn't live out – is that a fact. Well let me tell you, I know of plenty of soldiers under twenty-five living and sleeping with their wives outside barracks.'

Robbie lit a cigarette. His mind was racing. He didn't want to marry anyone. He didn't want his life changed – he didn't want to be accountable to any woman. What was he going to do? Yet he didn't want to desert Dolly. He loved her. Maybe eventually he would have married her – but not now – not like this. He loved Alice. Not that he had ever seen much prospect of marrying her. But all the same he didn't want to lose her, not yet.

'Did you hear what I said?' When he didn't answer Dolly repeated herself, her voice raising. Robbie lit one cigarette from another, gazing into the fire, continuing to ignore her. She felt the blood pounding in her head. 'Answer me. Are you going to marry me?' Still he said nothing. She got up and with shaking hands raised the wick. She turned the knob too high so that the flame flared and sent up a spiral of reeking smoke. She adjusted the wick and faced Robbie, hands on hips, her face ugly with fury. 'Did you hear me?' she screamed. 'I'm talking to you.'

'I know you're fucking talking to me. I'd have to be deaf not to.'

'You white-livered cur! How dare you talk to me like that. I'm a decent girl. I wasn't hatched under a hen.' For minutes she lashed him with her tongue. She wanted a response – anything other than him looking through and beyond her. 'Look at me. *Answer me*.' Her voice now had an imploring note. Robbie ignored the supplication. She pushed him so that he fell back against the sofa, his face forced upwards. Then into the sullen face with the eyes she had once likened

427

to chestnuts she spat. An expression of disbelief quickly replaced by one of disgust transformed his features. With one hand he fingered the spittle then lashed out and hit her hard across the mouth. She staggered back, bewildered, the fight gone out of her. She moaned with the pain and tasted the salt blood. It trickled through her lips and fell in beads like ripe redcurrants onto her dress.

'Oh Jesus, I'm sorry. I didn't mean that.' He was on his feet, his voice full of concern. 'Let me see. Open your mouth.'

She felt weak, dizzy, her legs shaking and leant against him with all her weight. He pressed his hankie against her lips, one arm supporting her. 'I'm sorry,' he whispered. 'It'll be all right. I love you. We'll manage. It'll be all right.'

They sat down and she put her head on his shoulder holding the hankie to her lips, looking at it now and then to see if the bleeding had stopped. She ran her tongue warily over the ragged edges of moist flesh and thought, he's left me a mark I'll carry to my grave.

He talked, explaining how things could be done. He would see the Company Commander, tell him the situation. Maybe he could get off the square, do clerical work, the money was better, and apply for a sleeping-out pass.

They made plans. Dolly told him he'd have to write to England for his Baptismal Lines and they'd have to see the priest.

'What's he like?' Robbie asked.

'To tell you the truth I don't know. All right, I suppose. You only see him at Mass or Confession. You know that because of the child we'll have to be married in the vestry in the evening.'

'I don't care.'

And Dolly said she didn't either. Thinking that she had no choice – the vestry was where you married if you were pregnant or marrying a Protestant.

*

'I thought Robbie might still be here,' Bridget said when she came in. Then she saw Dolly's swollen mouth and asked what had happened.'

'We had words. He didn't mean it.' Dolly said defensively.

'He'll never mean it. And you'll always have words.' She hadn't meant to say anything. She tried to say no more. But the sight of Dolly's face, the face that to her was always a child's, incensed her. 'He's a cur to have done that. And many's the time when I'm dead and gone he'll make you cry salt tears.' She checked herself from adding, 'but I told you what he was like. A vain, handsome, spoiled boy and you wouldn't listen.' Instead she asked where they intended living.

'In the parlour for the time being.'

'I'll do it up for you. There's a few rolls of paper and Maggie will help me.' She asked Dolly when the child was expected and when they planned on marrying. While Dolly was telling her, Bridget thought that all she could do now was help them however she could.

Whatever happened after he was married, there was no reason why he should stop seeing Alice beforehand. And if there was a way to keep seeing her then he would take it. He loved her. He loved Dolly, too. He was even glad about the child. He didn't suppose he and Alice could ever have married. Her family would have raised such a stink. And in the long run what sort of a life could he have given her? Dolly would be able to take the rough with the smooth. It was no good kidding yourself – you were better off marrying your own kind. But he dreaded the thought of a time without Alice. There was a magic about her: on the surface she was so gentle and demure, but in bed she became a different person. Except once or twice lately, when she had wanted to talk instead. Asking him what he thought about a soldier deserting the army. Arguing with him when he said that in no circumstances was desertion justified. She tied him in knots with the reasons she put

429

forward. Almost convinced him that a man who loved someone enough would do anything for them. In the end he agreed
just to shut her up. 'If it was for you, I'd desert. For you I'd
do anything,' She was so delighted anyone would have thought
she was pleading her own case.

Chapter Twenty-One

Once the marriage was arranged Dolly took Bessie into her confidence. 'I don't want anyone else in the house to know I'm pregnant, nor the wans in work either.'

'I wouldn't breathe a word,' Bessie said, 'though in the long run it's a hard thing to hide. Look at me.' She touched her great mound of a belly.

'Long before I'm that size we'll be gone away out of the neighbourhood, England even.'

'I hope you'll be very happy, please God.'

'We will – only . . .' Dolly looked away from Bessie's face.

'Only what?' Bessie gently prompted.

'I don't know – it's just a feeling I get sometimes that he doesn't want to be tied.'

'I'm sure most men feel that way, beforehand, maybe now and then afterwards,' she said consolingly.

'It's more than that. Mind you, it's not always that I think like this. Most of the time I'm beside myself with happiness, but every so often I feel he never intended marrying anyone. Do you know what I mean – that he only wants to enjoy himself.'

'Don't torment yourself with doubts. I used to do that because I'm older than Liam. Sometimes made myself sick with worry.'

'And that's another thing – he's younger than me, too.'

'No one would think it.'

'You've had no bother with Liam?'

'Never, and with the help of God neither will you with Robbie.'

Bridget came in from the other room. 'Will you go till Christmas?' she asked Bessie.

'I'm hoping I will.'

'Call me whatever hour of the day or night it is. I'll give Nurse Gannon a hand and don't worry about the washing or meals for yourself or Liam – I'll see to that.'

'What would I do without you?' Bessie said, getting up to go. 'Say a prayer the child stays where it is till Christmas.'

Not long after Bessie went there was a knock on the door and a voice called, 'Are you 'ithin?'

'Yes, come on,' Bridget replied. Her face dropped and so did Dolly's when they saw who it was. The woman who lived on Bessie's landing, was a skinny, crabby woman with no children who knew everyone's business. Her husband, according to Bridget, was an oul moff who wore a pinnie, washed the delft and was only short of wiping his wife's arse.

The woman was holding a parcel. 'I never knew a word till I heard the priest calling the Banns. Not a word.' She offered the parcel to Dolly. 'For you daughter,' she said, her eyes scanning Dolly's face and figure.

Bridget told the woman to sit down, but didn't offer a cup of tea, an unmistakable indication that she wasn't welcome.

Dolly undid the twine. 'Ah, you shouldn't,' she said, delving into the parcel and lifting out a blue chalk ornament of a simpering child holding out the hem of her dress with both hands. 'You're awful kind. I wasn't expecting anything, really thanks very much.' And said to herself that at the first opportunity she'd drop the figure, smashing it into smithereens. A bloody awful-looking thing.

The woman settled herself in the chair. Bridget got the sweeping brush, and Dolly knew the woman would be run like a redshank. 'You won't mind me sweeping the floor,' Bridget said.

'Indeed I won't, sure you must be run off your feet with a rush of a wedding. Aren't the young impatient all the same?'

'It's not the young but the military posting him back to England in the New Year and him afraid if we don't get married I'll throw him over.'

'Just imagine! But sure why would he be afraid you'd do a thing like that?' the woman asked as the fibre tufts of the brush sneaked towards her feet.

Dolly decided a double onslaught was necessary to shift the neighbour and picked up a mop with which she began following her mother before replying, 'It's because of him not being a Catholic. He thinks me mother has a down on him, you know. And she might try to put me off of him if he wasn't here. But you haven't, have you mother?' Bridget looked in dismay at Dolly who stared her out. Then said to the woman, 'I'll have to shift you while I run the mop over.' The woman admitted defeat and left.

'May God forgive you for being such a liar,' Bridget said when the door closed.

'What else could I do? Bringing me a present . . . moryah, all she wanted was information.'

'I'm well aware of that. But all the same how will the lies stand up when Robbie's seen at Mass and Communion?'

'You needn't worry about that – he doesn't go.'

'God between us and all harm!'

Bridget made the Sign of the Cross and Dolly said, 'That oul hypocrite'll be more scandalized with me marrying a Protestant than if I admitted being out on the town. For the time being it'll put any other suspicion out of her mind. By now she'll have it all over the house that he's not a Catholic.'

'She will. But what'll you gain in the long run? What'll you do when the child arrives, please God?'

'What everyone else does – lie till I'm blue in the face and let on it came before time. And in any case, anything could happen by then. I could be dead and buried or in England.'

433

'I hope it keeps fine for you. And that you don't take after me and have a nine-pound child. That would be hard to pass off as coming before its time.'

'I don't care,' Dolly said defiantly.

The next day she laced her stays tighter, looked at herself sideways in the mirror and running her hands over her belly was sure no one could suspect anything. Though she could well imagine the comments once the baby arrived. 'God bless him, isn't he a fine child for one that came early. Look at the size of him! And his nails, they're perfect. I hope he's not hard to rear, him being premature.' She'd heard it all before.

'You got caught all right this time, old son,' Robbie's mate Badgie said.

'I don't want to talk about it, shut up,' Robbie said.

He lay on his bunk smoking, looking up at the ceiling, thinking. He didn't want to marry Dolly, he didn't want to marry anyone. The whole world was in front of him. All the women in it to choose from. His freedom to come and go as he pleased. His money to spend as he liked. Jesus, the last thing he wanted was a wife.

It still wasn't too late to duck out. He could see the CO – tell him a girl was after him. A casual pick-up, he'd only seen her half a dozen times – the child could be anyone's. The CO would post him out; the army looked after its own.

The idea was tempting, but still – rough on Dolly. He liked her, in his way he loved her. The trouble was, he loved them all. He'd have to go through with it. Anyway, he couldn't spin that yarn to the CO, not after involving the welfare, getting permission to sleep out – he'd have to give it a go. But that didn't mean he was turning over a new leaf.

Christmas would be unbearable. Cooped up for days with her parents and Stephen. Keeping up appearances while all the time her heart ached for Robbie spending the holiday in barracks. Lady Basset had been so uncooperative when she had volunteered to serve in the canteen on Christmas night. 'Absolutely not. What would Stephen think of me if I allowed such a thing? Besides, the men have a marvellous time. Dinner, plum pudding, all the trimmings served by the officers. Free beer – gallons of it. Few of them will be sober enough to come to the canteen.'

Poor Robbie. Poor me. How awful it will be for both of us, Alice thought as she served tea to the soldiers. Each time the canteen door opened her eyes went to it – looking for Robbie. He was late. She hated the waiting, the fear that he might not come, that even the brief encounter – the smile, the touched hands, the whispered words – would be denied her. But soon all that would end, all the waiting, all the partings. Her plan was perfected. Canada was the choice. Canada greatly attracted Robbie, she had discovered. And he had agreed that a man who truly loved a woman must put her before all else. So he would desert. On the first Wednesday after the holidays she would tell him their wonderful news. Present him with the tickets, money and the civilian clothes she had bought for him. Tonight she would slip across the counter his Christmas present. A silk cravat bought in Gallaghan's, it was yellow with foxes' heads. She could picture him wearing it on their farm in Canada.

When she looked again to the door he was coming in. Her heart turned over. How much she loved him. Just then, someone began playing the piano and a soldier sang the tune *If You Were the Only Girl in the World*. He didn't have a good voice and the piano needed tuning. The canteen wasn't romantic yet Alice knew, this song, this scene, this moment, would be forever etched in her memory.

Lady Basset, while pretending to busy herself rehanging a red paper bell near the till, watched Robbie approach Alice. He was a handsome fellow and he was young – it was natural he should flirt with the girls. But – and she must be fair and

435

careful not to jump to conclusions – Alice sometimes seemed to over-respond. She had noticed it several times. Perhaps she should have reprimanded her sooner. Of course it was harmless, a smile, a blush – an accidental brushing of hands. But the fellow was about to be married. The flirting must stop. Maybe she was just a foolish old woman. Maybe she read more into the situation than there was.

Good heavens – that was too much! He was forward. Reaching and actually caressing Alice's sleeve. And what was the girl thinking of! One could take the season of goodwill too far. Alice was giving him something, not bothering to conceal it – a ribbon-decked box. They were gazing into each other's eyes. Alice was saying something. He was nodding, smiling, winking. Really, this had gone too far. Just let him leave the counter . . . he took his time. When he did, she restrained the urge to march down and order Alice to the office. Appearances must be kept up, nothing done to draw attention. Carefully, she arranged the bell, stepped back to admire it, then slowly approached Alice. 'Alice dear,' she said. 'There's something I need your help with in the office. Let Louise take over here. Then come along.'

'Yes, of course,' Alice replied, her voice bemused, her thoughts faraway. The smile she smiled at Lady Basset was meant for someone else.

'Sit down, child.' Lady Basset indicated a chair in front of her desk.

Alice sat, arranged her skirt, sucked in her breath. In the last few weeks she had become aware that sitting made holding in her stomach more difficult. What bliss it would be once the subterfuge was done with, she thought while Lady Basset rummaged through a drawer, then shifted a pile of papers from one side of the desk to the other. As if she were alone – about to start some clerical task. Alice coughed.

'Sorry to keep you. Something I'm looking for,' Lady Basset

said, slightly losing confidence now that the moment was here
– playing for time. Ridiculous woman, she scolded herself,
you're not fit to be in charge of young women. Pull yourself
together and say what needs to be said.

'Well now, Alice, I've been delighted with you. I think
you're one of my best girls. So sweet and charming. I'm sure
it's a pleasure to be served by you. Ah – yes, you bring
graciousness if only for a few moments into the lives of these
poor fellows far from home.'

'Thank you, Lady Basset,' Alice said. Lady Basset smiled
and Alice thought, Nella is right, she does look like an old
sheep. One expects her to bleat.

'But the trouble is, many of them are incapable of dis-
tinguishing between good manners and encouragement, don't
you know?'

Alice became wary. Lady Basset might resemble a sheep –
the resemblance was to do with her hair, the length of her
face . . . It had nothing to do with her eyes which now held
Alice's gaze.

Play the fool, Alice told herself. 'I'm not sure I understand
you.' She remembered the occasions when she had suspected
Lady Basset observing her and Robbie. 'I always try to be
pleasant.'

'And you succeed – perhaps too well, sometimes. Not that
it's your fault, my dear. Oh no, it's as I say, some of these
men are forward. Associate pleasantness from women in an
entirely different way to which it was intended. Wouldn't you
agree?'

'I'm not sure. I've never thought about it,' Alice said.

'Not even when that dark, handsome infantry chap flirts
outrageously with you?'

'There are so many dark ones – gunners, infantrymen –
I hardly know one from the other.' Alice's voice was
steady, her gaze candid. I am becoming an expert liar, she
thought.

'But Alice – tonight I saw you pass a gift across the counter. I saw that man hold your hand.'

'Oh, that.' Alice's heart beat faster, her mouth began to dry. She must get this right. Mustn't get flustered. So much depended on allaying Lady Basset's suspicions. She must not deny vehemently Robbie's advances. Must not appear to defend him. Must do nothing that would cause a whisper of gossip or endanger her and Robbie's getaway. 'Yes, you are right. He is a forward fellow. Last night he gave me the gift. Naturally, I refused. But he pleaded with me, said it was only a token, please to take it. Actually, I thought he might be drunk and that accepting it was the tactful thing to do . . .' She paused.

'Do go on,' Lady Basset said.

'Well, when I opened it at home I got a shock. It was an expensive scarf. Dreadful, but expensive. Of course, I couldn't accept it. So tonight I gave it back. That's what you saw. Mind you, he made quite a fuss. Caught my hand, insisting I should take it.'

'Good girl. You were absolutely right. You see – that's exactly what I mean, they just don't understand.'

'No,' Alice agreed. 'And that one is forward. I don't think it's intentional. All the same, in future I'll be guarded with my smiles.'

'His poor wife. She'll have her work cut out.'

Alice's senses swam. Lady Basset's face grew longer, it swayed from side to side. The desk appeared to tilt. I must do something quickly. My head is singing, I'll faint. I must get air, I'm choking. She took a handkerchief from her pocket, dropped it, bent and took moments to retrieve it. Breathing deeply before sitting up on the chair. 'He spends a lot of time in the canteen for a married man.' Her voice, she was sure, would give her away.

But Lady Basset didn't notice its shaking tone. 'He isn't yet. After Christmas. It's a welfare case. I sat on the committee yesterday – the girl is pregnant.'

438

'Oh dear – the poor thing and him spending money on scarves.'

'Well, dear, I'm glad we straightened that out. Would you like a cup of tea?'

Alice looked at the clock. 'Oh, is that the time, then I'd better not. I'd intended asking to finish early. You know, with Stephen coming home there's so much to do. Last-minute wrapping of presents – otherwise he'll peep.'

'Of course, of course,' Lady Basset rose, Alice did too. Her legs felt hollow. She held the back of the chair for support. Lady Basset kissed her. 'Good-night Alice, have a lovely Christmas and I'll see you after the holiday.'

'Good-night,' Alice said, embracing the older woman, wanting to cry, to say, 'You've made a mistake, it's not Robbie marrying a girl who's pregnant. I'm having his child. We're going to Canada after Christmas. You've made a mistake. Tell me you've made a mistake. Please, please.'

For the first time in her life she took a tram. Riding down the quays she sat looking out through the window, seeing nothing. Passing the gutted eating house, the four courts, the chapels, seeing nothing. Dead inside. 'Miss, Miss,' the conductor was shaking her arm. 'All change here, Miss.' She looked around. The tram deck was empty. 'Are you all right, Miss?' the conductor asked.

'I must have fallen asleep.' She shook her head to clear it. 'I have to go to Foxrock.'

'Foxrock, is it?' The conductor looked at her wan face, the staring eyes. 'That's a good way. If I were you I'd get a cab. You'll get one over there.' He pointed out through the window. She saw the lights reflected in the Liffey, the crowds passing. She swayed and clutched the conductor's arm.

'Hold on there now. Here, sit down.' She heard him shout down the stairs, 'Mikey, there's a girl up here after taking a quare turn. Would you ever get a cab for Foxrock?'

439

He came back to Alice. 'It does be stuffy up here. All the smoking. Are you better now?'

'Yes,' she nodded.

'Are you all right for the cab fare? I could take a lend outta this,' he rattled the bag hung round his neck.

'Thank you very much. I'm all right.'

He helped her down the stairs and into the cab. 'Your address, Miss?'

She told him and he gave it to the jarvey, 'Good-night now. You'll be home in no time.' Alice opened her bag. The man was so kind. She must tip him.

'That's all right, Miss. Don't bother.' He touched his cap, closed the door and was gone. She lay back against the seat and closed her eyes. She must keep her mind blank. Not allow herself to remember Lady Basset's words, not think beyond getting home. In the safety of her bedroom she could remember, think what their implication meant for her. In bed – in the dark, she could look beyond this night. Not here. Here, the handle of the door was too close . . . the night flying past, within her reach – just the stretch of an arm – the oblivion she longed for. But she mustn't. Keep her eyes closed and listen to the horse's hooves. Make rhymes to fit them – silly words. Anything as long as she didn't think.

'Where on earth have you been? Boyne went as usual to the canteen. Now he's searching the city for you.'

'I felt ill, Mama. I needed to walk a while. I still feel ill. I must go to bed.'

So many times Lady Delahunt had hoped, only to be disappointed. Lately she had hoped again. There was Alice's refusal of breakfasts and now – yes – she wasn't imagining it, Alice's waist had thickened. She wanted to embrace her daughter, congratulate her, fuss over her. But one didn't. No doubt Alice was waiting for Stephen's arrival before she made her announcement. She must be patient. 'You should have arranged to have yourself brought home. But never

440

mind, go along to bed. A good night's sleep and you'll feel fine.'

Alice heard the clock strike the hours and prayed to die. Death would be preferable to lying awake thinking how Robbie had used her. Made her believe he loved her. Went from her to another woman, a woman he was going to marry.

Once during the long night she grasped at hope. Lady Basset had got it wrong, it was some other man who was getting married. Lady Basset sat on so many welfare committees. Of course – that was it . . . she had made a mistake.

But then Alice remembered his long silences. Those she had attributed to their familiarity. You couldn't chatter all the time. You didn't need to – it was being comfortable with each other. Now she recognized them for what they were – preoccupation. His mind was on the other girl – her pregnancy. She let go the hope. Lady Basset hadn't made a mistake. It was Robbie. She had lost him. And without him she didn't want to live. What was there to live for? Like a butterfly's wings fluttering in a closed hand the child in her womb moved. She lay very still scarcely breathing, waiting. The sensation began again. This time, as though having tried and found it possible, the child moved once more, the movement stronger and lasting longer. Yesterday – two hours ago – how thrilled, how excited I would have been to feel that, Alice thought. Now it terrified her. Now it was a living thing that would grow and grow – as she would grow and grow. A child without a father! A bastard! Oh God, let me die. Let me fall asleep and never waken. For my sake, for everyone's sake – let me die. But she knew it was unlikely that her prayer would be answered. Death didn't come that easily. She would have to help it. Get up. Do something. Walk into the lake. Go into the gardener's shed, find poison. Get a rope and hang herself. Steal a razor – unsheath its gleaming blade and . . . No. No. I couldn't. I wouldn't. I don't want to die. Then what will you do? I don't know. I don't know.

Morning came and still there were no answers. She had

441

considered using the tickets – going to Canada alone – and dismissed it, admitting her cowardice. Without Robbie she couldn't face all Canada entailed. Without Robbie! She would never see him again. Never touch him. Never look into his lovely face. For the rest of her life she would be without him. The child moved again. Alice laid her hand over the place where it had fluttered. *I'll have you. I'll see him in you.*

It was some consolation. But not enough, not yet. It was too soon for anything to assuage her terrible pain. Yet the child had to be considered. The child mustn't suffer, she felt pity for it – a child without a father. When the thought began to form she dismissed it. It was ludicrous! She couldn't ask him. He would never agree. But the thought persisted. He owed her something. She had guarded his secret, preserved his respectability. Now she would ask the favour in return. It was blackmail. Yet she would do it – confess her plight to Stephen. Ask him to acknowledge the child as his. Only then did she cry – for Robbie her lost love, for the life they would never have together . . . for her travesty of a marriage.

Robbie tried on the cravat. He liked it. A pity he had no civvies to wear it with. He took it off, and put it back in the box. Dolly would ask where he got it – better give it away. He hadn't told Alice the Wednesday after Christmas was off. Maybe the next one, too. Dolly, since the wedding was arranged, made greater demands on his time. But that would stop. Once they were married she had to learn who was boss.

He would drop Alice a line at the flat, fix up another time. He had no intention of losing Alice.

Bessie kissed the face of her newborn son. 'You could have waited, you bold boy, only two days and you'd have been a Christmas baby. But thank God you're here and all in one piece.' She nuzzled his neck. It was soft and sweet-smelling. He opened his eyes and stared blankly at her. 'My little love,'

442

she crooned. 'My little son.' He stretched and she thought how small and how helpless he was. How helpless all human infants were. A calf or a colt in no time could fend for itself, follow its mother, demand food. But a baby left unattended died. And even attended, in this part of Dublin had a hard road in front of him.

Her son would be all right. God helped them that helped themselves. There was a good home for her son. A decent place, fine fresh air and green fields to grow up in. Only this week another letter had come from the Maguires. This time, Mrs Maguire acknowledged that Bessie had written. Scolded Liam for his neglect and sent a pound for Bessie to help with the expenses of the birth. The money was a godsend. It would get them through Christmas.

But one thought was prominent in her mind. The time had come to begin working on Liam that a return to the country could do nothing but good for all three of them. 'I'll mention it tonight,' she talked to the child, stroking his head. Making the Sign of the Cross over the fontanelle so that it would be protected and close.

She heard Liam at the door. 'God love you, you look perished,' she said. He came to the bed, touched the baby's cheek, then kissed Bessie lightly on the lips. 'Did you manage all right?' he asked.

'Grand. Bridget washed him and made me a bit of dinner. There's some for you in the pot. Eat it now.'

'I'm not hungry.' He sat on the bed. 'How long will you be laid up?'

'I should lie for the fourteen days – that's another ten in the bed.'

'Do then,' he said.

'I feel great. The bed kills you. I'll be up by the end of the week.'

'I got nothing, Bessie.'

'You will tomorrow,' she said with a conviction she didn't

443

feel. A ganger would need to be desperate starting Liam. He didn't look strong enough to hold a pick, never mind swing one. The change in him was terrible. The weight had dropped off of him, he was all eyes and teeth. She held his hand and looked at the other one. They were softening, and so thin.

'I was thinking,' she said, 'we should write to your mother. They've a right to know about the child. And maybe – you know – if things didn't improve . . . You know like – with the bad weather – building work isn't easy to get. Well – then we could go back if only for a while.'

'Never,' he said, his eyes growing cold, his expression bitter, so that Bessie was reminded of his mother the day she threw the milk over her. 'What in God's name put that idea into your head?'

'Well, to tell you the truth I wrote to them.'

'You didn't mention that I was out of work – or about here – this place? Anyway, you had no business writing. None at all.'

'Sure I know. Only I thought they should know about the child. But I never mentioned anything else.'

'Did they answer it, so?'

'Your mother wrote. You can read it.'

'I won't. What did she say?'

'That we're always welcome.'

'Huh – she would. They're old now. Want someone to run the farm. And wouldn't they have the great laugh. Me that went off with a fortune, back with my tail between my legs.'

'You should put pride aside and think of the child.'

'The child'll be fine. I'll see to that. I'll look after the two of you.'

'I know you will, love. You were always a grand provider. Don't think any more of it.'

He coughed, short dry coughs.

'You need another strengthening bottle. It'll make a new man of you.'

He lay down and closed his eyes. She looked from him to the child. The resemblance wasn't as striking as at the moment of birth. Then the likeness had been uncanny. But already the infant's face was filling out, becoming rounder.

Liam slept for a while. When he woke Bessie was suckling the baby. Liam touched her breast. 'Lay down the child,' he said. She laid him down. Liam kissed her mouth with urgency.

'Liam,' she said, taking away her lips, 'at a time like this them kisses can lead nowhere.' He let go of her, his face sulky. 'Sure I know love, it's been a long time. Be patient for a while yet.'

He turned away from her. Poor Liam and his wants, she thought. Whatever else ailed him it never affected his urges. Morning, noon and night he wanted her. Sometimes she wondered if she only imagined he needed her oftener than when they were first married. Though wasn't it more likely she was getting past it. As her mother had said – the gaminess was gone out of her while Liam was still a strip of a lad.

Or maybe pregnancy had cooled her desires. She hoped it was that. Now while Liam slept she tried to remember when she first found his demands too much. It was before the child was conceived. She remembered now. It started with his feverishness – them terrible night sweats. That's when it was, definitely. She was relieved. It wasn't her age at all, but something to do with Liam's health. Once she was up and about she'd get him well again. She'd take in washing, find a few days' cleaning. The priest would know of someone wanting a cleaner. And with the money she'd buy nourishment for Liam. Stallfeed him. And say no more about the farm for the present.

Chapter Twenty-Two

Stephen changed from his uniform into a lovat green tweed suit. He decided against wearing a cap – at least in the car. His fine fair hair was thinning. Every day it combed and brushed out. He was convinced that years of wearing a service cap, especially during the war when for weeks on end his head had been permanently covered, was hastening his baldness.

It was a fine crisp December day. He looked forward to the drive to Dublin. With luck, he should be there for dinner. It would be lovely to see Alice again. She seemed in great spirits these days. Her voluntary work in the canteen had been a good idea. You could tell from her letters how relaxed and happy she was. Well, he supposed, as happy as it was possible for one to be in her situation. Poor Alice, she was a wonderful person. Unique really. She deserved so much more from life. He wished it was within his power to undo the wrong his marrying her had done.

Coming from the opposite direction two children passed, a boy and a girl, twelve, thirteen perhaps. Their arms were filled with well-berried holly branches. The girl smiled shyly and the boy inclined his head. Stephen waved to them. Lovely, friendly children bringing home the Christmas holly. What lay in store for them, he wondered? Would they in a year or two become part of the young men and women fighting for this sad beautiful land?

Surely it must stop before then. The killing, the ambushes, reprisals and rebellions. The murders, executions. The troubles. Different names – labels used by the different sides for the same deeds. Dead men, women and children, shot, hanged, starving to death by choice. So many deaths.

Kevin Barry was not that much older than the boy with the holly. A boy with a future, a profession, hanged last month. And his victim another youth, an escort on a van collecting bread from a bakery. An English soldier in a situation he would neither understand nor care about. Just another dead man.

All the dead men. Irish, English, Catholics and Protestants. Terence MacSwiney, Lord Mayor of Cork, condemning himself to die for his belief in liberty. Taking seventy-three days, on any of which he could have broken his hunger strike, to die in Brixton Prison.

Who was right and who wrong? Certainly the politicians earned no credit. There was Lloyd George unleashing a force of savage, brutal, undisciplined men, the Black and Tans and Auxiliaries, who exulted in their reign of terror. A reign Lloyd George proclaimed successful with his 'We have murder by the throat' . . . a dramatic phrase, no doubt delivered with all his practised Welsh oratory. Two weeks later on Bloody Sunday, the phrase was exposed for what it was – words in the mouth of a politician. Fourteen English officers were shot in cold blood – in their homes – in their beds, some lying beside their wives. Men Michael Collins believed to be Intelligence Agents. Bloody Sunday gorged before the day was out. Another eleven dead, a child amongst them: spectators, players at a football match, victims of the trigger-happy Tans.

He was more than halfway to Dublin. Time to stop for tea. While eating ham sandwiches, tiny lemon-sprinkled pancakes and rich fruit cake he pursued his thoughts. An end *must* be near – Anglo-American relations were being damaged and criticism of the situation in Ireland was gathering momentum. It came from Europe, from England itself.

A deal would have to be done, involving bargaining and

447

compromise. The North wouldn't agree to the South's demands. The hard line Sinn Feiners wanted the struggle pursued but there were enough men in the republican movement to settle for a compromise. Peace might be restored – for a while at least. For everyone's sake, he hoped so.

Refreshed by his tea and the optimistic turn his thoughts had taken, Stephen resumed the drive to Dublin. Tomorrow he would take Alice shopping for her Christmas present. No more surprises – this year she must choose. Tonight he would tell her, 'You know what an ass I am when it comes to choosing gifts. All the things I've bought you in the past, unbecoming peignoirs, tasteless jewellery, gloves that didn't fit . . . now you must tell me what you really want and it shall be yours.'

He hadn't passed a cottage, a farm, or seen anyone for miles. The way seemed unfamiliar. Lost in his thoughts of Alice he must have taken a wrong turn. He didn't like this road – didn't like the way walls of rock rose on either side then gave way to large boulder-strewn areas. There was plenty of cover for snipers. Still, he was in mufti, in a private car and ammunition was scarce. The Sinn Feiners weren't likely to waste it on him.

The road began to twist. He drove slowly to negotiate the bends. Turning one of them, he saw the Crossley Tender pulled into the side. There wouldn't be room to pass. He stopped – better have a word with the driver, tell him he'd reverse. It wasn't far – the Tender could then come on.

Before he had time to open the door a Black and Tan Sergeant, pistol aimed, followed by a Corporal, came running to the car. Stephen rolled down the window. 'Out!' the Sergeant ordered. He was drunk, his speech slurred, but the pistol pointing at Stephen didn't waver.

The fellow's only doing his duty, Stephen thought. It's a lonely road. Only last week nine of them had been ambushed in Macroom, killed. They'd be extra cautious, vengeful. After all, I could be anyone. Follow correct procedure. Identify

448

myself. 'Out!' the Sergeant barked again. What am I doing, not identifying myself? I'm provoking him – why, for God's sake? I resent him, that's why. His drunken stance. That pistol aimed at my head. You're a fool. He's drunk, armed – an undisciplined hooligan. Identify yourself. Order him to put down the gun. Take his name and unit. Place him under arrest.

Stephen did none of those things, choosing instead to behave as if he was a civilian. An irrational impulse, wanting to witness how this man would treat an apparently inoffensive, respectable traveller. He got out of the car.

'Where are you going?' the Sergeant asked.

'Dublin, actually.'

'Dublin, actually,' the Sergeant mimicked in a West Country accent. 'Search him Corp., then the car.'

Stephen felt afraid. He had let this thing go too far. 'Look here,' he said, his hand about to go to his pocket, to produce his papers. 'I'm Major Whitehead. Be a good chap and put away the gun.'

'Keep your hands where they are. Do the car first, Corp.'

They'd find his gun. Accuse him of being – what? Anything they chose. God, he was a fool. He had to prove who he was quickly. The gun was inches from his face. He was sweating, his heart thudding. It was a crazy, unbelievable situation. The man was insane – you could see it in his eyes. Could he disarm him? Would the Corporal come to his assistance? He doubted it. Anyway, a sudden move and the madman would use the gun. But somewhere in that twisted brain must remain a vestige of respect for rank. It would have been drummed into him. It became as natural as breathing. It had the power to make men move puppet-like on barrack squares, charge to certain death, perform meaningless, degrading tasks. That a remnant of it still existed in this drink-sodden brutal vicious man was his only hope.

'Sergeant,' he said, summoning all his power of command,

pitching the timbre of his voice correctly, keeping his gaze unwavering, 'I am Major Stephen Whitehead. Put that gun away. I will produce my . . .'

The Sergeant fired the gun into his face.

'You mad bastard! He wasn't Irish. Supposing he was who he said? Why didn't you look at his papers,' the Corporal shouted while he went through Stephen's pockets.

'There's fucking Irish that talk like foreigners and fucking Irish that talk like him. Bleeding toffs. In this hole of a country how do you know who anyone is?'

'I told you. Look – Major Stephen Whitehead. You mad bastard! Now you've done it. Now we're in the shit. You've murdered an officer.'

'Listen, mate – I've done nothing. You've seen nothing. Who knows who kills anyone here if you're not seen – right?'

'Right,' the Corporal said.

'Put his papers back. There'll be a gun in the car, get it. The Shinners always take the guns – take his money as well. Then let's get out of here.'

'I've a feeling he won't come until morning,' Lady Delahunt said, as the clock struck midnight.

'In that case why hasn't he phoned?' Alice asked.

'Mightn't have been possible – trouble with the car probably. A Packard's not as reliable as a Rolls. He's holed up in some hotel. Telephone lines down. No point in staying up.'

'Your papa is right. Alice, you look all in. Let's go to bed.'

Alice dreamed she was on a ship. Robbie was with her, they were going to Canada: she was very happy. Then a storm came. Waves like sheets of green glass rose up all around the ship. She was surprised at their smoothness, for the wind blew furiously and the waves until they reached the ship heaved and rolled.

Robbie held her tightly and told her not to be afraid. It was

450

only a nightmare. Soon she would waken and everything would be as it was before.

Then a wave, an enormous one, came rolling in, towering high above the ship, higher even than the funnels. It hovered, began to descend and showers of green translucent glass fragments fell about her head and Robbie's. He let go of her. The wave swirled about them, lifting them from the deck. She reached out searching for a hold, grasping some solid structure, holding on tightly. She heard Robbie laughing. Saw him go willingly with the wave into the sea, swimming purposefully away from the ship, his laughter floating back. Further and further away he went. She screamed. People came. A woman scolded her for making such a noise. And another voice insistently told her to wake up.

She opened her eyes and saw her mother bending over her and her father standing at the foot of the bed. 'He's gone. I've lost him,' she whispered.

'Did you dream about him?' Alice's mother was crying. 'How did you know? Arthur, she knows. She knows he's gone!'

Alice woke fully and knew her mother wasn't talking about Robbie. 'Stephen, he . . . ?'

'You'll have to be brave. He'd have wanted that. We heard an hour ago. I let you sleep. You need your sleep.'

Her father came and sat on the bed. 'A terrible thing, a tragic waste. I loved him like a son.' He patted her hand. He looked awkward, embarrassed.

Bridie came in with a tray of tea-things. She was crying. 'I'm sorry for your trouble, ma'am. The poor man. Lord have mercy on him.'

Her mother insisted Alice should drink hot sweet tea. 'For the shock. You must. You have to think of the baby.'

'You knew.'

'For ages. I guessed you were waiting until Stephen came home before telling us. Did he know?'

451

Alice shook her head. 'What happened? Was it . . . an accident?'

Her mother told her as much as she knew. Her father added, 'They're not sure yet who's responsible. A cowardly thing to do. A waste, a terrible waste.'

Alice tried to feel grief, shock, horror. She couldn't. She kept thinking, now I won't have to ask him to pretend the baby is his. But if he had to die – why couldn't he have died years ago? Months ago even, before I met Robbie. Before Robbie made the other woman pregnant. Oh please God, don't let me think like this! It's wrong. I'm sorry for Stephen, I'm sorry he's dead. He was kind. He was a good person . . . only I didn't love him. I can't help it. I never loved anyone – only Robbie. She thought about the dream. How real it had been. How wonderful, to feel Robbie's arms around her. To hear him tell her everything was all right. Then she heard him laughing, remembered how purposefully he had swum away and away from her.

She began to sob, her body shaking with the force of her crying.

'The poor child, she's broken-hearted. Arthur, do something! Ring for the doctor. Crying like that isn't good for her. We have to think of the baby – we mustn't let anything happen to Stephen's baby.'

The doctor came and said: 'You're to stay in bed. Have complete rest, and try to take a little nourishment.'

The following day he visited again. 'You're a brave girl, a brave, strong girl. But we want no heroics. No going to Horsham for the funeral. Stephen wouldn't have wanted anything to endanger you or his baby, would he?'

'No,' Alice said. 'He wouldn't.'

Dolly worked her notice. During the week the girls in work brought her presents – a pair of pillow-slips, two statues of Our

452

Lady, a sugar bowl and a set of three jugs. The management presented her with a wedding cake.

She talked about Robbie's father. How well-off he was, all the money he had sent them, all he would do for them when Robbie was posted back to England.

'When will you be going?' the girls asked.

'Oh, any time now,' Dolly told them.

On the afternoon of the day she was to be married, she stood pressing the black, semi-fitted coat she had bought for her father's funeral and consoled herself aloud. 'Wouldn't I look grand going out in white silk sweeping the ground in this weather.' She looked towards the window at the snow that had fallen during the night.

'Indeed you would – get your end, so you would. The coat's grand and warm,' her mother said and grieved silently for poor proud Dolly. Poor Dolly, with all her fads and fancies, full of grand notions of lovely wedding dresses, wreaths and veils, houses with shut hall doors . . . all her dreams come to this – a hole and corner wedding and worse than any of that, a husband who'd bring her sorrow.

Later on it stopped snowing. A watery sun shone and melted the snow which had clung like cake-icing to walls and roofs. It fell with a whooshing sound and covered the ground with slush.

Dolly and the wedding party trudged through it, their feet soaked before they had gone far. Through the narrow streets they went, past the hucksters' shops that sold paraffin oil, coal by the stone, babies' soothers, penny packets of tea, toffee apples and gur cake.

They turned into a tree-lined street with houses well back from the road. Behind gardens with iron railings, mellow lights were shining through pale linen blinds and figures in the rooms moved, casting shadows on the blinds. On the top branches of monkey-trees, snow still lay like crumpled ruffs.

453

A little way down the road on the side they were walking, the church loomed. Its tall thin spire was etched against a few stars in the sky from which the snow clouds had gone.

The church was set far back from ornamental black railings, surrounded by beds of evergreen shrubs, approached by a gravel drive which branched into many narrow paths. Turning into one of them the wedding party followed it around the side of the chapel to the vestry.

Robbie knocked on the brass-hinged oak door, then moved back to wait with the others on the edge of the step. The door opened and the sacristan regarded them with hostile eyes, his fat face creased with apparent annoyance. 'Yes?' he asked, his voice no more welcoming than his appearance.

'We've come to see the priest, we . . .' Robbie hesitated.

Maggie pushed forward, elbowing him aside. 'They're getting married, now, tonight. They've an appointment.'

'Come in, then,' the man said ungraciously. 'I'll see if the priest's ready.'

'Oul shite,' Maggie whispered as they followed him in. 'Fecking well he knew what we wanted. It'd be down in his book.'

The room in which he left them was brown-painted and gloomy. There was an overpowering smell of incense. Dolly felt a wave of nausea and hoped she wouldn't be sick. In an effort to control the sick feeling she concentrated on things in the room, looking intently at the presses lining one wall, the packets of charcoal, boxes of matches and spills of half-burnt paper on a shelf.

Tom whispered that this was the altar boys' room. The cupboards were for their gear, and the charcoal and matches for the incense burners. 'The vestry's next door,' he said. Dolly conquered the nausea and linked her arm through Robbie's. Maggie, unabashed by the gloom or solemnity of the place, moved about inspecting objects, opening doors and

454

peeping into the presses at the black cassocks and white surplices.

The man with the face like a cranky infant came back and with a curt nod directed them to the next room. 'Wait there. Father'll be along in a minute.'

The vestry, like the other room, was painted brown. Its walls, too, were lined with presses and rows of wide drawers. There was a collection of processional crosses, hymn books, brass and bronze church ornaments arranged and stacked, and a row of thuribles hanging by their chains from cuphooks screwed into a shelf. Through the open door a strong draught swayed them. Their chains rattled and the smell of incense was stronger than in the other room.

Even Maggie's indomitable spirit was subdued by these surroundings. Nervously, the four of them waited for the priest. From the wall the agonized face of Christ on the Cross looked down on the wedding party.

The priest's face was no more welcoming than the sacristan's, who hovered beside him, handing him papers, checking a form. The two figures were garbed in black like the bride and her matron of honour. There was nothing to lift the darkness except for the priest's white stole.

Robbie and Dolly stood where they were bade. They listened to the familiar sound of Latin without understanding a word, not one word of their marriage service, until in English the priest asked for their vows. In low voices they gave them. The priest made the Sign of the Cross, nodded to them and left. Tom handed the sacristan two pounds in an envelope. It was all over.

'Well!' Maggie said when they were outside. 'I've been to better funerals. May God forgive them. And then to stretch their hand for money!'

All the way home, Dolly with her right arm through Robbie's, held her other hand, fingering her wedding ring, thinking – I'm married and sure what matter that it wasn't the kind of wedding I'd always planned. The man was. Robbie was her husband, she loved him and always would. She squeezed his arm close to her body.

Bessie and Bridget had the table set and the meal ready. A ham that Tom had given had been boiled, skinned, covered with breadcrumbs and toasted before the fire. The wedding cake was on the chiffonier and beside it, a bottle of port.

Liam was there holding the baby, sitting near the fire where Bridget had insisted he stay because he had a chill on him.

Tom proposed a toast for the bride and groom, and Dolly was persuaded to break her Confirmation Pledge with a sip of port.

After the supper Tom, Liam and Robbie went to the public house from whence they returned, as Tom said, 'Well able for any bloody oul sacristan!'

'Don't remind me. He looked as if his mother sat on him while he was still hot,' Maggie said and everyone laughed.

Dolly was dying to sing, to let Robbie hear her voice. 'Could I, Mother?' she asked.

'So long as it's not loud. After all, we're still in mourning.'

Robbie gave her great praise, saying she had a beautiful voice. 'I was going to have it trained once, a long time ago, but nothing came of it.' Maggie and Tom gave a song. Liam was a good singer, Bessie said, but tonight his cold was bad and she herself couldn't sing a note. Towards the end of the night Bridget was coaxed to sing *Down in the Valley, Sweet Alice, Ben Bolt*, but broke down halfway through. Robbie put an arm around her, talked to her, then plied her with stout and after a little cry she finished the song.

Dolly had mixed feelings about going into bed with Robbie. She longed to lie in his arms on the soft feather mattress, and have him touch and kiss her. It was such a long time since he had, ever since she had promised that never again would she commit that sin. Now it wouldn't be a sin, they were married. Only – her mother would be next door – hearing, maybe

456

listening. But when eventually they did go to bed, Robbie fell asleep immediately and began to snore.

'How is it that on Wednesday when you're on guard you can come home and the other times you have to stay all night in the barracks?'

Looking up from the book he was reading Robbie said: 'Wednesday's a special picket duty – to do with the troubles here. You're not complaining – you don't mind me coming home?'

'You know well I don't. But it's queer all the same, you'd think they'd change the night sometimes or at least have a fixed time for finishing.'

'That's the way it is in the army,' Robbie lied and went back to his book.

He'd been in very bad humour lately, so she wouldn't keep on about the Wednesday nights. It didn't take much to rise his temper and then he was ready with his hands. She had felt the weight of them more than once. Afterwards, he was always sorry. 'I didn't mean it,' he would say. 'I'll never do it again,' and he'd kiss her and make a fuss. But the hurt still hurt, and one day she was afraid he might mark her. So for the time being she'd hold her tongue, but she'd find out – she'd ask a woman she knew whose husband was a soldier. She wouldn't let him blind her up to the two eyes.

They went to bed and Robbie lay pretending sleep, thinking about Alice. It was nearly six weeks since he'd last seen her. She had vanished. Wednesday after Wednesday night he went to the flat, knocked and waited. Then walked around the city, coming back several times, hoping that in the meantime she would have arrived. Several times he had knocked at neighbouring houses: servant girls answered his questions. They knew no one answering Alice's description. A tall, red-headed woman went in and out of the basement flat. No, they didn't know her. She had no servants, so they couldn't find out.

457

His inquiries in the canteen got him nowhere, either. Neither did the letters he posted to the flat or pushed through the letterbox. If by next Wednesday Alice wasn't in the flat, he would speak to the woman with the white hair, the one Alice had called 'sheep's head'. He'd demand to know where Alice was, how he could get in touch with her.

Dolly moved in her sleep, shifted so he felt the warmth of her body. He put an arm round her and pulled her close. She woke and turned to him. He undid her nightdress, his hand going inside, fondling her breasts. After a while he left her breasts, his hand moving to pull up the nightie.

'No,' she said. 'Not yet. Listen – my mother's still up.'

'Christ!' He pushed her away. 'It's always the same. Your mother's up! Your mother will hear! You're ashamed or afraid. I'm sick of it. Not only in bed – it's the same with everything. We're never on our own. If it's not your sister here, it's one of the neighbours.'

'We're on our own now,' Dolly said.

'And a lot of good that does,' Robbie said getting up, going to the window and drawing back the curtains. By the light that shone in from the street lamp he found his cigarettes and matches. He lit a cigarette and pacing the room said, 'Every time I go to touch you you have an excuse. If it's not your mother it's the harm I might do to the child.'

'I can't help it. Men don't care. I do feel ashamed knowing my mother can hear you.'

'Fuck your mother. I was better off in the Park.'

'Yes,' Dolly retorted, 'and look what the Park did for me.'

'Well, I'm telling you: either we get out of here or I'm moving back into barracks.'

'Go,' she said. 'Go tomorrow.'

'Ah, listen.' He was sorry for shouting at her. Sorry for swearing. He loved her. The trouble was, he loved Alice too. He missed her. He knew it wasn't fair to compare the flat with Dolly's home . . . to compare Alice's joyous love-making with

458

Dolly's cautious embraces, one part of her constantly aware that her mother was near by. She hadn't been like that in the Park. 'Listen, I'm sorry. But we should look for a place of our own. Honestly, it would be better for both of us – not just in bed, but in every way.'

'What would I do with myself all day?' Dolly asked.

'I don't know. Whatever women do.'

'But supposing it was far away? When you'd go to the barracks I'd be on my own for hours. I've never been on my own.'

'Oh Jesus, Dolly, you're making excuses. All right then – look for a place near your mother. Near Maggie. But you'd better start getting used to the idea of being on your own. The Troubles won't last forever. I'll be sent back to England. You'd have to come.'

'Oh, but England would be different.'

'You're mad,' he said affectionately. 'Listen, there's not a sound from out there. Your mother's unconscious. All right?'

'All right.' She pushed back the bedclothes. 'Only don't make too much noise.'

Alice received the visitors. Not too many at a time, the doctor advised. They brought her flowers and books, sweets and token gifts for the baby. They seldom mentioned Stephen out of reticence and consideration for her condition.

Letters of sympathy came by the dozen. From schoolfriends of Stephen's and brother officers stationed all over the world. She read them, passed them on to her mother and father, who afterwards told her to keep them safe. Stephen's child would be proud one day to read in what high regard his father had been held.

She was deeply moved by the letter from Stephen's parents . . . their concern for her, their grief that she was left alone. Of their own tragedy they said nothing. They urged her to take good care of herself and were regretful that their poor health prevented them from coming to see her. She cried bitterly for their loss, for the deception she must practise on them.

Every day she missed Robbie. She wondered where he lived, what his wife was like. Nella passed on the notes, but refrained from commenting. One day, Alice asked her if she was ever there in the evenings, not wanting her to be but at the same time wishing for her to say, 'Yes, and he comes knocking on my door, not that I ever answer it.'

'I'm never there at night any more. I told you about my gorgeous man. His flat is much nicer, so I spend my nights with him.'

Alice read and re-read Robbie's letters. They were brief. He asked, was she sick? Why the silence? Would she please get in touch, please, please.

There was no address on the notes. Not that she would have contacted him. He was married. Was it because of that – or because he had deceived her? Yes, that was the reason. There was no use deluding herself. She wasn't moral enough to consider his wife or believe that adultery was a sin. She loved him, she always would. But she could never trust him again. Sometimes, she daydreamed that he came to see her, to beg her forgiveness, to plead with her to run away with him. Resolutely she refused him – reminded him of his deception and the hurt he had inflicted on her, the trust he had broken. He went away abject. She congratulated herself. Then, in reality she considered the same situation . . . and feared a different ending. No, she must never seek him out. Must never know where he lived, never be tempted to send a letter to the barracks. As she had once cherished his flower, so now she would cherish the memory of the time before Lady Basset spoke.

Dolly went with her mother to look for a room. They found one in a small, red-bricked house by the side of the canal.

460

'This is the one,' the woman said, opening the parlour door. 'It's clean and dry and I've had the gas put in.'

'What are you asking?' Bridget inquired.

'Half-a-crown. It's part-furnished, I couldn't let it go for a penny less.'

Bridget felt the wafer-thin mattress, examined its tucks and corners, inspected the bedsprings and satisfied there were no bugs, nodded her approval to Dolly. There was a gas-ring on a small table, a large picture of the Mother of Good Counsel and a wardrobe with a badly-fitting door.

'We'll take it,' Bridget said. Dolly gave the half-crown and got the latchkeys and a rent-book.

'It's a desperate-looking place,' Dolly said on the way home.

'It's clean and in a respectable neighbourhood. What more do you want?'

'Not that, but I suppose it'll do for the time being.'

That's what every young woman says, Bridget thought. For the time being. And before you knew it the children came and you could never afford anything else.

Maggie and Bridget donated an assortment of tables, a marble-topped washstand, sheets, quilts, a pair of pillows and some blankets. A man with a handcart pushed the furniture and the tea-chest with odds and ends and Dolly's wedding presents round to the new room.

Robbie borrowed a hammer from the landlady and knocked in nails for a mirror and two small pictures above the mantelpiece. Dolly made the bed – Robbie suggested they should hansel it. Dolly laughed and said there was too much to do, but half-heartedly. And when Robbie kissed her and lowered her on to the bed, protested no more.

They both agreed that living on their own was lovely. Robbie showed her how to use the gas-ring. At first she was nervous, jumping back and dropping the lighted match when the gas hissed and ignited. But she soon got used to it and fried rashers and eggs for their tea. The table was rickety.

Robbie fixed it by wedging a piece of cardboard under one leg. They laughed a lot and before very long were back in the bed again. All during that weekend Dolly congratulated herself for taking the room. Living on their own was wonderful. But on Monday, with Robbie gone to the barracks, the day stretched in front of her. Half an hour would see the place cleaned and tidied. She'd go mad all day on her own. So she went to her mother's. And did the same each day, returning in time to make Robbie's dinner. When she and Maggie were alone they talked about the baby. Never with their mother. She believed that was unlucky. You prayed to God for a safe confinement and a healthy child, but otherwise you didn't prate about it.

One day, on her way back to the room, Dolly met the soldier's wife and asked her about the guard duties.

'Ah go way out of that, Dolly. If you're on guard you're there all night. He's having you on. Out in a card school that's what he's doing of a Wednesday. Fellas are all the same.'

Playing cards – or was it something else, Dolly wondered. She'd seen the glances pass between her mother and Maggie when Wednesday after Wednesday Robbie went on duty. It couldn't be a wan. Surely to God, not already. Though they did say this was the time they strayed, when you were pregnant. And now that she was six months she was refusing him. Her mother said you had to.

She'd keep her eyes open from now on. Watch for any signs. And one of these nights tell him she knew the truth about guard duties.

'I was thinking, Bessie, I'll do what the nuns suggest and go in for a rest.'

Bessie's heart constricted with fear. No one ever came out of the Hospice. You went in there to die. Liam wasn't that bad, not that near the door. The nuns had been very kind, but now she wished they had never come bringing the loaves,

462

tea and sugar and an odd half-crown. If they'd never come, Liam wouldn't be talking about going in.

The nuns were only considering her and the child. With Liam in the Hospice her relief money would stretch further. But he wasn't going in, not yet. Not going under that arch spanning the drive, with the big gilt letters across it spelling out *Our Lady's Hospice for the Dying*. Nothing ailed him that nourishment and fresh air wouldn't cure.

If only he'd agree to go down the country. A few weeks on his father's farm and he'd be a new man. If he'd even talk about it, but no. After the last time she mentioned it he made her promise never to bring the subject up again, and never, ever, to let his parents know he was sick and idle. She regretted giving her word. A few pounds from the Maguires would have been a Godsend. But once his mother and father got word of his bad health they'd be up on the next train and Liam would never forgive her.

'You're not listening to me,' Liam complained.

'I am so, I heard every word. And you'll do no such thing. The summer is coming – you'll be grand then. What would I do here on my own?'

'A great help I am. Not able to carry up a bucket of water or a stone of coal. And dragging you and the child out of your sleep with the coughing.'

'Carrying buckets is good for me – look at the figure of me. And the coughing doesn't bother me. Making a cup of tea in the night's no trouble.'

'Aye, I've watched you down on your knees, the fire contrary and not even a few sticks to start it.'

'That was only once or twice. I've bundles of sticks now, thanks to Bridget, God bless her.'

'Oh, Bessie, this wasn't how I wanted it! This wasn't what I brought you to Dublin for. You that should have had everything, that I'd have decked in diamonds. And you got nothing.'

463

'Nothing! Only you and Michael. Is he nothing? Listen to me, Liam Maguire, you're not stirring from here. You're going to get better, wait'll you see. You'll be well again, and we'll get the compensation, and you'll get work. I'm telling you.' She watched his face. Saw hope return to it. With hope you could work miracles.

Chapter Twenty-Three

Tomorrow there would be a letter from Alice. Robbie imagined the scene. Going to the postroom, inquiring casually, 'Any mail, Corp?' The Corporal, Woodbine in the corner of his mouth, smoke curling up one nostril taking his time about looking in the pigeon hole. Taking his time about finding the letter. But it would be there . . . a thick creamy envelope with Alice's handwriting. He'd recognize it. She'd say:

'Darling Robbie,

I've been away for ages. I should have written – you must have worried so. But I had to go suddenly, a relation in England was desperately ill. Everything was so hectic I never had a moment to spare.

Except at night, when I couldn't sleep because I missed you and longed for you. Thank heavens my cousin recovered and as you can see I'm back in Dublin and will be at the flat on Wednesday. Please, please come.

Your loving,
Alice'

'Any mail, Corp?'
    Reluctantly, the Corporal left the table and his copy of the *News of the World*. The Corporal had a reputation for meanness. He didn't buy a Sunday newspaper but collected

the out-of-date ones and read them through the week. Deliberately taking his time sorting the letters. He looked pleased
when he said, 'Nothing for you.'

So convinced was Robbie that Alice had written he didn't
believe him. 'Are you sure? I'm expecting one.'

'Of course I'm bloody sure. Do you think I'm blind?'

Now he had to ask in the canteen. They had to tell him who
she was. Where she was. He would go to the fountain-head,
to Lady Basset herself. She was a sour-faced old bitch and he
didn't enjoy the prospect of an encounter with her. Still, he'd
face a lion to get what he wanted. He combed his hair, gave
a hitch to his tunic and went to the canteen. Lady Basset was
on her throne by the till.

'Excuse me, ma-am.'

'Yes, what is it?'

'There was a girl.' Her look was trying to intimidate him.
She was wasting her time. She was only a woman, he could
get round her. 'A pretty dark girl, serving until some weeks
ago.' He leant on the counter and smiled charmingly at Lady
Basset.

'Yes,' she answered, her face expressionless.

'I was wondering if she's ill.'

'She is quite all right. Her health is no concern of yours.'

'I want to get in touch with her. I've something belonging
to her a – a book. I don't know where to send it.'

'Leave it here. I'll see she gets it.'

'No. I'd like to get in touch with her. It's important.'

'Young man, we don't encourage our helpers to mix with
the men. Surely you're aware of that.'

'That's not right. Not fair,' Robbie said, his efforts to charm
deserting him, an edge of hostility to his voice.

'Perhaps you have a point. Tonight I'm dining with your
Adjutant. Shall I pass on your views?'

You bitch, you're threatening to report me! Robbie
thought. 'On second thoughts you're probably right – I mean

466

about leaving the book here. I'll drop it in tomorrow. Thank you.'

And if you think by pulling rank you'll stop me seeing Alice, you don't know me. I'll never give up. I'll find her. One of my letters will reach her. I'll make her answer. I've *got* to see her again, I can't get her out of my mind. Maybe she has no more time for me – but I want her to say that, to tell me why. I must see her, even if it is for the last time. There could be a genuine reason for her being away. His mind considered this possibility. They would be reunited. The Wednesday nights would begin again. She need never know he was married. She was so gentle, so softly-spoken. So even-tempered. Never like Dolly – who was moody. Flew into rages, provoked him to do the same, belittled him with her tongue. With Alice it was all pleasure. And he would find her.

His previous letters had been no more than notes. He would write another, make her understand how he felt about her. Write a letter she couldn't ignore.

'Come on, come on. Waken up. Open your eyes, Alice.'

She opened her eyes and wrinkled her nose. 'What a horrid smell,' she said.

'Good girl. That's the chloroform. Had to give you a little whiff. You've a big baby, a fine son. He needed a bit of assistance.'

'He's born?'

'Born and bawling – can't you hear him? He's being dressed.'

'I think I'm dreaming. Everything's fuzzy.'

'That'll clear in a minute. Well, I'm finished with you for the time being. I'll let your parents come and you can hold the baby.' The nurse brought him and laid him in her arms. Red and ugly, crumpled like a monkey. But to her he didn't look like that. His skin was pale and smooth, his hair close to

467

his scalp in flat curls. He was exquisite. She fell in love with him.

'What a perfect infant,' her mother said. 'I think he looks like you. Though they change so quickly, and of course the hair rubs off. It could grow back fair like Stephen's.'

'A fine little chap,' her father said. 'No mistaking that chin for a girl's. Well done, Alice.'

Alice smiled at her son, stroked his dark hair and his square chin with its hint of a cleft. Whoever he grew to look like, it wouldn't be Stephen.

'You can put him to the breast but only for a few seconds,' the nurse said, and holding the back of his head guided him to Alice's nipple. Like a limpet he fastened on and began to suck.

'We've made arrangements for a wetnurse. She's clean and healthy, the doctor has examined her.'

'Yes, all right,' Alice said. She was too tired, too happy to tell her mother that no other woman would suckle her son.

'We've sent word to the Whiteheads. They'll be ecstatic. I wouldn't be surprised if already arrangements are being made to put his name down for Stephen's school.'

Alice changed the baby to the other breast and nodded to indicate she was listening and in agreement.

Then Lady Delahunt began to cry. 'I can't help thinking how sad it is his father can't see him.' Alice felt a stirring of the earlier hatred she had felt towards her mother. Since her affair with Robbie it had diminished until she had come to see it as a destructive thing and her mother a stupid, foolish, ageing woman with ambitions. Sorrow was more appropriate for her. But looking at her beautiful son who would never know his father, the hatred flamed again briefly.

'Yes,' she said, 'I feel bitter about that, great bitterness towards those responsible. But I won't nurture it. It serves no purpose.'

*

468

'Ma'am,' Bridie said. 'It's like your wedding day all over. There's that many telegrams and bouquets of flowers and the phone doesn't stop. Though I'm not supposed to be listenin', I overheard that Lord and Lady Whitehead is coming over.'

'Oh no, she's too frail.'

'Well, she is. Sure it's amazing the strength you get to see your only grandson and after what happened to his poor father, the Lord have mercy on him.'

Alice dreaded their arrival. Dreaded hearing them acknowledge the baby as Stephen's. Could she go through with it? She longed for a sudden fever, some indisposition, but her pulse and temperature were normal. The poor, poor things, she was very fond of them and despised herself for the deception she would practise on them. But do it she would, for the sake of the child.

Nella came in the afternoon and winked knowingly as she inspected the baby. Alice hated her for the wink. She no longer trusted her friend. She was amusing, good fun, but several times lately Nella had let slip things in conversation about Stephen and Paris, revealing by her remarks that she had more than just suspected Stephen. And even though they were bosom friends, she hadn't spoken out before Alice's wedding. It would have been better had Nella not been involved – for Nella was a threat to the child. In a malicious moment, she could spread a rumour.

'He's rather sweet, the image of you,' Nella said.

'Boys often look like their mothers,' Alice said in a voice that unmistakably meant she didn't wish to discuss it further.

'You're very tetchy.'

'I'm not, only tired.'

'I'll call again.'

'Do,' Alice said.

She had forgotten how frail both the Whiteheads were, how sweet and how much Stephen had resembled his father. They looked with awe and adoration at the baby. Lady Whitehead held out her arms for him and cradled him against her. 'He's beautiful. Bigger than Stephen was, so you're not afraid to hold him.' She traced the outline of his face, her fingers lingering on the well-formed chin. 'So handsome. Such a manly face.'

Lord Whitehead touched the baby's hand. The tiny fingers uncurled and grasped the old man's finger. 'Look at that,' he said proudly. 'Look at how strong he is.'

Alice couldn't bear it any longer. She began to cry. The nurse took the baby and Lady Whitehead with difficulty got up from the chair, came to Alice and held her. 'I know. I know what it's like. But you mustn't cry. You must think of the baby, be strong for his sake. Stephen would have wanted that. That's a good brave girl. There now, dry your tears. You're exhausted. We'll leave you to have a little rest.'

'He's the future Lord Whitehead. You'll bring him up at Rudgewick Park. It will be expected of you.'

'Yes, Mama,' Alice said.

'Lady Whitehead is having the nurseries redecorated. I'll miss you dreadfully but we'll visit often. Now, what's this I hear about the wetnurse? You're not serious about feeding the infant yourself?'

'I am.'

'Really, Alice – you can't. You do get the strangest notions. I don't know. Once I used to think Nella influenced you, now I'm not so sure any more. However, this feeding thing may be just another silly notion. Like the buttercups you wanted in your wedding bouquet . . . Fancy me thinking about that! I don't suppose you remember?'

'Oh yes, I remember,' Alice said.

'All the same doesn't time fly, three weeks since Liam went into the hospice. How was he this evening?'

470

'He doesn't complain, but he's not improving. Was the child any trouble?'

'Not a bit,' Bridget said. 'Dolly's getting her hand in, look at her.'

Dolly was rocking the baby in her arms. 'I think he might be hungry, he keeps trying to suck his fingers.' Bessie took the baby and gave him the breast.

The conversation continued about the hospice, Maggie, Dolly and Bessie arguing with Bridget that the sign should be taken down. It was very callous – what heart could you have passing under an arch that told you you were dying. Bridget said by the time you were that sick it wouldn't matter. And that if it did, the nuns soon reconciled you to it. Everyone died, wasn't it as natural as being born.

'Have you let his mother and father know he's gone in?' Maggie asked.

'I haven't. They'd be on the first train up and that would kill him altogether.' She began to cry.

'Come on now, don't be upsetting yourself,' Maggie told her.

'I can't believe it's happening, not to Liam. And there's that many things I'd like to get for him. I know you're all very good natured and send him in plenty, but it's not the same as getting them yourself. What am I going to do? I can't manage any more, not on what I get.'

'May God look down on you. It's the first time I've heard you complain or admit your straits. You're a good proud woman. Don't be ashamed in front of us. We'll help you what way we can, won't we?' Bridget said, and Dolly and Maggie agreed.

'You've done enough.' Bessie wiped her eyes. 'Minding the child every night, buying his christening robe, you've done more than enough.'

Bridget, realizing that Bessie's pride was reasserting itself, made a suggestion. 'Wouldn't the solicitor lend you something on the head of it?'

'I tried him and he refused.'

'Have you nothing for a pledge?' Maggie asked.

'A pledge?'

'Something to pawn. Sweets, quilts, Liam's razor – if you've nothing I'd lend you a bundle. You wouldn't have to feel beholden to anyone then. Lending a bundle of bedding isn't like money somehow.'

'No thanks, I'll manage. I just lost myself there for a minute.'

Bridget made a sign to Maggie to leave the subject alone.

'There's someone at the door,' Dolly said.

'Well, answer it then,' said Bridget.

Dolly opened the door. There was a young boy outside. 'This is for a Miss Dolly Devoy,' he said, holding out an envelope. 'The man says I've to wait for an answer.'

'What man?' Dolly asked.

'Who is it?' her mother called.

'A man at the corner,' the child replied.

'I don't know, Mother, be quiet.'

She opened the unaddressed envelope and unfolded the sheet of paper. There was no address, so she looked at the end of the note. 'Jesus, Mary and Joseph!' she exclaimed.

'What's the matter? What's up? Is it Robbie? Has there been an accident?' Her mother and Maggie were at the door questioning her.

'No, it's not Robbie, it's Jem O Brien at the corner. Let me read the note, stand out of my light.'

'Dear Dolly,

I'm at the corner of Blackpits. If you're in come down, please. I have to see you and this time won't take no for an answer.

Jem'

'Here,' Dolly said, taking a penny she had in her pocket and

472

giving it to the boy. 'Go back and tell the man I'll be down in a minute.'

'You're not going on a mission like that! He's married and so are you. Why didn't he come to the house?' Bridget asked.

'I don't know, but I'll soon find out,' Dolly said, putting on a loose coat, that would hide her condition.

'Will I come with you?' Maggie asked.

'You will not.'

'Don't be long in your condition and it's lashing rain,' Bridget called after her.

In case he was watching she wouldn't hurry, though she wanted to and felt as excited as a child on Christmas Eve. She saw him standing under the street lamp. The eejit – where everyone could see him. He looked taller, bigger.

'What are you doing here,' she said. 'I thought you were in America. You're hardly there and back already?'

'You haven't changed – still giving out the pay!' Jem laughed with delight. 'Oh my God, Dolly, I've missed you so much.' He took her arm.

'Let go of me – you're a married man.'

'I'm not, that's what I've come to tell you.' He took her arm again, and decisively said, 'Walk down Blackpits with me. I've something to say to you.'

She let him take her down the lane. They stood at the bottom. 'You'll be soaked,' Jem said. 'Let me open this.'

'An umbrella!'

'Stand under it.'

'You're very bossy and you've grown, and you're too sure of yourself,' she said and thought how lovely it was to see him again. She had forgotten what a nice face he had. 'America's certainly changed you. Anyway, what do you want?'

'Listen Dolly, we're back where we started. That's why I came over – why I'm here. We can start again.'

'You're a widower?'

'No, I'm not.'

'Then what do you mean – start again?'

'I'm not with Josie – she left me. Do you see – I went over to an uncle – a baker. I never knew he had tuppence. But he had – a bakery and a string of cake shops. He made me a partner. Honest to God, I've never had so much in my life. Josie was living in the lap of luxury, managing one of the shops.'

'Her, that only knew about herrings! Go on – so why did she leave you?'

'I didn't love her, I suppose she knew that. Anyway, to cut a long story short she ran off with a traveller.'

'That's terrible. What about the children?'

'She took Danny's boy. My little fellow died with diphtheria not long after we went out.'

'I'm sorry. Didn't you have any more?'

'No,' Jem said. 'No more.'

'I'm awful sorry, Jem.' Dolly took his hand. 'I wouldn't have wished any of it on you. Stand in by the wall and lower the umbrella. Quick, cover my face, someone's coming. I wouldn't want to be seen.'

They remained silent until the person had passed. Then Jem said, 'I love you, Dolly. I've come over to take you back with me.'

'Have you lost your mind? Go to America with you! You're mad. Whether Josie's run off or not you're still married. Now listen – I only came to see you for old times' sake. You'd better go now about your business.'

'I won't. I told you in the note I wasn't taking "no" for an answer. I'm not making the same mistake twice. I can get a divorce – you can in America.'

'You, talking about divorce – you that never missed Mass in your life! America did more than make you rich.'

'Dolly, listen to me.' Jem put his arm around her. 'We love each other. All the time we were grown up we loved each other.'

'Speak for yourself,' Dolly said.

474

'I understand your contrary ways. I love them – they're you. I wouldn't want you different. I love you. Please say you will.'

'What about if Josie hadn't run away?'

'But she did.'

'But if she hadn't?'

'I'd have stayed with her. I made that vow.'

'And one to stay married until one of you died. Supposing she comes back?' Dolly moved out of his embrace.

'Don't twist me up in arguments. She went. I'm not that much of a saint – I wouldn't have her back.'

The rain had stopped. Dolly told him to put down the umbrella. Up, it would draw attention to them.

'You really have changed. The big Bow Wow – the Yank. You just took me for granted, didn't you? Come back – snap your fingers and I'm off to Philadelphia in the morning.'

'I'm not the thick I was. But I haven't changed that much. I never took you for granted.'

'Well, let's see how you take this! Look at that.' She held up a hand. 'That's my wedding ring. And what's more I'm having a baby and what's more again I love my husband, so now who's not a thick?'

'Oh Jesus! Oh Dolly, Dolly, I never thought of that. Why didn't I? While I was here married to Josie I never thought of anything else. But you were single when I went away and you know when you're away you think of everything staying the same. You see it that way in your mind.'

'Jem! You're crying – ah, don't cry! Don't now, come on, stop it. Start walking back.' She told him about Robbie, all the good things and lied about when the baby was expected, forgetting that she hadn't said when she was married, and where she lived.

'You were lucky to catch me in my mother's. We have a gorgeous flat in Rathmines and his people send us pucks of money.'

475

'He's good to you?'

'The best in the world.'

'You'd tell me if he wasn't – or if he ever altered?'

'I might, but he won't.'

'Can I write to you? Please?'

'I can't stop you, but I won't answer.'

'I'll write anyway.'

'Then you'd better send them to Maggie's. Don't cross with me,' she said when they came to the corner, 'and you'd better go now.' She reached and kissed his face. 'Goodbye, God bless you and a safe journey back to America. I'll never forget you, or forget that you came to say what you did.'

She hurried away from him.

Bessie went down to talk to Bridget when no one else was in.

'I was thinking,' she said, 'about pawning something like Maggie suggested. But do you know, I'd be ashamed going into one of them places.'

'Why would you, it's your own you'd be pledging. The poor do it but so do the richest in the land. There's always been pawnbroking in one way or another. I'll do it for you, if you like. What have you anyway?'

'My ring.'

'Ah, not your wedding ring, don't do that. Maggie'll lend you a bundle – if you weren't too proud, she'd lend you a few shillings.'

'It's not my wedding, it's the Mizpah.'

'That's not so bad, will I take it for you?'

'No thanks, if I do it I'll do it myself. Maybe you'd tell me how and where and mind Michael.'

'Of course I will. Go to Winetavern Street – the fella there's a decent skin. Ask for ten shilling, you won't get the colour of it but you have to leave him room to cut. If you're bashful about going in the main place there's cubicles and you needn't pawn in your own name. I know many a woman uses her maiden name. Take it off now and give it a rub with a soft cloth.'

The ring wouldn't budge until Bessie soaped her fingers well. 'I must have got fat,' she said.

'That's not fat. Like my own, your knuckles are swollen from scrubbing and washing and freezing water for rinsing,' Bridget said. 'It's a beautiful ring. Haw on it with your breath and give it a rub – it'll look like new.'

Chapter Twenty-Four

'I hope Robbie never finds out my part in this. Jem O'Brien must be writing every day of the week with the way letters keep coming.'

'He'll tire of it,' Dolly said, taking the latest one from Maggie and hoping Jem never would. She loved getting the letters, there was no harm in them. They lifted her spirits on the days Robbie was surly with her, critical of her and how they lived. Then she would take them from their hiding place and read them again, and for a while imagine she was living in America and married to Jem . . . never fearing his temper if she was a bit short in her manner, never having the fear inside her that dragged like a cold heavy weight. Not that she'd ever show it and let Robbie know he had that power over her.

Jem wrote about the business, described how far ahead America was with everything: Ireland was only in the ha'penny place. Each letter spoke of different things – only the ending of each one was the same. He wrote that everything he had told her that night was still true. He loved her and if things ever changed in her life, if she was unhappy, just to say the word and he'd send the fare. He would write always unless she sent word for him to stop.

'Listen.' Liam caught hold of Bessie's hand, drawing it onto the bed. His voice was hoarse. Lately he had complained of a soreness in his throat. She had mentioned it to the nun, suggested a salt gargle.

'It wouldn't help,' the nun said. 'The consumption has gone to his throat – it does sometimes. Tell him not to be talking so much.'

Now Bessie leant close to him. 'Don't tire your voice, love. I won't say another word about telling your mother and father.'

He smiled at her and his fingers stroked hers. His long fingers that were once so strong and brown, pale now like candles, soft, the callouses gone. The nails cut short and too clean.

Then fear gripped her heart as his fingers stopped their caressing and his hoarse whisper asked, 'The ring! The Mizpah ring. It's not there. Where is it?'

'The ring – I – well, I was using soda this morning. You know that shore in the yard – the way it smells. It was blocked – I had to flush it with a strong solution of soda. So I took off the ring and rushing out just now, forgot to put it back on.' Please God let him believe the lie. He appeared to.

'The man in the next bed never has a visitor. Give him a drink of minerals.'

The man thanked her. He said it was a pity Liam had a bad throat. He missed the chats they used to have. 'And he was a grand reader. I loved him reading bits out of the paper.'

Bessie went back to Liam's bed. She told him about the baby and that now the weather was improving she'd bring him up one evening. He said that would be grand. They held hands and Bessie convinced herself he was looking better. She was sure his face was filling out. He could get better. God could answer her prayers. No matter what words were up above the hospice gate, God spoke before them.

A nun came to the ward door carrying a bell and began ringing it. The visitors got ready to leave, standing, stacking things into lockers, pushing chairs into their place. Bessie kissed Liam. 'I'll be up tomorrow night.'

'Be on time.' His voice was fretful. 'I do be watching the door. You were late tonight.'

'I'm sorry, love. I had to wait for Bridget to take the child.'

The nun rang the bell again. The visitors started to go. Liam clung to her hand. 'I wish I was coming with you.'

'You will soon. Another few weeks and you will. I'll have to go, she's giving me terrible looks.'

At the door Bessie stopped and waved. He was smiling. He looked grand, she thought.

'Mrs Maguire!' Bessie stopped in the corridor and turned to see who called her. It was another nun, the one in charge. The nun came gliding towards her, the beads hanging from her leather belt rattling.

'Did you want me, Sister?'

'Only for a minute.' She had a smooth round face. Looking at it Bessie thought it was hard to tell a nun's age. Their hair and their necks, the things that gave away a woman's age, were hidden. The nun smiled at her. 'I only wanted to ask you to bring in a shirt and a pair of socks for Mr Maguire.'

'Oh Sister! Then he's improving you're letting him up!' I knew it. God didn't let me down. Her mind raced. The nun had forgotten to mention trousers. But she'd bring them as well, and his jacket.

'Sister, isn't that grand? He's getting up!'

'No, he's not. I'll want them for under the habit. Good-night now, Mrs Maguire.' The nun sailed away down the corridor.

Afraid she might collapse Bessie walked slowly, reaching out now and then to touch the wall for support. It was cruel, callous of the nun to tell her like that. To be making arrangements like that. To raise her hopes – then dash them. They were dealing with death every day, helping to ease the suffering of the dying – she knew all that. They were grand

480

women. They brought comfort to those near death, created an atmosphere in which they could accept what was happening to them. But it was still cruel and callous to have told her like that, to be so careless with how she worded it. It was the most heartless thing she had ever known.

How was it possible for someone to disappear without trace in Dublin, Robbie asked himself. He knew where Alice worked, he knew that the red-headed woman spoken of by the servants owned or rented the flat and that she was Alice's friend. It was as if they had all closed ranks against him. That white-haired witch in the canteen certainly had and all his inquiries to find the red-headed woman were as fruitless. He'd gone back again knocking on area doors, using his charm on the girls who answered.

'You must know something,' he insisted. 'Something about the woman who owns the flat. Servants always do.'

'Only if other servants tell them and didn't I explain that there's no one works there. In a normal house we'd know everything about everyone, but not here. You're wasting your time,' the girl who had flirted with him on his previous visit said.

He left the door not sure if she spoke the truth or was bribed to keep her mouth shut.

There was nothing for it now but the letter.

That evening and at work the following day he wrote and rewrote the letter over and over again in his mind. And after supper that night he began to put it down on paper.

Halfway through writing the letter he asked Dolly if she had a stamp.

'Where would I get a stamp at this hour of the night?'

'Why couldn't you just say, no, I haven't a stamp?'

'That's the way I talk and anyway, what do you want a stamp for?'

'Oh, for Christ's sake, there you go again! If you must know

481

I'm writing to my Aunt in America. That's why I want a stamp.'

'Well, I haven't got one. Don't forget to thank her for the money order.'

She made two cups of cocoa and drank hers while Robbie's went cold as he finished his letter.

'I sent her your love,' he said as he put the letter in an envelope, sealed it and, without addressing it, put it in the pocket of his tunic hanging on the back of a chair. He drank his cocoa and they went to bed.

'I suppose you're on guard duty again on Wednesday,' Dolly said.

'I was hoping to change with Badgie. You'd have liked that, we could have gone out. But he wouldn't change.'

'I hate it when you're out late. I'm always afraid. I'm sure there's rats in the place, it's so near the canal.'

'You should sleep in your mother's. One of these Wednesdays I might have to do an all-night duty. Maybe this week.'

Warning her that he might be out all night on Wednesday . . . it was fishy. But she said nothing yet – let him believe she suspected nothing. She'd wait for definite proof. Change the conversation.

'Badgie – that's a queer name. What's his real one? Why do they call him that?'

'He was a boy soldier in the artillery, a trumpeter – they're all called Badgie. The nickname stuck.'

'What's his real name?'

'Jim, I think.'

Jim, Jem. Jem O'Brien. She thought of his letters under the mattress and memories of their time together came floating back. The morning of the Rebellion when he hadn't turned up. How would their lives have been if he had? They'd have passed this house the night of the hooley . . . A scurrying sound interrupted her thoughts. It came from near the door, from behind the skirting-board.

'Robbie, listen!'

'What, listen to what?' he asked impatiently.

'Whisht, there it is again. Rats. The place is infested. It's too near the canal.'

'For Christ's sake go to sleep, you're imagining it.'

He always shut her up, never listened, never took her worries or fears seriously. Really, he wasn't what you could call caring. She closed her eyes and tried not to hear the skittering and scuffling from behind the wainscot. Robbie's arm reached and encircled her, his hand resting on her belly. He slept and for once she welcomed his snoring which drowned out the other sounds.

Through the thin curtains the moon shone into the room. Although the sounds of the creatures scratching and burrowing were no longer audible, she imagined them behind the walls. Down by the river bank, fat and sleek, brown ones and black ones with whipcord tails. Her skin crawled. And stories she had heard about them came to terrorize her. If you cornered one it went for your throat. A woman in Newmarket with milk in her breasts woke one morning with a rat sucking at her. Oh Jesus! I have to get out of here. I can't bring a newborn infant into this place.

In an effort to divert her frightened thoughts she looked around the room. Some things she could make out in the moonlight. The gas-ring, the chair with Robbie's tunic on it. The picture frames but not the pictures. They were ordinary, comforting things. Then her eyes shifted to the wardrobe. It looked like a coffin propped against the wall. That's foolish, she told herself. It's too big. It could be a big coffin, though. Tomorrow she would shift it. Move it so the moon didn't shine on it. And throw out that toque. Fancy someone leaving that awful oul thing. Stiff as a board, all wired between the lining and covered in jet beads. An oul wan's hat. How was it left? Maybe the woman who owned it died. Maybe here! In this bed.

483

Sacred Heart of Jesus, banish unpleasant thoughts from my mind. Blessed Mary, send pleasant ones instead and close my eyes in sleep. Her prayers went unanswered.

I don't want to die when I have the child. Women having babies died all the time. You saw them today, well and walking around. And tomorrow they'd be in a coffin with a dead child at their feet. That's where the saying came from about not talking too much about pregnancy. 'It might be your coffin you're carrying in front of you.' Sacred Heart of Jesus, I put all my trust in You. Holy Mary Mother of God, bring me safely through my confinement. Welcome be Thy Holy Will.

Afraid to get out of bed she ignored the pressure in her bladder. It got worse. Still she didn't get up. That was a queer thing tonight, Robbie not reading out the letter to his aunt. He'd never done that before. If she didn't get up now she'd wet the bed. Rats or not she had to go. The oilcloth was cold under her feet. She stood over the bucket, one hand lifting her shift, with the other tilting the bucket forward. That way you didn't make so much noise. She'd hate Robbie to wake and hear her. And after all that it was only a drain.

His jacket was there within arm's reach, the letter in his breast pocket. There was something peculiar about that. *Why* hadn't he read it out? Why hadn't he addressed it? There'd be no harm taking a look. He'd never know. Keeping an eye on the bed she undid the pocket and slipped out the envelope. Robbie stirred restlessly and called her name.

'It's all right, I've cramps. I'm making a sup of tea. Go back to sleep.' She put the letter under a paper on the table before lighting the gas-mantle. Robbie sighed deeply. He was asleep again. She half-filled the kettle with scoops from the enamel water pail, lit the gas-ring and put it on. Then she got a pencil and the letter and waited for the kettle to boil. She held the letter over the gushing steam, inserted the pencil under a corner of the flap, and carefully rotated it as the steam undid

484

the gum. She took out the two sheets and standing near the gas-bracket began to read:

'*Dearest Alice,*

Do you know how much I miss you? What these endless weeks have been like? How, every Wednesday, I've gone to the flat hoping you'd be there.

I don't know why you've gone from my life. If it was on purpose perhaps I did something to offend you. It wouldn't have been meant. I'd never do anything intentionally to hurt or displease you. You must believe that.

I keep hoping your reason for not seeing me is something simple – family matters that have taken you away for a while. Then I get frightened in case it's another man and terrified when I think you might be seriously ill and I couldn't come to you.

Please don't leave me like this. Even if you are tired of me, let me see you again. If only one more time.

My mind is full of beautiful things I want to say to you. I can't write them. But for all the times when it seemed there was no one in the world but us, be there on Wednesday.

As ever,

Your loving,

Robbie'

Dolly felt a weakness come over her. She was going to faint, fall to the floor, lose her senses and Robbie would find her there with the letter. She had to put it back. She mustn't let go. The feeling of faintness passed, anger replacing it. She wanted to scream, to pull Robbie out of his sleep, tell him she knew about the Wednesday nights, about Alice. She wanted to kill him. With the letter in her hand she went to the bed. He was sleeping on his back. She wanted to see his face, his eyes when she accused him. Her head began to swim again. She remembered how quickly his hand lashed out, hurting her, sometimes splitting her lip. She backed away, talking to herself. I'll have to close it, put it back. While she

485

returned the letter to its envelope, pressed and smoothed the edges, closing her fist and rubbing it hard over the envelope, she continued talking. My mother was right. Alice, Alice who? And where's the flat? If I only knew. On Wednesday I'd be outside the barracks and dog him every foot of the way. If only it was morning. If only there wasn't the landlady in the house I'd rise murder.

She put the letter back in Robbie's tunic. Behind the skirting the rats began their scratching. Too afraid to cross the room in the dark, Dolly left the gas-light burning and went back to bed. She lay as far away from Robbie as the sagging spring would allow, thinking of what she would do in the morning.

When morning came and Robbie got up he found the gas gone and put a penny in the meter. Gas hissed from the light-bracket. He turned it off and looking at Dolly sleeping like a child with one hand under her face, knew she had been up during the night. She often forgot to turn out the light. Or let on she forgot. He wouldn't give her a cup of tea. Let her sleep. Before leaving for the barracks he reminded himself he must post Alice's letter.

Dolly slept on, not wakening until the landlady going out to Mass banged the door behind her. God Almighty, I've slept my senses away, she thought seeing the time. And let Robbie go out without a bit in his stomach. She sat up in the bed then remembering the letter, fell back dejectedly on the pillows where she lay for a long time with a tormented mind.

Her mother's words: 'He's full of himself and any woman's fancy,' added to her torment. How could she tell her, or Maggie either? See the pity on their faces, the sorrow on her mother's. Listen to Maggie say what she would have done, middle of the night, landlady or not. And Maggie was right, she should have accosted him there and then. But wait until he came home! I'll give him Alice. I'll find out who she is. I'll put a stop to it. And I'll never lay aside on a bed with him again.

486

Remembering the child she was carrying and that for its sake she must eat, she got up and put on the porridge that had steeped overnight. She wet tea and cut bread but had no mind for food. The porridge tasted sour and the bread dry. She pushed them away and sat stirring her tea, wondering what to do for the best.

If she raised too much of a scene he might walk out on her. How would she live? Who would keep her and the child? But how could she live with him, allow him ever to touch her again? The other woman would be there in front of her. Jesus, direct me what to do. Show me how to carry on, how to keep him. But not let him get away with it. I couldn't keep it bottled up – I'd have to have my say. I'd want his promise that it was over. I'd forgive him, I'd have to. I love him. I'd forgive him – I would.

Though she talked and reasoned with herself and asked God's help, she felt no peace. Her mind like her heart, raced. She paced the room. She could smash something, kill someone. She needed something to do, something to burn up the fury in her. She looked around the room – two minutes was all that would take to tidy. But the wardrobe, she could move that, throw out the black toque. First she washed and dressed, cleared the table and made the bed. Already she felt calmer, able to decide not to tell Maggie and her mother, not yet. She'd tell no one else, either. For wouldn't she be a laughing stock, married no time and him out whoring it.

She opened the wardrobe door. The rat sat on the shelf above the hanging rail next to the black toque. It looked at her inquiringly. Fear engulfed her. If she moved it would go for her throat. If she shut the door quick? But the catch could slip, the door swing open, the rat land on her neck. Without conscious thought, she raised her hand. The rat inched backwards. Her hand darted forward, picked up the stiff, bead-encrusted hat and dropped it over the startled animal. She held onto the toque. Through its wired frame she felt the rat squirm and the racing of its heart.

A loathing for the wriggling creature filled her. Squeezing the hat tighter around it, she screamed: 'Help me! Help!' No one came. She lifted the bundle, her fingers digging into the stuff, terrified she might let it fall and the rat turn on her. Walking backwards to the door, holding the bonnet well away from her, she reached behind, opened the door and ran into the yard. Frantically, she looked around for somewhere to throw the thing – an ashbin with a lid, anything to contain it. The rusty, lidless bins were piled with ashes. There was nothing else – except the washtub full of steeping clothes. That would do. She had to get rid of it. Kill it. Squeeze the life out of it, drown it.

In its black silken prison the rat squirmed and made high-pitched squeaking noises. There was a yardbrush leaning against the wall next to the tub. With her free hand Dolly picked it up then dropped the toque into the water. The rat surfaced, its head streaked with suds. Dolly forced it under again and again, plunging the long brown twigged broom into its body. It escaped once and swam feebly to the far side of the tub tangling in the soaking clothes. Not until it lay still and sodden did Dolly cease to jab and stab. Then she leant against the whitewashed wall, trembling, soaked with sweat, and vomited into the drain.

Robbie's letter was delivered at midday, to Nella's flat. Shortly afterwards she set out for Alice's.

'This came for you. From him, I suppose.'

'Yes,' Alice said and put the letter under her pillow.

'Will you be wanting the flat again?'

'I don't think so.' Alice wished Nella would go. Wished she hadn't delivered the letter. Knew curiosity was the reason Nella had come.

'I didn't think it would last.'

488

'You were right,' Alice said.

Nella bent over the cradle. 'He is quite beautiful. I don't care much for infants, but he is rather lovely. Such a pity his father never saw him.'

'A terrible pity,' Alice said.

Nella knew she had had a lover. She now felt guilt and fear in Nella's presence.

'Aren't you going to read your billet doux?'

'Later. They're very tedious. Just asking when I'll be at the flat.'

'That's the trouble with some men – they do tend to hang on,' Nella said, sitting down, producing her cigarettes and an elaborate holder.

'I'd rather you didn't, Nella.'

'My God, you sound just like your mother.'

'Oh Nell – I'm sorry.' She was sorry for the sharpness of her tone. Sorry that she no longer trusted Nella. 'You know it's nothing to do with disapproval. It's because of the baby. It wouldn't be good for him.'

'Of course not,' Nella said. 'I'll have one later. Anyway I have to go. I'm meeting someone in town. You know, I'm thinking of going to France. You remember the gorgeous man? Well, we've decided that if there's anything in all these rumours of a Treaty with the Irish running the show, can you imagine how dreary the place will become! So we're off and soon.'

'But not before I'm about again.'

'Not that soon. There'll be time to celebrate my leaving.'

And celebrate I will, Alice thought. Once, the idea of Dublin without Nella would have been unbearable. How sad it was that relationships changed. That people changed. That innocence and trust were replaced by guilt and suspicion.

When Nella left she read Robbie's letter, crying quietly, tempted to answer it. Tempted to cover page after page with her love, her awful loneliness, her need for him. She'd describe

489

the baby, tell him how much like him his son looked. Beg him to fly with her far away from Ireland.

She cried until she was exhausted. Until her mind was purged of rash thoughts, thoughts that acted on, would be self-indulgent – bringing happiness for a while, perhaps. But she wanted more than that. She needed to trust . . . and knew that whatever else Robbie inspired it was not trust.

The baby would learn to love him, depend on him. Want him always there. Robbie couldn't be counted upon. Robbie mustn't be allowed to trifle with something as precious as a child's love.

Calmly now, she re-read the letter. She would like to keep it, but it was a dangerous souvenir. A faded flower pressed in a book was anonymous. Anyway, she had no need of souvenirs. She had her son – a living reminder of all that had once been beautiful. She tore the letter into fragments.

In another few days she could get up. Lying in bed was so tiring – being bathed, with everything done for you. I'll probably have to learn to walk again. She stretched her legs and flexed her feet.

Soon it would be summer. The baby would be taken for long walks in his perambulator. First, of course, there was the christening. Stephen's mother was bringing the family christening gown. It was sweet of her to travel again so soon and to have relinquished the idea of the baby having his christening in Horsham.

For once, Alice thought, Mama supported me. I was surprised. She can't wait for Lord Whitehead to die . . . and her grandson, Stephen Arthur Edward, to inherit the title. I'm surprised she didn't side with the Whiteheads. I suppose it's because she loves him so much, and having the christening here gives her extra time with him. She'll miss him when I go to Horsham.

Like a sudden shower of icy water, the shock hit her. *Robbie came from Horsham*. If the rumours about a Treaty proved true, the army would be withdrawn from Ireland. And Robbie, if only for leaves, might return to his home. She remembered him saying: 'It's a small place, you know most people.' He would know Rudgewick Park, get to hear about the young widow from Dublin. He could even leave the army, settle in Horsham. They would inevitably meet.

Why haven't I realized this before? How could I have overlooked it! I did. What can I do now? Stephen should be brought up there – or should at least spend a great deal of time there. I couldn't justify doing otherwise. And I wouldn't have him separated from me.

If I go, and if I meet Robbie, will I have the courage to nod and pass him as I would any one of the locals? I'd see his wife, perhaps, his children – half-brothers and sisters of Stephen's. That wouldn't stop me, I know myself. I know what I feel inside me. Reason is one thing: I can tell myself I don't want to be hurt, that I could never trust Robbie again. That's in my head, when there is a distance between us. But if he stood close to me, smiled, looked into my eyes, I'd start meeting him again. I'd cheat and lie. I know myself. I know. I know. The rest of my life would be spent in rapturous moments – and hours of torture, while I thought of him with his wife, his family . . . other women.

Stephen may grow to resemble him even more. Grow to be his image. Country towns soon put two and two together. I don't want him sniggered at – acknowledged to his face as Lord Whitehead or his heir, and behind his back as Robbie's bastard. I won't go. I don't care that it breaks the Whiteheads' hearts. Though I'm sorry for them but not sorry enough. I don't care that Mama will have forty fits or Papa threaten to disinherit me. I have my own money and Stephen's money. I am not going to Horsham. Nor staying in Ireland. This is my life and my son's. I'll put oceans between us all. I'll go to Canada after all. I will have the apple orchards. There we'll be safe. It'll be safe.

*

Dolly had to get out of the house. She kept thinking about the rat tangled in the clothes, the scene the landlady might create when she came back from Mass and found it. Every sound startled her. How many more rats were waiting, in the press, under the bed? She put on her coat and ran out. It was a cold damp morning and she regretted not wearing a scarf. She turned up the collar of her coat and tried to walk quickly but her legs felt heavy. All the way along the canal she thought of her mother's welcoming presence, the bright fire and the cup of hot sweet tea. She was shivering and had a pain in the bottom of her stomach. It was, she told herself, only from retching on an empty stomach, or maybe the strain of using the brush. It would go in a minute.

She turned onto the bridge and the pain got worse and her legs were giving out. She'd rest for a minute, lean on the bridge, let on she was looking at the water. It was easing, she would go on. She turned and saw Bessie carrying Michael, and Bessie was crying.

'Oh Bessie, what happened? Is it Liam, is it bad news?'

'He's dead. They sent for me. Your mother was out and I hadn't the price of a cab. I ran all the way but it was too late. Oh Dolly, what am I going to do?'

'You'll come home with me. Let me link you. I've a bit of a weakness. I'm terrible sorry. Poor Liam, you're heartbroken. You'll be all right. My mother will console you.'

Pushing open the door of ninety-seven, Dolly called, 'Mother! Oh, I forgot – it's Wednesday.'

'I said she was out.'

'She cleans for Mrs Margolis today.'

Though the fire blazed, without her mother the room was cold and cheerless. And she wanted her mother and Bessie needed her, too.

'You're not well, Dolly. What is it?'

She looked up into the kind, sorrowful face. 'I strained myself shifting something, but I'll be all right.'

492

'Are you sure? I've a lot to see to but I'd stay with you.'

'You will not, I'm grand.'

'Then I'll make you a cup of nice hot tea, we'll both have one.'

'That'll be grand,' Dolly said, her head spinning, not wanting to alarm or delay Bessie. 'What about the child? I don't think I could manage him, but Maggie will. Take him into the shop.'

'I want him with me, he's a comfort.'

'You're very brave,' Dolly said, admiringly.

Bessie made the tea and after they'd drunk it, left the child on the chair beside Dolly while she went upstairs to get her policy. 'Stay where you are by the fire till your mother comes and I'll be in later.'

When she came back downstairs, Bessie went on, 'I was thinking I'll call on Mrs Margolis on my way and let your mother know you're not well.'

'Thanks very much.' She didn't want Bessie to leave, she was afraid on her own. 'She's a nice oul wan, very kind to my mother.' Dolly made conversation to delay Bessie going, telling her things from her childhood, incidents she had forgotten herself until now, things she and Bid did.

'I'll have to go, love, I'd be afraid the society man wouldn't be in. Can I get you anything?'

Dolly said for Bessie to go, she'd be all right, and apologized for not being able to mind the child.

With Michael wrapped in the shawl Bessie went down the street hearing the laughter, the sound of voices, women calling to one another, children playing, a drunken man singing. The sun came out and was warm on her. Everyone and everything was going about their business. No one knowing that Liam was dead, her world taken from her. The warm sun and him so cold. All the sounds and him so still.

She was glad Michael was too young to feel grief and sorry that he would have no memories of his father, only those she

493

would instil in him, and those his grandparents would pass to him. For her mind was made up: Michael was going back to the farm. They were all going back to the farm. She had broken her word to Liam, written to his parents the day after the nun asked for the shirt and socks. She told them the truth. They were coming to Dublin – tomorrow they'd arrive. God help them, she thought, there was a sad end to their journey. That they may find some consolation in their grandson. And they would, of course. For that was what life was – with all its sorrow there were the children and their children and life, as it did in the fields, constantly renewing itself. And Liam wasn't suffering any more. He was in Heaven and she'd see him again. Oh, Liam, my love. My handsome laughing boy. We only had a short time together but it was the sweetest, most beautiful time anyone could ever have. And I'll cry no more today. I've a lot to do – see to the child and make arrangements, get the insurance money. There now, I'm breaking my word already and crying again. But isn't it the sad thing you had to die for me to have a few pounds insurance money? Tomorrow I could have showered you with sweets and minerals. Ah God – how the poor have to live. Angrily she wiped at her eyes. But I'll do something you'd have wanted. I'll redeem the Mizpah ring and wear it till I die. Then we'll take you back. The men will meet the train and shoulder you home. And when my time comes I'll be laid beside you. Only for a little while we'll be parted.

After Bessie left, Dolly moved closer to the fire, her mind hazy, thoughts of Bid, Jem, Robbie, of the rat, drifting in her mind . . . along with memories of playing in the street, herself and other children making sport, knocking on doors and running away. Calling after the beggars and tramps. Laughing at Mrs Margolis who sometimes nodded off sitting out in the sun. Laughing because her wig slipped. Jeering at the little dwarf who waddled up to the shops. Memories of lighting the

494

gas or putting a match to the fire on Saturday for the Jews. And Mrs Margolis offering her black bread instead of a penny. And she wouldn't take it and demanded the money.

She was too warm, sweating and her stomach hurting. And she must keep thinking about Mrs Margolis, the bread and her childhood, not Robbie and the letter, nor the rat, only nice things.

Maybe she could doze until her mother returned. She closed her eyes and strange dreams came . . . Mrs Margolis chasing her round the kitchen with a loaf of black bread, telling her to light the fire. Going to the stove with the spill of burning paper and on the hob instead of the singing iron kettle, a rat sat. A rat whose face changed to that of Robbie's as the lighted paper ignited the sticks and newspapers and the tongues of flames flared and licked over Robbie's face.

She woke startled, saturated in sweat, the pain in her stomach worse, spreading into her thighs. If she lay down maybe it would get better. In the other room she used the chamber pot and saw blood on her knickers. She lay on the bed, thinking she could lose the child. A thread haemorrhage, that's what she was having, that's how the women described it – she was having a six months' mis. Afraid to move, she lay still for what seemed hours, thinking her mother would never come. Like poor Bid, she'd be on her own having a dead child.

Then her mother was there, telling her everything would be all right. It was all God's will. To lie still for a minute and she'd call a neighbour. The pain got worse. Her head was bathed with cold cloths and her back rubbed. She was praised and encouraged for being a good girl and to give one more push, hard. One more and it would all be over.

'Don't cry now, it was God's will. You'll have plenty more children,' her mother was saying.

'What was it?' Dolly asked.

'A little girl. Usually they're boys. Boys are harder to carry.

495

I'll get word to the barracks, maybe they'll let Robbie come away early.'

She was washed and her belly bound, then wrapped in a blanket. Her mother and the neighbour talked in low voices as they cleaned and tidied. Dolly heard the sound of newspaper being crumpled, wrapped round something, and buried her head under the clothes.

There was an ache in her belly where the child had been. Her hand lay on the place; it was still big, swollen and the child was gone. Wrapped up in newspaper to be taken and burnt. Under the covers she cried.

'If I'm not there by nine go on without me,' Robbie told Badgie.

'It's worth a visit. You're still trying to find that piece from the canteen, then?'

'I am and I will,' Robbie replied.

'You know what it is with you, don't you? You can't stand anyone throwing you over.'

'Probably,' Robbie said. 'If she doesn't show up I'll come and give Monto the once-over.'

Badgie left the office and was back almost immediately. 'There's a kid outside looking for you.'

Robbie went and spoke to the boy who told him his wife was sick and could he come home. 'What's the matter with her and who sent you?'

'I don't know. It was Mrs Devoy who sent me, I live across the road. She said to come quick if you could.'

'Is Dolly in her mother's, she's not in hospital?'

'No, she's in the house all right.'

'Right then, here's sixpence for yourself, and you tell Mrs Devoy I'll be down as soon as I can.'

Robbie went back into the office and considered the situation. Whatever ailed Dolly couldn't be that serious or she wouldn't be in the house. If it was dangerous she would have

496

been taken to hospital. Tomorrow would be soon enough, he had the afternoon off and plans for the evening.

'What time is it?'

'Ten after ten,' Maggie said.

'I must have slept for hours.'

'You did.'

'So he didn't come, then.'

'No,' Maggie said. For a moment she considered lying to Dolly, saying, 'He mightn't have got the message,' but decided not to. In the long run it would be cruel. 'And I spoke to the young fella me ma sent. Robbie got word, the child spoke to him.' Dolly said nothing and Maggie continued: 'You should leave him. Now is your chance before he lands you with another child.'

'I love him,' Dolly said quietly.

'You do not. I don't think you ever did. You fell for what you thought you were looking for – some dream, some notion of yours. He's no good.'

'I know that.'

'Well, at least that's a start in the right direction.'

'How's Bessie?' Dolly asked. 'For a minute I forgot about her.'

'Brokenhearted and why wouldn't she be. There was a man! She'll cry many a day for him.'

'They make you cry one way or the other,' Dolly said, remembering the tears she'd shed since meeting Robbie.

'There's different kinds of tears. You'll cry for someone you loved who loved you. Those tears will help to console you, heal your grief. But the ones from a scalded heart heal nothing, settle nothing,' Maggie said in a sad, solemn voice.

'What's come over you all of a sudden, you never talk like that.'

'It must be my age,' Maggie said in her normal voice. 'You have my advice, throw that fella over. My mother's heating a drop of gruel for you. Is there anything you want before I go?'

'No, thanks.'

'Then I'll see you in the morning.'

Dolly drank the gruel and let her mother make her comfortable for the night. Before she left the room she asked, 'The young fella you sent with the message, he was telling the truth? He gave word to Robbie?'

'I'm sure he did, and you'd be as well to believe it. He's no good, your husband. He's no good.'

Dolly thought about it for hours, lying there listening to the clock striking the hours. He went to see Alice! He'd have posted the letter early and she'd have got it at lunchtime. Alice, whoever she was, wouldn't be the last. After her, there'd be another and another. She couldn't live like that. With a mind full of suspicion and her heart like a lead weight, every day watching for signs, searching his pockets, steaming open his letters, reading what he wrote to other women, not able to hold her tongue, provoking him, rising his temper.

That wasn't love. It had to be something more. A handsome face wasn't enough. Anyway – you got used to a face. You weren't looking at a face every five minutes and thinking – his eyes are gorgeous, his teeth are lovely, his skin is soft. Nor bed either, that wasn't enough. There were the little, everyday things, just living together, the kindness, the trusting one another . . .

God, hadn't she made an awful hash of her life. She was paying now for all her contrary ways, for all her fads and fancies. She heard the clock strike two before falling asleep.

Robbie came the next day, full of contrition and lies. There had been no one at the flat and no word from Alice. He had returned to the room late after spending the evening with Badgie in Monto, too drunk to wonder why Dolly hadn't come back from her mother's.

Had he known it was serious he'd have found some way of coming. It was terrible about the baby, but she wasn't to worry, only to hurry up and get better. She let him kiss her. He sat on the bed, holding her hand.

'How long will you be laid up?' he asked.

'A fortnight. You'd be better off moving into barracks.'

He protested unconvincingly. 'I'll hate that. I'll miss your cooking.'

'And another thing,' she said, 'I'm not going back to the room.'

'Well, I won't live here, not with your mother.'

'I know, we'll find somewhere else. Don't create a scene, I'm not able for one and there's a death in the house.'

'All right, I won't. Only I want us on our own. I love you, I want us together.'

You love no one but yourself. We shouldn't have married. It was my fault as much as yours, Dolly thought. He was very attractive, nothing would change that. She could still admire him, but knew she would never think herself in love with him again. She didn't know what she would do in the future. For the present it was enough to know she wasn't going back to the room and that Robbie would be living in. She needed the time to think.

'I'll come down every evening except . . .'

'Except the nights you're on duty, I know,' Dolly said. 'That'll do grand.'

'What time are your in-laws coming?' Bridget asked Bessie.

'Half-two, I'll meet them.'

'Do you want me to mind the child?'

'You've enough to do, looking after Dolly. And anyway, the child will be a help. There was bad feeling between me and the Maguires. No love lost on either side.' Bessie sat down and began to cry. 'His mother didn't want me to have Liam. There was a terrible scene.'

499

She told Bridget about the milk-churn, stopping as the crying overcame her, broken-hearted thinking about the incident which seemed such a short while ago. Only yesterday, when Liam was her beautiful boy, the finest, handsomest young man in the country. All the resignation she had prayed for and believed she had been granted and fully accepted, deserted her. And she cried for the loss of him, for the senselessness of life, the unfairness of it, talking aloud asking '*Why*, Bridget? Why him? Why my Liam?'

'There are no answers,' Bridget said. 'Time and time again the question is asked: why him? why her? What harm have they ever done? Look at this one and that, idlers and wasters, neglectful mothers and cruel fathers, sons, husbands, alive and well. Why was mine that never harmed anyone taken? I asked them myself when Richard was killed. No doubt Dolly is doing the same, asking why her little child was taken.'

'Poor Dolly, for a minute I forgot all about her.' Bessie wiped her eyes. 'How is she?'

'Broken-hearted over the child and with a tormented heart – that louser never put in an appearance until the next day.'

'Did he know for sure?'

'Oh, without doubt. He's no good. A charmer as I've told you many times, a likable man that if he wasn't married to your daughter you couldn't but take to. My poor daughter, she'll walk a sorrowful road with him.'

'Will I go in and see her?'

'Do, she'd be glad of the company.'

Dolly was sleeping. She stirred when Bessie came in, opened her eyes and sat up.

'Oh Bessie,' she said. 'I was sorry about Liam and I won't be able to go to the funeral.' All Dolly's own grief and the sorrow she felt for Bessie overwhelmed her. Bessie sat on the bed and put her arms round her and they cried for each other.

Chapter Twenty-Five

Bessie took a cab to Kingsbridge station. Driving along the quays she looked at the eating house as the cab passed by. The stairs were still there and a bedroom wall, tatters of wallpaper flapping in the wind. The bricks and mortar and old paper lasted and Liam was gone. She remembered the day she bought the paper, was delighted with its bargain price – a job-lot, the man had told her, a flaw here and there but there were over a dozen rolls. Out of them she'd get enough that weren't flawed. Pink and white roses it was, which she loved and Liam said looked like overgrown cabbages. In the end they'd had a row which didn't last long and he'd helped her trim the paper. She found herself smiling at the memory.

Waiting for the Maguires' train to arrive she felt nervous. How would they take her? What way would Liam's mother take the news? Would she say it was all her fault, for taking him from the country, from the clean, fresh air and bringing him to the city where he got consumption?

The train was coming in. Bessie was tempted to turn and run, avoid the scene. The train stopped, people got out and purposefully walked towards the exit. They hadn't come. Her fears had been for nothing. The crowd was thinning now, twos and threes, then passengers alone, then no one only the guards unloading sacks and boxes from the guard's van. Not a sign. They must have changed their mind at the last minute. She'd go home. Michael began to whimper. 'Whisht now, astoir.' She rocked and soothed him. 'Mammy will take you home

501

now. Your granny didn't come. There now, there's a good boy, don't cry.'

Just as she was about to turn away, Bessie saw two old people far down the train, dressed in black, linking each other, walking slowly, looking lost. Could it be them? Surely they weren't that old, that bowed! She hadn't remembered them like that. The man raised a hand and waved in her direction. It was them all right. A great feeling of pity engulfed her. Liam was their son, they'd loved him, too. She hurried down the platform.

'He's gone then,' Mrs Maguire said before Bessie had time to open her mouth. 'I knew it. I woke in the night feeling lost and I knew then. I woke you, didn't I, Pat? I shook him and said "Liam's dead. I feel it in my heart – an emptiness."'

'What time was that?' Bessie asked.

'Three in the morning.'

''Twas at that hour he died,' Bessie said, not knowing whether or not to embrace her mother-in-law, to offer her comfort. It was true that Mrs Maguire looked older, but as fierce as ever. Then the old woman's face softened as she looked at Michael.

'God bless and spare him to you, he's a fine child and the image of his father. My poor lovely son. My lovely Liam.' She held out her arms for the baby. 'Let's rest for five minutes,' she said, holding the baby close, kissing him and still not shedding a tear.

'Aye, let's sit,' the old man said, taking Bessie's arm. 'We're sorry for you Bessie, sorry indeed. And sorry for many a thing. Parents think they know what's best but sure many a time they don't. We were talking coming up on the train. We were very wrong. It's late in the day we're telling you, but there it is. We'll do what we can to make up for it when you all come home, isn't that so?' he said, addressing his wife.

'It's so, every word he says.' She turned to look at Bessie, her face wet with tears. 'Oh girl,' she said, 'I'm that sorry. I'll

502

spend the rest of my life making amends. You'll come home, won't you?'

'I'll come home,' Bessie said. 'Yes, we'll come home.'

Alice and her mother were in the nursery. Alice was feeding the baby and Lady Delahunt keeping her eyes averted from the sight of Alice's bared breast. When the baby was satisfied, Alice laid him in his cradle. Her mother stood up and suggested it was time to give the nursery back to Nannie.

'Not yet, there's something I want to tell you. Sit down.' Lady Delahunt wanted to know if the telling couldn't be as well told downstairs. Alice said no, she wanted to speak here and now. Her mother sat again and Alice stated: 'I'm going to Canada.'

'For a holiday? I didn't know you had friends there.'

'For good, me and the baby. I've booked a passage on a boat to New York and will go the rest of the way by train.'

Her mother gasped. 'You can't be serious! You've taken leave of your senses. You can't go to Canada – you can't take my grandson away. Horsham would have been bad enough – but Canada! I won't allow it.'

'Don't shout, you'll waken him and let Nannie know our business – you wouldn't want that, Mama, not before it's absolutely necessary.'

Lady Delahunt lowered her voice. 'I know you've had a hard time, are still grieving for Stephen and having a baby can put strange ideas into one's mind and . . . but I won't allow it. I'll speak to your father!'

'I haven't taken leave of my senses and there's not a thing you or my father can do to stop it, so don't use that argument.'

'But you can't,' Lady Delahunt said with less conviction. 'What about the Whiteheads? He's their heir, he can't be brought up in the wilds of Canada.'

'He's Stephen's son, he'll be the Whitehead heir no matter where he lives.'

'Have you no feelings – they'll be broken-hearted.'

'Hearts mend,' Alice replied with a callousness she didn't feel.

'I can't believe it – the change in you, you're . . . I don't know . . . nowadays it's difficult sometimes to remember the sweet girl you once were.'

'I grew up.'

'I suppose Nella's had a hand in this. Is she going with you?'

Alice laughed. 'Why should she? Nella has her own life and it has nothing to do with me or Canada. And now I'm going to write to Stephen's parents.'

'Don't think I've given up – I'll talk to your father, he'll change your tune.'

Alice found the letter difficult to write. She knew it would distress the Whiteheads greatly. Taking the baby away from them was her only regret. They were kind gentle people with an enormous capacity for love and their hearts would not, as she glibly told her mother, mend easily. So to be kind she lied, promising that she would return often with their grandson. And wrote the truth when she said she hoped they would visit her. Resorting to lies again she told them how lost she was without Stephen, that it was her reason for going away. A new country, a new way of life might ease her pain and sense of loss. She sealed the letter but decided not to post it until nearer her departure date. She didn't wish for their reply until she was in Canada.

She anticipated a scene with her father, but Sir Arthur's mind was preoccupied with other things, with the changes that were coming in Ireland. How the country would be in the hands of the Catholic peasants – his way of describing those who, when the time came, would wield power – and how he and his kind would fare under such a régime. So the scene in which Alice had imagined herself flaunting her new-found independence, calmly but definitely telling her father that nothing he could say or do would make the slightest difference

504

to her plans, never materialized. Instead, there was only an expression of regret that the boy was going away and that she must, when the time came, send him back to England to be educated.

Dolly got her strength back and went in and out of the house, shopping with her mother, visiting Maggie, going to the chapel to pray that God would help her with the decision she had to make. Sometimes after her prayers she wondered if it wasn't a sin to be asking God's help when the decision she might reach would be to leave her husband and go off with a married man. Going off with Jem she knew would be sinful, of that she was in no doubt. And so she supposed that kneeling before the altar thinking of such a thing was sinful, too. But she had to do it and maybe, she reasoned, God would persuade her to stay with Robbie, so asking His help was right.

She often thought of the lies she had put about to hide the fact she was pregnant. How, when her mother had asked what she would do when the child was born before its time, she had flippantly replied, 'Anything could happen by then. I could be dead or in England.' She had never considered losing the baby. The lies hadn't been necessary, after all.

When she told Maggie that she was thinking about going to Jem, her sister gave her encouragement. 'You've got sense at last. Make a new life for yourself. Jem will be kind to you, whereas if you stay with the other fella you'll have a life of Hell.'

Robbie came on his free nights and always wanted to stay the night, but each time Dolly fobbed him off. He accepted the excuses for a while then one night dug in his heels and reminded her that she was his wife. She hadn't intended telling him she was going to America – she hadn't fully decided that she was. But suddenly, seeing his smiling face, putting on the charm as he had when he courted her, she wanted to take the smile off it.

505

'I won't be for much longer.'

'What are you talking about – you won't be for much longer?'

'I'm leaving you. I'm going away.'

'Where? Where could you go? You can't leave your husband.'

'Wait and see,' Dolly replied. He didn't believe her, she could see that, though he looked less sure of himself. He tried to put his arms around her, to kiss her. She wouldn't let him. 'Don't think you can get round me that way either, that's finished too.'

'Christ Almighty, you're mad. I've been kicked out of my home such as it was, not allowed to sleep with you and now I can't even touch you. I won't stand for much more of this. You talk about leaving me – watch it that it's not the other way around.'

'Where would you go – to Alice?'

'What do you mean Alice – I know no one called Alice.'

'Along with everything else you're a liar. The night before I lost the child I found and read the letter.' She watched his face go pale. 'You were with her when I was lying here, for all you knew losing my life's blood.'

She saw him recover himself, his face changing expression, a smile, a false one on his mouth and in his eyes. 'I forgot about her – she was nothing. Someone who worked in the canteen, a skivvy. I had a bet with Badgie that I'd write her a love letter – a joke, that's all it was.'

'Was that all? Well, it doesn't matter any more. I'm leaving you and that's an end to it.'

'We'll see about that. I'm going to the Curragh for two months, and by the time I get back you'd have better changed your tune.'

She was about to tell him he was a bully as well as a liar and a cheat, but thought better of it. He wasn't worth the waste of breath. Let him go to the Curragh. And in the meantime she would make up her mind about America. 'Leave it until you come back from the Curragh then,' she said amicably.

'Then can I stay the night?' Robbie asked, full of smiles again.

'You'd better not. I'm not over the mis yet, you know, and it would be knocking my mother about, pulling her out of the big bed and that.'

Robbie shook his head, 'I don't know, you're a contrary woman. Will you at least let me kiss you good-night?'

She didn't want to, but agreeing would be the quickest way of getting rid of him. With all his expertise he kissed her and she felt herself beginning to respond. She mustn't, that's what he had banked on. That was how he solved everything. Well, she had been duped many times by his body and her own, but not tonight, not any more. She pulled away from him.

'I'll write to you,' he said. 'And make sure you write back.'

'I will, honest to God.' And she would, to allay suspicion, stop him coming up to Dublin and creating a scene.

After he went she knew that the time had come for her to make up her mind about writing to Jem, telling him she wanted to come to America. If only it wasn't America. It was so far away. Maybe she'd never see her mother again. She couldn't imagine life without her, or Maggie either. Even loving Jem, how could she live without her family? And Dublin – what would she do without that? Every street in America would be a strange one. Every voice a strange one. She'd never be able to walk across town of a Saturday, see the Liffey or go to the Park or the Green. Though she supposed they'd have parks and rivers in America and that you'd get used to the strange way of talking. But in the heel of the hunt there was her mother and that she wouldn't be there. Everything else she could get used to, yes, even leaving Maggie and Tom and Christie. She'd miss them, of course, but they were young and had all the time in the world to come out. It was different with her mother.

The next day she went down to Maggie's and told her what she had been thinking.

'So my mother's the only thing holding you back,' Maggie said when Dolly had finished talking.

'Really, yes.'

'And what makes you so sure you'd never see her again? Me mother's got years in her, please God, she could outlive the lot of us. And in any case, you're not talking about the coffin ships when it took months to get to America. I was reading the other day that the *Mauretania* can cross the ocean in five days. Jem's not short of money – what's to stop you coming back for a holiday or me ma going over, she'd be landed. Imagine her telling the neighbours, "I'm going on me holidays." "Down the country is it?" "The country how are you, I'm going to America." Cut the ground from under them that would.'

Dolly laughed. 'Especially oul frosty muzzle that gave me the dancing girl for a wedding present. Yes, you're right. I could come back or take her over, I never thought of that.'

'Well now, there you are. Will you do it?'

Dolly thought for a few minutes before saying, 'Yes, I'll do it. I'll go home now and tell me mother and then I'll write to Jem.'

'I'll pray for God to forgive you and Jem O'Brien. You'll be living in sin, not able to receive the Blessed Sacrament. Oh Dolly, Dolly, it's a terrible thing you're doing and I should be trying to stop you. But I know what you've been through. And I know you'll be happy with Jem. You couldn't see it but he was the one meant for you all the time.'

Dolly was amazed with how her mother took the news. She had expected at least a threat of the priest even though she knew her mother, no matter how outraged she might be, would never bring the priest on her. And she was surprised

508

at the way her mother cried, never having seen her cry like that before.

'I'm sorry for all the hasty words I've said to you. Sure I never meant the half of them. It's only my way. It wasn't that I didn't love you. Alanna, I'm sorry. And you're going to the other side of the world.'

'Ah Mother, don't. Don't cry. America's not the end of the world any more. I'll send for you and I'll come back, honest to God I will.' Dolly herself was crying and holding Bridget in her arms, saying, 'You called me Alanna, me da used to do that, Lord have mercy on him. Do you remember?'

'As if I could forget,' Bridget said. Then asked Dolly when she would be leaving and Dolly told her she was going to write this minute. 'It'll take a few weeks for it to get there and the answer come back. Then I'll take the first boat that's going.'

Back from Jem came a letter full of dollars and instructions. She was to come first-class. She was to go to Thomas Cook's – they would see to everything. And as soon as she had a sailing date she was to write and tell him and he'd begin counting the minutes. But even after she had arranged her passage, doubts still troubled Dolly. Would she love Jem when she saw him again? How could you be sure when you had only seen someone for but a few minutes after not seeing them for years? She thought she loved him, but might it not be because she was looking for an escape from Robbie and her unhappiness with him? And what about living in sin?

Maggie as usual was her sounding-board. While she talked about her worries and listened to Maggie's answers, her doubts about her feelings for Jem vanished. And to her fretting about living in sin Maggie replied, 'You were living in torment and misery with your husband. Sin can't be worse than that. Anyway, let God be the judge.'

On the third morning at sea Dolly woke and felt well. The churning nausea was gone and so was the dipping and swaying of the ship. She got up, washed and dressed and was wondering if she would venture out of the cabin when the steward came with her early morning tea and biscuits.

'So you've got your sea legs, ma'am,' he said, putting down the tray.

'Is that what you call them?' Dolly smiled at him, remembering his kindness when she had felt so ill.

'That's what you call them, though to tell you the truth the weather's changed for the better and that makes all the difference. I'd say you'll be able for your breakfast. Then have a walk on the deck. Fresh sea breezes, that's the thing to put the roses back in your cheeks.'

'Am I pale, then?'

'A little bit, love. Have a promenade after your breakfast. Then I'll see to a deckchair and rug.'

'Thanks very much,' Dolly said.

At breakfast there was a dark pretty woman sitting at the next table. Her face seemed familiar. Dolly smiled at her and the woman smiled back. Dolly thought how nice it would be to get into talk with her, but after the initial smile the woman didn't look her way again and left the dining room before Dolly began to eat.

So much food for breakfast: porridge, kedgeree, kippers, haddock with poached eggs, bacon, sausage, kidney, chops, eggs boiled, fried, scrambled, coddled, toast, hot rolls, white bread and brown, jam, honey, marmalade. 'Does anyone eat it all?' Dolly asked the waiter after reading the menu.

'A few attempt it, but most have only the one or two courses. If I were you I'd have the bacon and scrambled and the rolls, fresh baked this morning.'

She mastered the menus and made a few friends by the time the boat reached New York. But she hadn't, though she had looked for her, seen the dark pretty woman again. Then on the morning they were docking she was on deck by the railings, holding a baby. Dolly went and stood beside her.

510

'The Statue of Liberty!' the woman said. 'Imagine – we are really looking at it.'

'My God, you're from Dublin!' Suddenly overwhelmed with the strangeness of the scene in front of her, thinking of what lay ahead, wracked with homesickness, the sound of an Irish voice delighted her.

'Yes, I'm from Dublin,' Alice replied.

'So am I. Are you staying in New York?' Dolly asked hopefully, thinking that maybe she would have a friend, a friend from home before she landed.

'At first, then I'm travelling on.' Alice was lonely and homesick, too. Apart from the one morning she had breakfasted when Dolly had seen her in the dining room she had spent the voyage in her cabin with the baby who was very unsettled. She longed to tell Dolly she was going to Canada. Chat to this attractive, friendly girl.

While Alice was struggling to overcome her natural reserve Dolly – annoyed that she couldn't place where she had seen her before – had decided that she was stuck up, you could tell by her voice, upperclass. They couldn't have been friends. So instead of asking any more questions she admired the baby. 'He's beautiful God bless and spare him.' She touched his soft smooth cheek.

'I'd better go down now, he'll want feeding and changing before I go ashore. I hope you'll be happy in America.'

'You too,' Dolly said.

She stood on deck looking at the waiting crowd. Several times she was sure she spotted Jem, then realized it wasn't him. Supposing he hadn't come. Supposing Josie had come back and he had changed his mind. She'd be stranded in New York without the money to go home. And if he was there, would he think differently of her when they met, fall out of love with her? She felt sick with nervousness and excitement, oblivious of everything except the crowd, straining her eyes for a glimpse of Jem. Then she saw him. He was waving, a

511

little speck moving his arm, but it was him all right. And he was taller. Oh Please God, let it all work out.

She disembarked and then the two of them were walking towards each other. He was gorgeous. Such a swank! Only look at his hair falling over his forehead. Wouldn't you think with all his money he could find a decent barber. Her eyes were full of tears and when they came closer she saw that his were, too.

'Oh Dolly, Dolly Devoy! I thought you'd never arrive.' He hugged her and kissed her until she could hardly breathe. They were laughing and crying. Then she pushed him away.

'Look at you,' she said. 'Look at the state of your hair, I never knew a man like you.'

And then she said, going into his arms again, 'Hold me, Jem O'Brien. Hold me and never let me go.'